Loss of Homes and Evictions across Europe

ELGAR LAND AND HOUSING LAW AND POLICY

Land and housing law and policy are currently undergoing upheavals which will certainly shake and reshuffle their fundamentals. Overpopulation, mass migration, climate change and other environmental disasters, the increasing scarcity of agricultural and urban land, as well as the social, economic and political problems resulting thereof, put under pressure land tenure and overshadow more technical but nevertheless persisting problems such as incompatibilities of conveyancing, registration and tenancy systems. Housing systems are additionally challenged by excessive shortages in urban areas, lack of public budgets, privatisation and restitution problems as well as, in many States, counterproductive tax, subsidy and tenancy regulation.

Against this background, the new Elgar Land and Housing Law and Policy Series sets out to analyse legal regulation in its political, economic, social and environmental context. Its focus is, thus, on the governance dimension of modern law and regulation. This basic orientation is in line with the TENLAW project, funded by the European Commission from 2011–2015, whose key participants serve as editors in the present series:

Elena Bargelli (University of Pisa),
Magda Habdas (University of Silesia),
Marietta Haffner (Delft University of Technology),
József Hegedüs (Metropolitan Research Institute, Budapest),
Padraic Kenna (University of Galway),
Irene Kull (University of Tartu and Estonian Supreme Court, Tartu),
Špelca Mežnar (International School for Social and Business Studies, Celje, and Slovenian Constitutional Court, Ljubljana),
Per Norberg (University of Lund),
Sergio Nasarre-Aznar (UNESCO Housing Chair, University Rovira i Virgili, Tarragona),
Hendrik Ploeger (Delft University of Technology),
Peter Sparkes (University of Southampton), and
Christoph U. Schmid (Centre of European Law and Politics, Bremen University), managing editor.

The editors welcome book proposals sharing the series' interdisciplinary and comparative orientation, irrespective of the substantive topics covered. Contact may be made with Christoph U. Schmid.

Published by
Edward Elgar Publishing Limited
The Lypiatts
15 Lansdown Road
Cheltenham
Glos GL50 2JA
UK

Edward Elgar Publishing, Inc.
William Pratt House
9 Dewey Court
Northampton
Massachusetts 01060
USA

A catalogue record for this book
is available from the British Library

Library of Congress Control Number: 2018954449

This book is available electronically in the **Elgar**online
Law subject collection
DOI 10.4337/9781788116992

MIX
Paper from
responsible sources
FSC
www.fsc.org   FSC® C013056

ISBN 978 1 78811 698 5 (cased)
ISBN 978 1 78811 699 2 (eBook)

Typeset by Columns Design XML Ltd, Reading
Printed and bound in Great Britain by TJ International Ltd, Padstow

Loss of Homes and Evictions across Europe

A Comparative Legal and Policy Examination

Edited by

Padraic Kenna

Director, Centre for Housing Law, Rights and Policy, School of Law, National University of Ireland Galway

Sergio Nasarre-Aznar

Director, UNESCO Housing Chair, University Rovira i Virgili, Tarragona, Spain

Peter Sparkes

Professor of Property Law, Southampton Law School, University of Southampton, UK

Christoph U. Schmid

Director, Centre of European Law and Politics (ZERP), Bremen University, Germany

ELGAR LAND AND HOUSING LAW AND POLICY

 Edward Elgar
PUBLISHING

Cheltenham, UK • Northampton, MA, USA

Contents

Editorial advisory board

Contributors

Elena Bargelli is Full Professor of Private Law at Pisa University. Her research is focused on national, European and comparative contract and tort law in general and tenancy law in particular. She is a Fellow of the European Centre of Tort and Insurance Law (Vienna), Italian reporter at the annual conference in Vienna and Member of the Council of the European Law Institute. She has published a book on comparative tenancy law under Italian, French and German law in 2004 and many articles on tenancy law.

Witold Borysiak is assistant professor at the University of Warsaw Faculty of Law and Administration and at the Institute of Justice. He has worked in the Department of Studies and Analyses of the General Counsel to the Republic of Poland and as a law clerk at the Polish Constitutional Tribunal. Between 2013 and 2015 he was a member of the Working Group on Succession Law of the Polish Civil Law Codification Commission. He has been a visiting scholar at many universities including the University of Florida Levin College of Law, the Institute for European Tort Law in Vienna and the Swiss Institute of Comparative Law in Lausanne. As a SCIEX Scholar, he worked as an assistant at the University of Geneva's Faculty of Law. He is the author of numerous publications on comparative private law, law of obligations, succession law, family law, medical law and constitutional law including co-authorship of commentaries on the Polish Constitution, the Civil Code and the Family and Guardianship Code.

Pascal De Decker is professor at the KU Leuven (P.PUL, Department of Architecture). He studied Sociology and Urban Planning and has a PhD in Political and Social Sciences.

Giulia Donadio is a Postdoctoral Research Fellow in Private Law at the University of Pisa. Currently, her research is focusing on the interactions between contract law and human rights, with special attention to the horizontal effects of non-discrimination principle in the European context. Dr Donadio obtained her PhD in Private Law, magna cum laude, at the Scuola Superiore S Anna (School of Advanced Studies) in Pisa in

May 2014, defending a thesis on contractual business networks. Her research interests have always included the development of European contract law, which has been the main topic of several articles, published works and seminars. She is a fellow of the European Law Institute (ELI).

Rosa Maria Garcia-Teruel (international Doctor in Laws and MSc in Corporate and Contract Law – URV) is a postdoctoral researcher at the UNESCO Housing Chair of the Rovira i Virgili University. Her PhD in civil law covered the legal aspects of tenancy agreements in which the tenant pays in kind (ie performing renovations), and it was funded by the Catalan Government (FI DGR 2015). In this field of research, she has published more than ten articles and book chapters, and she has presented her research in several national and international conferences (Denmark, Portugal, France, Hungary, United Kingdom, Albania, the Netherlands). She is a researcher on several competitive projects and has carried out a research stay at the Zentrum für Europäische Rechtspolitik, University of Bremen (Germany) and at the University of Groningen (the Netherlands). She is a lecturer in the Degree of Law at the Rovira i Virgili University and for the Real Estate Agent's Course. Her fields of research are tenancy law, construction law, property rights, housing policies and alternative funding for real estate development.

Maša Filipovič Hrast is an associate professor at the Faculty of Social Sciences, University of Ljubljana, Slovenia. She is a member of the Sociology department at the Faculty of Social Sciences, University of Ljubljana and lectures at both undergraduate and postgraduate level. Her main research topics are social and housing policy and social exclusion and she has been involved in several international and national research projects linked to wider housing issues and homelessness in particular. She has been a member of the European Observatory on Homelessness and is a member of the Women's Homelessness in Europe Network.

Caroline Hunter is Head of School at York Law School, and has published extensively in housing law and related areas. Prior to her academic career, she worked as a barrister and developed a specialist practice in relation to housing and local government.

Padraic Kenna lectures in real property, equity, housing law, regulation, local government law and related topics at NUI Galway. He has published widely in property and housing journals and is on the editorial boards of the *International Journal of Law in the Built Environment* and the *Queen Mary Human Rights Law Review*. Padraic contributes at European level on housing rights developments and established the Centre for Housing Law, Rights and Policy at NUI Galway. His book

Housing Law, Rights and Policy (Dublin, Clarus Press, 2011) provides a comprehensive examination and critical analysis of Irish housing law and policy, while his *Contemporary Housing Issues in a Globalized World* (Ashgate, 2014) examines international developments in this area. Recently, he acted as Project Director and lead author on an EU Commission research project on evictions across the 28 EU Member States, published in 2016.

Sergio Nasarre-Aznar (Tarragona, 1974) is Full Professor of Civil Law and Director of the UNESCO Housing Chair at the University Rovira i Virgili (Spain). He is European Doctor in Law and holds an MPhil in Land Economy from the University of Cambridge. Since 2008 he is a Corresponding Member of the Spanish Royal Academy of Jurisprudence and Legislation. He has been granted the ICREA Fellowship to the excellence of research 2016–2020. Sergio is also a consultant of the EU Commission, the Catalan Parliament and Government, Amnesty International, the FAO and the Association of German Pfandbrief Banks. Since 2018, he has been advisor to the German Ministry of the Interior, Construction and Community for the implementation of housing policies in Europe in its European Presidency in 2020. He has been Deputy Judge in the Court of Appeal of Tarragona for 15 years (2004–2018). He is the author of four books and has edited seven more. He has published more than 90 research works and has delivered over 160 invited speeches in 15 countries. He has taken part in drafting five laws related to housing. He is the main researcher in ten national and international projects and has taken part in some projects of the EU Commission and the European Parliament about tenancies, evictions and homelessness, cross-border acquisition of land and collaborative economy.

Sofija Nikolic is a PhD student at the Faculty of Law, University of Belgrade (Serbia). She was a teaching associate at the same faculty for the subject Civil Law – General Part and Property Law. She was research associate at the Faculty of Law, University of Bremen (Germany).

Nicholas Pleace is a faculty member of the University of York, Centre for Housing Policy. His work centres on the successful housing and social integration of people with support needs. His work ranges from evaluation of homelessness services and strategies, through to exploring innovative approaches aimed at tackling long-term unemployment and improving social supports for homeless and formerly homeless people. He also has a particular interest in the measurement of service outcomes and service cost effectiveness. Nicholas also works for the European Observatory on Homelessness and is on the Editorial Committee for the

European Journal of Homelessness, both of which operate under the auspices of Fédération Européenne d'Associations Nationales Travaillant avec les Sans-Abri (FEANTSA).

Christoph U Schmid was postdoctoral fellow at the EUI Florence from 1995–2005 and has been Director of ZERP and Professor of European Private, Economic and Constitutional Economic Law at Bremen University since 2005. His research revolves around the Europeanization of private law in general and consumer, tenancy and real property law in particular. He is a member of several transnational Study Groups on European Private Law and has acted as an expert for the EP and the European Commission, for which he has authored and coordinated key studies in the field of land and housing law. He has acted as adviser to the governments of Portugal, Estonia and Germany and the OECD in land and housing law reforms.

Eszter Somogyi is a researcher at the Metropolitan Research Institute (MRI), Budapest. She has participated in numerous research and consultancy projects, among them the evaluation and elaboration of national and local housing policies, housing finance systems and urban regeneration programmes. She particularly focuses on housing affordability problems and the development of inclusive housing policy schemes for segregated areas, and disadvantaged groups. She also gathered special experience on the use of EU Structural funds for the housing and urban development problems of marginalized social groups.

Nóra Teller (Metropolitan Research Institute, Budapest) has research interests including spatial processes of housing exclusion, homelessness, social housing systems in Central and East Europe, housing conditions of the Roma in the region, and the use of EU funds in tackling social exclusion. She is one of the co-editors of the *European Journal of Homelessness* and a member of the European Observatory on Homelessness.

Nóra Tosics is a lawyer specialized in European law and in civil law including tenancy law, having worked in European institutions as well as in the private sector. Nóra is currently working at the European Institute for Innovation and Technology and pursuing a Phd at the University of Pécs, Hungary.

Marc Uhry is a European consultant on housing rights and housing policies, and lecturer at the University of Lyon Faculty of Law, on housing rights. Previously, he worked as a researcher and a legal adviser in the NGO sector, and with the European Housing Rights Expert Group set up by FEANTSA (European Federation of NGOs working with homeless people).

Diederik Vermeir is researcher at the University of Antwerp (Faculty of Law) and the Policy Research Centre for Housing (Steunpunt Wonen). Within the field of housing law, his research focuses on rental legislation, housing quality and housing exclusion.

Jana Verstraete (P.PUL, Department of Architecture, KU Leuven) is a PhD researcher. She studied Adult Educational Sciences and Sociology. Her research focuses on housing exclusion and new housing initiatives.

Michel Vols is Full Professor of Public Order Law at the University of Groningen, the Netherlands. His main fields of research are anti-social behaviour law and housing law. He is one of the chairs of the Housing Law Research Network within the European Network on Housing Research. Michel is (founding) editor of the peer reviewed book series Studies in Housing Law (Eleven Publishing).

Foreword

This publication is the result of several years of hard work to better understand how evictions and repossessions lead to housing exclusion and homelessness. It examines the extent to which evictions can be considered a violation of the right to housing and related human rights.

This publication was made possible by the desire and perseverance of Professor Padraic Kenna to make the high, and indeed, often rising, rates of evictions, an issue of urgent concern for policy makers and civil society organizations in Europe. I am convinced it will reach a large audience and hopefully will incite stakeholders to take action.

The support of the European Commission has also been crucial to the research on which the chapters in this publication are based, following the EU-wide study on the evictions in the context of the right to housing, published in 2016.

The book makes it clear that evictions and repossessions are not only a problem in countries that experienced housing booms and busts, such as Spain and Ireland. The issue concerns *all* EU Member States, and is more widely related to the housing affordability crisis in Europe. Housing is becoming increasingly unaffordable, especially in large urban areas, and the divide between rich and poor is growing for most, if not all, of the common housing exclusion indicators.

This publication shows that tackling the high eviction rates is not only a human rights obligation, but also makes good economic sense. There is abundant proof that preventing evictions is cheaper than rehousing people after a period of housing exclusion, or, in extreme cases, a situation of homelessness.

These well-researched chapters from European-wide experts come at a timely moment. The European Union is putting pressure on commercial banks to sell off their non-performing loans portfolios to non-bank entities, which might create a spike in evictions in several Member States. It also comes after the solemn proclamation of the European Pillar of Social Rights by the Parliament, the Commission, and the European Council of the European Union. The Pillar will probably guide EU social policy in the next decade and includes a commitment to protect vulnerable people against forced eviction.

I am confident you will find this a thought-provoking read.

Freek Spinnewijn
Director, FEANTSA

Introduction

Padraic Kenna

1. EVICTION

Eviction from home strikes at the core of human rights and civilized society. The forced removal of people from their homes evokes a primordial response, related to the primary human need for shelter.[1] All civilized societies have protected the homes of their inhabitants from arbitrary violations and forced eviction.

Across the world, today, most countries have adopted international human rights standards to protect people and households from forced eviction from their homes.[2] Often, these are based on the need to protect people's dignity and rights to habitation from powerful property owners or political forces. The concept of rights to respect for privacy, home and family life has emerged as a key legal principle. But inadequate public management of the control and use of property and private and public spaces, often leads to legally approved evictions. Indeed, lack of state regulation of property and spaces can facilitate illegal forced evictions. Even in developed European Union Member States, with constitutional and legislative protection, forced evictions are legally permitted in certain circumstances. Integrating housing rights protection into modern housing systems remains an undeveloped area of study.[3]

Today, protection from arbitrary eviction is often ascribed to the security of property ownership and property rights in liberal societies, and is finely balanced in law between occupiers and property owners in social democratic societies. It is, of course, regularly asserted that,

---

[1] The need for shelter is recognized as a fundamental need. See AH Maslow, 'Theory of human motivation' originally published in (1943) 50 *Psychological Review* 370–396.

[2] United Nations, Commission on Human Rights, Resolutions 1993/77 and 2004/28.

[3] P Kenna, 'Can housing rights be applied to modern housing systems?' (2010) 2 (2) *International Journal of Law in the Built Environment* 103–117.

without the possibility of repossessing rented or mortgaged housing, investment in a functioning mortgage and rented housing market would cease to exist. Of course, in the real world it is much more complex.

Across Europe evictions are taking place every day. This book examines evictions across eleven European countries: Belgium, France, Germany, Hungary, Ireland, Italy, the Netherlands, Poland, Slovenia, Spain and the United Kingdom covering the period between 2010 and 2015/2016. Each chapter has been written by a national expert in the field and represents the most developed national research to date on this issue.

It follows and builds upon the EU Commission-funded study *Pilot Project – Promoting Protection of the Right to Housing – Homelessness Prevention in the Context of Evictions, Final Report*[4] (hereinafter 'the EU Pilot Project Report'). The EU Pilot Project Report examined evictions across the 28 EU Member States between 2010 and 2013, in the context of the protection of the right to housing, encompassing the prevention of evictions, early intervention, the provision of support for the rapid rehousing of those evicted and the measurement of the impacts of eviction on homelessness.

This introduction and each chapter examines evictions within the relevant social, policy, legal/human rights, and substantive frameworks. The social context considers wider issues relating to housing systems and social conditions set out in research by national experts. The policy section considers the general housing policies of the selected countries, as well as specific policies focused on evictions. It summarizes the range of measures which prevent and counter evictions. The legal/human rights context involves a range of human rights and legal frameworks applicable to evictions. These originate from international, regional and national constitutional and legislative provisions. The legal basis and procedures for evictions across tenures are explored as well as an outline of key emerging developments. The substantive section examines the structural and other risk factors which lead to evictions, as well as examining the nature and extent of evictions across tenures and countries. Data availability issues are summarized and examined.

---

[4] P Kenna, L Benjaminsen, V Busch-Geertsema and S Nasarre-Aznar, *Pilot Project – Promoting Protection of the Right to Housing – Homelessness Prevention in the Context of Evictions* (VT/2013/056). Final report (2016). European Union: European Commission, Directorate-General Employment, Social Affairs and Inclusion. Freek Spinnewin of FEANTSA, who acted as scientific adviser for the project, has assisted in this research.

1.1 The Concepts of 'Home' and 'Eviction'

The issue of eviction is closely related to respect for home. Today, the notion of home is viewed as much more than a physical setting. In contemporary societies, home is associated with safety, belonging, esteem and self-actualization. Housing and home are intertwined with health, child development, poverty/wealth and opportunity in general.[5] 'Home' can be seen as a physical structure; as a territory implying security, control and rootedness; as identity; as a social and cultural phenomenon; and as a base for relationships. Home also acts as a geographical space from which a person or household can access other services and amenities, and is regarded as necessary for the enjoyment of all human rights.[6] International human rights law regards 'home' as involving 'rights of central importance to the individual's identity, self-determination, physical and moral integrity, maintenance of relationships with others, and a settled and secure place in the community'.[7]

> 'Home' is an autonomous concept which does not depend on classification under domestic law. Whether or not a particular premises constitutes a 'home' which attracts the protection of Article 8 §1 will depend on the factual circumstances, namely, the existence of sufficient and continuous links with a specific place ... Thus, whether a property is to be classified as a 'home' is a question of fact and does not depend on the lawfulness of the occupation under domestic law ... .[8]

Lorna Fox-O'Mahony suggests that, as yet, there is no established coherent concept of home in law. Indeed, she points out that in many ways 'home-type' interests are anathema to legal reasoning, especially as 'home' is seen as essentially a subjective phenomenon:

---

[5]   L Fox O'Mahony, *Conceptualising Home: Theories, Laws and Policies* (Oxford, Hart 2007).

[6]   According to the ECtHR, whether accommodation is classified as a 'home' is a question of fact and does not depend on the lawfulness of the occupation under domestic law – *Buckley v UK* (1996) 23 EHRR 101; *McCann v UK* App No 19009/04, 13 May 2008, §50.

[7]   *Connors v the United Kingdom* App No 66746/01, 27 May 2004, §82.

[8]   For the purpose of the Article 8 ECHR, 'home' has an autonomous meaning and the ECtHR refers to 'the existence of sufficient and continuous links' as being a prerequisite for a 'home' with the domestic legal status of the occupier being irrelevant. See also *Orlic v Croatia* App No 48833/07, para 54.

It does not appear to be easily quantifiable, and the value of home to its occupiers is not readily susceptible to legal proof. Nevertheless, there are compelling arguments to support further analysis of the idea of home in law. For one thing, while it may be true to say that the nature of home attachments presents obvious impediments to the development of a coherent legal concept of home, and that this explains, to a certain extent, the relative neglect of home-oriented analysis in law, the centrality of 'home' to human dealings and the deep significance of rights and obligations relating to home render the lack of rigorous analysis in this area difficult to defend.[9]

There are many personal and social consequences linked to an eviction. It is generally accepted that forced evictions from homes can result in severe trauma and can set back the lives of those already marginalized or vulnerable in society.[10] Research shows that, although the experience varies, victims of home loss frequently experience feelings of painful loss; continued longing; a general depressive mood; frequent symptoms of psychological, social or somatic distress; a sense of helplessness; and occasional expressions of both direct and displaced anger.[11] Some households may be exposed to a great psychosocial burden, especially when children and/or adult dependents are involved. There are particularly negative consequences for children in the loss of home and the experience of homelessness.[12] Research shows that at least two years after their eviction, mothers still experienced significantly higher rates of material hardship and depression than their peers.[13] Yet, generally, there is a paucity of research into the effects of eviction, especially its links to

---

[9]   Fox O'Mahony (n 5) 4–5.

[10]   See United Nations, Office of the High Commissioner for Human Rights (UN OHCHR). 'Forced Evictions and Human Rights Fact Sheet No 25/Rev 1' (New York and Geneva, UN 2014) <http://www.ohchr.org/_layouts/15/Wopi Frame.aspx?sourcedoc=/Documents/Publications/FS25.Rev.1.pdf&action=default &DefaultItemOpen=1>.

[11]   Fox O'Mahony (n 5) 110. Fox points out that the personal consequences of evictions, such as attachment, grief or loss, are seen as intangible, immeasurable and difficult to articulate, which means that they are easily ignored in cost-benefit and legal approaches to evictions.

[12]   Fox O'Mahony (n 5) 440–441.

[13]   M Desmond and RT Kimbro, 'Eviction's fallout: housing, hardship, and health' (2015) 94 (1) *Social Forces* 295–324. Compared to matched mothers who were not evicted, mothers who were evicted in the previous year experienced more material hardship, were more likely to suffer from depression, reported worse health for themselves and their children, and reported more parenting stress.

suicide.[14] One study of 22 000 Swedish households showed that those who had lost their legal right to their home, where a landlord had applied for the eviction to be executed, were approximately four times more likely to commit suicide than those who had not been exposed to this experience.[15]

Matthew Desmond, author of the iconic study on evictions in Milwaukee, suggests that:

> Eviction's fallout is severe. Losing a home sends families to shelters, abandoned houses, and the street. It invites depression and illness, compels families to move into degrading housing in dangerous neighbourhoods, uproots communities, and harms children. Eviction reveals people's vulnerability and desperation, as well as their ingenuity and guts.[16]

Foundation Abbé Pierre and the European Federation of National Organisations Working with the Homeless (FEANTSA) have described eviction in Europe as:

> … one of the worst forms of violence that can afflict someone. It is not one of life's ups and downs; it is a mark of infamy inflicted by society through institutions such as the police force and the legal system. Eviction is not only a punishment, it is a collective abandonment of other people; prioritising one individual's right to own property over another individual's most basic needs. Whether a property owner cannot meet mortgage repayments because of soaring interest rates, or a tenant cannot manage to pay rent while awaiting work-injury benefits, or a family deprived of the right to work is forced to seek shelter in a run-down barn; all are at risk of being forced from their homes, not just in a physical sense, but also psychologically in that the outside world invades the private sphere. Eviction is a humiliating and traumatising experience, which risks pushing the victim down a slippery slope

---

[14] M Holl, L van den Dries and JRLM Wolf, 'Interventions to prevent tenant evictions: a systematic review' (2015) *Health Soc Care Community* 1–15. See also C Hartman, 'Evictions: the hidden housing problem' (2003) 14 *Housing Policy Debate* 461–501.

[15] Y Rojas and S-Å Stenberg, 'Evictions and suicide: a follow-up study of almost 22 000 Swedish households in the wake of the global financial crisis' (2016) 70 *Epidemiol Community Health* 409–413 <http://jech.bmj.com/content/70/4/409>.

[16] M Desmond, *Evicted – Poverty and Profit in the American City* (New York, Crown Publishers 2016) 5. These low-income tenants are disproportionately African American women with children. See also AD Dana, 'An invisible crisis in plain sight: the emergence of the "eviction economy", its causes, and the possibilities for reform in legal regulation and education' (2017) 115 (6) *Michigan Law Review* 935–953.

towards destitution and poor self-esteem. It constitutes a violent rupture of one's home life that directly feeds into the problem of homelessness.[17]

1.2 Defining an Eviction

The actual physical removal of occupants from a physical space is colloquially and generally regarded as the moment of eviction. However, that moment may represent the culmination of a lengthy and complex social and legal process involving a number of stages prior to, and leading to, the physical eviction. The trauma associated with physical eviction, however, is almost always avoided by occupiers, when possible. Indeed, occupiers may choose to leave before that moment, albeit involuntarily, and the physical removal will not be necessary for an eviction to occur.

While people move voluntarily and change accommodation all the time, it is the involuntary or forced moves which constitute eviction. In the Milwaukee study, some of those who were surveyed did not go to court, but Desmond concluded they were undeniably evicted, although they did not see it in this way '"When you say 'eviction'," Rose explained, "I think of the sheriffs coming and throwing you out and changing the locks … That's an eviction. We were *not* evicted."'[18] Desmond points out that:

> I learned that asking why someone moved was no simple task. Tenants often provided an explanation for a move that maximized their own volition … as tenants tended to have strict conceptions of eviction.[19]

In the Belgian research for this publication, the social workers' advice that 'tenants [should] disappear' when summoned to court, or in order to avoid the experience of eviction, was described thus:

---

[17] Foundation Abbe Pierre – FEANTSA, *Second Overview of Housing Exclusion in Europe 2017, Evictions in Europe: Useless, Expensive and Preventable* (Brussels, FEANTSA 2017) 82.

[18] See Desmond (n 16) 330–331. Desmond's detailed study revealed that one in eight of Milwaukee's private renters experienced at least one forced move, formal or informal eviction, landlord foreclosure, or building condemnation, in the two years prior to being surveyed. Nearly half of these forced moves were informal evictions; off-the-books displacement not processed through the courts. Formal eviction was less common, constituting 24 per cent of forced moves. Thus, for every eviction executed through the judicial system, there were two others executed beyond the purview of the courts, without any form of due process.

[19] Desmond (n 16) 330.

I always tell people to make sure that they go away of their own accord. Certainly, if it concerns a family when children are involved. (...) There is police, with a bailiff. Everyone in the street is watching. Just not a good experience. Avoid that, and we'll agree that you leave the key somewhere.[20]

The EU Pilot Project Report identified the process of eviction as beginning at the moment when an occupier is formally instructed to leave the home.[21] This excludes situations where an occupier willingly moves out, including leaving at the natural end of a tenancy.[22] In many cases, occupiers vacate their accommodation after the instruction to leave, but before the completion of the full formal eviction process. The formal instruction to leave the premises may involve a notice from the owner, mortgagee or landlord requiring the occupant to vacate the property; the service of proceedings for possession; the service of a barring order or divorce papers; or some other such instruction.[23] In this context, across Europe there are both judicially supervised and non-judicially supervised evictions; and some of the latter evictions may be illegal, as illustrated in Table I.1 below.

In developing a deeper analysis, the EU Pilot Project Report identified the judicially supervised eviction process as comprising three distinct phases. The first phase is the pre-court phase and begins from the moment of issuance of the formal instruction to leave.[24] The second phase involves the court process itself. The third phase encompasses the period between the court order for possession and the actual physical eviction (if it actually takes place). There is a possible link with homelessness at every stage of this process, and indeed, people may become homeless even at the first stage, as they may leave their homes on receiving formal notice to quit.

---

[20] Interview with Public Centres for Social Welfare (PCSW) social worker.

[21] Kenna et al (n 4) Part 1.

[22] A significant exception is the assured shorthold tenancy arrangement used for the private rented sector in England. These tenancies provide legal protections during an agreed period (usually 6 or 12 months) but do not provide any legal protection once the agreed period of the tenancy has expired.

[23] The issue of those fleeing domestic violence is one that does not easily fit into these descriptions of eviction, but nevertheless it involves dispossession from the home.

[24] Prior to the instruction to the occupant to leave, there may be exchanges of letters, etc; however, only materials and data from the moment that the formal eviction process has begun can usually be researched (in many cases these informal exchanges may not lead to any eviction being instigated, and they are impossible to access).

Table I.1   Phases of eviction process for judicially supervised and non-judicially supervised evictions[25]

Judicially supervised evictions	Non-judicially supervised evictions	
	Legal	Illegal
Phase 1. Pre-court from formal instruction to leave	Notaries/ Administrations/ Police/Auction Houses	Usually linked to housing shadow market (often use or threat of force, bullying, cutting off of utilities, etc)
Phase 2. Court proceedings to eviction order		
Phase 3. Execution of eviction/possession order		

In this context, it is widely accepted that officially recorded numbers of evictions do not reflect the full extent of evictions, as those at risk or issued with notices to leave may leave their home or indeed move at any stage of the eviction process.[26] For instance, in Ireland, two-thirds of mortgaged homes repossessed by lenders between 2009 and 2016, were voluntarily surrendered or abandoned.[27] The EU Pilot Project Report on evictions found that in some countries, seven times more households had eviction proceedings initiated against them than were actually physically evicted.[28] Thus, actual evictions may not involve court appearances, or physical removal, but are involuntary or forced surrenders of rights of occupation.

A 'forced' eviction is defined by the UN Committee on Economic, Social and Cultural Rights (UN CESCR) in their General Comment No 7 (1997) on the right to adequate housing as 'the permanent or temporary removal against their will of individuals, families and/or communities from the homes and/or land which they occupy, without the provision of, and access to, appropriate forms of legal or other protection.'[29] Of course,

---

[25]   See Kenna et al (n 4) 22.

[26]   Hartman (n 14).

[27]   Department of Finance/Central Bank *Report on Mortgage Arrears* (Dublin, Central Bank of Ireland 2016) 33. Of course, this took place in the course of eviction proceedings having been instigated, and the action taken by distressed home loan borrowers avoided the traumatic physical eviction from taking place. Unfortunately, there has been no research by the Central Bank or Department of Finance on the fate of those who left their homes in these circumstances or how many children were involved.

[28]   Kenna et al (n 4).

[29]   UN Committee on Economic, Social and Cultural Rights (UN CESCR), General Comment No 7 (1997) The right to adequate housing (Art 11.1): forced evictions. UN Doc. E/1998/22 (Sixteenth Session 20 May 1997) Annex IV.

many evictions take place lawfully, with due process, and in conformity with international human rights norms and under judicial supervision. This can involve legally balancing property rights and human rights with managing control and use of private and public spaces.

2. SOCIAL CONTEXT

2.1 Prevention and Risk of Evictions

Most European welfare state systems seek to mitigate the personal and social costs of evictions. A variety of social inclusionary counter-measures, remedial services for victims, and other measures, act to prevent or delay evictions.

Clearly, most evictions arise from loss of income, poverty, over-indebtedness and other economic issues.[30] People threatened by eviction are typically weak actors: many do not apply for assistance and are unable to defend their rights by themselves.[31] Yet, there are differences in the prevalence of evictions between types of tenure. Eviction for mortgage arrears is more common in some countries, and eviction from tenancies in others, although there are some common causative factors. Desmond and Gershenson, in a dataset of Milwaukee renters, empirically evaluated several potential mechanisms for understanding disparities in eviction among renting families. These included: discrimination (individual demographics); life shocks such as job loss or relationship dissolution (individual misfortunes); gentrification and concentrated disadvantage (neighbourhood characteristics); and social isolation (network composition).[32]

---

[30] One of the major deficits identified in that research (EU Pilot Project Report) was that the Eurostat EU-Survey on Income and Living Conditions (SILC) on change of dwelling, in the special housing module of 2012 (which found that 700 000 people in EU Member States had changed dwelling due to an eviction in the previous five-year period) was based on households and did not survey those living in hostels, hotels, homelessness services or on the street. The EU Pilot Project Report recommended that improving the basis for the EU-SILC question on housing evictions requires a reason for 'change of dwelling'.

[31] C von Otter, O Bäckman, SÅ Stenberg and CQ Eisenstein, 'Dynamics of evictions: results from a Swedish database' (2017) 11 (1) *European Journal of Homelessness* 1, 3.

[32] M Desmond and C Gershenson, 'Who gets evicted? Assessing individual, neighbourhood, and network factors' (2016) *Social Science Research* 1, 2

In Europe, public policy interventions to prevent/restrain evictions are often closely linked with anti-poverty, social inclusion and social policy measures. Of course, individual cases also reveal a complexity of human, financial, social, relational and health factors.[33] The risk of eviction is shaped by economic and social mechanisms that operate on structural, systemic, interpersonal and individual levels. Structural factors such as poverty, unemployment and lack of affordable housing interact with individual vulnerabilities such as low educational skills, psychosocial vulnerabilities, weak family ties and lack of social support networks in shaping the risk of eviction for the individual. These risks are mediated by systemic and institutional factors, such as the functioning of social welfare and protection systems and the legal standards and procedures regulating repossessions and evictions. The EU Pilot Project Report identified irresponsible mortgage lending, inadequate consumer protection and liberalization of the private rented sector as factors which increase the risk of evictions. Table I.2 shows a conceptual model of risk factors on the structural, systemic, interpersonal and individual levels.

Table I.2   Analytical framework of risk factors for evictions[34]

Level of cause	Factor	Comment
Structural	Poverty	High level of poverty
	Unemployment	High unemployment rate, financial turmoil
	Lack of affordable housing	High housing and rent prices, supply shortage of affordable housing
Systemic/ institutional	Legal systems	Legal procedures on evictions and repossessions contain few mechanisms to prevent eviction
	Social protection systems	Weak protection against unemployment and loss of income, low subsistence benefits

<https://scholar.harvard.edu/mdesmond/publications/who-gets-evicted-assessing-individual-neighborhood-and-network-factors>.

[33]   The EU Pilot Project Report showed that in the EU Member States where evictions are widely concentrated among people with complex support needs, about one-quarter of those can become homeless.

[34]   Kenna et al (n 4) 79.

Level of cause	Factor	Comment
	Availability of support services	Shortage of social support, prevention and outreach for high-need groups, ie individuals with psychosocial vulnerabilities
	Housing allocation systems	Insufficient social housing available for low-income and high-need groups
	Integration and coordination between existing services (including housing)	Lack of holistic approaches to housing and support
Interpersonal	Family status	Single persons more vulnerable
	Relationship situation	Abusive partners
	Relationship breakdown	Death, divorce, separation
	Lack of social network	No support from family, friends or social networks
Personal	Economic/ employment status	Low disposable income, no job, working poor, low savings
	Ethnic status/ minority background	Cultural barriers, discrimination
	Citizenship status	Lack of access to social protection
	Disability/long-term illness	Includes mental ill health and learning disability
	Educational attainment	Low attainment
	Addiction	Alcohol, drugs, gambling
	Age/gender	Young/old, male/female/transgender/ other
	Immigrant situation	Refugee status/recent arrival

Source: Adapted from W Edgar and H Meert (2005) 'Fourth Review of Statistics on Homelessness in Europe. The ETHOS Definition of Homelessness' (Brussels, FEANTSA).

Across the European Union, unemployment and financial instability in households are highlighted as major risk factors for eviction. The economic crisis since 2008 has reinforced this pattern, especially in the countries of southern Europe and the parts of the Central and Eastern European Countries (CEECs) that were most adversely affected by the crisis.[35] The EU Pilot Project Report showed that in southern Europe, evictions were associated mainly with unemployment and household breakdown, whereas in most CEE countries, evictions were associated primarily with more general poverty-related problems. In CEE Member States, low income and lack of savings, among both the working poor and people on subsistence benefits, are associated with the risk of eviction, in combination with the often weaker social protection systems in those countries. Rent and mortgage arrears, frequently related to consumer debt, in addition to utility arrears (often due to high heating costs in cold winters, especially in housing estates in need of renovation), are highlighted as important or key reasons for evictions.

In northern and western European Member States,[36] unemployment, financial instability and household breakdown played a significant role in the risk factors for evictions. However, there is evidence of significant levels of eviction among individuals with complex support needs due to mental ill health and substance abuse. These groups were prevalent among evicted people in the eastern and southern European states too, but in these countries, more general poverty and unemployment problems are significant. This is a pattern which can be explained by the variations in general economic conditions and the welfare systems in these countries.

2.2 Structural/Societal Factors Related to Evictions in the Selected Countries

UN Habitat has pointed out that the commoditization of housing has strengthened the perception of shelter as a speculative financial asset, generating an artificial sense of wealth and an unsustainable cycle of debt, which culminated in the housing foreclosure crisis and the global economic downturn of 2007–2009.[37]

---

[35] Southern European Member States in this classification include Cyprus, Greece, Italy, Malta, Portugal and Spain. The Central and Eastern European (CEE) Member States include Bulgaria, Croatia, the Czech Republic, Estonia, Hungary, Latvia, Lithuania, Poland, Romania, Slovakia and Slovenia.

[36] This category of northern and western European States includes Austria, Belgium, Denmark, Germany, Finland, France, Ireland, Luxembourg, the Netherlands, Sweden and the UK.

[37] UN Habitat, *Housing at the Centre of the New Urban Agenda* (Nairobi, UN-Habitat 2015) 9; see also MB Aalbers, *The Financialization of Housing* (Oxford, Routledge 2016).

Land and housing markets have reproduced this speculative practice in the urban domain reinforcing instead of attenuating socioeconomic and spatial inequalities. The challenges to create, preserve and improve affordable housing have grown across the globe. Indeed, this is one of the most critical problems of housing today with an increasing number of households in developing and developed country cities financially stretched by housing costs.[38]

Across Europe, there are similar reports of structural challenges around expensive housing markets. The lack of affordable housing in larger cities exacerbates the financial problems of many low-income families. It forces them into housing they can barely afford, which also increases their risk of rent arrears. Moreover, changes in demographics and household composition reinforce the structural lack of affordable housing, as more and more households become single-person households, creating a need for additional housing. A shortage of social housing, with lengthy waiting lists in many countries, forces low-income and vulnerable households into the private rental markets, where, depending on the market situation and legal regulations, increasing rent levels limit their options, and enhance the risk of eviction.

Housing affordability can also be a key factor in the pathway to evictions. In 2015, an 11.3 per cent share of the EU-28 population lived in households that spent 40 per cent or more of their equivalized disposable income on housing. The proportion of the population whose housing costs exceeded 40 per cent of their equivalized disposable income was highest for tenants with market price rents (27.0 per cent), and lowest for persons in owner-occupied dwellings without a loan or mortgage (6.7 per cent).[39] The EU-28 average masks significant differences between the EU Member States. At one extreme, there were a number of countries where a relatively small proportion of the population lived in households where housing costs exceeded 40 per cent of their disposable income, notably Malta (1.1 per cent), Cyprus (3.9 per cent), Ireland (4.6 per cent) and Finland (4.9 per cent). At the other extreme, just over two out of every five people (40.9 per cent) in Greece and just under one in six of the population in Romania (15.9 per cent), Germany (15.6 per cent) and Denmark (15.1 per cent), spent more than 40 per cent of their equivalized disposable income on housing.

---

[38] UN Habitat (n 37) 9.
[39] See Eurostat, 'Housing Statistics 2015' <http://ec.europa.eu/eurostat/statistics-explained/index.php/Housing_statistics#Housing_affordability>.

Social housing has traditionally provided affordable housing to those on low incomes. It has a long history in Europe, where it has also played a vital role in the economy, in regeneration and in meeting housing need.[40] However, a report by the European Parliament in 2013 showed that state budgets dedicated to housing policies were significantly reduced in a number of countries.[41]

In Chapter 1, Jana Verstraete, Pascal De Decker and Diederik Vermeir point out that in Belgium, a high level of rented housing is occupied by low-income households (who cannot afford to buy), and these tenants bear a high rent burden. Private rented housing is regarded as a tenure of last resort, although some 'buyers under duress' purchase inferior quality dwellings and cannot then afford to make necessary improvements. One-third of social renters cannot afford a dignified lifestyle after rental costs. In Chapter 2, Marc Uhry suggests that in France prevention of evictions has been part of social policy for many decades, although recent decades have seen the emergence of new challenges in the form of undocumented migrants and the development of squats and slums.[42] Mortgage lenders are held liable for their 'irresponsible lending', and accordingly, there are low levels of mortgage possession cases in France. The social effects of the banking crisis of 2008 were delayed in France; there was no house price collapse or rise in interest rates, and only a gradual increase in unemployment.

Christoph U Schmid and Sofija Nikolic point out, in Chapter 3, that in Germany, eviction is mostly a consequence of rent or mortgage arrears. As in France and the UK, there is a developed welfare state system of support for tenants and others in arrears. Evictions mainly arise as a result of unemployment, relationship breakdown or personal difficulties.

In Chapter 4, Nóra Teller, Eszter Somogyi and Nóra Tosics show that in Hungary, the 2008 financial crisis increased the vulnerability of many households. There has been a dramatic increase in the number of severely materially deprived people, which grew from 18 per cent of the population in 2008, to 30 per cent in 2016. General indebtedness has

---

[40] K Scanlon, CME Whitehead and M Fernández Arrigoitia (eds), *Social Housing in Europe* (London, Wiley-Blackwell 2014); Housing Europe, *The State of Housing in the EU 2015* (Brussels, Housing Europe 2015); M Elsinga, 'Changing housing systems and their potential impacts on homelessness' (2015) 9 (1) *European Journal of Homelessness* 15.

[41] European Parliament, 'Social Housing in the EU' (2013), Brussels, IP/A/EMPL/NT/2012-07 PE 492.469.

[42] Some 400–500 such slums were counted in 2014, where 17 000–20 000 people lived, and in that year some 13 000 people experienced forced evictions.

increased dramatically, while utility, loan and housing arrears are common. There is growing housing insecurity, and evictions have almost doubled in the period 2012–2016.

The current economic crisis facing Italy has been identified as the main causative factor in the rising level of evictions, although as Elena Bargelli and Giulia Donadio observe in Chapter 6, the mortgage market has not been affected by the speculative bubble of some other European countries. Lending policies have been conservative, and this is now reinforced by the Mortgage Credit Directive.[43] Indeed, this Directive has been transposed by many EU countries, and limits the levels of mortgage lending according to strict means tests and property valuation tests. In Ireland, the banking collapse led to a severe recession and unemployment of 15 per cent in 2012. However, the rise in rents and shortage of affordable rented housing is the main cause of evictions.

In Chapter 8, Witold Borysiak shows that in Poland, the main reasons for evictions are viewed as economic, in the context of a 12 per cent unemployment rate. This leads to arrears of rent, or mortgage or other debts. Psychosocial factors also have an impact, and sometimes a combination of economic, social and personal issues precipitates an eviction. Poland lacks a national support system for local authorities to deal with the need for social housing, and there are an estimated 1.5 million housing units required.

In Slovenia, since 2008, unemployment levels have increased, but are now declining, although the EU at-risk-of-poverty rate increased from 9 per cent in 2009 to 14.3 per cent in 2015, and for those who are unemployed the rate was 45 per cent in 2015. Maša Filipovič Hrast suggests, in Chapter 9, that these financially vulnerable households face a higher risk of eviction due to arrears of mortgage, rent or other costs.

In Chapter 10, Sergio Nasarre-Aznar and Rosa Maria Garcia-Teruel explain that the absence of any alternatives to home ownership rendered Spanish households vulnerable, due to their reliance on mortgages. This has been facilitated by tax and policy incentives for developers and purchasers, and the establishment of a mortgage system with fast foreclosure, until EU consumer law (the iconic *Aziz* case) began to be applied. This case exposed irresponsible lending and very strict enforcement of security, often extending to family guarantees as recourse. The rental sector remains undeveloped and often in the shadow economy; and

---

[43] Directive 2014/17/EU on Credit Agreements for Consumers Relating to Residential Immovable Property and Amending Directives 2008/48/EC and 2013/36/EU and Regulation (EU) No 1093/2010.

this affects greatly the housing security of those who are at risk of poverty. Spain has only 2 per cent social housing stock. The banking crisis and subsequent recession, with unemployment of 20 per cent, exacerbated the problems, with major levels of evictions.

In Chapter 7, Michel Vols affirms that in the Netherlands the economic crisis and unemployment have been significant factors in mortgage-related evictions, but another factor is the approach of local authorities to squatting and housing-related crime, such as drug-dealing and cannabis-growing.

In the UK, since 2010 government policy has sought to assert a 'free market' approach to renting. Even earlier, legislative and policy changes reduced the protection of private tenants to the lowest level in Europe, with six- or twelve-month assured shorthold tenancies. These give an automatic right to possession for the landlord once the required notice is given. Indeed, such is the insecurity of these tenancies that one-quarter of renters are in their homes for less than one year. Taking place against a background of reduction in welfare and social housing expenditure, this leaves fewer and fewer options for poor households. Housing affordability is poor in the UK, and the gap between income and housing costs continues to grow. As Nicholas Pleace and Caroline Hunter suggest in Chapter 11, there is an inherent dysfunctionality in the private rented sector, which needs to be addressed, as the current model exacerbates the risk of eviction. Law plays a central role in the UK. It is the law which makes the private rented sector an inherently insecure tenure for tenants, with major imbalances in rights in favour of landlords.

3. POLICY CONTEXT

3.1 General Housing Policy

There are significant variations in the housing systems of the eleven countries in this study. Levels of owner-occupation vary between 92 per cent in Hungary to 45 per cent in Germany, with concurrent variations in the levels of private and social rented housing. Germany exhibits some 50 per cent of tenures in the private rented sector, while Spain, Italy and Hungary have less than 5 per cent. Significantly, the UK, which has had a liberal market-based approach to its housing system, has less than 18 per cent private rented housing. Housing cooperatives or similar condominium ownership systems account for 16 per cent, 9 per cent and 14 per cent of tenures in Poland, Italy and Slovenia respectively.

The housing systems vary considerably in the proportions of social rented housing, with France, the Netherlands and the UK reflecting the legacy of welfare state post-World War II public housing provision (see Table I.3). These variations have significant implications for security of tenure in cases of potential eviction, as well as the opportunity for state agencies to provide alternative accommodation in cases of eviction. Indeed, as shown by Nicholas Pleace and Caroline Hunter, general housing policy in the UK in the years after World War II, involving a range of welfare state measures, has had a major impact on evictions and related homelessness. This model is being dismantled in the UK, but still exists there to a greater extent than in many other European countries. For instance, while legislation and policy since the 1980s have diminished tenant security and affordable rented housing, nevertheless there are local authority supports and interventions which protect tenants and ensure that those evicted do not become homeless. However, lack of government investment in the UK in new social housing means that poorer families now occupy private rented housing and cannot pay increasing rents. State housing benefits are paid to five million households at an average of £5460 (€6150) per annum. UK government policies may be creating systemic general inequality in health care, education and housing, but with state assistance reduced to a safety net.

In France, as Marc Uhry suggests, the legacy of the post-World War II welfare state with relatively high levels of social housing (4 million dwellings or 17 per cent of total stock), is significant. However, there is a paradox, whereby poor households have a relatively low housing costs burden yet are relatively more often involved in rent arrears cases and evictions.

In Germany, legislative competences and government responsibilities for housing policies have been transferred from the federation to the regional states (*Bundesländer*). However, legislation regulating housing subsidies (*Wohnraumförderungsgesetz* – WoFG), the control of rents in the private rented sector, and tenancy protection (all of which are regulated in the Civil Code (*Bürgerliches Gesetzbuch* – BGB)) remains at the national level. There is a good level of protection against eviction, which includes reporting obligations on courts, support with rent and arrears, curial discretion to suspend evictions and obligations on authorities to provide shelter for those who are involuntarily homeless. In Hungary, some 90 per cent of dwellings are in private ownership (20 per cent with a mortgage), with 3–4 per cent social rentals. The housing allowance scheme (devolved to local government in 2015) covers 500 000 households or 3.8 million people and 10–15 per cent of normative housing costs. Although some municipalities run local arrears management schemes, these are ineffective as most private sector tenancies are now unofficial. Non-governmental organizations (NGOs) operate tenancy support and eviction-prevention schemes.

Table I.3   Variations of housing tenures across the eleven countries[44]

Country	Owner-occupied (%)	Private rented (%)	Social rented (%)	Other (%)
Belgium[45]	64.8	27.5	6.5	1.2
France	57.9	23	16.8	2.4
Germany	45.4	50.7	3.9	
Hungary[46]	92	4	3	1[47]
Ireland[48]	67.6	20.6	8.7	3.1
Italy	71.9	14.8	3.7	9.6
Poland	75.4	0.8	7.6	16.2[49]
Slovenia	77	3	6	14
Spain	77.1	13.8	2.5	6.5
The Netherlands	60	10	30	
United Kingdom	63.1	19	17.6	

In Ireland, evictions are a socially and politically charged issue, and politicians of all parties denounce such actions. Yet, as Padraic Kenna suggests in Chapter 5, evictions are quite common, largely in the private rented sector, but also due to mortgage arrears arising from the credit boom up to 2007. Following the banking collapse of 2008, the subsequent economic recession led to high unemployment and many mortgages becoming unsustainable, particularly where reckless lending had taken place. General housing policy related to evictions involves significant support to help with unaffordable rents, social supports, and extensive homelessness supports delivered through non-state bodies.

---

[44]   Housing Europe, *The State of Housing in the EU 2017* (Brussels, Housing Europe Observatory 2017) <http://www.housingeurope.eu/resource-1000/the-state-of-housing-in-the-eu-2017>.

[45]   European Commission, Population and Housing Census 2011; Housing Europe General Survey 2016.

[46]   Census 2011, European Mortgage Federation (EMF) *Hypostat 2017* (Brussels, EMF 2017).

[47]   Cooperatives.

[48]   Census (Ireland) 2016.

[49]   Cooperatives.

There have been a number of codes for lenders and a major revision of Irish personal bankruptcy/insolvency legislation. This enables households to achieve a fresh start after one year of personal bankruptcy, or six years of an insolvency arrangement.

The Polish Ministry of Infrastructure and Development has adopted new guidelines for national development of housing, although there are no specific policies on evictions. Witold Borysiak points out that local governments or municipalities are obliged by law to provide shelter, meals and essential clothing for those who are evicted. In Slovenia, Maša Filipovič Hrast discusses how debt levels are low, despite a high level of home ownership. The new 'Resolution on Housing Policy 2015–2025', includes increasing security of tenure and reducing illegal renting, but also contains measures which would enable quicker/swifter evictions.

Spain has been among the countries worst affected by the banking crisis, with reports of some 210 000 mortgage related evictions between 2010 and 2015. In the rented sector, there were some 206 000 evictions in the period. Despite the large numbers of households evicted, only a small number become homeless. Reliance on family supports and accommodation in such cases of emergency is a significant feature of the response of Spanish society. Various enactments by the Spanish government and the Autonomous Regions have sought to address the levels of repossession, often in response to findings of the Spanish Supreme Court or the Court of Justice of the European Union (CJEU). However, as Sergio Nasarre-Aznar and Rosa Maria Garcia-Teruel point out, there is a lack of rented housing, or intermediate tenures, and reliance on mortgages to access homes remains a significant element of housing policy.

Government policy in the Netherlands supports home ownership, although levels of social rented housing are comparatively high, amounting to some 30 per cent of housing stock. One significant feature of the Dutch mortgage system is the National Mortgage Guarantee Scheme (NMGS), which, for a premium of 1 per cent of the mortgage, paid at the outset, guarantees to cover any shortfall in the event of default and sale of the mortgaged property. Michel Vols points out that in 2015, some 78 per cent of buyers availed of this surety. Another unique feature is that following EU decisions on State Aid, Dutch housing associations who provide social housing must rent the great majority of new tenancies to those on annual incomes below €36 000.

3.2 Policy Measures which Prevent Evictions

The EU Pilot Project Report identified a range of primary, secondary and tertiary measures across EU Member States which prevent evictions or mitigate their impact. Primary prevention measures are macro-level measures related to increased housing supply and affordability. In some cases, the state takes on a direct provision or appropriation role, or sponsors NGOs or housing organizations and others to do so. This may require investment in major social housing programmes.

The general availability of income benefits, housing benefits, employment protection and other supports can have a major impact on preventing evictions, alongside the more focused and targeted secondary and tertiary prevention measures. Indeed, social transfers reduced the at-risk-of-poverty rate by around 50 per cent or more in the Czech Republic, Germany, Finland, Ireland, the Netherlands, Sweden and the United Kingdom.[50] However, the EU Pilot Project Report identified an increasing gap between combined welfare and housing benefit levels, compared with increasing rent levels, particularly in urban growth centres, where a high level of evictions from private rented housing is evident. The specific nature of this problem varies, depending on whether the focus is on very high rent levels in cities, such as London, Munich, Paris or Stockholm, or on general poverty problems for lower-income people in CEE Member States. There is a major current challenge in aligning welfare and housing benefit levels with housing costs so as to enable low-income and vulnerable persons to access secure and affordable housing.

Evictions can be prevented in many ways. Availability of financial and social support from family and friends can be significant factors. Public assistance to cover rent arrears/mortgage instalments and the provision of housing counselling and advice are also significant. Holl et al suggest that debt advice and legal assistance can be most effective in preventing evictions of tenants.[51] Evictions can be prevented or suspended through measures which support tenants to deal with arrears and debt, as well as developing realistic repayment options for arrears. There are a range of measures which can be taken in cases of mortgage arrears which would prevent evictions.[52] Other secondary prevention measures

---

[50]   The greatest impact was in Ireland, where the rate was reduced from 38.5 per cent to 14.1 per cent in 2013 through social transfers.

[51]   Holl et al (n 14) examined all existing international (English language) published research on preventing tenant evictions and concluded that '[A] scientific foundation of knowledge for the development and implementation of preventative practices and policies regarding tenant evictions is almost absent and more research is needed.'

[52]   European Central Bank (ECB), *Guidance to Banks on Non-Performing Loans* (ECB 2017) 49; EBA, *Final Report on Guidelines on Arrears and Foreclosure*, EBA/GL/2015/12 (EBA 2015). These include forbearance measures such as

include notification by courts of state/welfare agencies of the planned eviction, legal aid and representation, adequate legal defences to eviction, general moratorium on evictions, winter and out-of-hours bans on evictions, and court suspensions of eviction orders. Measures which reduce the negative impact of evictions include rapid or emergency rehousing of those evicted, protected minimum income and debt relief schemes, and access to effective homelessness services.

A critical limitation in any European research on evictions is the absence of data and reports on evictions in the informal or 'shadow' housing sector, particularly among migrants (documented and undocumented) and other excluded people. These include people with disabilities, asylum seekers and others who experience insecure housing, precarious employment and a high risk of eviction, and those who are not included in state, court or NGO bureaucracy and/or (any other) record-keeping. Data exists on such evictions in only a few northern European countries; although anecdotal accounts would suggest that there are many evictions in the informal or 'shadow' sector. The risk of homelessness among those evicted is clearly related to economic and social resource levels, with the poorest people (always including migrants) generally becoming homeless in the absence of state or family support.

Specific policies related to evictions in the eleven countries in this study vary considerably. All countries have a range of state and charitable funds which support those at risk or after eviction. In France, the Housing Solidarity Fund can assist those in arrears, and courts are obliged to allow a tenant three years to repay arrears, while the social agency CCAPEX can intervene at any time to provide alternative housing. In Germany, there is a housing allowance (*Wohngeld*), for those on low incomes with high housing costs, and a social protection system. In the UK, there is a welfare state safety net involving emergency homelessness provision, social protection measures and housing benefits to assist with housing costs, in addition to a range of statutory and policy measures. For instance, legislation from 1977 on protection from evictions enables local authorities to intervene and support tenants at risk of eviction. There is also a statutory obligation on local authorities, since the 1970s, to provide accommodation for homeless people who are in

---

interest-only payments; reduced payments; grace period/payment moratorium; arrears/interest capitalization; interest rate reduction; extension of maturity or term; additional security; sale by agreement or assisted sale; rescheduled payments; conversion of currency; other alteration of contract conditions or covenants; new credit facilities; debt consolidation; and partial or total debt forgiveness.

priority need (those with children, disabilities or a vulnerability), are not intentionally homeless, and have a local connection with the authority.

In France and Belgium, there are a range of policies to prevent evictions such as an obligation on landlords or courts to notify public authorities of an impending eviction. Relevant Italian housing policy measures include support for vulnerable people, suspension of evictions and measures to alleviate temporary economic hardship. Italian legislation which allows the suspension of enforcement of evictions has resulted in mortgage lenders becoming more conciliatory. Faced with a lengthy process, lenders often opt for some form of debt restructuring or forbearance, which usually results in lower levels of evictions. As pointed out by Elena Bargelli and Giulia Donadio, the Solidarity Fund of 2007 finances the suspension of mortgage payments in cases of death, total impairment or unemployment. There is also an alternative dispute-resolution system focused on the mortgage market. The Social Fund for Rent and Fund for Tenants in Default, assists those who cannot afford rents in the private rented sector. Tenancy laws initiated in 1978 act to suspend evictions and allow late payments of arrears to avoid eviction.

The foreign exchange loan crisis in Hungary led to government action in 2012, with the establishment of the National Asset Management Company, which took over those mortgages. Loans were taken at 35–55 per cent of origination value, and debtors converted to tenants, thereby avoiding evictions. By 2016, some 25 000 mortgages had been converted to tenancies in this way. In Spain, as Sergio Nasarre-Aznar and Rosa Maria Garcia-Teruel point out, the national government did not react to the crisis until 2011, and the Autonomous Regions, such as Catalonia, were the first to address the issue of evictions. However, almost all these steps by the Autonomous Regions have been challenged before the Spanish Constitutional Court. This has led to the rise of social movements and judicial activism by some judges to mitigate the worst effects of the situation. In 2011, legislation protected a minimum income of the debtor from being attached as part of the enforcement of the security on the defaulted mortgage. There are public and charitable funds to assist those evicted by the provision of temporary shelter.

3.3   Best Practice Models for Preventing, Tackling and Reacting to Evictions

There are a range of good practices examined in this study across the eleven countries, although most are tenure specific. In relation to mortgage arrears, the caution of lenders against reckless lending was highlighted as a key issue in Belgium, German and Italy, and as a major factor in avoiding mortgage-related evictions. In Germany, prevention of eviction from mortgaged property is also advanced through conservative lending practices, and long-term mortgages with fixed interest rates, which avoid sudden increases in costs for the borrower. The harmonization of responsible lending, as a result of the EU Mortgage Credit Directive, is generally viewed as beneficial.

A second example of good practice was the linkage of a range of support agencies, particularly when combined with an early-warning system; for instance, where there is an obligation on landlords or courts to inform social services of impending eviction, as in Germany. Other best practices include the Flemish 'fund to prevent evictions', compensating a small number of affiliated landlords for a shortfall between a court-agreed payment schedule and the actual payments made by the tenant. The French GIP Charente Solidarités (Charente Solidarities Public Interests Group) coordinates all actions preventing evictions in the Department of Charente. It manages the Fund for Solidarity for Housing (FSL), and a personalized support service, making reports to the court and the Prefect at all stages of the procedure. Two-thirds of those who engaged with GIP Charente Solidarités found a concrete housing solution to the eviction process. In Ireland, a tenancy protection service operated by the Threshold housing advice agency renegotiates rents and levels of assistance to ensure continued occupation of tenants at risk of eviction, and a tenancy protection service operated by Focus Ireland, a housing NGO, are examples of good practice. Another example is the provision that a landlord cannot penalize a tenant for referring a dispute, including a threatened eviction, to the State Residential Tenancies Board.

There are special protections available in Poland for vulnerable groups of tenants such as pregnant women, minors, persons with disabilities and the unemployed, who must be provided with alternative accommodation in the event of eviction, and this applies to some 60–65 per cent of cases. Other groups of tenants can be evicted, but the court will examine *ex officio* whether special conditions exist which require alternative social housing. Witold Borysiak points out that there may be a delay of two to four years in the provision of such housing and that no eviction can take place in the meantime. Other best practices include the protection of tenants from excessive rent increases and other fees, as specified in Polish legislation dating from 2001.

Maša Filipovič Hrast highlights that in Slovenia, while free legal aid is inaccessible to vulnerable people at risk of eviction, social tenants are protected from eviction under 2003 legislation in cases of a death in the family, unforeseen loss of employment, serious illness and other factors. In Germany, pursuant to Article 721 *Zivilprozessordnung* (ZPO), the court may, *ex officio* or upon a request, grant to the debtor a reasonable period to vacate premises (up to twelve months), taking into account all relevant circumstances. According to Article 765a (1) ZPO, the eviction may be suspended if 'the measure entails a hardship that due to very special circumstances is immoral (*contra bonos mores*)'.[53]

Best practices in Spain, as described by Sergio Nasarre-Aznar and Rosa Maria Garcia-Teruel, include moratoria on evictions and codes of good practice for lenders. These include new insolvency measures allowing a 'fresh start', measures to facilitate separating parents, a social fund of dwellings, assistance by the authorities with securing a new dwelling, and judicial discretion allowing more time before evictions.

In the UK, as described by Nicholas Pleace and Caroline Hunter, legal advice and support is available from a range of agencies for tenants at risk of eviction, along with mediation services and tenancy-sustainment teams in social housing. Legislation obliges local authorities to provide access to temporary rehousing for homeless people with a priority need and a local connection. There is also a network of court duty schemes whereby anyone facing possession proceedings can get free legal advice and representation. In Ireland, the *Abhaile* scheme (which is attached to the state Money Advice and Budgeting Service) provides for a consult-ation with a solicitor in mortgage possession cases, although this does not actually cover legal representation. The Human Rights Ombudsman in Slovenia has argued for changes in legislation regarding the principle of proportionality in cases of eviction.

In addition to the moratoria on eviction in winter in France, Hungary, Poland and the northern Italian cities, moratoria on evictions have been introduced in Italy and Spain.[54] Italian legislation in 2013 provided a moratorium on evictions in the private rented sector in cases arising from unemployment, reduction in working hours, economic hardship or health issues. Spanish legislation in 2012 provided for a mortgage possession moratorium until 2020, but this is, however, quite limited (covering around 2000 cases in 2017).

Michel Vols draws on research which shows that in the Netherlands, combinations of personal and circumstantial factors which create risk of eviction can be addressed only through individualized and tailor-made approaches to effectively prevent evictions.[55] Research in 2015 highlights that debt advice, monitoring, agreements between housing agencies and

---

[53]   Art 765a (1) ZPO.

[54]   In Poland this does not apply to squatters.

[55]   D Wewerinke, W De Graaf, L van Doorn and J Wolf, *Huurders over een dreigende huisuitzetting* (Nijmegen, RUMC 2014) 54.

debt support organizations, and community mental health networks that respond to vulnerability of households, proved to be valuable interventions to prevent evictions.[56]

Of course, rapid rehousing and effective homelessness services are a major part of the policy response to evictions. In Germany, according to laws of regional states relating to police, security and regulatory issues, it is a duty of municipalities to provide temporary accommodation for persons who would otherwise be homeless, with homelessness considered a serious threat to public safety. In Belgium, rehousing is not guaranteed, although social support agencies can offer assistance including financial support, and are obliged to do so in the Brussels and Wallonia Regions.

In Italy, as described by Elena Bargelli and Giulia Donadio, there is assistance through social services for households that become homeless, although this is limited by available regional and local resources.

Other examples of good practice involve initiatives where the state purchases distressed mortgages and arranges for occupants to become tenants, as in Hungary, a practice described by Nóra Teller, Eszter Somogyi and Nóra Tosics. Ultimately, as Nicholas Pleace and Caroline Hunter point out, the key to avoiding homelessness or housing exclusion following eviction is a strongly integrated strategy involving housing advice, homelessness prevention and other services working seamlessly.

4. LEGAL AND HUMAN RIGHTS CONTEXT

4.1 Housing Rights and Evictions

Evictions can involve a gross violation of human rights, especially the right to adequate housing. Forced evictions can result in other severe human rights violations, particularly when they are accompanied by forced relocation or homelessness.[57] Unsurprisingly, therefore, evictions

---

[56] G Schout, G De Jong and I Van Laere, 'Pathways toward evictions: an exploratory study of the inter-relational dynamics between evictees and service providers in the Netherlands' (2015) 30 (2) *Journal of Housing and the Built Environment* 183–198.

[57] See UN OHCHR (n 10) 1.

which involve interference with the home by state or non-state institutions have been the subject of many constitutional and legal provisions establishing strict legal limitations.[58]

Fundamental human rights and housing rights are rooted in the social and political order of society, social justice, the development of children, the securing of a stable home life, security of tenure, a corrective to markets and advancing the public interest. The term 'right to housing' often refers to wider rights of housing access, quality and other factors, as well as protection from eviction and homelessness prevention. The right to housing is primarily framed, defined, implemented and enforced through national constitutional, legislative, regulatory and institutional provisions.[59] Across EU Member States, there is a complex interplay between national law, EU law and various international human rights instruments in relation to evictions.[60]

Illegal or unauthorized evictions are generally regarded as a violation of housing rights, and there are growing obligations on EU Member States, in relation to particular classes of people, to rehouse those evicted before authorizing actual evictions.[61] While the rights of those being evicted can include criminal law remedies for illegal or unauthorized evictions, the EU Pilot Project Report found few enforced criminal sanctions in relation to illegal/unauthorized evictions across EU Member States. Countries with a relatively high level of renting in the 'shadow market' reported significant levels of illegal evictions.[62]

---

[58]   B Bengtsson, S Fitzpatrick and B Watts, 'Rights to housing: reviewing the terrain and exploring a way forward, housing' (2014) 31 (4) *Theory and Society* 447–463; See also S Fick and M Vols, 'Best protection against eviction? A comparative analysis of protection against evictions in the European Convention on Human Rights and the South African Constitution' (2016) 3 *European Journal of Comparative Law and Governance* 40–69; S Gerull, 'Evictions due to rent arrears: a comparative analysis of evictions in 14 countries' (2014) 2 *European Journal of Homelessness* 137–155.

[59]   M Oren, R Alterman and Y Zilbershats, 'Housing rights in constitutional legislation: a conceptual classification' in P Kenna (ed) *Contemporary Housing Issues in a Globalized World* (Aldershot, Ashgate 2014); P Kenna (ed), *Contemporary Housing Issues in a Globalized World* (Aldershot, Ashgate 2014).

[60]   See Kenna et al (n 4).

[61]   Significantly, the Tenants Charter of the International Union of Tenants 2004, Article IX (b), suggests that '[E]victions on social causes cannot be accepted without the tenant obtaining another dwelling' <http://www.iut.nu/aboutiut.htm#Tenants_Charter>.

[62]   The EU Pilot Project Report recommended the development of a prohibitory injunction against illegal or unauthorized evictions similar to that in

4.2 Housing Rights at UN Level

Protection from eviction forms part of the protection of the right to housing and is recognized at the level of international human rights.[63] The right to housing is included within the United Nations International Covenant on Economic, Social and Cultural Rights (ICESCR)[64] and the European Social Charter of the Council of Europe,[65] both of which have been ratified by all EU Member States.

Article 11 (1) of the ICESCR obliges States Parties to recognize the right of everyone to an adequate standard of living for himself and his family, including adequate food, clothing and housing, and to the continuous improvement of living conditions. The States Parties should take appropriate steps to ensure the realization of this right, recognizing to this effect the essential importance of international cooperation based on free consent.[66] State obligations with regard to the right to housing should be interpreted together with all other human rights obligations and, in particular, in the context of eviction, with the obligation to provide the family with the widest possible protection. The obligation of States Parties to provide, to the maximum of their available resources, alternative accommodation for evicted persons who need it, includes the protection of the family unit, especially when the persons are responsible for the care and education of dependent children.

The UN Committee on Economic, Social and Cultural Rights (UN CESCR), General Comment No 7 on Forced Evictions, sets out the

---

environmental cases and consumer protection under Directive 98/27/EC of the European Parliament and of the Council of 19 May 1998 on injunctions for the protection of consumers' interests, 11 June 1998, OJL 166/51.

[63] See J Hohmann, *The Right to Housing: Law, Concepts, Possibilities* (Oxford, Hart 2013); M Kolocek, *The Human Right to Housing in the Face of Land Policy and Social Citizenship – A Global Discourse Analysis* (London, Palgrave Macmillan 2017); N Moons, *The Right to Housing in Law and Society* (Abingdon, Routledge 2018).

[64] Art 11 International Covenant on Economic, Social and Cultural Rights (1966) UN Doc. A/6316. There are also a range of housing rights in relation to children, persons with disabilities, migrants and others groups at risk of eviction; See P Kenna, 'Can housing rights be applied to modern housing systems?' (2010) 2 (2) *International Journal of Law in the Built Environment* 103–117.

[65] Council of Europe, European Treaty Series – No 35: European Social Charter, Turin, 18 October 1961. (Revised) Council of Europe, Strasbourg 3 May 1996, Articles 16, 30 and 31.

[66] All EU Member States have adopted the ICESCR.

international human rights norms.[67] In cases of forced evictions,[68] UN human rights standards oblige states to ensure the presence of government officials, or their representatives, during an eviction, and ensure proper identification of the persons carrying out the eviction.[69]

However, evictions should not render individuals becoming homeless. Where those affected do not have the means to acquire alternative housing, States Parties must take all appropriate measures to ensure, where possible, that adequate alternative housing, resettlement or access to productive land, as the case may be, is available.[70] States Parties should pay particular attention to evictions that involve women, children, older persons, persons with disabilities or other vulnerable individuals or groups who are subject to systemic discrimination. The State Party has a duty to take reasonable measures to provide alternative housing to persons who are left homeless as a result of eviction, irrespective of whether the eviction is initiated by its authorities or by an individual, such as the lessor.

The obligation to provide alternative housing to evicted persons who need it implies that, under Article 2 (1) ICESCR, 'States Parties must take all necessary steps, to the maximum of their available resources, to uphold this right.'[71] States Parties can choose a variety of policies to achieve this purpose, including the establishment of housing subsidies for those unable to obtain affordable housing.[72] However, any measures adopted must be deliberate, specific and as straightforward as possible to fulfil this right[73] as swiftly and efficiently as possible. Policies on

---

[67] UN Committee on Economic, Social and Cultural Rights (UN CESCR), General Comment No 7 (1997) (n 29).

[68] According to the UN CESCR, General Comment No 7 (1997) (n 29).

[69] UN CESCR, General Comment No 7 (1997) (n 29) 4, para 15 (d).

[70] UN CESCR, General Comment No 7 (1997) (n 29) 5, para 16.

[71] UN CESCR, General Comment No 3: The Nature of States Parties' Obligations (Art 2, Para 1 of the Covenant) 14 December 1990, E/1991/23 (Adopted at the Fifth Session of the Committee on Economic, Social and Cultural Rights).

[72] UN CESCR, General Comment No 4: The Right to Adequate Housing (Art 11 (1) of the Covenant). Adopted at the Sixth Session of the Committee on Economic, Social and Cultural Rights, on 13 December 1991. (Contained in Document E/1992/23), para 8 (c).

[73] UN CESCR, General Comment No 3 (1990) (n 71). See also the letter of 16 May 2012 from the Chair of the Committee to the States Parties to the Covenant.

alternative housing in case of eviction should be commensurate with the need of those concerned and the urgency of the situation and should respect the dignity of the person. Moreover, States Parties should take consistent and coordinated measures to resolve institutional shortcomings and structural causes of the lack of housing.[74]

In 2015, the UN CESCR stated that there are state obligations to ensure the accessibility of legal remedies for persons facing mortgage enforcement procedures for failure to repay loans. States must adopt appropriate legislative measures to ensure that mortgage enforcement procedures contain appropriate safeguards before evictions take place, in accordance with the ICESCR and General Comment No 7.[75] It is significant that, in this case, inadequate notice of possession proceedings was held to be a violation of the right to housing.[76]

In a significant decision relating to eviction, the UN CESCR, on a complaint under the Optional Protocol, held that an eviction in Spain without a guarantee of alternative housing by the authorities of the State Party, constituted a violation of the right to adequate housing.

The protection against forced evictions applies to persons living in rental housing. In the case of *Mohamed Ben Djazia and Naouel Bellili v Spain*, the UN CESCR set out the state obligations to ensure the horizontal nature of the protection against forced eviction, ie the state has a duty to ensure that the protection extends to relations between private individuals in eviction proceedings.[77] Significantly, the State Party contended that the eviction took place at the initiative of the lessor and that the state/judiciary intervened only as a mediator. However, the UN

---

[74] See, for example, the submission in this case of the Special Rapporteur on adequate housing as a component of the right to an adequate standard of living, and on the right to non-discrimination in this context, and her report (A/HRC/31/54, paras 28–38). See also UN Doc. A/72/128, Farha, L, UN Special Rapporteur, 'Adequate housing as a component of the right to an adequate standard of living, and the right to non-discrimination in this context' and UN, Committee on the Rights of Persons with Disabilities, General Comment on Article 19: Living independently and being included in the community. UN Doc. CRPD/C/18/1.

[75] UN CESCR, Communication No 2/2014, Views adopted by the Committee at its fifty-fifth session (1–19 June 2015 Spain) UN Doc E/C.12/55/D/2/2014.

[76] Ibid para 13.7.

[77] See UN Doc. E/C.12/61/D/5/2015, Committee on Economic, Social and Cultural Rights. Views adopted by the Committee under the Optional Protocol to the International Covenant on Economic, Social and Cultural Rights with regard to communication No 5/2015. Adopted by the Committee at its sixty-first session (29 May–23 June 2017).

CESCR reiterated that the state's duty to protect tenants involves taking measures to protect ICESCR rights, even when the action which undermined the right was in the first place carried out by an individual or a private entity. An eviction due to the expiry of the term of a rental contract is regarded as a dispute between individuals (lessor and lessee), in which the eviction is not directly initiated by the state. Thus,

> An eviction related to a rental contract between individuals can, therefore, involve Covenant rights. Accordingly, the State party's argument that the communication deals with a dispute that is exclusively between individuals and therefore does not fall under the Covenant does not stand.[78]

The UNCESCR stated that:

> ... States parties do not only have the obligation to respect Covenant rights, and, it follows, to refrain from infringing them, but they also have the obligation to protect them by adopting measures to prevent the direct or indirect interference of individuals in the enjoyment of these rights. If a State party does not take appropriate measures to protect a Covenant right, it has a responsibility even when the action that undermined the right in the first place was carried out by an individual or a private entity. Thus, although the Covenant primarily establishes rights and obligations between the State and individuals, the scope of the provisions of the Covenant extends to relations between individuals. An eviction related to a rental contract between individuals can, therefore, involve Covenant rights. Accordingly, the State party's argument that the communication deals with a dispute that is exclusively between individuals and therefore does not fall under the Covenant does not stand.[79]

The UN CESCR held that in some circumstances the eviction of people living in rental accommodation may be compatible with the ICESCR, as long as the eviction is provided for by law, is carried out as a last resort, and that the persons concerned have had prior access to an effective judicial remedy in order to ascertain that the measure in question was duly justified. This could apply, for example, in the case of persistent non-payment of rent, or of damage to rented property without just cause. In addition, there must be a real opportunity for genuine prior consultation between the authorities and the persons concerned, there must be no less onerous alternative means or measures available, and the persons

---

[78]   Ibid para 14.1.
[79]   Ibid para 14.2.

concerned must not remain in or be exposed to a situation constituting a violation of other Covenant or human rights.[80]

In 2015, UN Member States unanimously adopted the 2030 Agenda for Sustainable Development, grounded in the international human rights treaties, and the Sustainable Development Goals (SDGs).[81] States made an undertaking that by 2030, to ensure access for all to adequate, safe, and affordable housing and basic services and upgrade slums. While there is no direct reference to protection from eviction, the development of access to housing for all will be a significant policy goal.

4.3 Housing Rights and the Council of Europe

All European countries have accepted the European Social Charter and Revised Charter of the Council of Europe.[82] The European Committee on Social Rights of the Council of Europe (COE, ECSR) has stated that evictions are subject to a range of human rights standards.[83] States must take action to prevent categories of vulnerable persons from becoming homeless. While illegal occupation of a site or dwelling may justify the eviction of the illegal occupants, the criteria of illegal occupation must not be unduly wide. The eviction should be governed by rules of procedure sufficiently protective of the rights of the persons concerned and should be carried out according to these rules.[84]

Legal protection for persons threatened by eviction must include, in particular, an obligation to consult the parties affected, in order to find alternative solutions to eviction and the obligation to fix a reasonable

---

[80]   Ibid para 15.1.

[81]   See UN Doc. See A/RES/70/1. SDG 11 provides targets for building sustainable cities and communities.

[82]   Council of Europe, European Treaty Series – No 35; European Social Charter (Revised) Council of Europe, Strasbourg, 3 May 1996. See <http://www.coe.int/t/dghl/monitoring/socialcharter/Presentation/AboutCharter_en.asp>. These charters include state obligations in relation to access to adequate and affordable housing; a reduction of homelessness; housing policy targeted at all disadvantaged categories; procedures to limit forced eviction; equal access for non-nationals to social housing and housing benefits; and housing construction and housing benefits related to family needs.

[83]   Council of Europe (COE), Digest of the case law of the European Committee of Social Rights <https://rm.coe.int/CoERMPublicCommonSearchServices/DisplayDCTMContent?documentId=090000168049159f>.

[84]   COE, European Committee on Social Rights (ECSR), *European Roma Rights Center (ERRC) v Greece*, Complaint No 15/2003 (Decision on the Merits 8 December 2004) 14, §51.

notice period before eviction. When evictions do take place, they must be carried out under conditions which respect the dignity of the persons concerned. The law must prohibit evictions carried out at night or during the winter period. When an eviction is justified by the public interest, authorities must adopt measures to rehouse or financially assist the persons concerned.[85] Domestic law must provide legal remedies and offer legal aid to those who need to seek redress from the courts. Compensation for illegal evictions must also be provided.[86]

The European Convention on Human Rights (ECHR), as adopted by all European countries, requires respect for the rights to 'home', and proper justification and a 'pressing social need' for an eviction, which must be proportionate to the legal aim pursued.[87] Evictions which impact on people's dignity and cause inhuman and degrading treatment are regarded as violating the ECHR.[88] The European Court of Human Rights (ECtHR) found that the living conditions and racial discrimination to which a family was publicly subjected after eviction, constituted an interference with their human dignity amounting to 'degrading treatment'.[89]

The application of Article 8 ECHR on the right to respect for privacy, home and family life is creating a common European standard in relation to loss of home or repossession. The ECtHR has held:

> The loss of one's home is a most extreme form of interference with the right to respect for the home. Any person at risk of an interference of this magnitude should in principle be able to have the proportionality of the measure determined by an independent tribunal in the light of the relevant principles under Article 8 of the Convention, notwithstanding that, under domestic law, his right of occupation has come to an end.[90]

These 'proportionality' questions arising from Article 8 ECHR housing-related issues were more elaborately defined in *Yordanova and Others v*

---

[85]   ECSR (n 83) 172.

[86]   COE, ECSR, *European Roma Rights Center (ERRC) v Bulgaria*, §52.

[87]   *Connors v the United Kingdom* (n 7) §9.

[88]   The relationship between Art 8 ECHR and housing in the jurisprudence of the ECtHR is summarized by the Council of Europe and European Court of Human Rights (2017). *Guide on Article 8 of the Convention – Right to respect for private and family life* 52–58, <https://www.echr.coe.int/Documents/Guide_Art_8_ENG.pdf>.

[89]   *Moldovan v Romania (No 2)* App Nos 41138/98 and 64320/01, 30 November 2005 (Final) 27, §113.

[90]   *McCann v United Kingdom* App No 19009/04, Fourth Section 13 May 2008, §50.

Bulgaria.[91] Assuming the eviction measures are legally permitted, on the question as to whether the interference is 'necessary in a democratic society' the ECtHR held:

> An interference will be considered 'necessary in a democratic society' for a legitimate aim if it answers a 'pressing social need' and, in particular, if it is proportionate to the legitimate aim pursued. While it is for the national authorities to make the initial assessment of necessity, the final evaluation as to whether the reasons cited for the interference are relevant and sufficient remains subject to review by the Court for conformity with the requirements of the Convention (see, among other authorities, *Smith and Grady v. the United Kingdom*, nos. 33985/96 and 33986/96, 27 September 1999, §§ 88, ECHR 1999-VI).[92]

While a margin of appreciation is left to the national authorities, this margin will vary according to the nature of the ECHR rights at issue. The margin of appreciation left to the national authorities will tend to be narrower where the right at stake is crucial to the individual's effective enjoyment of intimate or key rights.[93]

> (ii) ... Since Article 8 concerns rights of central importance to the individual's identity, self-determination, physical and moral integrity, maintenance of relationships with others and a settled and secure place in the community, where general social and economic policy considerations have arisen in the context of Article 8 itself, the scope of the margin of appreciation depends on the context of the case, with particular significance attaching to the extent of the intrusion into the personal sphere of the applicant (see, among many others, *Connors*, cited above, § 82);

> (iii) The procedural safeguards available to the individual will be especially material in determining whether the respondent State has remained within its margin of appreciation. In particular, the Court must examine whether the decision-making process leading to measures of interference was fair and such as to afford due respect to the interests safeguarded to the individual by Article 8 (see *Buckley*, cited above, 1292–93, § 76, and *Chapman*, cited above, § 92). The 'necessary in a democratic society' requirement under Article 8 § 2 raises a question of procedure as well of substance (see *McCann*, cited above, § 26);

> (iv) Since the loss of one's home is a most extreme form of interference with the right under Article 8 to respect for one's home, any person at risk of an interference of this magnitude should in principle be able to have the

---

[91]   *Yordanova and Others v Bulgaria* App No 25446/06, 24 September 2012.
[92]   Ibid §117.
[93]   Ibid §118.

proportionality and reasonableness of the measure determined by an independent tribunal in the light of the relevant principles under Article 8, notwithstanding that, under domestic law, he has no right of occupation (see *Kay and Others v. the United Kingdom*, no. 37341/06, § 67–8 and 74, 21 September 2010 and *Orlić v. Croatia*, no. 48833/07, § 65, 21 June 2011). This means, among other things, that where relevant arguments concerning the proportionality of the interference have been raised by the applicant in domestic judicial proceedings, the domestic courts should examine them in detail and provide adequate reasons (*ibid.*, §§ 67–69).[94]

Key 'proportionality' issues around interference with Article 8 ECHR rights regarding respect for privacy, family life and home as identified in *Yordanova* are:

- the individual's identity
- self-determination
- physical and moral integrity
- maintenance of relationships with others
- a settled and secure place in the community
- the extent of the intrusion into the personal sphere of the applicant.

In *Yordanova and Others v Bulgaria*,[95] the European Court of Human Rights stated that those at risk of eviction should be afforded the following procedural safeguards:

1. The decision-making process leading to measures of interference has to be fair and must afford due respect to the interests safeguarded to the individual by Article 8.
2. Any person at risk of the loss of his/her home should in principle be able to have the proportionality and reasonableness of the measure determined by an independent tribunal, notwithstanding that, under domestic law, he/she has no right of occupation.
3. National authorities, in their decisions ordering and upholding the applicant's eviction, must give an explanation or put forward arguments demonstrating the necessity of eviction.

More recently, the European Court of Human Rights has requested that Spain make arrangements for housing and social care for a household with children that was subject to potential eviction to ensure compliance

---

94   Ibid.
95   (n 91).

with international human rights standards.[96] Together, these human (social) rights instruments, which have been adopted to varying degrees by the EU Member States being examined, oblige countries to ensure that evictions do not result in individuals being rendered homeless or vulnerable to the violation of other human rights. Where those evicted are unable to provide for themselves, Member States must take the maximum appropriate measures allowed by their available resources to ensure that adequate alternative housing or resettlement is available.[97]

There is, however, a major limitation in the application of Article 8 ECHR in the context of evictions in the 'private' arena. The horizontal impact of the Article, ie whether it applies in evictions from private rented housing, or as a result of mortgage repossessions, has been subject to much discussion. The *McDonald* case[98] in England (the UK) held that Article 8 protection and the need for a proportionality test did not apply in circumstances where legislation governed the contractual rights of the landlord. The Housing Act 1988 section 21, entitles a landlord to possession at the expiry of an assured shorthold tenancy after having served the required notice in writing on the tenant.[99] In *Vrzic v Croatia*,[100] the ECtHR addressed the 'horizontal' application of Article 8 in a case where the home was sold, as it had been pledged as collateral for a business loan which had not been repaid. The ECtHR held that in all previous such Article 8 cases involving eviction, the applicants were living in state-owned or socially owned accommodation flats, and an important aspect of finding a violation was the fact that there was no other private interest at stake.[101] Furthermore, the applicants in those cases had not signed any form of agreement whereby they risked losing their home. In the *Vrzic* case, the parties involved a bank, and the

---

[96] *Ceesay Ceesay and others v Spain*, App No 62688/13, Decision of 15 October 2013.

[97] UN CESCR, General Comment No 3: The Nature of States Parties' Obligations (Art 2, Para 1 of the Covenant) (n 71).

[98] [2016] UKSC 28. See Emma Lees, 'Horizontal effect and Article 8: McDonald v McDonald' (2014) *Law Quarterly Review* 131. For a modern critique of *McDonald* see S Pascoe, 'The end of the road for human rights in private landowners' disputes?' (2017) 81 (4) *The Conveyancer and Property Lawyer* 269–286.

[99] The order can be suspended for a maximum of six weeks in cases of exceptional hardship under the Housing Act 1980, s 89(1), and therefore no proportionality test can be effectively carried out.

[100] App No 43777/13 Judgment 12 July 2016.

[101] Ibid §66.

borrowers had voluntarily used their home as collateral for a loan.[102] There was no violation of Article 8, despite the absence of a proportionality assessment. However, the ECtHR held that this does not mean that the court will not examine the procedures in cases involving private parties:

> The Court is mindful of the fact that the present case concerns proceedings between private parties, namely the applicants and their creditors on the one hand and the applicants and the purchaser of their house on the other hand. However, even in cases involving private litigation, the State is under an obligation to afford the parties to the dispute judicial procedures which offer the necessary procedural guarantees and therefore enable the domestic courts and tribunals to adjudicate effectively and fairly in the light of the applicable law (see *Anheuser-Busch Inc. v. Portugal* [GC], no. 73049/01, § 83, ECHR 2007-I; *J.A. Pye*, cited above, § 57; and *Zagrebačka banka d.d. v. Croatia*, no. 39544/05, §§ 250 and 251, 12 December 2013).[103]

4.4 Housing Rights and the European Union

Evictions from residential, commercial or state property usually require the invocation and enforcement of property law. Each country has its own property law regime, based on national law. National property law systems are very closed, and the development of European harmonized standards has been slow and indirect.[104] Indeed, Article 345 Treaty on the Functioning of the European Union (TFEU) specifically precludes Treaty primacy over national systems of property ownership, and the principles of subsidiarity and proportionality are highly significant.[105] This means that the rules relating to property ownership fall within the sole competence of Member States. But, although national constitutional law

---

[102]   The situation involving a state owned or majority state owned bank seeking possession for a mortgage debt was not considered, even though this situation is common in Ireland.

[103]   *Vrzic v Croatia* App No 43777/13 Judgment 12 July 2016 §73.

[104]   See S Van Erp and B Akkermans, *Cases, Materials and Text on Property Law* (Ius Commune Casebooks for the Common Law of Europe) (Oxford, Hart 2012) Ch 10; P Sparkes, *European Land Law* (Oxford, Hart 2007); CU Schmid, C Hertel and H Wicke, *Real Property Law and Procedure in the European Union* (European University Institute (EUI) Florence/European Private Law Forum, Deutsches Notarinstitut (DNotI) Würzburg 2005).

[105]   See Sjef Van Erp, 'Article 345 TFEU: a framework for European property law' in Jaume Tarabal Bosch, Elena Lauroba Lacasa (coords) *El derecho de propiedad en la construcción del derecho privado europeo* (Tirant lo Blanch, 2018).

protects private property rights, there is an increasing Europeanization of these rights, especially through the jurisprudence around Article 1 of Protocol 1 to the ECHR, as well as the effects of Article 8 ECHR. Indeed, both these provisions have been replicated in the EU Charter of Fundamental Rights, in force since 2009.[106] European Union Treaty provisions on establishing and ensuring the single market (Article 26 TFEU) can impact on national property law. Consumer law provisions, and especially the Unfair Contract Terms Directive, are leading to harmonized standards in relation to the enforcement of mortgage security over property. Perhaps the most significant and far-reaching harmonization of property law in the EU has taken place through the adoption of the Mortgage Credit Directive (MCD).[107]

The MCD proposed an EU harmonized legal framework on mortgage law, including significant measures in relation to home possession in cases of mortgage arrears. This was created:

> In order to facilitate the emergence of a smoothly functioning internal market with a high level of consumer protection in the area of credit agreements relating to immovable property and in order to ensure that consumers looking for such agreements are able to do so confident in the knowledge that the institutions they interact with act in a professional and responsible manner, an appropriately harmonised Union legal framework needs to be established in a number of areas, taking into account differences in credit agreements arising in particular from differences in national and regional immovable property markets.[108]

Article 28 of the MCD deals with this concept of arrears and foreclosure, creating a harmonized approach to the enforcement of security for mortgages on property and of course, the concurrent exclusion from occupation of the debtor. Subsection 1 of Article 28 states that 'Member States shall adopt measures to encourage creditors to exercise reasonable forbearance before foreclosure proceedings are initiated.'[109] This concept

---

[106] Consolidated versions of the Treaty on European Union and the Treaty on the Functioning of the European Union Charter of Fundamental Rights of the European Union (OJ C 83/13, 30 March 2010).

[107] Directive 2014/17/EU on credit agreements for consumers relating to residential immovable property and amending Directives 2008/48/EC and 2013/36/EU and Regulation (EU) No 1093/2010. See M Anderson and EA Amayeulas (eds), *The Impact of the Mortgage Credit Directive in Europe* (Groningen, Europa Law Publishing 2017).

[108] Directive 2014/17/EU Preamble 5.

[109] While Art 43(1) of the Directive disapplies the Directive to mortgages created before 21 March 2016, Peter Sparkes points out that this is quite

of reasonable forbearance was solidified by the European Banking Authority (EBA) and the European Central Bank (ECB), bodies created as part of the mechanism of the European System of Financial Supervision, which was in turn set up to ensure cohesion and consistency of the EU financial system, promoting the proper functioning of the internal market.[110] Following the enactment of the MCD, the EBA published its *Final Report on Guidelines on Arrears and Foreclosure*[111] (the *Guidelines*) to assist Member States in complying with their obligations under Article 28 of the MCD.[112] The *Guidelines* cover all stages of the mortgage process from 'establishment of policies and procedures' prior to the engagement with consumers,[113] through the initial and ongoing engagement with the consumer,[114] to the resolution of a situation where a consumer has fallen into arrears.[115] Guideline 4, on the 'resolution process', provides more extensive information on what Article 28 of the MCD considers 'forbearance measures'. This gives a non-exhaustive list of possible modifications a credit institution should consider when exercising forbearance in the resolution of a credit account in payment difficulties. These are: 'a) extending the term of the mortgage;

---

illogical: 'as things stand, the full benefits of the legislation [MCD] will not be felt for twenty or twenty-five years when all loans in circulation will be covered by post-Directive agreements and there is no solution on offer to the millions of borrowers burned by the conduct of lenders leading up to and during the financial crisis'. See P Sparkes, 'What is mortgage credit?' in M Anderson and EA Amayeulas (eds) *The Impact of the Mortgage Credit Directive in Europe* (Groningen, Europa Law Publishing 2017) Ch 2. The EBA Guidelines on Arrears and Foreclosures (2015) appear to suggest that these are now applied to existing mortgages as described in Article 3 MCD rather than just post March 2016 mortgages.

[110]   See Council Regulation No 1024/2013 of 15 October 2013, conferring specific tasks on the European Central Bank concerning policies relating to the prudential supervision of credit institutions (Single Supervisory Mechanism [SSM] Regulation). See ECB website for explanation of the significance of the SSM Regulation, <https://www.bankingsupervision.europa.eu/about/thessm/html/index.en.html>.

[111]   EBA/GL/2015/12. The EBA's authority to issue guidelines stems from Article 16(1) of Regulation (EU) 1093/2010.

[112]   Section 3 of the EBA *Final Report on Guidelines on Arrears and Foreclosure* (1 June 2015) EBA/GL/2015/12.

[113]   Ibid Guideline 1.

[114]   Ibid Guidelines 2 and 3.

[115]   Ibid Guideline 4.

b) changing the type of the mortgage ... ; c) deferring payment ... ; d) changing the interest rate; [and] offering a payment holiday'.[116]

Forbearance measures are considered more closely by the ECB in Part 4 of its *Guidance to Banks on Non-Performing Loans* (the *Guidance*) of March 2017.[117] It should be noted that unlike the *Guidelines* of the EBA, the *Guidance* is not limited to mortgage credit agreements, but rather applies to all non-performing loans (NPLs), as its title suggests. This includes those mortgages excluded from the MCD provisions ie pre 2016 mortgages. The centre of focus is not the consumer in payment difficulties, but rather the financial institution itself when affected by a high level of NPLs. These (also referred to as non-performing exposures), for the purposes of the *Guidance*, are 'material exposures which are more than 90 days past due' and/or situations where 'the debtor is assessed as unlikely to pay its credit obligations in full without realization of collateral, regardless of the existence of any past-due amount or of the number of days past due'.[118] The list of forbearance measures proposed by the ECB in the *Guidance* is non-exhaustive, similar to the list provided by the EBA in its *Guidelines*, in the understanding that there are 'national specificities' to which financial institutions of each Member State must mould their system.[119]

The short-term forbearance measures proposed in the *Guidance* are: (i) interest only; (ii) reduced payments; (iii) grace period/payment moratorium; and (iv) arrears/interest capitalization.[120] The long-term measures are: (v) interest rate reduction; (vi) extension of maturity or term; (vii) additional security; (viii) sale by agreement or assisted sale; (ix) rescheduled payments; (x) conversion of currency; (xi) other alteration of contract conditions or covenants; (xii) new credit facilities; (xiii) debt consolidation; and (xiv) partial or total debt forgiveness.[121] The most severe long-term forbearance measure listed in the *Guidance* is partial or total debt forgiveness. This latter measure entails a settlement between the parties, whereby the debtor agrees to pay a certain amount of

---

[116] Ibid Guideline 4.1.2.

[117] Although the *Guidance* is 'currently non-binding in nature', non-compliance could 'trigger supervisory measures' as prescribed by the Single Supervisory Mechanism of the EU.

[118] European Central Bank, *Guidance to Banks on Non-Performing Loans* (ECB March 2017) 49.

[119] Ibid 43.

[120] Ibid 42.

[121] Ibid 42–43.

the debt within a given time-frame in return for which the creditor waives any legal claim over the remaining amount.

There is also much developing harmonizing jurisprudence across Europe which indirectly impacts on property law through other elements of EU and ECtHR jurisprudence. Today, there is a developing jurisprudence linking national, EU and international human rights law on evictions, which also encompasses EU consumer protection law.[122] This impacts in different ways, creating unique sets of circumstances for evictions in each EU Member State. Through a combination of EU consumer law and the EU Charter[123] of Fundamental Rights (CFREU),[124] a developing CJEU jurisprudence is developing whereby mortgage-related evictions are engaging consumer and human rights protections for those at risk of eviction.[125]

Article 51 (1) CFREU provides that the Charter is binding on the institutions, bodies, agencies and offices of the EU, and these include the European Central Bank and the European Banking Authority.[126] Article 7 CFREU states that: 'Everyone has the right to respect for his or her private and family life, home and communications.' According to the *Explanations* on the CFREU,[127] this corresponds with Article 8 of the ECHR. Indeed, the Court of Justice of the European Union (CJEU) has drawn on the jurisprudence of the European Court of Human Rights (ECtHR), in mortgage consumer law cases. In Case C-34/13, *Monika Kušionová v SMART Capital a.s.*, the CJEU held:

> The loss of a family home is not only such as to seriously undermine consumer rights (the judgment in *Aziz*, EU:C:2013:164, paragraph 61), but it

---

[122]   Case C-34/13 *Kušionová v SMART Capital* a.s.

[123]   All provisions of primary and secondary EU law must be interpreted according to the provisions of the Charter, including Art 24 (The rights of the child), Art 25 (The rights of older people), Art 26 (Integration of persons with disabilities) and Art 47(2) and (3) (Fair and public hearing and legal aid).

[124]   Consolidated versions of the Treaty on European Union and the Treaty on the Functioning of the European Union Charter of Fundamental Rights of the European Union (OJ C 83/13, 30 March 2010).

[125]   Case C-415/11 *Aziz v Caixa d'Estalvis de Catalunya*; Case C-280/13 *Barclays Bank* [2014]; Case C-280/13 *Sánchez Morcillo and Abril García* [2014] ECLI:EU:C:2014:2099; Cases C-482/13, C-484/13, C-485/13; Case C-539/14 *Sánchez Morcillo and Abril García* [2015]; Case C-8/14 *BBVA* [2015]; Case C-49/14 *Finanmadrid EFC* [2016]; Case C-421/14 *Banco Primus* [2017].

[126]   Steve Peers et al, *The EU Charter of Fundamental Rights: A Commentary* (Oxford, Hart 2014).

[127]   *Explanations Relating to the Charter of Fundamental Rights* (OJ 2007/C 303/02).

also places the family of the consumer concerned in a particularly vulnerable position (see, to that effect, the Order of the President of the Court in *Sánchez Morcillo and Abril García*, EU:C:2014:1388, paragraph 11). In that regard, the European Court of Human Rights has held, first, that the loss of a home is one of the most serious breaches of the right to respect for the home and, secondly, that any person who risks being the victim of such a breach should be able to have the proportionality of such a measure reviewed (see the judgments of the European Court of Human Rights in *McCann* v *United Kingdom*, application No 19009/04, paragraph 50, ECHR 2008, and *Rousk* v *Sweden*, application No 27183/04, paragraph 137). Under EU law, the right to accommodation is a fundamental right guaranteed under Article 7 of the Charter that the referring court must take into consideration when implementing Directive 93/13 [Unfair Terms in Consumer Contracts Directive].[128]

The emerging trend is a closer link between mortgage law, consumer law and human rights law, with the Unfair Contract Terms Directive providing the nexus between all three areas.[129] The treatment of consumer mortgage contracts by the CJEU has the potential to radically improve the rights of home loan borrowers in the EU context.

In November 2017, The European Parliament, the Council and the Commission solemnly proclaimed the European Pillar of Social Rights[130] laying down 20 key principles for delivering stronger protection of social rights for citizens. The 19th Principle is focused on the right to housing and assistance for the homeless as follows:

1. Access to social housing or high-quality housing assistance shall be provided for those in need.

---

[128] Case C-34/13 *Kušionová* v *SMART Capital a.s.* paras 63–65.

[129] Anthi Beka points out in 'The Protection of the Primary Residence of Mortgage Debtors: Embedding a "Basic Needs" Principle in Mortgage Repossession Proceedings' in Luca Ratti (ed) *Embedding the Principles of Life Time Contracts* (The Hague, Eleven Publishing 2018), that the MCD also provides a link in European legislation between credit default, indebtedness and the family home. Of course, the proposed Directive on credit servicers, credit purchasers and the recovery of collateral Com(2018)135 final 2018/0063(COD), which advances the use of extra judicial enforcement of collateral default, proposes that 'Even for business borrowers, the main residence of a business owner will be excluded from the scope, based on social considerations.' Thus, the development of three EU legislative areas are viewing contracts relating to home loans as a special type of consumer contract subject to different considerations than other loans.

[130] See <https://ec.europa.eu/commission/sites/beta-political/files/social-summit-european-pillar-social-rights-booklet_en.pdf>.

2.   Vulnerable people have the right to appropriate assistance and protection against forced eviction.
3.   Adequate shelter.

Abbe Pierre Foundation and FEANTSA have welcomed the European Pillar of Social Rights as giving 'hope of a positive change in relation to social rights in Europe'.[131]

> This provision makes use of Article 34.3 of the Charter of Fundamental Rights of the European Union which recognises the right to social and housing assistance to ensure a decent existence for all those who lack sufficient resources.
>
> Although the Commission's initiative was welcomed, a point of concern was that of the legal nature of the principles. The principles and rights enshrined in the Pillar are not directly enforceable and non-binding. They need to be translated into concerted action and legislation. In the case of principle 19, Member States are invited to adopt measures to support universal access to accommodation.
>
> The Secretary General of the Council of Europe believes that the Pillar is an opportunity. However, he expressed concerns that 'while the standard-setting systems of the European Union and Council of Europe constitute a comprehensive and structured whole, the persisting inconsistencies between them could jeopardise effective enforcement of the rights that they guarantee.' Many European stakeholders believe that the provisions of the European Social Charter should be formally incorporated into the European Pillar of Social Rights as a common benchmark.
>
> Indeed, the proclamation states that: 'nothing in the European Pillar of Social Rights shall be interpreted as restricting or adversely affecting rights and principles as recognised, in their respective fields of application, by Union law or international law and by international agreements to which the Union or all the Member States are party, including the European Social Charter signed at Turin on 18 October 1961 (…)'.[132]

Housing Europe has pointed out that neither the Pillar nor the associated social scoreboard makes an express reference to the right to housing. Thus, the EU Commission will not supervise housing affordability, the number of people in housing need or, generally speaking, the policies

---

[131]   FEANTSA/Abbe Pierre Foundation, *Third Overview of Housing Exclusion in Europe 2018* (FEANTSA 2018) 91/92.
[132]   Ibid.

adopted to comply with the provisions enshrined in the Pillar.[133] Yet, the Pillar adds to the *acquis* of housing rights instruments in Europe.

4.5 Constitutional and Legislative Protection from Evictions

Among the EU Member States, some eleven countries, all of them with civil law systems, make specific reference to housing in their constitutions.[134] The 'inviolability' of the home is specifically protected in the constitutions of most EU Member States.[135] This is often juxtaposed with the universally recognized right to property, enabling expropriation and regulation of property rights for public purposes, with compensation required in some cases.[136] Article 30 of the Polish Constitution, on the obligation to respect and protect the inherent and inalienable dignity of the person, was invoked by the Polish Constitutional Court in 2001 to rule that, 'evictions to nowhere' (in the absence of alternative temporary housing) were unconstitutional.[137] Nevertheless, express terms on housing rights in constitutions or laws are not always an indicator of stronger protection from eviction.

Public policy measures enable a court to suspend, postpone or restrict the execution of eviction orders for specified purposes. Winter bans on evictions exist in Austria, the Brussels-Capital and Wallonia Regions of

---

[133] Housing Europe, *Housing in the European Pillar of Social Rights: A Critical Review* (Housing Europe, April 2017) <http://www.housingeurope.eu/resource-930/housing-in-the-european-pillar-of-social-rights>.

[134] For the essential differences between and development of civil and common law systems in property law in Europe see S Van Erp, 'From "classical" to modern European property law' in *Essays in Honour of Konstantinos D Kerameus/Festschrift für Konstantinos D Kerameus* Vol I (1517–1533) (Athens/Brussels, Ant. A Sakkoulas/Bruylant) <https://papers.ssrn.com/sol3/papers.cfm?abstract_id=1372166>.

[135] While the Constitution of the Czech Republic, the Constitution of the Fifth Republic of France (1958), and the Constitution of Sweden do not specifically refer to this, the protections in Arts 6 and 8 ECHR apply in these countries, providing similar protection. The Human Rights Act 1998 incorporates these ECHR provisions into UK law, adding the requirement for the principles of fair procedures, due process and the rule of law to be taken into account in evictions, as well as court rules, since there is no single written constitutional document.

[136] In Poland, there is also a constitutional commitment to protecting the rights of tenants; see Art 75 Constitution of Poland 1997.

[137] Polish Constitutional Court Decision of 4 April 2001, K 11/00, OTK-ZU [Official Journal of the Constitutional Court; Polish: *Orzecznictwo Trybunału Konstytucyjnego. Zbiór Urzędowy*] 2001, No 3, item 54.

Belgium, France, Hungary and Poland. There have been moratoria (either legal or *de facto*, with broader or narrower scope) on actual evictions in Cyprus, Greece, Ireland, Italy, Spain (for vulnerable households until 2017) and Portugal. In Italy, a state fund operates to permit the temporary suspension of mortgage repayments where the debtor fulfils certain requirements. The suspension of 'evictions to nowhere' in Poland and Slovakia protects those with children, pregnant women, larger families, people with disabilities, old people and other vulnerable people. In some cases, such as in Spain, Lithuania and Poland, courts have linked evictions to the right to respect for home and family life under Article 8 ECHR, European Union law and the human rights of children.

In Belgium, Article 23 of the 1994 Constitution declares that everyone has the right to a decent living, which includes the right to decent housing. This can be used to contest the appropriateness of an eviction, as well as giving direction to the interpretation of legal norms.[138] No one can be evicted without a court order except in the case of a municipal or regional administration for an uninhabited dwelling. The right to housing is endorsed in the Housing Codes of all three Regions (Brussels-Capital, Walloon, Flanders) in Belgium.

Marc Uhry recounts that in France, housing is not a constitutional right, although the Supreme Court held in 1995 that the right to housing was a constitutional goal. Legislation in 1989, 1990, 2007,[139] 2009, 2013 and 2014 refer to housing rights in the various tenures and in relation to measures addressing homelessness. German law does not guarantee an individually enforceable right to housing, although states such as Bremen, Bavaria and Berlin have regulations on housing rights which

---

[138]   See N Moons, *The Right to Housing in Law and Society* (Abingdon, Routledge 2018); N Bernard, 'L'article 23 de la Constitution: pas une botte secrète, mais pas non plus dénué de toute effectivité (judiciaire)' (2015) 23 *JLMB* 1080–1089.

[139]   Droit au logement opposable (DALO) 2007 [Enforceable Right to Housing Act], Art 1, states: 'the right to decent and independent housing is ensured by the State to any person residing on French territory who cannot access it by his own means or keep it'. This provides for a two-tier remedial mechanism with local mediation committees, and an administrative court. See K Olds, 'The role of courts in making the right to housing a reality throughout Europe: lessons from France and the Netherlands' (2010) 5 (21) *Wisconsin International Law Journal* 170–199. The Prefect must secure housing or pay a penalty as determined by a court for as long as the person has not been rehoused.

enable local authorities to develop housing policies.[140] There are obligations on municipalities to provide temporary accommodation for people who would otherwise be homeless, as involuntary homelessness is considered a serious threat to public safety. Occasionally, to prevent homelessness, the authorities may require that a tenant remains in situ after a lawful termination of tenancy, with rent support provided.

Article 12 of the Constitution of Hungary 2012 states that: 'Hungary shall strive to ensure decent housing conditions and access to public services for everyone.' There is an obligation on the state and local municipalities to ensure accommodation for persons without a dwelling, although it is illegal to use a public space as a habitual dwelling. In Italy, in 1988 the Constitutional Court recognized rights to housing as a consequence of the mandatory duties of social solidarity in Article 2 of the Constitution, and also Article 3 dealing with equality. Indeed, this is a right with horizontal effects among private parties. On the other hand, the suspension of eviction orders in densely populated municipalities was held to be in breach of European Convention on Human Rights (ECHR) property rights guarantees, although such moratoria can be used in areas of housing stress.[141] There is no fundamental right to housing in the Irish Constitution, although there is a right to protection of the inviolability of the home, in line with almost all European countries. Legislation permits local authorities to provide social housing, and social welfare supports are provided by government and voluntary agencies.

In Poland, as Witold Borysiak describes, the Constitution guarantees the inviolability of human dignity, as well as obliging public authorities to pursue policies to combat homelessness and grant statutory protection to tenants. A combination of the Act on Tenants Rights and Municipal Housing Stock 2001, together with Article 146 of the Code of Civil Procedure, and the Act on Social Assistance 2004, creates a duty to provide a place to sleep in a shelter to every evicted person. Constitutional Court decisions have led to the principle of 'no evictions to nowhere' as the combination of constitutional, statute and human rights

---

[140] Constitution of the Free Hanseatic City of Bremen (1947). Art 14 (I) states that: 'Every citizen of the *Hansestadt Bremen* has the right to an adequate dwelling. It is a duty of the state and the municipalities to facilitate the realisation of this right.'

[141] See *Spadea and Scalabrio v Italy* App no 12868/87 (Chamber) Strasbourg, 28 September 1995; *Immobiliare Saffi v Italia*, 28 July 1999, no 22774/93; *Stornelli and Sacchi v Italia*, 28 July 2005, no 68706/01; *Cuccaro Granatelli v Italia*, 8 December 2005, no 19830/03.

protections are applied.[142] Indeed, the courts have ordered that social housing be made available in a significant number of cases. Courts, in 2010, established the right of a person entitled to such social housing to claim compensation from a local authority where it was not provided. The Polish Ombudsman has established that it is not possible to evict a person where the court has made such an order unless temporary accommodation at least is provided. The Polish Constitutional Court applies the approach that an eviction without adequate alternative housing violates Article 8 ECHR, which, combined with the Constitution, requires minimum safeguards in relation to housing rights. Case law in 2013 established that this also applies to social housing evictions. In Poland, illegal eviction is punishable under Article 191 of the Criminal Code and 2065 such proceedings were initiated in 2015, with convictions in 1551 cases, which involved a fine or suspended jail sentence.

Although Article 36 of the Constitution of the Republic of Slovenia guarantees the inviolability of the dwelling, there is no fundamental right to housing per se. Legislation from 2003 protects tenants from eviction for rent arrears where they are faced with extraordinary circumstances, such as death in the family, illness or unemployment.

In Spain, the right to housing is not a fundamental right but is considered a programmatic principle which guides legislation and the courts. The Spanish Supreme Court has defined this right as a fundamental right of freedom, which includes the sanctity of the home and promotes the free development of the personality. Judicial activism has led to many new interpretations on the extent and nature of housing rights. This, combined with an increasing number of CJEU judgments on consumer law and human rights, as well as ECtHR rulings on the eviction of squatters, and United Nations reports, means that legal development in the area of evictions in Spain is the most active in Europe. The Order of the Court of First Instance No 39 of Madrid 6/3/2013, suspended the eviction (by the Municipal Housing Company of Madrid) of a tenant with three minor children on the basis of both the Convention on the Rights of the Child of 20 November 1989, and the relationship between the right to housing and other constitutional rights enshrined in the Spanish Constitution such as the right to personal and family privacy (Article 18.1), the freedom of residence (Article 19), the

---

[142] Polish Constitutional Court Decision of 4 April 2001, K 11/00, OTK-ZU [Official Journal of the Constitutional Court; Polish: *Orzecznictwo Trybunału Konstytucyjnego. Zbiór Urzędowy*] 2001, No 3, item 54.

right to education (Article 27) and the right to health (Article 45). Moreover, the Court, taking as a starting point the case *AMB* v *Spain*,[143] required the local authority to take concrete measures to guarantee the right of the children to adequate housing. The court made reference to Article 8 ECHR and other international treaties concerning the protection of children that have been ratified by Spain.[144] More recently, the decision of the Spanish Supreme Court 23 December 2017, held that the Court must consider the Convention on the Rights of the Child where the local authority were seeking possession of housing, even if illegally occupied, where minors may be affected by the execution of the eviction order.[145]

The Constitution of the Netherlands does not contain a right to housing, but courts draw on Article 8 ECHR as well as on Article 12 of the Constitution on the inviolability of the home. Article 8 ECHR requires that any interference with the respect for home, such as an eviction, must be approved by a court, and the principle of proportionality applied. Michel Vols points out that although these substantive and procedural protections can lead to a dismissal of the action, or a suspension of the order of eviction, this does not happen very often, and most eviction actions are approved by courts.

In the UK, as Nicholas Pleace and Caroline Hunter specify, there is no written constitution, and no universal right to housing. However, legislation provides something quite close to this, with statutory obligations on local authorities to provide temporary accommodation for specific categories of homeless people who are in priority need, are not intentionally homeless, and who have a local connection. Scottish local authorities have statutory obligations to provide permanent accommodation to a wider group of homeless people.

4.6 Law Relating to Owner-occupation

There is a significant difference in the process of possession and eviction in mortgage arrears between the civil law and common law countries (the latter being Ireland and the UK). Civil law systems usually enable a

---

[143] *AMB v Spain*, App No 77842/12 (ECHR, 20 February 2014).
[144] According to Sergio Nasarre-Aznar, '"Robinhoodian" courts' decisions on mortgage law in Spain' (2015) 7 (2) *International Journal of Law in the Built Environment* 136.
[145] ECLI: ECLI:ES:TS: 2017:4211.

lender, after a period of arrears,[146] to engage the legal system, a notary or a bailiff, who then arranges for a forced sale (where no agreement has been reached with the debtor). The new purchaser then uses the resources of the legal system to evict the former owner. There are various discretions and appeals within the court process, such as 24-month suspension in France to enable a payment plan.[147] In Germany, where a court responsible for the execution of the eviction finds that the eviction entails 'a hardship that due to very special circumstances is immoral (*contra bonos*)', it is entitled to reverse, prohibit or temporarily stay the enforcement of the eviction.[148] Since 2016 and the transposition of the Mortgage Credit Directive, under Dutch law, the mortgagee is no longer able to sell the mortgaged property in default without a court order, although there were some 4500 forced sales by the National Mortgage Guarantee Scheme (NHGS) in 2015. In Spain, enforcement of the security on a mortgage involves a civil procedure, with the possibility of a forced auction. The case of *Aziz*[149] challenged the compatibility of the procedure with the requirement of the effectiveness of EU consumer law, which regards mortgages as consumer contracts.

In Ireland, legislation, the mortgage contract and principles of equity enable a lender under a defaulted mortgage to acquire possession of the property, prior to sale. However, legislation of 2009 distinguishes between 'housing loans' and other mortgages, and gives more discretion to courts to adjourn or suspend cases where there is a possibility of

---

[146]　After three months' arrears in Belgium and Spain; 30–180 days' arrears in Italy, but only after seven occasions. In Italy, the forced sale may take up to three years after proceedings are initiated and generally the process is slower, which encourages lenders to seek more conciliatory approaches, and therefore finding agreement with the debtor, which avoids eviction, is more likely. In Germany, the highest bid in the forced auction must exceed 50 per cent of the estimated value.

[147]　The Code of Civil Procedure provides that in cases of sale as a result of mortgage debt, the contract can oblige the new owner to allow the debtor to remain in occupation. The Overindebtedness Commission (*Commission de surrendettement*) can suspend an enforcement procedure for two years.

[148]　Art 765a (1) ZPO. Serious illness that may deteriorate owing to the execution of the eviction is one of the circumstances where this provision may be applied. Consequently, the eviction may either be prohibited altogether, or it may be carried out when the illness is controlled through medication.

[149]　See Case C-415/11 *Mohamed Aziz v Caixa d'Estalvis de Catalunya*; Case C-280/13 *Sánchez Morcillo and Abril García* [2014], ECLI:EU:C:2014:2099; Cases C-482/13, C-484/13, C-485/13; Case C-539/14 *Sánchez Morcillo and Abril García* [2015]; Case C-8/14 BBVA [2015]; Case C-49/14 *Finanmadrid EFC* [2016]; Case C-421/14 *Banco Primus* [2017].

repayment. The 'equity of redemption' and the legislation in place require that the courts firstly grant an order for possession. This is followed by a sale (with obligations on the mortgagee to get the best price). While the mortgagor is liable for any shortfall, they can also receive any surplus after all debts are paid from the sale price.[150] There are few defences to possession in mortgage arrears cases, and failure to respond to the initial proceedings quickly can result in a summary judgment of eviction.[151] However, most cases are treated sympathetically by judges and registrars, who adjourn proceedings to enable an arrangement to be made. United Kingdom property legislation since 1925 enables a mortgagee to take possession of a property where there are mortgage arrears, although in practice, it is necessary to obtain vacant possession before sale, unlike in most EU civil law systems. Legislation of 1970 in England and Wales gives powers to courts to adjourn or suspend cases.

4.7 Law Relating to Private Renting

The laws on private renting vary considerably across European countries and procedural protections differ. Generally, the procedure is that after a period of arrears or some other breach, the landlord will issue a legal claim for possession and the court will have some discretion to order, suspend or enforce that order. However, the UK is unique in that assured shorthold tenancies give an automatic right to possession for the landlord, after either the prescribed six- or twelve-month tenancy. There is an accelerated procedure in England and Wales which does not require a court hearing. Similar legislation was introduced in the Netherlands in 2016, although Michel Vols points out that Dutch courts continue to carry out proportionality assessments in line with Article 8 ECHR.[152]

Protections for tenants at risk of eviction vary, including landlords' obligations to inform housing benefits services, and, as Marc Uhry points out, the Prevention of Eviction Commission (CCAPEX) has played a

---

[150] Unlike civil law countries, Ireland, with its common law system, does not use the term foreclosure, although it is widely used in ECB, EBA and European Commission literature. Foreclosure was abolished in Irish law through legislation in 2009, although this does not change the rights of mortgagees to acquire rights of possession and sale in default.

[151] SI No 171 of 2016, Circuit Court Rules (Actions for Possession, Sale and Well-Charging Relief) 2016.

[152] Similar legislation was introduced in Spain in 2013, providing for short contracts, limited security of tenure and market rents.

significant role in its interventions to avoid evictions in France.[153] In Germany, the law on private renting is regulated by the German Civil Code (*Bürgerliches Gesetzbuch* – BGB),[154] and tenancies can be terminated only on specific grounds unless it is a fixed-term tenancy, but tenants can defend the action on grounds of hardship, or seek an extension of occupancy of up to one year.

There are few protections for tenants where an unregulated private market persists, and this applies in Hungary, where illegal or unauthorized evictions are common. In Italy, tenancy laws of 1978 and 1998 provide protection to tenants, enabling late payment of arrears and suspending the eviction order for up to 180 days in densely populated areas (as identified by the government).

In Ireland, the law on evictions from private rented dwellings is contained in legislation dating from 2004 and requires statutory periods of notice and allows an appeal to the Residential Tenancies Board (RTB) by a tenant (or former tenants who have been illegally evicted). Where a tenant does not leave after a notice from the landlord or an order from the RTB, it is necessary to obtain a court order to enforce the eviction. There are limited grounds for eviction, although sale of the property is one of these. There is a three-step process for evictions for rent arrears. Most landlords have one or two properties, and in some cases where landlords have defaulted on mortgages, receivers are appointed by lenders who then evict tenants prior to sale, one of the main causes of family homelessness in Ireland.

4.8 Law Relating to Social Renting

In most countries, evictions from social housing are rare and take place only when all other supports and efforts have been exhausted. However, the exceptions are the UK and the Netherlands. In the UK, the structure of social housing provisions has changed, and many housing associations use tenancies comparable to the private sector, including 'probationary' and 'flexible' tenancies. Nicholas Pleace and Caroline Hunter show that the UK courts have interpreted the obligations under Article 8 ECHR to consider the proportionality of any possession order in a somewhat

---

[153] Tenants can request extension of time of up to three years before vacating after an order is granted.

[154] German Civil Code (*Bürgerliches Gesetzbuch* – *BGB*), in the version promulgated on 2 January 2002, I Federal Law Gazette [*Bundesgesetzblatt*], 42, 2909; 2003 I, 738, last amended by Art 4 para 5 of the Act of 1 October (2013), I Federal Law Gazette, 3719.

narrow way, resisting the notion that this created any 'horizontal' rights between a tenant and a landlord, except in state tenancies. Michel Vols indicates that under social housing eviction litigation in the Netherlands, requiring court assessment of proportionality, tenants do not successfully defend these actions. In Ireland, a small portion of social housing tenancies with approved housing bodies has been merged with the regulatory system for private rented tenancies. In Germany, the definition of social housing includes municipal housing and public–private arrangements involving development subsidies for cost-based tenancies of fifteen years' duration to low-income households; thus, the law applying to private tenancies applies, as in Poland.

4.9 Law Relating to Unauthorized Occupancy

Generally, the law relating to evictions from unauthorized occupancy has two elements. Firstly, it can involve evictions from personally owned property of unauthorized occupants. A mix of property law and criminal law operates in all countries and involves the removal of the occupants, usually, but not always, after a court hearing. In the second instance, large settlements of people, often Roma, Sinti, Travellers or migrants, in unauthorized encampments in districts are mostly tolerated by state authorities. However, there are instances of evictions of these groups and indeed, such evictions have been examined for compatibility with the ECHR.[155]

Inviolability of the dwelling protects against arbitrary evictions by the property owner, but where squatters are not identifiable a speedy eviction process is usually authorized by a court of first instance. The laws on 'no eviction to nowhere' in Poland do not apply to squatters. In Italy, where almost 5 per cent of public buildings are squatted, particularly in southern Italian cities, legislation dating from 2014 seeks to prevent unauthorized occupiers from using public services such as energy or telephone. However, the eviction process is lengthy and there are few evictions, which usually requires police intervention.

Squatting is considered a criminal law issue in Spain, although social movements, such as PAH,[156] have been encouraging people in mortgage arrears to squat empty bank-owned properties, as a means of negotiation. There are also some 10 000 temporary dwellings occupied by Roma. Indeed, in Italy, Spain and Slovenia, there are unauthorized settlements of

---

[155] *Winterstein v France* App No 27013/07 (ECHR, 17 October 2013).

[156] Plataforma de Afectados por la Hipoteca (Platform for People Affected by Mortgages).

Roma, Sinti or Caminanti, with some camps of 40 000 people or more, which are tolerated by the public authorities.

4.10 Law Relating to Temporary Dispossession – Domestic Violence, Urban Development and Other Issues

In all eleven countries examined, legislation provides that abusive partners can be excluded from the dwelling. The situation in cases of divorce or relationship breakdown is more protracted, but generally the party with custody of any children retains the right to occupancy of the dwelling, with the other party being excluded. Sergio Nasarre-Aznar and Rosa Maria Garcia-Teruel estimate that there are almost 100 000 male partners in divorce cases seeking new accommodation annually in Spain.

The temporary closures of buildings by public authorities on grounds of breach of building codes, nuisance or crime has been highlighted by Michel Vols as significant in the Netherlands. Surprisingly, these grounds are used to close down 200 buildings per year and to evict those involved in drug-related crime or cannabis cultivation. In Spain, the declaration of ruin of buildings by the state administration can result in occupiers being forced to leave, while recorded evictions from unauthorized occupancies range between 2500 and 3000 per annum, according to Sergio Nasarre-Aznar and Rosa Maria Garcia-Teruel.

In Slovenia, as well as in Poland and Hungary, those living in denationalized dwellings face an increased risk of eviction with title restored to the heirs of former owners who wish to convert or sell the property. Changes in tenancy protection and increases in rents make these occupancies less secure than other tenancies and this has been held in some cases to amount to a breach of the European Social Charter housing rights protection.[157]

4.11 Soft Law/Codes and their Effectiveness

There are situations where Codes of Guidance or Conduct in the procedures leading to eviction can have an impact. In relation to mortgage arrears, there are Codes of Conduct or Pre-action Protocols in Ireland, Hungary and the UK, which, although not legally binding, offer some procedural protections against arbitrary evictions. Protocols between landlords, municipal administrations, NGOs and consumer or

---

[157] European Committee of Social Rights (ECSR), *European Federation of National Organisations Working with the Homeless (FEANTSA) v Slovenia* CC53/2008, Complaint No 53/2007, 8 September 2008.

support services in France, Germany, Italy[158] and the Netherlands,[159] can reduce or effectively suspend evictions.

5. SUBSTANTIVE CONTEXT

In almost all countries in the study, the data available on evictions is limited and fragmented over the period 2010 to 2015/2016. While states collate court statistics, very often possession cases do not distinguish between property types or tenures and whether the property is inhabited and by whom. The ECB is now engaged in monitoring the levels of non-performing loans in EU Member States, and this involves direct supervision of significant lenders in each Member State in the euro area.[160] However, even this data does not distinguish between loans on properties which are used as homes, and those which are not.

5.1 Mortgage-related Evictions

Good data is available for some regions of EU Member States, or various dispute-resolution systems, and it is possible to generate some estimation of the levels of evictions in a number of countries, for some tenures. However, while some records exist for court proceedings, often there is no data available on the pre-court proceedings (the point at which many leave their accommodation involuntarily). For instance, in Ireland, some 40 per cent of instigated mortgage arrears actions result in possession, and this occurs in 70 per cent of cases where the creditor is an investment or 'vulture' fund.[161] Indebted borrowers are actually more likely to voluntarily surrender or abandon their homes before the conclusion of court proceedings than be forcibly repossessed.[162] Of the dwellings

---

[158] Between March 2015 and December 2016, 11 338 families obtained a twelve-month suspension <https://www.abi.it/Pagine/news/Raggiunta-intesa-su-nuova-moratoria-famiglie.aspx>.

[159] Between 2004 and 2014, the Dutch government and the four biggest cities implemented an action plan to address homelessness and reduce the number of evictions, which was effective in reducing evictions by 22 per cent. There are inter-agency agreements in the main cities to prevent evictions.

[160] European Central Bank, *Stocktake of National Practices and Legal Frameworks Related to NPLs* (Frankfurt, ECB 2016 and 2017).

[161] Overall, in Ireland, court proceedings for mortgage possession rose from 300 in 2010 to 1300 in 2015, and then fell to 1000 in 2016.

[162] In Ireland, the government and the banks are strongly resisting debt write-downs in favour of a policy of mortgage forbearance. Forbearance involves

repossessed by lenders between 2009 and 2016, some 66 per cent were repossessed by lenders after voluntary surrender or abandonment.[163]

In France, the numbers of evictions instigated rose from 155 874 in 2010 to 168 775 in 2015, with over 90 per cent the result of arrears.[164] Some 75 per cent of cases involved a court decision. A police request for assistance in the execution of the eviction order was requested in some 35 per cent of the decisions, and effective execution by police in 30 per cent of requests.

While there are no universal official statistics in Germany, data was obtained from juridical reports on enforced auctions. These show some 68 723 cases of real estate repossessions in 2010, and a reduction to 42 670 in 2015. In terms of evictions from private rental(s), while there is no official national data, research in Saxony indicated that there were 3037 cases in 2010, rising to 4762 in 2015. There are some 10 000 eviction cases each year in Berlin, of which 50–70 per cent are executed. Research indicates that approximately 20 per cent are the result of divorce or separation.

In Hungary, there is no overall data collected on the extent of evictions, but some information exists for parts of the country. There were approximately 40 000 procedures for possession of immovable property (which includes all buildings) instigated in 2013, but this resulted in some 2500 housing units being designated for sale in the process, and 517 ended with an eviction. In 2016, there were 3400

---

restructuring a debt's contractual terms to ease a debtor's repayment schedule. In practice, forbearance has been a strategy of 'extend and pretend' whereby lenders have been slow to offer restructurings or have relied on temporary interventions that impose minimal costs upon them. Forbearance benefited lenders by negating the pressure to enforce possession of devalued property, while ensuring borrowers remain solely responsible for outstanding debts. See R Waldron and D Redmond, '(For)Bearing the costs of reckless lending: examining the response to the Irish mortgage crisis' (2016) 16 (3) *International Journal of Housing Policy* 267–292.

[163] Department of Finance/Central Bank (2016) 33. In Ireland, data is available on possession orders through the Courts Service of Ireland and the Central Bank of Ireland, and from the Residential Tenancies Board in relation to the private rented sector. However, there is no exact data on the numbers of evictions from owner-occupied dwellings as a result of mortgage enforcement, although observations suggest that the number is very low, and the data from the Courts Service does not accord with data prepared by the Central Bank of Ireland.

[164] This data includes evictions from squats and slums but may be an underestimate in those situations.

housing units made for sale, and 1734 evictions. Political initiatives led to a situation where lenders agreed to cap the number of evictions arising from defaults on foreign exchange mortgages. Based on their research, Nóra Teller, Eszter Somogyi and Nóra Tosics suggest that in Hungary, some 3000 auctions take place each year in relation to real estate, resulting in about 300 households being evicted as a result of actions on debt.

The Polish Ministry of Justice collects data on the number of evictions. Although the Ministry does not distinguish between the different types of housing, it records the numbers of cases in the District Courts and the numbers of bailiffs' actions. The data shows some 34 500 cases submitted in 2010, and 32 863 cases resolved, compared to 26 286 cases submitted in 2015, and 27 000 resolved.[165] Of these cases, the obligation to provide social housing was upheld in 50 per cent of cases. The number of bailiffs' actions was 6569 in 2010, of which two-thirds required the provision of social housing to proceed. The numbers increased to almost 9000 in 2015.

In Belgium, mortgage arrears rarely lead to evictions, as alternative solutions are pursued. The figures indicated that just over 1 per cent of mortgage accounts are in arrears.

There have been significant increases in mortgage-related evictions in Italy, concurrent with the economic crisis, with one report by a banking federation showing increases of 160 per cent between 2008 and 2014, and a further increase of 18 per cent in 2015. In Slovenia, Ministry of Justice data covers repossessions of all immovable property, both residential and commercial. Maša Filipovič Hrast suggests that the figure is less than 300 per annum, and the level of evictions from mortgaged property is quite low.

While no comprehensive data is collated by Spanish state agencies, research by Sergio Nasarre-Aznar and Rosa Maria Garcia-Teruel shows that the number of evictions was approximately 40 000 per annum between 2010 and 2013, and 30 000 per annum for 2014 and 2015. In the Netherlands, mortgage arrears are the main reason for owner-occupier evictions, but there is no central register of systematically collected data on these evictions. Figures from the NHGS reveal that forced sales of mortgaged properties rose from 1335 in 2010 to 4477 in 2015. Overall, according to Michel Vols, it is estimated that there are also 7500 pre-court evictions from mortgaged properties. In the UK, pre-court actions are not recorded and court data on mortgage cases is collated by the Ministry of Justice. This shows that in England and Wales, claims for

---

[165] Cases resolved may date from earlier years.

possession dropped from 75 000 in 2010 to 20 000 in 2015, while execution of possession orders by bailiffs decreased from 21 000 in 2010 to 2000 in 2015. Available data indicates a two-thirds fall also in the period for Scotland and Northern Ireland.

5.2 Evictions from Private/Social Rented Housing

The data in relation to evictions from private/social rented housing is not universally collated, although studies in some regions, and on types of tenure, have yielded some useful estimates. One major issue identified in the Italian, Hungarian and Slovenian research, was the absence of records in relation to the unofficial private rented sector. In some cases, this can amount to a larger element of housing stock than the regulated sector, and therefore statistics on eviction for rented housing will almost always be a gross underestimate. The exceptions are Belgium, Germany and Ireland, where the sector is somewhat better regulated. In Belgium, some 12 000 eviction procedures are instigated in Flanders annually, and about one in three instigated procedures results in eviction for rent arrears. When behavioural problems are the issue, tenants are evicted in six out of ten cases. A combination of both rent arrears and behavioural problems leads to 80 per cent of cases resulting in eviction.

In Hungary, less than a dozen households are officially evicted from the private rented sector, although the figure is estimated to be much higher in reality. In relation to social housing, the figure can reach 500 to 1000 per year, according to the Hungarian experts.

Elena Bargelli and Giulia Donadio have found that evictions from private rented accommodation in Italy are increasing, though not dramatically, and in any case, there is a significant unofficial market. In the rented sector, between 2008 and 2014 there was an increase of 50 per cent. In the private rented sector, eviction notices for non-payment of rent doubled between 2007 and 2013. Evictions from social housing are not widespread in Italy.

The trend in evictions from private sector tenancies in Ireland as published by the RTB involved a growth in eviction-related cases from 580 in 2010 to 3000 in 2015 – a five-fold increase. Padraic Kenna shows that evictions from social housing remained at relatively low levels.

For Slovenia, a report on social housing from Ljubliana revealed very small numbers of evictions, between 10 and 30 per annum. However, a study in Ljubliana dating from 2013 and described by Maša Filipovič Hrast, found that 11 per cent of private landlords wished to rent without a contract, thus avoiding inclusion in official data. In Spain, the estimates are 23 000 in 2010 to 36 000 in 2015, but again the data is not universal, and includes some other buildings and mainly relates to private and social rented housing. Comprehensive data is not available in the Netherlands either. However, research by AEDES (Dutch organization of housing associations), indicates 19 000 to 23 000 eviction judgments per annum, with 25–30 per cent of these executed by bailiffs. The actual number of evicted tenants is higher, as a further 1700 to 2800 tenants left before the execution of the eviction order according to Michel Vols.

In the UK, eviction claims by private and social landlords in England increased between 2010 and 2015, although actual evictions were less common. Data from the Ministry of Justice shows that claims issued rose from 135 000 in 2010 to 154 000, while the use of the accelerated procedure rose from 22 600 cases in 2010 to 38 400 in the period. Actual evictions from this sector increased from 26 700 in 2010 to 41 500 in the period. In Scotland, where data includes evictions from both private and social rented housing, the figures remain broadly similar over the period.

5.3 Profile of Those Evicted

Many countries do not collate data on the profile of those evicted, although local and regional studies have proven very valuable in creating an impression of the key profiles. Research by Jana Verstraete, Pascal De Decker and Diederik Vermeir suggest that, in Belgium, among evicted tenants, some 50 per cent are men and 21 per cent are couples composed of a man and a woman. Some 40 per cent were single persons with children. One study in the city of Namur in 2010 showed that almost all those evicted were dependent on social welfare and households with children were involved in 50 per cent of cases. In Germany, research in Rhine Westphalia in 2012 showed that single persons without children made up 57 per cent of those evicted, while couples without children amounted to 9.6 per cent, and couples with children to 16.7 per cent. Single parents made up 12 per cent of those evicted, and people with a migration background constituted 22 per cent of the total. There is no research on this issue in Ireland, Italy, Poland, Slovenia, Spain or the UK.

5.4 Risk Factors Identified Leading to Evictions

In all the chapters of this book, compiled by the experts across the eleven countries, there is a clear pattern in the analysis of the risk factors for evictions. Unemployment, relationship breakdown, loss of a family member or illness are the key determinants of risk of eviction. This leads to mortgage or rent arrears, or other breaches of the housing arrangements.[166] The sudden drop in income following unemployment often triggers mortgage or rent arrears, which may be attenuated by other debt commitments claiming a higher priority. Other factors mentioned include substance abuse, and, for mortgage-related evictions, Christoph U Schmid and Sofija Nikolic identify incorrect estimation of financial capacity of borrowers and underestimation of all costs as the main risk factors. Some researchers, including Nóra Teller, Eszter Somogyi and Nóra Tosics, identified energy and utility costs as risk factors leading to eviction, as well as situations where a guarantee has been offered on another person's loan, which becomes non-performing. They also highlight the situation of foreign exchange loans with increased repayments due to devaluation or interest rate increases. For Elena Bargelli and Giulia Donadio, economic circumstances in Italy were observed as the main risk factor.

In Ireland, there are clear factors associated with risk of eviction from private rented housing, such as low income, insecurity of tenure and relationship breakdown. For mortgage debtors, Central Bank of Ireland studies have shown that low income (or unemployment) and relationship breakdown are the main risk factors, in addition to overindebtedness. Witold Borysiak suggests that in Poland, unemployment, poverty, debt, misuse of alcohol and release from prison are viewed as key risk factors. Another risk factor, which was also highlighted for Slovenia, is the reprivatization of property appropriated by the state during the socialist period, where the new owners are converting the property for re-use. Michel Vols suggests that in the Netherlands, rent arrears are the main reason for evictions, amounting to over 80 per cent of cases, with nuisance, illegal sub-letting and drugs at approximately 5 per cent each. In social housing evictions, landlords execute eviction orders for arrears only in 30 per cent of cases; however, they do so in over 90 per cent of cases involving drugs. Mortgage-related evictions are often the result of relationship breakdown, accounting for 60 per cent in 2015, with unemployment or loss of income accounting for 29 per cent in the same year.

---

[166]   Sarah Nield, 'Secured consumer credit in England' in M Anderson and E Arroyo Amayuelas (eds) *The Impact of the Mortgage Credit Directive in Europe. Contrasting Views from Member States* (Groningen, Europa Law Publishing 2017) Ch 5, 199, points out that 'Changes in macro-economic climate in the labour and property market thus present immediate risk for the mortgage borrower as do higher divorce rates and the instability of the modern family. However, evaluating these risks and the prospect of default present a challenge to economic experts, let alone consumers. A borrower may understand their responsibilities and the risks they face but is unable to do much about them.'

Nicholas Pleace and Caroline Hunter point out that in the UK, risk of eviction is clearly linked to socio-economic position. Job loss, relationship breakdown and loss of income are major risk factors. Although the UK still has a comparatively extensive and relatively generous welfare state system, housing costs are very high relative to incomes. In areas of housing stress, housing costs can be much higher than the level of welfare supports. In the private rented sector, high rents, limited regulation and restricted legal protections for tenants create insecure tenancies and high risk of eviction. In the social rented sector, there is evidence of over-representation of women, lone parents and unemployed people among eviction cases. Problems in the administration of housing benefits can be a significant factor in arrears cases. Research on mortgage possessions also show a strong association between loss of income and arrears, leading to actions for possession.

5.5 Links between Evictions and Homelessness

There are complex links between evictions and homelessness. As the EU Pilot Project Report shows, persons who are evicted seek the assistance of family and friends initially and only when these support networks are inadequate or break down does the household rely on homelessness services. Of course, this pathway may not be linear or consistent, and particularly in the case of those with complex support needs, there may be a recurrent pattern of evictions and homelessness. Research shows that it is only the most vulnerable who become street homeless directly after eviction.[167]

The availability of eviction-prevention services, even after a court order has been granted, can have a significant impact in breaking the link between eviction and homelessness. Indeed, supporting those at risk of eviction, even at the earlier stages of the process before court, to remain in their homes can be a critical element in mitigation of homelessness. According to the report of National Coalition of Services Working with the Homeless in Germany (*Bundesarbeitsgemeinschaft Wohnungslosenhilfe e.V.* – BAG W), in 2014, some 172 000 households were threatened with eviction and approximately 50 per cent availed of preventative measures. Of the 86 000 persons who lost their homes, 40 per cent lost them as a result of the execution of eviction orders, whereas 60 per cent left in the course of, or before, the conclusion of the eviction proceedings. Some 30 per cent had left after receiving a notice to quit.

---

[167] Kenna et al (n 4).

However, Marc Uhry suggests that in France, there is scant evidence that evictions are leading to homelessness, although homeless people with multiple needs regularly experience eviction. Generally, people with multiple needs, especially those suffering from psychiatric disorders, seem particularly vulnerable to the pathway from arrears to eviction, and consequent homelessness.

Nóra Teller, Eszter Somogyi and Nóra Tosics describe a study in Hungary in 2011 which showed that persons losing their home was the direct cause of their homelessness in 44 per cent of cases. Elena Bargelli and Giulia Donadio suggest that in Italy, the link between evictions and homelessness is considered a 'social bomb', and the highest risk of homelessness is among those with poor social networks, such as immigrants or old people. In Ireland, there are clear links between evictions and homelessness. A doubling of family homelessness between 2014 and 2017 is directly linked with evictions from private rented housing. Sergio Nasarre-Aznar and Rosa Maria Garcia-Teruel point out that in Spain, of the 23 000 homeless people studied in 2012, over 50 per cent had lost their jobs and remained unemployed, while 12 per cent were homeless as a result of eviction. A quarter of homeless people stated that they were homeless because they could not pay their housing costs. However, in the vast majority of cases, those evicted return to their parents' home, as there is a legal obligation in Spanish law to provide for relatives in need, an option not effectively open to immigrants. There is insufficient social housing to rehouse those evicted in Spain.

Nicholas Pleace and Caroline Hunter indicate that in the UK, the end of a time-limited assured shorthold tenancy can be a trigger for homelessness, although the safety net of housing benefits to cover rent, legislation to deal with threatened homelessness and the provision of temporary housing, all mitigate against homelessness in eviction cases. Indeed, in England, some 3.5 million households were provided with temporary or permanent housing as a result of becoming homeless in the period 1979–2015.

Michel Vols highlights research on homeless people in the Netherlands which showed that the three main pathways to homelessness were evictions (38 per cent), relationship problems (35 per cent) and other reasons (28 per cent). Finally, the difficulty of avoiding homelessness through access to new rented housing was emphasized by Jana Verstraete, Pascal De Decker and Diederik Vermeir for Belgium, since, where rents are high, landlords can be selective and may not look favourably upon applicants with a history of eviction.

6. CONCLUSION

Evictions are legally justified on the basis of enforcing property, mortgage, contract or tenancy law, as well as for public and social policy reasons. All EU Member States have a unique blend of constitutional, legislative, human rights, administrative and procedural norms, as well as distinct political/policy approaches to evictions. An array of complex legal, social and procedural anti-eviction and support measures are in place in many countries, but in others there are significant gaps in the protection of housing rights in the context of evictions.[168] The risk factors are the same – a combination of structural, personal and social impacts – and the prevention of eviction can be enhanced through state measures. This book shows that in the various different social, policy, legal and substantive contexts of evictions in eleven selected countries, cross-country comparisons are difficult, and with varying national systems, a clear comparison is not always possible.

Each of the eleven countries has its own pattern and interaction of public policy, law, social inclusion measures, and, indeed, societal structures that impact on the prevalence and nature of evictions. The situation in the UK – with very limited security for tenants – stands out. But the situation generally is one where a clear overall picture can be formed only by assembling available data and reports, which are often limited. Although it is clear that comparative data on evictions in any particular tenure does not universally exist, permitting robust comparisons, there are similar factors that create a propensity for evictions. Poor security of tenure, high housing costs, unemployment or income shock, illness, relationship breakdown or death of a partner, combined with personal difficulties and lack of social or personal support create a high risk of evictions everywhere. The level of legal and social protection determines whether an eviction takes place in these circumstances or not; and whether those evicted become homeless and experience one of 'life's tragedies'.

While some examples of innovative legal and human rights development shine out, particularly in Poland and Spain, the analysis in the chapters shows little evidence of systematic application of EU consumer and human rights law across the eleven countries. Witold Borysiak demonstrates that the courts in Poland have developed an advanced jurisprudence in this area, combining constitutional rights to dignity with ECHR rights on home and national legislation to create an innovative

---

[168] Kenna et al (n 4) 1.

matrix of protection against eviction where alternative accommodation is not made available. In Spain, the EU consumer law cases have established obligations on Spanish courts to carry out own-motion assessments for unfair terms in mortgage possession cases, and to interpret the compatibility of the whole process with respect for the rights of the EU Charter of Fundamental Rights. However, this does not appear to have been followed elsewhere to any great extent. While Germany has a somewhat unique approach to the issue of harm caused by an eviction, in practice this does not lead to any significant legal developments. Equally, this research shows that in the Netherlands and the UK (for social housing only), where the courts comply strictly with the Article 8 ECHR proportionality assessment, in reality the balance between those who own or control property and those being evicted remains generally in favour of those owners or controllers. One area which seems to be undeveloped in any of the jurisdictions is that of the rights of household members who may not be party to the mortgage or the tenancy, such as children or adult dependents. Their rights do not seem to figure in any of the cases and only marginally in policy measures. While most states have policies to protect children from homelessness, the integration of these rights with the right to continue living in an established home seems to be largely relegated to post-eviction protection measures.

Blanket bans or moratoria on mortgage-related possessions are in force in Italy and Spain, although the ECB states that debt-enforcement procedures in Germany, Ireland and Spain are not an obstacle to NPL resolution. However, the ECB suggests that the 'foreclosure' procedures are an obstacle in Italy and Slovenia.[169] Many states and regions have winter or night-time bans on evictions.

Developing a European narrative on loss of home must be viewed in the context of the difficulties of creating EU harmonized standards, and the disparate but emerging human rights jurisprudence. However, all eleven countries have adopted a set of common housing rights norms and are adapting these to a greater or lesser extent into the corpus of national law. The obligation on all states which have accepted the ECHR to ensure that any person at risk of losing their home must have the

---

[169]   European Central Bank, *Stocktake of National Practices and Legal Frameworks Related to NPLs* (Frankfurt, ECB 2016) 18. The term 'non-performing loans' (NPL) as used by the ECB and EBA includes home loans as part of the overall lending, and do not recognize the fact that actions in relation to realizing the security on a home loan, which involves eviction, raises human rights issues. The word eviction is entirely absent from the reports, guidance and guidelines of the ECB and EBA in relation to non-performing loans.

proportionality of the measure determined by an independent tribunal in the light of the relevant principles under Article 8 ECHR provides a sound common protective base.[170] This human rights norm has been clarified further in *Yordanova*,[171] which identified that the proportionality issues relate to the effect of an eviction on the individual's identity, self-determination, physical and moral integrity, maintenance of relationships with others, and settled and secure place in the community, and the extent of the intrusion into the personal sphere of the applicant being evicted. Since Article 8 ECHR is replicated in Article 7 of the EU Charter of Fundamental Rights, this norm can become part of EU law, and indeed has been so regarded by the CJEU. The MCD, although not yet transposed by all EU Member States, has the potential to create a harmonized and consumer-oriented mortgage market, as well as a more coherent mortgage arrears process across EU Member States. The treatment of mortgages as consumer contracts by the CJEU has the potential to radically improve the rights of home loan borrowers in the EU context. The emerging trend is a closer link between mortgage law, consumer law and human rights, through the nexus between all three areas provided by the Unfair Contract Terms Directive.[172] It is perhaps useful to view mortgage contracts and tenancy contracts more as Life Time Contracts which provide the necessities for living, rather than a purely commercial contract.[173]

As Nogler and Reifner point out:

> At the heart of this class of contracts there is an individual human being, with his or her physiological and ethical requirement, in terms of security, belonging, success and self – fulfillment in other words the existential need to be able to enjoy essential goods (*lebenswichtige Güter*), services, labour opportunities and income opportunities. Satisfaction of such needs is normally an essential pre-condition for the pursuit of a happy life, or self-realization and participation.[174]

---

[170] *McCann v United Kingdom*, App No 19009/04, Fourth Section 13 May 2008, §50.

[171] *Yordanova and Others v Bulgaria* No 25446/06, 24 September 2012.

[172] Case C-34/13 *Kušionová v SMART Capital a.s.*; H-W Micklitz and N Reich, 'The court and the sleeping beauty: the revival of the Unfair Contract Terms Directive (UCTD)' (2015) 51 *Common Market Law Review* 771–808.

[173] E Bargelli, 'Exploring interfaces between social long-term contracts and European law through tenancy law' in L Nogler and U Reifner (eds) *Life Time Contracts* (The Hague, Eleven 2014) 627 ff.

[174] See Nogler and Reifner (n 173).

Many of these objectives are already included within human rights instruments in Europe, yet, there seems to be little interaction between countries in the implementation of these human rights norms, good practices or better policies on evictions. There is a great need for a European Open Method of Coordination-type approach, similar to that suggested in relation to rented housing by Christoph Schmid in his book on tenancy law in Europe.[175] This would involve a process similar to the Open Method of Coordination advanced by the European Commission in key areas of social policy, whereby comparative data is collated across Europe and best practices are promoted.[176] However, evictions raise important human rights issues, which go to the core of civilized societies and the mainstreaming of eviction preventative measures with budgetary and policy instruments represents an innovative approach. In this context, the UN report on European Added Value (2018)[177] has set out a set of recommendations on combatting forced evictions and ending homelessness, which should apply to the Multiannual Financial Framework (MFF) of the EU budget from 2020. These are:

- The MFF should explicitly recognize the principle that the EU budget must contribute to the advancement of security of tenure and the right to adequate housing more broadly.

---

[175]   CU Schmid, *Tenancy Law and Housing Policy in Europe* (Cheltenham, Edward Elgar Publishing 2017).

[176]   <http://www.europarl.europa.eu/EPRS/EPRS-AaG-542142-Open-Method-of-Coordination-FINAL.pdf>.

[177]   UN Office of the High Commission for Europe, *European Added Value, The EU Multi-Annual Financial Framework Post-2020. A Tool to Close Human Rights Gaps in Europe?* (Brussels, UN Regional Office for Europe 2018). The report suggests that EU funding in the next cycle should be directly linked to international human rights treaty provisions, as well as the authoritative guidance and recommendations from the UN human rights mechanisms, Council of Europe monitoring bodies, as well as EU bodies. The report also suggests that the EU should fund, directly and independently from Member State intervention, academic institutions, media, and other civil society organizations that are essential for the functioning of democracy, in particular those working on the protection and promotion of human rights. Such funding should be readily available for a range of entities including for grassroots organizations and human rights defenders. Such funding should cover, as appropriate, the variety of activities of civil society organizations, such as service provision, watchdog activities, advocacy, litigation, campaigning, human rights and civic education and awareness-raising. In addition, the EU should review current funding criteria to remove rules barring the use of EU funding for human rights litigation.

- The MFF should support the use of EU funds for actions that advance the implementation of policies for realizing the right to adequate housing.
- The MFF should fund the advancement of alternative accommodation to ensure that evictions do not result in households being rendered homeless or vulnerable to the violation of other human rights.
- The MFF should fund initiatives aimed at overcoming shortages of social housing and advance affordable housing, as well as ending homelessness.

The development and implementation of housing rights norms, on adequate housing and prevention of evictions across Europe compares poorly with the position of national property law, and ECB directions to lenders on non-performing loans, encouraging evictions. There is a major imbalance in the national and European legal and policy architecture around evictions and the position of those who are engaged in advocacy, litigation, campaigning, human rights and awareness-raising on evictions enjoy very little media recognition.

Acknowledgements

Special thanks are due for the valuable support of Christoph U Schmid, University of Bremen, without whose support this book would not have been published, and the dedicated work of Dr Ingrid Cunningham in editing drafts of this book.

1. Evictions in Belgium, a neglected yet pressing issue[*]

Jana Verstraete, Pascal De Decker and Diederik Vermeir

1. INTRODUCTION

The EU Survey of Income and Living Conditions (SILC) 2012 shows 0.27 per cent of the Belgian population had moved in the preceding five-year period because of an eviction.[1] Regrettably, with this record, Belgium ranks in third place for the highest rate of evictions among the 28 countries of the European Union.[2] Despite this ranking, the extent and nature of evictions remain a blind spot in Belgium. Twenty years ago, a 'General Report on Poverty' criticized the lack of official data on the number of evictions.[3] In 2005, the same critique was raised by the research agency charged with alleviating poverty, social insecurity, and social exclusion. After yet another decade, not much has changed. Data on the matter is both limited and fragmented. Hence, a clear picture of the number of evictions, the profile of those evicted, and the housing paths following an eviction is indeterminate. In this contribution, an attempt is made to consolidate existing data and to shed light on this phenomenon.

* We wish to thank Prof. Dr. Nicolas Bernard (l'Université Saint-Louis – Bruxelles) for his profound reading of and valuable comments on previous versions of this text.
¹ European Commission, *European Union Survey of Income and Living Conditions (EU-SILC)* (2012).
² P Kenna, L Benjaminsen, V Busch-Geertsema and S Nasarre-Aznar, *Pilot Project – Promoting Protection of the Right to Housing – Homelessness Prevention in the Context of Evictions* (Brussels, European Commission 2016).
³ Koning Boudewijnstichting, ATD-Vierde Wereld België and VVSG, *Algemeen Verslag over de Armoede* (Brussel, Koning Boudewijnstichting 1994).

As a background to the research, the chapter starts with a brief discussion of the Belgian housing market and Belgian housing policies. Thereafter an overview of the different eviction procedures that apply for different situations is provided including: judicial procedures to evict owner-occupiers, social and private renters, and squatters; temporary dispossessions in the case of family disputes and administrative eviction procedures related to housing quality. The chapter then elaborates on the judicial eviction of both owner-occupiers and renters. A discussion on the extent of the problem for these tenure types as well as the profile of those involved, their rehousing trajectories and risk factors for evictions is then provided. An outline of a limited number of 'good practices' in preventing eviction or in mitigating its harmful consequences is presented. The chapter concludes with some final observations on the issue.

2. POLICY BACKGROUND

2.1 General Housing Policy Related to Evictions

Belgium is a country of homeowners. Ever since the initiation of a public housing policy during the nineteenth century, the Belgian government has encouraged and supported the construction or the purchase of a home of one's own.[4] This objective has been pursued in policy ever since and the share of homeowners has continually risen. In 2015, 64.8 per cent of all Belgian households were owner-occupiers.[5]

2.2 Structural Factors Related to Evictions

Nonetheless, homeownership is not attainable for all. This especially applies to low income households who are not in an equal position to purchase a property.[6] The rental sector offers a solution for those unable

---

[4] L Goossens, *Het sociaal huisvestingsbeleid in België: een historisch-sociologische analyse van de maatschappelijke probleembehandeling op het gebied van het wonen* (PhD, Leuven Faculteit Sociale Wetenschappen KU Leuven, 1982).

[5] Housing Europe, *The State of Housing in the EU 2015: A Housing Europe Review* (Brussels, Housing Europe, the European Federation for Public, Co-operative and Social Housing 2015).

[6] The Foundation Abbé Pierre and FEANTSA, *Second Overview of Housing Exclusion in Europe 2017* (2017) <http://www.feantsa.org/en/report/2017/03/21/the-second-overview-of-housing-exclusion-in-europe-2017> accessed 14 April 2017.

(or unwilling) to become a homeowner and whose income is below a certain threshold. However, the provision of social rental housing has always been a goal of secondary importance.[7] As a result, social rental housing has remained a lacking sector, representing only 6.5 per cent of the housing market. Approximately 186 000 households are registered on waiting lists to be assigned a social rental dwelling.[8] Consequently, those unable to enter the social rental sector (SRS) have to find alternative housing. Some of them, who may be called buyers under duress, resort to homeownership. They purchase a dwelling of inferior quality but do not have sufficient financial means to make the necessary improvements.[9] Others without access to social rental housing turn to the private rental sector (PRS). The PRS can, therefore, be seen as a last resort for those looking for housing and unable to enter homeownership or social rental housing.

Unsurprisingly, problems that violate different aspects of the right to housing, affordability, quality and security, are mostly found within the (private) rental market. First, a remarkable share of renters bear a very high rent burden. For instance, in Flanders, one out of two private renters (51.7 per cent) spend more than 30 per cent of their income on rent. For the 20 per cent lowest-income group, the share is no less than 78.1 per cent. In the SRS, rent prices are set in relation to income. Nonetheless, one-third (34.5 per cent) of its renters cannot afford a dignified lifestyle owing to lack of money after paying their rent.[10] Secondly, quality problems are concentrated on the rental market as well. Almost half of both private and social rental dwellings (47 per cent and 44 per cent respectively) in Flanders do not meet the official housing quality criteria.[11] Thirdly, tenure security is limited. Legally, the length of leases in the PRS is nine years, however (under certain conditions) short-term contracts are permitted and landlords can relatively easily, that is, cheaply, terminate an existing lease.[12] Until recently, tenure security for

---

[7]   Goossens (n 4).

[8]   Housing Europe (n 5).

[9]   L Vanderstraeten and M Ryckewaert, 'Het verhaal van noodkopers en 'captive renters' in P De Decker, B Meeus, I Pannecoucke, E Schillebeeckx, J Verstraete and E Volckaert (eds) *Woonnood in Vlaanderen, Feiten/Mythen/ Voorstellen* (Antwerpen, Garant 2015) 87–106.

[10]   K Heylen, *Grote woononderzoek 2013. Deel 2. Deelmarkten, woonkosten en betaalbaarheid* (Leuven, Steunpunt Wonen 2015).

[11]   Vanderstraeten and Ryckewaert (n 9).

[12]   M Dambre, 'Woninghuur in Vlaamse handen: nieuwe kansen voor het grondrecht op behoorlijke huisvesting?' in B Hubeau and T Vandromme (eds)

social renters was assured by lifelong contracts. However, as of March 2017, this principle was abolished and nine-year contracts will now be applied in the SRS also. As an eviction can be seen as an abrupt end to housing security, its magnitude can be considered an indicator of housing (in)security. The sections following will show that evictions are, by far, most common in the private rental market. Importantly, evictions in Belgium are closely linked to affordability and quality issues, as rent/mortgage arrears (judicial procedures) and a lack of quality (administrative procedures) are the key reasons leading to an eviction.

3. LEGAL AND CONSTITUTIONAL BACKGROUND TO PROTECTION AGAINST EVICTIONS

In Belgium, no one can be evicted from their home without the authorization of a judge, except for renters who can be evicted after a decision of a municipal or regional administration in case of an inhabitable dwelling. In any other case, specific judicial procedures are installed by federal and regional legislation. Legal frameworks differ according to the housing tenure. Before expounding on these procedures, a brief discussion on how the right to housing is enshrined in Belgian law is presented.

3.1 Housing as a Fundamental Right

International declarations of the right to housing have been largely ratified in Belgium. Article 25 of the Universal Declaration of Human Rights, Article 11 of the International Covenant on Economic, Social and Cultural Rights and Article 38 (3) of the EU Charter of Fundamental Rights have been approved at federal (and regional) level.[13] However,

---

Vijftien jaar Vlaamse Wooncode. Sisyphus (on)gelukkig? (Brugge, Die keure 2013) 273–282; P De Decker, 'Jammed between housing and property rights: Belgian private renting in perspective' (2001) 1 (1) *European Journal of Housing Policy* 19–39.

[13] Belgium also ratified the European Convention on Human Rights. It is well known that the right to housing is not formally protected by this Convention, but has gained relevance as a protectable interest at the very least. N Van Leuven and F Vanneste, 'De inroepbaarheid van het recht op wonen' in N Bernard and B Hubeau (eds) *Recht op wonen: naar een resultaatsverbintenis?* (Brugge, Die Keure 2013) 221–252; F Tulkens and S Van Drooghenbroeck, 'Le droit au logement dans la Convention Européenne des droits de l'homme. Bilan

Belgium did not ratify Article 31 of the Revised European Social Charter (RESC) (Right to Housing). As a result, the right to housing is only protected under the RESC as part of the right of the family to social, legal and economic protection[14] and the right to protection against poverty and social exclusion,[15] both of which have been ratified by Belgium.[16]

In 1994, the right to housing was enshrined in the Belgian Constitution. Article 23 declares that everyone has the right to a decent living, which includes, among other economic, social and cultural rights, the right to decent housing. In the Belgian legal doctrine it is often assumed that this article has no direct effect and that it is up to the competent legislator to implement this fundamental right. Some case law, however, shows that this should be put into perspective. First, the right to housing is frequently invoked when balancing the interests of the tenant and the landlord. References to Article 23 of the Constitution are then made to underpin the interests of the tenant and, among other possible goals, contest the appropriateness of an eviction.[17] In addition, the right to housing gives direction for the interpretation of (open) legal norms, while it also constitutes a standard for the assessment of their legality.[18]

Further, Article 23 (3) of the Constitution states that the different branches of government are responsible for the realization of the right to housing, each within the limits of their powers. This is important as housing is a regional policy matter. Consequently, the right to housing is also endorsed in the Housing Codes of all three regions. The Flemish Housing Code (Article 3) confirms that everybody has the right to

---

et perspectives' in N Bernard and C Mertens (eds) *Le logement dans sa multidimensionnalité. Une grande cause régionale* (Namur, 2005) 311–324.

[14]   Art 16 RESC.

[15]   Art 30 RESC.

[16]   For example, ECSR, International Federation on Human Rights Leagues (FIDH) against Belgium, nr. 62/2010 (21 March 2010). See also N Moons, *The right to housing in Flanders-Belgium: international human rights law and concepts as stepping stones to more effectiveness* (doctoral thesis) (Antwerpen, Universiteit Antwerpen, 2016); Van Leuven and Vanneste (n 13).

[17]   Eg Voorz. Rb. Namen 11 May 1994, *Dr.Q.M.* 1995, 54, note Fierens, J.; Peace Court Elsene 6 March 1995, *TBBR* 1996, 296, note B. Hubeau. See also: Moons (n 16) and N Bernard, 'L'article 23 de la Constitution: pas une botte secrète, mais pas non plus dénué de toute effectivité (judiciaire)' (2015) 23 *JLMB* 1080–1089.

[18]   For example, a measure implying that social leases could be annulled without authorization of a judge was found incompatible with Art 23 of the Constitution (Constitutional Court, nr. 101/2008, 10 July 2008).

dignified housing. For this purpose, the provision of an adapted dwelling of good quality, in a decent environment, against an affordable price and with housing security, should be promoted. The Housing Code of the Brussels-Capital Region (Article 3) includes the right to housing as well. To reach this goal, the code prescribes that accessibility, minimal quality and security standards and a decent living environment have to be pursued. The Walloon Housing Code (Article 2) imposes on the regional and other authorities, within their competences, to realize decent housing as a place to live, to emancipate and the development of individuals and the families. Each region also has its own administration and institutions to monitor the right to housing and the housing situation in practice.

In all three regions, municipalities and public local organizations are also responsible for the right to housing. A key partner in this regard is the Public Centres for Social Welfare (PCSW), and these agencies will be discussed in the sections following dealing with social support for households that are threatened by an eviction.

3.2 Law Relating to Owner-occupation

Owner-occupiers can only be evicted in cases where they fail to redeem their mortgage. Before a judicial procedure is started, the creditor (bank) and debtor (owner-occupier) usually come together to find a solution on how to prevent arrears from accumulating and on how to rearrange the mortgage agreement. When no solution is found, or in the event the debtor does not meet the new arrangements, the bank can follow a certain legal procedure. The Law on Mortgage Loans regulates, among other things, the course of this procedure.[19]

First, a prerequisite is that the arrears accrue up to three months. When this condition is met, the bank has to inform the debtor by registered mail about the consequences of defaults by virtue of Article 45 Law on Mortgage Loans. The bank also has to inform the Central Individual Credit Register, which will register the client as a defaulter and retains this information for one year. If the debtor is, thereafter, still unable to repay his/her mortgage, the creditor has to start a procedure before the Attachment Court. Here, an attempt at reconciliation, for instance spreading out repayments over time, is compulsory and has to precede any attachment of property.[20]

---

[19] Wet op hypothecaire kredieten, 04/08/1992 (Law on Mortgage Loans).
[20] Art 59 Law on Mortgage Loans.

If no agreement is found, the creditor can exploit all guarantees given by the debtor (for example an attachment of earnings or other property), or the creditor can start a procedure of executory attachment of the property. This execution of attachment has to be preceded by a command to pay, noticed by the bailiff, stating that non-payment will result in an executory attachment. The command also notifies the debtor that he can inform the judge of any offer to buy his property by first hand sale.[21] An important legal consequence of the command is that the debtor can no longer alienate his ownership on the property by any means. The command itself expires after six months, unless it is followed by a writ of attachment.[22] Within 15 days after the command, no executory attachment is possible.[23]

The writ of attachment has to be registered to the mortgage registry office under Article 1569 of the Judicial Code. Within a month following registration of the writ, the creditor is obliged to ask the Attachment Court to appoint a notary to sell the house. The notary is authorized by law to access the dwelling; for example, to visit it with potential buyers, under Article 1580 of the Judicial Code. The property will be assigned to a buyer on one court hearing, by auction. Within 15 days after this hearing, anyone can make a higher bid.[24] When the house is sold, the client has to leave within a legally defined period of time, usually four months after the agreement on the sale.

3.3 Law Relating to Private and Social Renting

In Belgium, a single procedure exists for both renters in the private and the social rental market. Yet it should be noted that some differences exist in the broader legal framework. First, additional and legally binding prevention measures have been introduced in the SRS and these will be discussed in the sections following. A second (but somewhat related) issue is that social housing agencies conduct a task of public interest (providing affordable and decent housing), linked to the right to housing and the right to human dignity. Consequently, the eviction of social renters is seen as an *ultimum remedium*.[25] Finally, the regions are

---

[21] Art 1564 Judicial Code.
[22] Art 1567 Judicial Code.
[23] Art 1566 Judicial Code.
[24] Arts 1587 and 1592 Judicial Code.
[25] T Vandromme, 'Het kraken van panden bekeken vanuit grondrechten, het strafrecht en het burgerlijk recht (inclusief het procesrecht)' (2014) 2014-2015 nr. 35 *Rechtskundig Weekblad*, 1363–1378. This means that an eviction will only be

competent to make amendments to the procedure for rental disputes since 2014.[26] At the time of writing however, the 'federal' procedure discussed below is still applicable for all three regions.

A first point of interest is how a judicial procedure to evict a renter can be prevented. This is possible by a 'reconciliation'; an informal and voluntary procedure before a justice of the peace. If no agreement is found, there are no consequences. If, however, a compromise is found, the agreement is translated into a procès-verbal, which makes it binding under Articles 731–733 of the Judicial Code. From 2002 onwards, this reconciliation procedure was an obligatory prerequisite and without a foregoing reconciliation attempt, a judicial procedure for a rental dispute could not be initiated. However, the obligation was discontinued in 2008. Alternatively, the landlord and renter can agree to refer their dispute to a (professional) mediator under Articles 1727–1737 of the Judicial Code or an arbitration procedure.[27]

A judicial procedure itself can be started in three ways: (1) both parties can agree on appearing voluntarily, (2) landlords can submit an appeal, and (3) landlords can involve a bailiff to cite renters to court (Articles 701, 706 and 1344bis Judicial Code). The judicial procedure is held at the Court of the Justice of the Peace (Article 591 Judicial Code).

The procedure starts with a session in the Court of the Justice of the Peace. It is important for the tenant to attend this session, as failure to do so can result in a claim for eviction by default (in absentia) under Articles 802–806 Judicial Code. When both parties are present, the judge will first make an attempt at reconciliation.[28] If reconciliation fails, the judge examines whether the renter protests the claim. If not, the judge can pass an immediate verdict. The judge can then help find a solution or approve the eviction under Article 735 Judicial Code. If any of the claims are contested by either of the parties, a period of time will be allowed for the parties to formulate their arguments and a subsequent session will be scheduled. During that next session, the judge may render a verdict or

---

authorized when 'sufficiently severe reasons' exist, thereby taking into account the consequences of an eviction, the possibilities of finding decent housing afterwards and the public interest (including, among other issues, the right to housing of other (candidate-)renters).

[26] B Hubeau, T Vandromme and D Vermeir, 'Het huisvestingsbeleid' in B Seutin and G Van Haegendoren (eds) *De bevoegdheden van de gewesten* (Brugge, Die Keure 2016) 85–119.

[27] Arts 1676–1723 Judicial Code.

[28] Art 1344septies Judicial Code.

accept an alternative solution proposed by one of the parties.[29] It is also possible for the judge to propose a solution (in reality, it would typically be a payment plan) to avoid eviction. In several follow-up sessions, the judge then evaluates the tenant's compliance with the agreement. If the tenant fails to comply, the judge can, at any time, pass an eviction verdict.

When a court renders the verdict of eviction, the tenant must be served with a writ to that effect by a bailiff.[30] The eviction cannot take place until one month has passed from the date the order was served. In exceptional circumstances, the landlord or tenant may petition to shorten that period, for instance when the landlord can show that the tenant has already vacated the dwelling, or, extend it. The bailiff has to inform the tenant of the exact date and time of the planned eviction at least five working days before an eviction may be carried out under Article 1344quater of the Judicial Code.

A bailiff and the police must be present on the day of the eviction. Municipal services will remove any remaining items from the dwelling and put them out on the street. If the items form a nuisance in the public space, they may be stored for up to six months by the municipality. The tenant will be charged for the cost of all these actions. Hence the bailiff has been tasked by law to inform the tenant in advance about the fate of any remaining items.[31]

3.4 Law Relating to Unauthorized Occupancy

In Belgium, squatting is subject to debate and many challenge the fact that squatters cannot be expelled immediately by the police as 'unfair'. Often it is also asserted that squatting is not a criminal offence and that changes to the law should be made to make squatting an offence. Although squatting itself was not a crime in Belgium in the examined

---

[29] Arts 736–763 Judicial Code.

[30] Due to a recent amendment, the Judicial Code upholds as a general principle that a provisional enforcement of a verdict (ie eviction) is possible, even when an appeal has been filed (Art 1397 Judicial Code). The Judicial Code also states that he or she who requests the provisional enforcement is responsible for the restoration to the initial situation when the appeal was successful (Art 1398 Judicial Code). In case of evictions, however, the consequences of a provisional enforcement seem hard to repair.

[31] Art 1344quinquies Judicial Code.

period of time,[32] a number of observations can be made in relation to it. First, the right to property is (and always has been) protected by criminal law. Hence squatters can, among others, be liable for damage to the dwelling or 'theft' of utilities, for instance water and electricity. Secondly, the inviolability of the home is guaranteed, as home invasion ('huisvredebreuk') is a criminal offence. Yet this requires the dwelling to be inhabited under Article 439 of the Criminal Code.

Squatters themselves do not have any title to occupy a dwelling. Consequently, evicting squatters is relatively easy. Nonetheless, legal procedures are in place, and as the inviolability of the home also applies to squatters, an authorization of a judge is necessitated for an eviction.

Whether a squatter(s) can or cannot be identified by the property owner, determines which procedure regulates the eviction. If squatters are not identifiable, the owner can submit a one-sided appeal before the President of the Court of First Instance under Article 584 of the Judicial Code.[33] The President will order the eviction and decides on the anticipated time before the actual eviction of the squatters takes place. To give notice to the squatters, a bailiff typically posts the eviction order at the squatted building and following the anticipated timeframe, the property can be emptied.

In the case where squatters are identifiable by the property owner, the owner has to start a contradictory procedure before the Justice of the Peace,[34] or, in cases of urgency, before the President of the Court of First Instance.[35] The procedure must be commenced via a notification by a bailiff. There will be a hearing, where squatters can defend their case. When the judge orders an eviction, she or he usually determines that the identified squatter(s) can be evicted 'together with everyone else in the dwelling'.[36] The judge will also prescribe the period that has to be respected before the actual eviction. No official rule or guideline on the respected time exists. However, according to one Judge of the Peace, this

---

[32] As a result of the ongoing discussion, squatting itself became a crime as of November 2017.

[33] In some cases, squatters intentionally identify themselves or even request a legal domicile. This prevents a one-sided appeal and makes it relatively harder for the landlord to evict them (K De Greve, 'Gekraakt leven – processuele actiemogelijkheden in het burgerlijk procesrecht' (2014) 1 *Huur* 7–20).

[34] Art 590 Judicial Code.

[35] Art 584 Judicial Code.

[36] De Greve (n 33).

usually entails a one-month period, similar to the procedure of private and social renters, in view of humanitarian eviction and the right to housing.[37]

Squatters have little basis to defend their occupation and sometimes the right to housing is invoked. However, according to a judge and a housing activist working with Roma families squatting in Ghent, a balancing test between the right of ownership and the right to housing often finds in favour of the owner.[38]

Lastly, a 'precarious lease' ('bezetting ter bede') with the owner is used as a measure for owners to prevent squatting. For squatters this can be a way to ensure their right to stay for a specific period of time. From a legal perspective, this 'lease' is not equal to a rental contract (for instance, quality standards for rental dwellings do not apply and the notice period is not regulated by law), however it is a legal agreement that states that the occupier can stay until a certain date or under certain conditions.[39] According to a Brussels housing scholar, increasingly, squatters in Brussels have such 'precarious leases'. The Brussels Regional Housing Code has even included the possibility for the Regional Housing Association to

---

[37]   In future, due to the legislative amendment of November 2017, a distinction must be made depending on the fact whether the dwelling is inhabited or not. In case of an inhabited dwelling, police officials can immediately evict the squatters. When this is not the case, but a complaint has been filed against the squatting, the police can request an authorization of a judge for the eviction. The squatters can then protest the decision before the Justice of the Peace.

[38]   This information was provided during interviews with a Judge of the Peace and a housing scholar/activist (see section 4 for more information on the interviews conducted by the authors). Both interviews took place in May 2014. See also P Debruyne, E Vandeputte and S Beunen, 'Uit de Marges van het Woonbeleid. De Strijd voor het Recht op Wonen in Gent' (2014) 5 (2) *Ruimte en Maatschappij* 9–45 and T Vandromme, 'Het kraken van panden bekeken vanuit grondrechten, het strafrecht en het burgerlijk recht (inclusief het procesrecht)' (2014) 2014–2015 nr. 35 *Rechtskundig Weekblad*, 1363–1378 on this matter. Relevant questions for a judge are both related to the condition of the squatters (do they have any other option to realize their right to housing?) and the situation of the landlord (does (s)he have any plans with the dwelling?). In the case law we know, the right to housing will only prevail when the answer to both questions is negative.

[39]   Because of the compulsory nature of the (house) rental legislation, however, a judge can reclassify any so called 'precarious lease' into a regular rental contract when the actual terms of the agreement rather indicate the existence of the latter. As a result, the provisions of the rental legislation, with a fixed length of the lease and statutory notice periods, will be applicable.

close precarious leases for dwellings for which a renovation is planned and for which the inhabitants receive social support.[40]

3.5 Law Relating to Temporary Dispossession

In case of disputes between married or legal partners, 'urgent and temporary measures' can be taken to alleviate the situation under Articles 223 and 1479 of the Civil Code. Previously, the Justice of the Peace was responsible for this matter; however, since 2014, the new Family Courts are responsible.[41] The judge can ascribe the right of residence of the family home, irrespective of the tenure type, to one of the partners. According to research carried out by the authors, in those cases, the person who should leave the family home is assigned a period to find a new place of residence.[42]

Moreover, a new law on domestic violence was adopted in 2012, which anticipates the possibility to evict any adult member of a household from the joint home in cases where the safety of other family member(s) is at issue. In contrast to the aforementioned 'urgent and temporary measures', this law is not restricted to married couples or persons officially living together. The public prosecutor can command an immediate restraining order for ten days. Within this period, a judge evaluates the measure and can either withdraw or lengthen this restraining order to a maximum of three months. In 2014, this jurisdiction was also transferred from the Justice of the Peace to the newly founded Family Court.

3.6 Uninhabitable Dwellings

Dwellings that do not meet minimal quality standards can be declared uninhabitable, in which case, the inhabitants can be evicted by an administrative instead of a judicial procedure. The eviction is based on the Belgian Municipal Law or on the Housing Codes of all three regions.

The Belgian Municipal Law is valid for all three regions. Based on Article 135 of the Municipal Law, the mayor himself can declare a dwelling uninhabitable in the case of acute risk or in view of the public

---

[40] Art 67 Brussels Housing Code.

[41] Art 572bis Judicial Code.

[42] Information provided by our respondent (Justice of Peace), interview May 2014. The same respondent, however, is not aware of any case in his jurisdiction where a person had been actually evicted by a bailiff due to such a measure.

interest, for instance if there is a fire risk. The mayor can declare any dwelling uninhabitable, regardless of the tenure status of inhabitants.

All three regions have their own Housing Codes that include minimal quality norms. Regional inspection services are responsible for technical controls to investigate whether dwellings meet these norms. In Flanders and Wallonia, the responsible administrations advise the mayor to declare a dwelling uninhabitable if necessary, based on their technical reports. This is the case when severe risks to the health and safety of the inhabitants exist. If the mayor declares a dwelling uninhabitable on the advice of the administration, the residents have to leave the dwelling.[43] In the Brussels-Capital Region, the responsibility is at the regional level under Article 6 of the Brussels Housing Code.

While there is no interference by a judge *prior* to an eviction order in these administrative procedures, a judge may be involved once a decision to evict a household is taken and the parties involved can appeal against this decision. An appeal against a regional decision has to be lodged with the regional governments at first instance; and to the Council of State in second instance. The decision of a mayor can be challenged at the Council of State.

In the Brussels-Capital Region and the Walloon Region, public land-lords are restricted from evicting their tenants in winter. Both regional governments have recognized a 'winter ban'. In the Brussels-Capital Region, such a ban was established in 2001.[44] From 1 December until 28 February, a 'winter prohibition' is in operation. Evictions are not prohib-ited outright; however, the eviction procedure becomes harder during this period. A household can only be evicted in cases of severe behavioural problems against other renters or staff of the social housing organization, and in the event that the renter does not respond to measures taken by the social housing organization.[45] Following Brussels, the Walloon Region has more recently recognized a stricter winter ban that interdicts public landlords from evicting renters. If a household is in receipt of social support by the PCSW, they will not be evicted between 1 November and 15 March.[46] If an eviction is ordered, it will only be executed after these dates. In Flanders, no winter ban has been established yet.

---

[43] Arts 15–17 Flemish Housing Code and Arts 3–13 Walloon Housing Code.
[44] Circulaire du 16 Novembre 2000.
[45] N Bernard and L Lemaire, *Expulsions de logement, sans-abrisme et relogement* (Brussels, Larcier 2010).
[46] Art 94 §1 Walloon Housing Code.

4. EXTENT OF EVICTIONS OVER THE PERIOD 2010–2015

4.1 Introduction

Sourcing data on evictions in Belgium has been a difficult task. Data on the number of evictions, the profile of those evicted and rehousing paths, is not gathered at a central level. Instead, the information derives from a number of different sources and accordingly is fragmented. To gather as much information as possible, the authors have (1) analysed related legislations, (2) collected existing reports by scholars, NGOs, policy administration, etc, (3) contacted over 60 organizations including associations of renters, landlords and bailiffs, anti-poverty organizations, local police offices, local governments, local social services, NGOs and ministries, (4) reviewed parliamentary debates on evictions, and (5) interviewed a limited number of respondents, each with a different link to eviction procedures.[47] Data was mainly collected in two periods: March–June 2014 and October–November 2014. An additional yet limited search for data was held in February–March 2017. This research has provided information on judicial evictions of owner-occupiers and renters. Therefore, the remainder of the chapter focuses on these groups. As no data has been found on the extent of evictions in situations of unauthorized occupancy or in the light of family law, nor on the profile of those involved in these specific types of evictions, we will not come back to these issues.

To shed light on the magnitude of evictions in the Belgian housing market, we have focused on three phases during the judicial procedures: (1) the initiation of an eviction procedure in court; (2) the authorization of an eviction by a verdict of a judge; and (3) the actual eviction.

4.2 Evictions from Mortgaged Property

There are no figures on the extent of evictions from owner-occupied houses as a result of mortgage enforcement. On the contrary, there are no indications that such evictions happen frequently. The fact that no public attention or debate was/is going on, may be an important indicator; given the importance of home ownership in Belgium.

---

[47] The respondents included two social workers from different PCSWs, a social scientist, a housing activist, a law professor, a Judge of the Peace and a bank clerk.

Evictions from owner-occupied dwellings result from the incapacity to redeem the mortgage. Therefore, an examination of the number of households confronted with this difficulty is outlined. Table 1.1 shows that only a minority of all mortgages are not redeemed as planned. The number of households with arrears has been rather stable, just above 1 per cent of all debtors. Two important remarks have to be made here. First, mortgage arrears rarely lead to actual evictions as alternative solutions are mostly pursued. Second, there is no distinction in the data between first or second homes.

Table 1.1   Mortgage arrears in Belgium (2010–2015)

	Number of mortgages	Number of arrears	%
2010	2 501 787	27 678	1.06
2011	2 689 587	28 974	1.08
2012	2 753 225	30 509	1.11
2013	2 797 148	32 340	1.16
2014	2 846 568	34 005	1.19
2015	2 900 013	33 709	1.16

Source: National Bank of Belgium, *Centrale voor kredieten aan particulieren Statistieken* (2016) 23.

4.3 Evictions From Private/Social Rented Housing

The search for data on the number of evictions taking place on the rental market in Belgium has been difficult, as mentioned above. This difficulty is highlighted in Table 1.2, where all the data is gathered. After an intensive search, the authors were able to obtain at least a partial view of the situation in Flanders and Wallonia. Nonetheless, owing to the lack of data, Table 1.2 is fragmented. The situation in the Brussels-Capital Region remains completely unknown.

The Association of Flemish Cities and Municipalities (VVSG) collects data from all PCSWs[48] on the number of judicial procedures that are commenced on a yearly basis (Table 1.2).[49] Until 2012, the number of eviction cases had increased slightly, a trend that started earlier on from

---

[48]   As we will discuss later, PCSWs are informed whenever an eviction case is started at court.

[49]   More specifically, the data refers to all cases whereby eviction was demanded as from the start of the procedure. The data does not contain those

2008. In 2012, a peak of 13 561 new procedures were registered. In the year following, the number of cases fell back on estimate, to 12 000 procedures a year. This translates to 230 procedures a week or 33 procedures per day.

Data from 2013 permits the comparison of the number of initiated procedures and the number of households in the (private and social) rental stock in Flanders. No less than 1.76 per cent of all tenants (households) were threatened with an eviction in that year.[50]

It is unknown how many verdicts resulted from this large amount of initiating activity. In the SRS and the social rental agencies (SRAs) respectively, 496 (in 2015) and 138 (in 2012) households were actually evicted by the bailiff (Table 1.2). To gain insight into the number of evictions that ensued in the entire rental stock, we have to rely on estimates. While some of the informants in our own investigation estimated that one out of three initiated procedures eventually ended with an eviction, a news item on the website of the Flemish public television VRT[51] asserted that no less than 90 per cent of all initiated procedures ended with an eviction. Depending on the estimation that is followed, between approximately 4000 and up to 10 800 households lost their rental dwelling owing to an eviction in 2015, which translates to between 76 and up to 207 evictions per week.

The authors were unable to ascertain how many judicial procedures had been initiated in Wallonia (Table 1.2). For two housing segments, namely public housing, among which the social housing associations account for 80 per cent, and SRAs, the overview provided by Deprez and Gérard (2015) is incomplete. While the authors contacted all public housing services[52] and all SRAs, the response rate was quite low. Therefore, the given figures of 1096 procedures in the public housing

---

procedures that started as a mere rental dispute and that evolved into a demand for eviction (filed during the procedure).

[50] Flanders counted 2 707 723 private households in 2014 (D Luyten and K Heylen, 'Hoe wonen gezinnen in Vlaanderen' in D Luyten, K Emmery, I Pasteels and D Geldof (eds) *De sleutel past niet meer op elke deur Dynamische gezinnen en flexibel Wonen* (Antwerpen/Apeldoorn, Garant 2015) 91, 100). In 2013, the most recent year for which data is available, 27.1 per cent of all Flemish households were tenants (ie 733 793 households), of which 20.4 per cent were in the private rental sector and 6.7 per cent in the social rental sector (K Heylen, *Grote woononderzoek 2013. Deel 2. Deelmarkten, woonkosten en betaalbaarheid* (Leuven, Steunpunt Wonen 2015)). In 2013, a judicial procedure for eviction was initiated against 12 938 tenants.

[51] F Bruggeman, 'Elke week belanden zo'n 250 Vlaamse gezinnen op straat' *De Redactie*, 10 June 2014 <www.deredactie.be> accessed 11 June 2014.

[52] Sociétés de Logements de Service Publics (SLSPs).

stock and 122 for the SRAs in 2012, understate the real magnitude. Neither were these authors able to obtain complete figures for the two subsequent stages. Within the part of the public sector for which they obtained data, 786 cases resulted in a verdict to evict, of which 134 were eventually carried out by the bailiff in 2012. The 122 initiated procedures by 15 SRAs, ended with 84 verdicts, resulting in 35 actual evictions that same year.

Table 1.2   Evictions on the rental market in Belgium (2010–2015)

	Flanders				Wallonia*			
Number of initiated procedures for eviction								
	Total	Private rental	Social rental**	SRA	Total	Private rental	Public rental****	SRA
2010	12 566		1539				869	89
2011	12 740						976	85
2012	13 561						1096	122
2013	12 958							
2014	12 000***		1542					
2015	12 000***		1431					
Number of claims for eviction								
	Total	Private rental	Social rental	SRA	Total	Private rental	Public rental****	SRA
2010							695	65
2011							717	65
2012							786	84
2013								
2014								
2015								
Number of actual evictions* **								
	Total	Private rental	Social rental	SRA	Total	Private rental	Public rental****	SRA
2010			463	99			151	30
2011				127			153	21
2012				138			134	35
2013								
2014			499					
2015			496					

Notes:

* Data for Wallonia are only partial. The calculations are based on only 26 of the 64 SLSPs and 15 of the 28 SRAs.

** Data for the social rental sector for the period 2014–2015 are only partial. A survey was sent to all 90 social housing companies, 77 of which returned the survey. These companies cover 90% of the entire sector.

*** The total number of eviction cases in Flanders (2014–2015) is an estimation by the VVSG (Association of Flemish Cities and Municipalities). All 308 PCSWs were contacted, of which 57% responded – including all large(r) PCSWs (in municipalities with a high(er) population). Based on data that had been collected, an estimation for the whole of Flanders is made.

**** Data cover the entire public rental sector. Social rental housing represents the large majority of this sector.

Sources: A Deprez and V Gérard (2015), Calculations by the Institut Wallon de l'Evaluation, de la Prospective et de la Statistique; H Ledegen, 'OCMW-barometer staat op betaalbaar en goed' wonen' *Lokaal* 2016 62–63; B Mallants, 'Uithuiszettingen door sociale huisvestingsmaatschappijen: focus op preventie' (2016) 107 (7) *De Gids op Maatschappelijk Gebied* 60–64; VVSG; VMSW; Annual reports VOB.

The amount of reliable data is clearly limited. Still, some general trends can be identified. First, the majority of the tenants threatened with eviction are in the PRS. In both Flanders and Wallonia, about 80 per cent of the eviction procedures are initiated by a private landlord.[53]

Secondly, the eviction procedure can be seen as a funnel. Households drop out throughout the procedure for various reasons, such as an agreement reached between a landlord and a tenant, a payment plan devised by a judge, or a landlord deciding not to have the bailiff serve and execute an eviction order. However, the gap between the number of initiated procedures and the number of actual evictions is not only the result of such 'solutions' that prevent the tenant from having to move. In some cases, tenants just disappear when they are summoned to appear in court or when a verdict is rendered so as to avoid the experience of an eviction.[54] One of the respondents in the research carried out by the authors stated that clients are advised to take such a course of action. The number of tenants who are forced to move after the initiation of a procedure is therefore higher than the number of actual evictions.

I always tell people to make sure that they go away of their own accord. Certainly, if it concerns a family when children are involved. (…) There is police, with a bailiff. Everyone in the street is watching. Just not a good

[53] E Meys and K Hermans, *Nulmeting dak- en thuisloosheid* (2014) Steunpunt Welzijn, Volksgezondheid en Gezin (Leuven); A Deprez and V Gérard, *Les expulsion domiciliaires en Wallonie: Premier état des lieux* (IWEPS, Belgrade Namur 2015).

[54] Deprez and Gérard (n 53).

experience. Avoid that, and we'll agree that you leave the key somewhere. (Social worker PCSW)

In this regard it is important to mention that initiated procedures in the SRS are not always meant to actually evict a tenant, rather they are used as a last resort to pressure tenants 'to face up' to existing problems, as stated by respondents in the research. This strategy seems to be effective when rent arrears are the motive for a procedure. When rent arrears are the main motive for an eviction procedure, only one out of three initiated procedures lead to an actual eviction. Yet when 'behavioural problems' are the main motive, tenants are evicted in almost six out of ten cases. A combination of both motives leads to an actual eviction of about 80 per cent of all procedures.[55] According to Deprez and Gérard, the strategy of pressuring tenants by a judicial procedure is also used by some private landlords in Wallonia.[56]

4.4   Profile of Those Evicted

An owner-occupier can only be evicted where they fail to redeem their mortgage. Information regarding the profiles of the small group of those who fail to do so is limited. However, recent data from National Bank of Belgium reveals that mortgage arrears are most common among people aged between 35–44 years and those aged between 45–54 years.[57]

A study by Meys and Hermans in 2014 was the first in Flanders to sketch a profile of renters confronted with an eviction on a large scale.[58] Records of the procedures initiated by 179 of the 308 Flemish PCSWs were examined, and the analysis showed that men run the highest risk of eviction and account for over half of all eviction orders served (53.3 per cent). The study found however that only one in five (21.4 per cent) of evictions are served to a couple of a man and a woman. Furthermore, tenants threatened with eviction are mostly in the age groups of between 30–39 years (28.5 per cent) followed by those in the 40–49 years age bracket (21.4 per cent). Thirdly, the study reveals that single persons

---

[55]   B Mallants, 'Uithuiszettingen door sociale huisvestingsmaatschappijen: focus op preventie' (2016) 107 (7) *De Gids op Maatschappelijk Gebied* 60–64.

[56]   Deprez and Gérard (n 53).

[57]   National Bank of Belgium, *Centrale voor kredieten aan particulieren. Statistieken* (Brussel, Nationale Bank van België 2016) 41.

[58]   Meys and Hermans (n 53).

without children run the highest risk of eviction (39.2 per cent). Nevertheless, children are involved in one out of four (26 per cent) eviction claims.[59]

No large-scale survey has been undertaken in Wallonia or Brussels. The PCSW of Namur, a city of approximately 110 000 inhabitants in Wallonia however, has gathered detailed information on households threatened with an eviction that are supported by the centre. Even though the city of Namur is not representative of the whole of Wallonia, it gives an indication of the profiles of people threatened by eviction. Data for 2010 gives the most detailed insight into the profile of the households threatened by an eviction and supported by the PCSW.[60] The data reveals information on the number of people reached by the PCSW, the household type, age, income and gender of those involved. In 2010, 312 initiations of eviction cases were reported. Following the notification of the procedure, the PCSW has been able to reach 236 persons.[61] In Namur, evictions mostly affect people aged between 25–34 (30 per cent) and between 35–44 (39 per cent). Figures show single persons (36 per cent) to be the most vulnerable in terms of being confronted with an eviction procedure, yet children are involved in half of all cases (52 per cent). Furthermore, most people involved in an eviction procedure are dependent on social benefits (mostly unemployment benefits and living wage[62]), and only one out of five have an earned income (22 per cent). The ratio of men and women are equal in eviction cases.

5. RISK FACTORS IDENTIFIED LEADING TO EVICTIONS

As stated above, very few owner-occupiers fail to redeem their mortgage. It has been asserted that information regarding the profile of those involved in evictions is scarce. No information on risk factors, except for the age factor shown in the previous section, are identified.

---

[59] Ibid.

[60] The PCSW of Namur has not published a report on evictions but has shared its data with the authors for the sake of the research.

[61] The number of people reached by the PCSW is higher than the number of initiated procedures due to the fact that the PCSW counts the number of persons in each household it supported.

[62] The living wage is the minimal financial allowance provided by the Belgian state.

The main cause of evictions in the private rental sector (PRS) is rent arrears. Therefore, an examination of the factors leading to arrears is necessary in order to understand the large number of eviction cases. The lack of affordable housing is a key element. As mentioned above, many tenants bear a high rent burden. Moreover, data on housing quotes[63] do not include the necessary expense(s) for heating and electricity and many households experience difficulties paying these utility costs.[64]

It becomes more difficult to cover all costs when a financial setback occurs. This can be the case, for instance, when a renter loses his or her income because of unemployment. A second example of a 'financial setback' is a relationship breakdown. If one of the partners stays in the rental accommodation while the ex-partner moves out, the former will have to pay all housing expenses with a tighter budget. Extra (un-anticipated) expenses, such as hospital bills or instalments for paying off debts, might put pressure on the available household budget. Accordingly, some households often have trouble making ends meet. In the research carried out by the authors, social workers identified such unexpected costs as a risk factor. When households choose to not pay rent, a large sum of money is released to pay other costs such as the electricity bill, the hospital bill etc.

Furthermore, respondents in the research expressed that rent arrears are often combined with other debts. Not paying rent is used to free an amount of money to pay off other debts, as the following citation illustrates. In addition, households underestimate the consequences of rent arrears and the risk of an eviction, which makes rent arrears grow.[65]

> Because people chose to pay the bailiff who is knocking at the door, to pay him as much as possible. And to buy food. And then they don't pay rent. Because they have to make choices and they chose to fix the machine … . (Social worker PCSW, own translation)

---

[63]   The housing quote is an indicator for housing affordability. The quote is determined by assessing the percentage of the household income that is spent on housing, usually the monthly rent or mortgage repayment. In international research, 30 or 40 per cent is generally used as an indicator of affordability, meaning that a household spending more than 30 or 40 per cent of its income on rent/mortgage repayment is experiencing affordability problems.

[64]   The Foundation Abbé Pierre and FEANTSA (n 6).

[65]   L Verbeeck, 'De gerechtelijke uitzetting uit het duister gehaald' in P De Decker, L Goossens and I Pannecoucke (eds) *Wonen aan de onderkant* (Antwerpen-Apeldoorn, Garant 2005) 337–350.

Frisque asserts that caution should be exercised in blaming individual tenants for the risk of an eviction and that the bigger picture should be kept in mind.[66] As affordable housing is lacking, households are forced to accept rent prices that place a constraint on their budget. In 2013, the average rent in the Flemish PRS was €562 per month. The average rent paid by the households in the lowest income quintile was only €40 less (€520). That same year, the 'living wage', a financial minimum benefit, was set at €817.36 per month for a single person and at €1089.82 per month, for a couple. Clearly, this tension between rent and income generates a great financial risk for many households in the PRS.

These risk factors in the PRS are also at stake in the SRS. Even though rent is adjusted to income, one out of three social renters do not have a sufficient income to have a decent life after paying rent.[67] However, payment difficulties are not the only risk factor in the SRS. Next to rent arrears, behavioural problems caused by renters is the second major motive for social rental organizations to start an eviction case.

6. LINKS BETWEEN EVICTIONS AND HOMELESSNESS

The procedures leading to an eviction and the eviction itself are serious events. In addition, what happens following an eviction also creates uncertainties as a new dwelling has to be found, and for many, this search is challenging.

As financial problems are undoubtedly a major issue leading to evictions, for both renters and owner-occupiers, the acquisition of a property is rarely an option, as it requires a relatively affluent and financially stable situation. Entering the SRS right after an eviction is hardly an alternative, due to long waiting lists.[68] Although social rental agencies allocate dwellings based on the level of urgency rather than

---

[66] C Frisque, *La prévention des expulsions locatives. Les paradoxes de la banalisation d'un nouveau risque* (2006). Rapport pour la DREES-MIRE, Ministère de la Santé et des Solidarités, Université Paris-X Nanterre – Institut des sciences du politique.

[67] Heylen (n 10).

[68] It should be noted, however, that the Social Rental Legislation foresees exceptions on the principle of chronology. First, a system of 'accelerated allocation' exists in cases of 'exceptional social circumstances', such as homelessness (Art 24 Social Rental Decree). Secondly, there are multiple priority rules. An example is the priority for inhabitants of uninhabitable dwellings (Art 19 Social Rental Decree).

chronology on waiting lists, the chances they can offer a dwelling immediately are small. Consequently, evicted households are, to a large extent, forced to revert back to the PRS, the same sector where most have lost their previous home.

Several issues hinder an easy search for a dwelling in the PRS. First, rent prices are high compared to incomes. Secondly, many private landlords are not eager to welcome low-income families, and certainly not if these households have a poor housing record. Research on discrimination in the PRS in Belgium has shown that some landlords contact the previous landlord or demand proof of recent rent payment at the previous address.[69] Obviously, landlords do not look favourably upon households that have been evicted after a judicial procedure.

Once again, the data that is needed to demonstrate the tedious path to rehousing is lacking; it is not possible to show how many households succeed or fail in finding an alternative rental dwelling after the eviction. From discussions with social workers, the authors learned that some do secure a new dwelling with or without aid from social service agencies; however, for others, the search remains fruitless. Households may have to fall back on unstable and temporary solutions, such as doubling up with family or friends, temporary housing, crisis shelters, or residential homeless services. For some, such an unstable solution only lasts until a suitable dwelling is found, but for others it marks the start of a much longer period of homelessness.

Researcher:	Do you know whether many people quickly find a stable housing situation, or does it often remain unstable?
Interviewee:	That is difficult to say. Actually, we don't keep track of that ourselves. We should really do that. (…) My gut feeling is that the situations are often not stable.
Researcher:	Temporary solutions?
Interviewee:	Yes indeed, many temporary solutions. Or we see young people who move back in with their parents or share with friends. Or maybe they just rent something else. But also that often fails in the end.
Researcher:	And that means that people actually end up on the street?

---

[69] J Verstraete and P De Decker, 'Discriminatie van financieel kwetsbare huishoudens op de private huurmarkt in België' in P De Decker, B Meeus, I Pannecoucke, E Schillebeeckx, J Verstraete and E Volckaert (eds) *Woonnood in Vlaanderen. Feiten/Myten/Voorstellen* (Antwerpen, Garant 2015) 281–296.

Interviewee: What does that really mean, on the street? If someone has a
                couch to get some shut-eye on each night, but hangs out on
                the street the entire day, is that one homeless? The way I see
                it, yes. But not according to the law.

(Interview fragment, social worker PCSW)

7. BEST PRACTICE MODELS FOR PREVENTING, TACKLING AND REACTING TO EVICTIONS

Eviction procedures are well-defined by law for all tenure types. At different stages throughout these procedures, owner-occupiers and renters are protected against a threatening eviction and its harmful consequences, either by law or by practices developed within the field. In this final section, some key practices aimed at preventing, tackling, or reacting to an eviction are discussed.

7.1 Preventing Evictions

First, the cautiousness of both the lender and the borrower in closing a mortgage is one of the most effective anti-eviction practices in Belgium, as arrears and consequently evictions among homeowners are very rare. Financial institutions are careful in providing mortgages to future owner-occupiers. Such institutions accurately check the capabilities of monthly repayments of a household, and only allow households to spend about one third of their income on their mortgage, and often decide on a minimal amount of money that the borrower has to have after repaying the mortgage. For instance, in the case of one respondent in the authors' independent research, the bank sets a threshold at €800 a month. Research by De Decker has shown owner-occupiers are very careful as well. Buying a dwelling is only completed after thorough considerations and calculations.[70]

Secondly, the Flemish regional government has imposed on social housing companies and social rental agencies, a number of basic support tasks for (candidate-) renters.[71] These tasks should enhance the early identification of problems in addition to supporting renters before more serious problems arise. The list of tasks includes assisting renters who are experiencing difficulties in fulfilling their rental obligations, assisting

---

[70] P De Decker, 'Eigen woning: geldmachine of pensioensparen?' (Antwerpen, Garant 2013).
[71] Art 6 Ministerial Order of 21 December 2007.

renters who are in rent arrears and closely monitoring their situation, and mediating in disputes where behavioural problems are the main concern. If necessary, social housing companies have to involve other (more specialized) social services to find a solution for reoccurring problems (eg addiction problems). In addition, social housing agencies in Flanders are required by decree to approach the PCSW to make a mediation attempt for tenants with a yearly income below €16 200 *before* they are allowed to initiate a judicial procedure for an eviction.[72]

The Centres for General Welfare (CGW)[73] have developed preventive housing support for all renters. It aims to intervene as early as possible when problems arise. As soon as a CGW has been notified by a landlord, it will contact the renter and sets up an outreach support trajectory. The umbrella organization of all CGWs (*Steunpunt Algemeen Welzijnswerk*) has evaluated this programme. The organization states, first, that the support service reaches more social than private landlords. While the social landlords often agree on partnership, the private landlords, in general, do not. Secondly, the overall success rate to prevent an eviction once a support trajectory is started lies at 71 per cent. Results are, however, much more positive within the SRS compared to the PRS. In general, private landlords only contact a CGW at a later stage in the process, when problems have already amassed and when the possibility of negotiating has diminished; and private renters face higher rent quotes, hence less capacities to repay debts.[74]

Lastly, the Flemish government introduced a 'Fund to prevent evictions'. This fund is not a general insurance for rent arrears but is applicable when a private landlord has requested an eviction due to rent arrears and the judge imposes a payment plan instead. More precisely, the financial intervention of the fund remains limited to situations where the tenant does not comply with the conditions of the plan: only the difference between the imposed and the actual reimbursement is covered. In this way, the fund aims to provide a reasonable alternative in case of rent arrears, next to dissolution of the rental agreement and eviction of the tenant. However, the system has been fiercely criticized. First, actual protection for tenants depends on whether the landlord is affiliated to the fund or not. Secondly, the fund only operates in cases where a request for

---

[72]   Art 33 §3 Social Rental Decree of 12 October 2007.

[73]   The CGWs are NGOs. There are eleven CGWs spread over the Flanders and Brussels-Capital Regions.

[74]   D Lescrauwaet and G Van Menxel, *Evaluatie van de preventieve woonbegeleiding van de CAW's gericht op voorkoming van uitzetting* (Berchem, Steunpunt Algemeen Welzijnswerk 2011).

eviction has been filed in court. The Flemish Housing Council has suggested that assisting the tenant at an earlier stage, however, could avoid such an escalation.[75] Lastly, the number of landlords applying to the fund is very low. Landlords' organizations indicate that the procedure, with several administrative steps and due dates, is far too complicated.[76]

7.2 Tackling Evictions

In 1998, an amendment to the Judicial Code was launched at federal level to 'humanize' the judicial eviction procedure ('Law on the Humanization of Evictions'). The law introduces a number of measures to protect renters throughout the procedure. First, it decides on the time range in between several steps, such as the one-month period in between the judgment and the actual eviction.[77] These 'pauses' should enable households to prepare in defending their case, to search for help, or to find a new place to stay. Second, and more importantly, the law introduced the obligation for a bailiff or a court clerk to inform the PCSW when an eviction case has been initiated at the Justice of the Peace, unless the tenant explicitly objects. Thereafter, the PCSW has to 'provide support in the most appropriate manner, within its legal mandate'.[78]

Consequently, at least in theory, every household threatened with an eviction should be offered social support. Yet in practice, several downfalls emerge. First, the objective of the law was that PCSWs would make an attempt to reconcile the tenant and landlord, and therefore it was anticipated that these social services would get involved from the start of the judicial procedure. In practice, the PCSWs are often not even notified until a few days before the first court session, which gives them insufficient time to take effective action and to help tenants preparing for that court session.

> The main problem is that we receive the information very late. Before we get it and have it properly registered (...). The sessions are always on Tuesday

---

[75] Vlaamse Woonraad, 'Advies over het ontwerp van besluit van de Vlaamse Regering houdende instelling van een tegemoetkoming van het fonds ter bestrijding van de uithuiszettingen' (Brussel, 2013) 6.

[76] B Hubeau and D Vermeir, *Een evaluatie van het woninghuurrecht. Deel II. Bevindingen werkgroepen 'Toegang, selectie en discriminatie', 'Procedure en bemiddeling' en 'Huurprijs', resultaten wegingsoefening en aanbevelingen expertencommissie* (Leuven, Steunpunt Wonen 2015).

[77] Art 1344quater Judicial Code.

[78] Art 1344ter Judicial Code.

afternoon. If I'm lucky [the notion arrives] on Thursday or Friday. But sometimes I don't find it in my inbox until Monday. (Social worker, PCSW, own translation)

Secondly, no funding was attached to this new task when it was assigned to the PCSWs in 1998. This omission has been contested several times in the past.[79] Consequently, the PCSWs cannot provide everyone with adequate assistance. Instead of making contact with the affected households in person, all PCSWs can often do is send them a letter. Yet many letters remain unanswered, leaving many households without help. If a PCSW wants to offer more extensive support, it is forced to prioritize certain groups. One of our respondents indicated the manner in which she deals with the situation. She not only writes to affected families but also makes house calls. Together with the tenant, she prepares for the first court session (if time allows). If the tenant wants her to, she will join the session. But because of budget and staff constraints, such an intensive approach means prioritizing certain groups of people that need the help most, and consequently exclude others.

Thirdly, PCSWs are only informed once a judicial procedure has been initiated. Later on during the procedure, there is no requirement to involve the PCSW, neither when the justice of the peace renders a verdict, nor when the actual eviction is scheduled.[80] An enlargement of the legally obliged involvement of the PCSW at later stages would enable support to households when a threat of eviction becomes even more pressing.

7.3 Reacting to Evictions

When households, either renters or owner-occupiers, are evicted after a *judicial* procedure, rehousing support is not guaranteed within the legal procedures. Some PCSWs intensively try to support evicted renters, such as the PCSW in Namur. Here, advertisements for rental dwellings are listed and volunteers support households in their contacts with landlords and join visits to increase their chances. Yet the possibility of PCSWs investing in rehousing programmes for evicted households is often limited due to financial and staff constraints.

---

[79]   Eg Verbeeck (n 65); Meys and Hermans (n 53).
[80]   Bernard and Lemaire (n 45).

In the case of evictions through an *administrative* procedure, local or regional governments are charged with rehousing the affected household. The extent of their obligation differs from region to region.[81]

In Flanders, local authorities are charged with an *effort* commitment, yet only for those households who comply with the income and property requirements of the Social Rental Decree.[82] The authorities can take an initiative to support others but are not obliged to. The commitment implies that all effort has to be done to relocate the household involved. To do so, households can be prioritized on the waiting list for a social dwelling, the municipality can collaborate with local housing associations, and it can provide transit housing or attribute a rent contribution.

In Wallonia, a *result* commitment for the local government has been introduced to relocate evicted households. Hence authorities are obliged to search for a solution. This solution has first to be found within the public housing supply within the municipality where the household was living. If unsuccessful, the dossier can be transferred to the regional social housing association, to find a social rental unit in another municipality. When relocation is not possible within public housing, a final option is to grant financial support for housing in the private sector.[83] Despite this result commitment, stable housing solutions are not always found. In the independent research, one respondent indicated that relocation can also include shelter in accommodation such as temporary housing or residential care settings.

In recent years, the Brussels-Capital Region adopted a mechanism similar to the obligation that exists in Wallonia; one difference, however, is that no financial support is possible.[84]

8. CONCLUSION

Evictions remain an under-documented problem in Belgium, despite the far-reaching consequences for those involved. Data on the magnitude of the phenomenon is fragmented and can only be traced through myriad sources. The fact that evictions are relatively undocumented is surprising as the limited amount of data that is available proves evictions to be anything but a marginal phenomenon. In Flanders, approximately

---

[81] N Bernard, 'Le relogement des personnes occupant un immeuble frappé par un arrêté d'inhabilité' (2013) 3 *Revue de droit communal* 34–46.
[82] Art 17bis Flemish Housing Code and Art 3 Social Rental Decree.
[83] Art 7 Walloon Housing Code.
[84] Art 12 Brussels Housing Code.

12 000 judicial procedures are initiated against renters on a yearly basis. At least some of the households threatened with an eviction do not find a stable place to live afterwards. Some will succeed in re-entering the housing market after a turbulent period, but others will remain homeless for a long time.[85]

Gaining a deeper insight on evictions in the rental market – the most vulnerable market segment – should not, however, require a major effort. The PCSWs are informed whenever an eviction procedure is initiated. Informing the PCSW at later stages in the procedure and, importantly, the collection of these figures at regional levels, would result in a much clearer picture.

Several measures have been developed to prevent evictions from taking place, mostly in the rental market. Due to budgetary and staff shortages, and due to less communication with private landlords, only a few of all initiated procedures for an eviction can be prevented, and only a few households are supported in their rehousing paths. Furthermore, the assistance of social support services is limited in the current rental market where problems of affordability and housing quality are commonplace. Importantly, we must not lose sight of these structural causes of the high incidence of evictions.[86] Social services can lend their support to households, while tenants can be called upon to meet their responsibilities as renters. However, as long as income and rent levels remain out of sync, there will always be people who find it hard to pay the rent each month. Assisting households in finding alternative housing is also very demanding, as long as the housing market remains so inaccessible for this group.

---

[85]   P De Decker and K Segers, 'Chaotic, fluid and unstable. On the complex housing trajectories of homeless people in Flanders, Belgium' (2014) 29 (4) *Journal of Housing and the Built Environment* 595–614.

[86]   Frisque (n 66).

2. Evictions in France

Marc Uhry

1. INTRODUCTION

France maintains the essential elements of a classic welfare state model, with extensive measures protecting borrowers and tenants' rights, social allowances, and a relatively large social housing stock. This is combined with a significant political commitment to universal equality, although in practice this is not always achieved. Indeed, while systematic policies seek to prevent and alleviate the effects of evictions, France has experienced an increase in evictions over the past two decades. This leads to a 'French paradox' – a country where poor households experience relatively lower housing costs overburden, but are more often in rent arrears, and more often evicted through a long process. Yet, despite this high level of evictions, this does not necessarily lead to homelessness, but homeless people have often experienced an eviction.

2. POLICY BACKGROUND

2.1 General Housing Policy Related to Evictions

For decades, forced evictions in France have affected mainly poor tenants, rather than distressed home loan debtors. The prevention of evictions rose on the political agenda in the late 1990s, and between 1998 and 2008, a range of legal initiatives and administrative tools were established in order to 'substitute a logic of social care to a logic of public order',[1] according to Louis Besson, the French Housing Minister

---

[1]   Law no 89-462 (6 July 1989) on landlord–tenant relations. Law no 90-449 (31 May 1990) on the implementation of the right to housing (the Besson Law). Law no 98-657 (29 July 1998) relating to the fight against social exclusion. Law no 2005-32 (18 January 2005) introducing a social cohesion programme. Law no 2007-290 (5 March 2007), 'DALO' law (Droit au Logement Opposable/

at that time. However, during that period, France also experienced a
re-emergence of squats and slums, providing shelter for Roma people and
those from the former Yugoslavia. At that time, there was a peak in
immigration arising from the civil war in Algeria. Indeed, this phenomenon became more extensive, with encampments in Paris and Calais,
despite the number of shelters opened. In 2014, the national administration (Dihal) calculated some 400–500 slums, where 17 000 to 20 000
people were living. In that year, approximately 150 forced evictions took
place, involving 13 000 individuals.[2] Thus, evictions on this scale are
often linked to extremely poor housing conditions for migrants and
refugees – evoking politically sensitive issues.

In relation to mortgage repossessions, the main prevention policy
stems from World War II measures to make banks responsible for
'irresponsible lending'. Banks are cautious in mortgage lending since
they can be held responsible for the risk taken in cases of default – a
factor which may explain the low level of mortgage repossessions in
France, compared to other European Union (EU) countries.[3]

A unique feature of the French housing system is the existence of a
large social housing stock, comprising 4 million dwellings – 18 per cent
of the total housing stock, as well as a high level of housing allowances
covering 20 per cent of the population. These two policies result in poor
French households paying less than other Europeans for their housing.[4]
When a household's housing expenditure exceeds a certain threshold,
established at 40 per cent of household income, the burden of this cost is
considered excessive. Such overburden threatens the security and well-
being of the household. In only two European countries (Malta and
Cyprus) are fewer than 15 per cent of poor households overburdened by
housing costs, followed by France and Finland (around 20 per cent).

Enforceable right to housing). Law no 2009-323 (25 March 2009) on mobilizing
for housing and combating exclusion. Law no 2014-366 (24 March 2014) for
access to housing and renewed urbanism (Law ALUR). Law no 2013.672 (26
July 2013) aimed at strengthening the protection of mortgage borrowers.

  [2]   Romeurope-Rapport (2014). 54 <http://www.lacimade.org/publication/
rapport-national-dobservatoire-2014-du-collectif-national-droits-de-lhomme-rom
europe-le-droit-et-les-faits/>.

  [3]   The Mortgage Credit Directive (2014/17/EU) may affect the current
position in this respect.

  [4]   FEANTSA/Foundation Abbé Pierre, *Second Overview of Housing Exclusion in Europe 2017* (2017) <http://www.feantsa.org/download/gb_housing-
exclusion-report_complete_20178613899107250251219.pdf>.

There is, however, a 'French paradox'. While France has one of the lowest rates of housing cost overburden it ranks highly in terms of arrears and evictions in Europe.

Lengthy judicial procedures fail to adequately explain this paradox.

2.2 Structural/Societal Factors Related to Evictions

The strong welfare system in France makes it difficult to trace a direct link between the social situation of households and risk of evictions. It is also difficult to connect structural factors with high eviction rates, given the extensive level of welfare provision.

Moreover, such analysis is made arduous by the poor quality of data available in France. For instance, there have been changes in the manner in which unemployment is recorded, and in police practices and the documenting of 'effective' evictions. In addition, there has been a cessation of documenting mortgage arrears.

France has only recently been affected by the 2007–2008 economic crisis. There was no housing market collapse, no jump in interest rates, and the slow rise of unemployment was dampened by the welfare system. Nonetheless, the social effects of the economic crisis were delayed, but not eradicated. According to the National Employment Agency, the number of registered unemployed people in France increased from 3 million to 5 million between 2007 and 2015. Whereas forced evictions were no longer on the political agenda, after a decade of preventative measures, the links between economic crisis, social difficulties and housing consequences have now become apparent. In 2015, forced evictions by police forces rose by 24 per cent in one year, to reach 14 363 cases, while forced evictions of tenants were estimated at 132 196 cases.

Young households, however, enjoy lower levels of social protection, particularly in respect to social housing access, and are more reliant on expensive private rented housing, with the precarious conditions of that tenure. Indeed, younger households are proportionally more affected by eviction than other groups.

2.3 Specific Policies Related to Evictions

There are many policies relating to evictions, where intervention takes place in the procedural aspects as well as the substantive situation. When rent arrears occur, a landlord must warn public authorities at least two months in advance of any litigation.[5] Public bodies then write to the tenant to suggest a meeting with a social worker. Under French housing law,[6] each *département* has a 'Housing Solidarity Fund' (Fonds Solidarité Logement [FSL])[7] that is partly dedicated to lending or giving money to households in arrears.[8] Social workers from public bodies are entitled to request this fund. However, where a social worker does not request this fund, the landlord may request a bailiff to serve the tenant with an order to pay. Where no payment is made, the landlord can institute proceedings in the civil court, and a judge can prevent eviction by making an order granting the tenant up to three years to pay arrears, with a monthly obligation. In the interim, if a tenant is only one day late with repayment, the lease is terminated, and the bailiff delivers an order to vacate. Where the tenant refuses to leave, a bailiff can then call the police, who make a social inquiry and decide whether to force the tenant to leave or not.

In terms of rehousing, at any stage of the process, a social agency, CCAPEX,[9] has the authority to suggest that the tenant be rehoused in a more sustainable dwelling. Following the commencement of litigation, tenants are eligible to invoke the justiciable right to housing, which means that the state has nine months to offer an alternative solution – although this process can take longer than the eviction process.

3. LEGAL AND CONSTITUTIONAL BACKGROUND TO PROTECTION AGAINST EVICTIONS

3.1 Housing as a Fundamental Right

There is no specific reference to a right to housing in the French Constitution. Indeed, there is only one word in French for both 'property' and 'ownership': '*propriété*', which essentially means 'ownership'. Thus, tenants have no property rights. However, the French Administrative Supreme Court (le Conseil d'Etat) established a subtle hierarchy of

---

[5]   Law ALUR (n 1), Art 27.

[6]   Besson Law (n 1).

[7]   Ibid Art 6.

[8]   Art 4 of the Besson Law establishes departmental plans for the housing of people in difficulty (Plans départementaux pour le logement des populations en difficulté [PDLPDs]).

[9]   Law no 2009-323 on mobilizing for housing and combating exclusion (n 1).

norms, recognizing the right to ownership/property as a constitutional *right*, but the right to housing as a constitutional *goal*.[10]

Various legal instruments however, refer to the right to housing as a fundamental right. The provisions of the Code of Civil Enforcement Procedures (CPCE), for instance, state that a court decision is required to proceed to eviction from a building or a 'housing place'.[11] Articles L. 412-1 (CPCE) set out a framework for the execution of an eviction decision made by a judge. These apply to occupation of 'spaces used for/as main residential housing' ('locaux affectés à l'habitation principale des personnes'), and the interpretation of this wording rests with the judge. Generally, these rules also apply to unauthorized occupation of housing (squatting) and to tenants without 'lease or title', but very rarely to occupants of land.

Law no 89-462 (6 July 1989) is aimed at improving tenancy relations. Article 1 provides that 'housing is a fundamental right'. Law no 90-449 (31 May 1990) on the implementation of the right to housing states that to 'guarantee the right to housing is a duty of solidarity for the whole nation'.[12] The law against exclusion, dating from 1998, aims to replace the public order approach to the eviction process with a social approach.[13] In the private sector, the law establishes a pre-court phase during which social services are warned of an impending eviction and contact the tenant household concerned.

The 2007 law establishing an enforceable right to housing[14] asserts that the state is legally responsible for the right to housing, and shall provide a dwelling to any household who has been declared 'priority' by the DALO Mediation Commission (COMED), which includes households involved in an eviction procedure. Law no 2009-323 (25 March 2009) on 'mobilisation for housing and combating exclusion' makes the establishment of 'commissions of coordination of actions of prevention

---

[10] Decision no 94-359 (19 January 1995). In this decision, the Constitutional Council declared that 'the possibility for any person to access to decent housing was an objective of constitutional value', in 'reference to the 10th and 11th paragraph of preamble of Constitution of 1946 but also to the constitutional principle of protection of human dignity.'

[11] Art L. 411-1 Code of Civil Procedure (CPC).

[12] Art 1 Besson Law (n 1).

[13] Law no 98-657 (29 July 1998), states in Article 1, that 'the right of fight against exclusion is a national imperative grounded on the equal dignity of all human beings and a propriety in all the public policies of the nation'.

[14] Law no 2007-290, 'DALO' law (n 1).

of eviction' (CCAPEX) mandatory for all departments. This law requires a social and financial report on a household involved in an eviction procedure to be presented to the judge at the moment of the hearing.[15] Law no 2014-366 (24 March 2014) for access to housing and renovated urban planning (ALUR) creates an obligation on landlords to inform the CCAPEX of any arrears of rent two months before the summons to attend the court hearing, failing which the application for eviction shall be declared inadmissible. In addition, this law extends the period of the 'winter break' (or 'winter truce'), ensuring that no household can be evicted from 1 November to 31 March.[16] ALUR also extends the time limits of an arrears payment plan, to a maximum of three years. A judge may grant terms of payment if the rehousing process requires it and may also grant similar extensions after the notice to quit has been delivered, to leave the dwelling.[17] The DALO Mediation Commission may request the judge to suspend the eviction process of households declared to be in 'a situation of priority' during the rehousing period.[18] From 1 January 2015, the (ALUR) law provides that landlords must report to CCAPEX on all cases involving notices to pay that have been sent to their tenants, in order to find alternative solutions before going to court.[19] Law no 2013.672 (26 July 2013) is aimed at strengthening the protection of mortgage borrowers and permits the granting of time extensions to overindebted owners facing an enforcement procedure by suspending the eviction procedure for a period of two years.

3.2 Law Relating to Owner-occupation

In France, limited data is available about owner evictions; a matter not considered as a public problem and not monitored by public authorities, agencies, or defence of housing rights organizations. Only repossession procedure cases leading to effective eviction of the owner are recorded within a global category, which does not distinguish between owner, tenant or illegal occupant.

The French Civil Code provides for the extension of time limits in the mortgage repossession process, through legal mediation and preventative

---

[15] The social report assists the judge in making a decision on eviction or alternative solution. Law ALUR (n 1) has made this report mandatory.

[16] Law ALUR Art 25.

[17] Ibid Art 27.

[18] Ibid Art 41.

[19] Ibid Art 27.

measures.[20] A judge can grant extensions of the time limits to a debtor in good faith up to a maximum of 24 months, allowing the debtor to reorganize the payment plan, or with a deferment of debt. The procedure for a forced sale, that is, a sale by auction, is then suspended by virtue of provisions in the Code of Consumption.[21]

In the case of an amicable sale in the context of mortgage distress and arrears a judge will ensure that the sale involves a 'fair price' by considering the economic conditions of the market, and the estimated value of the property – indeed the judge will establish a minimum price below which the property cannot be sold. The conditions of sale can also impose an obligation on the new owner to allow the debtor to remain in the property for a period of time.

As soon as the debtor's case has been accepted by the 'over indebtedness commission' (Commission de surendettement), the enforcement procedure is suspended.[22] The Commission can gain a court order to suspend the adjudication hearing, for serious and duly justified reasons, provided the debtor has informed the commission of the situation. Any such demand for a suspension of the enforcement and forced sale must be made within 15 days before the planned date of sale. The duration of suspension cannot exceed two years and ends as soon as the decision of the Commission has become effective.[23]

The borrower may ask for legal assistance (aide juridictionnelle) if she or he cannot afford a lawyer. Legal costs are covered by the state at different rates according to the household's incomes.[24]

3.3 Law Relating to Private Renting

The main law regulating private renting is the aforesaid Law no 89-462 of 6 July 1989 on landlord–tenant relations.[25] Despite the various preventative measures in force, the reality is that many evictions take place. Indeed, the eviction prevention commissions and measures have

---

[20] Civil Code Arts 1244-1 and the Code of Consumption Arts 1244-2.

[21] Code of Consumption L.313-12.

[22] Suspension of enforcement (Code of Consumption: L.331-3-1, L.331-5, L.333-2-1, R.331-11 and R.331-11-1).

[23] Law no 2013.672 (aimed at strengthening the protection of mortgage borrowers) (n 1).

[24] Law no 91-647 (10 July 1991) on legal aid, Art 2.

[25] However, there are still a few dwellings regulated by a former law (Law no 48-1360 (1 September 1948) amending and codifying the rules concerning the relationship among landlords and tenants or occupants of residential premises or of premises for professional use and establishing housing allowances).

reacted in a very disparate way.[26] The social report, which assists the judge in making a decision on eviction or alternative solution,[27] is not consistently prepared, and relies on contact being made with the tenant at risk of eviction. Where this has not taken place, no solutions are proposed to the court.

Contrary to what was required in application of the DALO law,[28] information about the enforceable right to housing is not systematically delivered to the households that are subject to an eviction process. In 2012 and 2013, less than 10 per cent of the households declared 'priority' by the DALO commission were recognized as being in a situation of 'eviction without rehousing solution', resulting in more than 155 000 eviction summons in both years.[29] This indicates that 95 per cent of households involved in a legal process of eviction have not been protected by the enforceable right to housing.

Yet, the different housing laws have provided a great number of supports to prevent eviction, applying at the first stages of arrears in order to avoid eviction and enabling the household to remain in the home.[30] At the local (that is, departmental) level, these mechanisms can be very efficient, which is, actually, the institutional level designed to implement solutions to rental housing problems.

A judge can grant an order setting out terms of payment to clear arrears,[31] thereby suspending the termination of a lease since the enactment of Law no 98-657 29 (Article 114).[32]

A judge may also terminate the lease, with or without granting extensions of time limits to pay or quit,[33] and in such cases, a judge orders the eviction. The decision shall be disclosed to the tenant, by deed of a bailiff.[34] Finally, the decision ordering eviction must clearly indicate the possibility of referring the matter to the DALO Mediation Commission.[35]

---

[26]   The eviction prevention commissions were created by Law no 2006-872 (13 July 2006) and made mandatory by Law no 2009-323 (25 March 2009).

[27]   Law no 2009-323 (n 26).

[28]   Law no 2007-290, 'DALO' law (n 1).

[29]   DALO, Commission report, 2013.

[30]   CCAPEX, FSL and CDAPL

[31]   Law no 89-462 (on landlord–tenant relations) (n 1) Art 24 al. 3, modified by Law ALUR (n 1) Art 27-V.

[32]   Code of Civil Enforcement Procedures (CPCE) Art L412-3.

[33]   Code de la construction et de l'habitation (Code of Construction and Housing) (CCH) Art L. 613-1, al. 2.

[34]   Law no 91-650 (9 July 1991) on the reform of civil enforcement procedures, Art 61.

[35]   CCH (n 33) Art L.441-2-3; Law ALUR (n 1) Art 27.

When an owner wants to sell their property ('congé pour vente'), or when they intend to regain the use of it, for themself or a family member ('congé reprise'), tenants of private rented housing may receive notices from their landlord obliging them to leave at the termination date of the lease, even if the tenant does not want to end the tenancy. If the tenant is perceived to be unable to pay their debts, a judge will be less likely to grant extensions and will pronounce more quickly the order of eviction.

The CPCE contains a provision which provides for minimum income which the evicted debtor is entitled to retain, which cannot be attached to cover arrears. Article L162-2 of the CPCE states that in the case of enforcement, the creditor cannot attach a minimum income, or unattachable bank balance (ISB), which equals the minimum social income, the Revenu de Solidarité Active (RSA).[36]

There are a number of legal aid, mediation, conciliation, defence appeals, alternative funding arrangements and preventative measures available to private renters facing eviction. For instance, the Civil Code provides that a tenant-defendant may ask the judge to grant an extension of terms of payment for his or her debts.[37] A tenant may also ask a judge to grant him or her an extension of the time limit before quitting a dwelling. In both cases, the duration of any extension cannot be less than three months or more than three years.[38] The execution of eviction can be suspended in the case of overindebtness, provided the debtor's case has been accepted by the overindebtedness commission, whereby the enforcement procedure is suspended.[39] The tenant may appeal the decision under Article 543 of Code of Civil Procedure, which provides that an 'appeal is open, in all cases, against the first instance decisions'. A tenant must then address the court within 15 days from the decision in a 'référé procedure'.

The 'winter truce' does not suspend the référé procedure, but does postpone the execution of eviction,[40] by virtue of Law no 2014-366, which states that 'eviction cannot be implemented between the 1 November and the 31 of March of the next year'.[41] The landlord has to inform the Housing Benefits Departmental Commission (CDAPL), or the social

---

[36] Equivalent to Income Support in the United Kingdom, and to Minimex (financial social help) in Belgium.
[37] Civil Code Art 1244.
[38] CPCE (n 32) Art L.412-4; Law ALUR (n 1) Art 27 V.
[39] Code of Consumption L331-3-2, R 331-12; Law no 2010-737 (1 July 2010) on the reform of consumer credit, Art 40.
[40] CCH (n 33) Art L. 613-3.
[41] Law ALUR (n 1) Art 10 A; CPCE (n 32) L.412-6.

services paying housing benefits (CAF, MSA)[42] about any non-payment problem of a tenant, in order to attempt to clear the debt, before starting a legal procedure.[43] When a tenant receives housing benefit (APL), or when the housing benefit is paid directly to the landlord, the landlord has to inform the CDAPL within three months after the non-payment debt has started.[44] Providers of housing benefits, such as the CAF and MSA, must apply to the Prevention of Eviction Commission (CCAPEX) as soon as the household is at risk of losing its rights and supports.[45] Under Law no 98-657 (29 July 1998), a bailiff has to inform the administration (préfet) of a notice to quit two months before the hearing date, under penalty of the notice being declared void (Article 114). A copy of the notice to quit must be disposed to the préfet by the bailiff.[46] The préfet must remind the CCAPEX and the household of the possibility to apply to the DALO Mediation Commission where a notice to quit has been sent by the bailiff.[47] As of January 2015, landlords have to report to CCAPEX all cases of notice to arrears sent to their tenants in order to find alternative solutions before going to court.[48]

3.4 Law Relating to Social Renting

A small proportion of the private rental sector is dedicated to social purposes, through an agreement between the landlord and public bodies.[49] The agreement includes provisions on financial support towards the renovation of dwellings and tax relief, balanced with a regulated rent. The lower this regulated rent is set over the longest period the higher the level of public support that is granted.

Social housing companies provide the largest part of social rented housing. While these companies can be public, privately or cooperatively owned, they are all regulated by law and must sign an agreement with the

---

[42]   Caisse d'allocations Familiales (CAF) (family allowance fund) and Mutualité Sociale Agricole (MSA) (social protection scheme for agricultural workers).

[43]   Law no 2005-32 introducing a social cohesion programme (n 1) Art 99; CCH (n 33) Arts L. 353-15-1 and L. 442-6-1.

[44]   Ibid Art R. 351-30.

[45]   Law ALUR (n 1) Art 27; CPCE (n 32) L.412-5.

[46]   Law no 91-650 on the reform of civil enforcement procedures (n 34) Art 62.

[47]   Law ALUR (n 1) Art 28; CPCE (n 32) L.412-5.

[48]   Law ALUR (n 1) Art 27.

[49]   Regulated by Art 74 of Law 2011-1977 (28 December 2011) of finances for 2012.

state.[50] The law on social cohesion programming enables state payments of housing benefits in social housing and suspends the eviction process, if an agreement protocol is signed between the landlord and the tenant.[51] In terms of legal procedure, process and protections, the social/public rented sector is very similar to the private rented sector.

3.5 Law Relating to Unauthorized Occupancy

The Code of Civil Enforcement Procedures (CPCE),[52] and the Code of Administrative Justice,[53] state that an eviction cannot take place without a court decision, for all types of 'inhabited constructions'. However, this does not include caravans illegally installed on land, which is regarded as a criminal law issue, and police are empowered to prevent this taking place or continuing.[54] For temporary constructions, including slums, the CPCE provides that a delay may be requested before eviction takes place.[55] Article L412-6 of the CPCE states that there can be no eviction in winter, except when the landlord can prove the occupiers entered by force. Here the burden of proof is reversed: the use of force is assumed unless the defendants can prove otherwise – a situation which makes the winter truce ineffective in these cases.

Unauthorized occupancy is addressed through three legal procedures and three different courts. The Court of First Instance (Tribunal d'instance) deals with unauthorized occupancy of housings; the High Court (Tribunal de Grande Instance) deals with unauthorized occupation (encampments, caravans, etc) of land owned by a private person or belonging to the private domain of a public person; an administrative court (tribunal administratif) deals with occupation (encampments, caravans, etc) of land belonging to the public domain.

The CPCE contains the obligation to obtain a court decision to proceed to eviction from a building or a 'housing place' and sets out the framework for implementing an eviction decision made by a judge,[56] and apply to the occupation of 'spaces used for/as main residential housing' ('locaux affectés à l'habitation principale des personnes'). Generally, these

---

[50] CCH (n 33) Art L351-2.
[51] Law no 2005-32 introducing a social cohesion programme (n 1).
[52] CPCE (n 32) Art L411-1.
[53] Art L21-3.
[54] Art 322-4-1 of the Criminal Law Code (Code Pénal).
[55] CPCE (n 32) Art L. 412-3 and Art L412-4.
[56] CPCE (n 32) Art L. 411-1, Arts L. 412-1 et seq.

provisions also apply to unauthorized occupancy of housing (squatting) and tenants without 'lease or title', but very rarely to occupants of land.

When an occupied property is in the public domain and belongs to a public entity, the owner must ask an administrative judge to order an eviction. Compared to the procedure before a civil judge, the procedure here is far less structured and offers inferior protection to those affected. The protection of occupants is within the discretionary power of the administrative judge.

Regarding unauthorized occupancy, the procedure for eviction varies depending on whether the occupants are identified or not. Where the occupants consent to be identified, a bailiff (on behalf of the owner) makes a report (proces verbal) and summons them to attend a hearing. The owner can go to court and ask the judge to order an eviction.[57] The order is enforceable and is delivered to the occupants by a bailiff. At the same time, the bailiff delivers an order to quit. When the occupants refuse to be identified or are absent the eviction procedure is 'par requête'. In this case, the owner can only make a request for eviction to the President of the High Court. This is an ex-parte (one side only) application and if the request is accepted, the judge gives an order, which is immediately enforceable. The parties to an unauthorized occupancy may opt for a conciliation agreement so as to avoid a legal procedure and this agreement must be reported to, and co-signed by the judge and parties.[58]

In accordance with the Article L412-1 CPCE, an eviction may not be executed within two months after the notice to quit and only a bailiff can execute the eviction. A bailiff cannot, however, enter an occupied dwelling with court authorization.[59] If an occupant is in the dwelling and accepts to leave, the bailiff makes a report (proces verbal), which must be signed by every person present.[60] If the dwelling has been abandoned, the bailiff can enter the dwelling in order to establish abandonment.

Where the occupants refuse to leave, a bailiff may request the préfet to intervene, and the préfet has two months to respond. Silence on the part of the occupants is deemed to indicate refusal.[61] The refusal must be justified, since the state is required by an administrative court to pay compensation to the landlord where repossession, duly authorized by a

---

[57] Arts 808 and 809 CPC.
[58] Code of Civil Procedure Art 130.
[59] Law no 91-650 on the reform of civil enforcement procedures (n 34) Art 21-1.
[60] Ibid.
[61] Ibid art 17.

court, does not take place. If the préfet accepts the request, the police assume responsibility for evicting the occupants. The 'winter truce' does not suspend the procedure, only the execution of eviction.[62]

3.6 Law Relating to Temporary Dispossession

Article L641-1 of the Building and Habitat Code provides for temporary dispossession (réquisition) of empty homes, for five years, with provision for compensation to be paid to landowners, although this law is seldom used. In cases involving domestic violence, the Civil Code introduces a specific emergency court procedure before a Family Judge (Juge aux Affaires Familiales), to prohibit access to the home by violent spouses. However, there is no possibility of ending the lease for one of the two members of a family in such cases, since this is considered a unilateral change in the contract, which would allow the landlord to terminate the lease for the remaining person.

The Expropriation Act (décret loi)[63] establishes permanent expropriation and is permitted by the French Constitution, where ownership/property is an absolute right, except in cases of public interest. Expropriation is possible, provided that all other means have been explored and after an administrative phase to justify a public interest. A public body then offers compensation to the owner of the building and if not accepted, the owner can challenge it in a civil court.

3.7 Soft Law/Codes and their Effectiveness

Public/social housing tenants may sign an agreement protocol with the landlord suspending the eviction during the period of repayment of a debt.[64] The tenant can receive housing benefits in the meantime. If the tenant complies with the payment plan, the landlord may propose a new lease for the same dwelling, within the time limits provided in the protocol. Details on the extent of the arrangements are not compiled nationally and it is unclear how many such arrangements take place.

---

[62] CCH (n 33) Art. L. 613-3.

[63] Décret loi 30 October 1935.

[64] Law no 2005-32 introducing a social cohesion programme (n 1) Arts L 353-15-2 and CCH (n 33) L 442-6-5.

Table 2.1   Extent of evictions for the period 2001–2015

	2001	2005	2010	2015
Litigation to obtain an eviction order	125 706	140 587	155 874	168 775
Litigation to obtain an order for payment of rent arrears	107 639	128 782	145 384	159 812
Court decision	No data	No data	115 205	132 196
Requests for police assistance	36 400	40 417	40 417	49 783
Effective execution by police	6 337	10 182	11 670	14 363

Source: Ministry of Justice, Ministry of the Interior (this data includes squats and slums, when there is a court case, although this does not always occur).

Data from the Ministry of Justice with regard to eviction litigation incorporates all types of actions – so it includes occupied and unoccupied buildings. Collectively, the numbers are increasing (see Table 2.1). As in other countries, the numbers of proceedings initiated and those executed show significant discrepancies, and of course, this does not mean that those persons were not evicted – just that they did not remain until the end of legal proceedings. According to data reported by the Ministry of the Interior, proceedings in relation to illegal occupancy of land or buildings were relatively low. However, the data does not differentiate between illegal occupants (squatters) and overholding tenants; that is, tenants who remain in the property after their tenancy has been legally terminated and are awaiting the execution of the possession order.

4.   DEFINITION OF EVICTION

According to European Commission research there are three stages to the legal eviction process: pre-court, court and post-court.[65]

---

[65]   P Kenna, L Benjaminsen, V Busch-Geertsema and S Nasarre-Aznar, *Pilot Project – Promoting Protection of the Right to Housing – Homelessness Prevention in the Context of Evictions* (VT/2013/056). Final report (Brussels, European Commission 2016). Freek Spinnewin of FEANTSA, who acted as scientific adviser for the project, has assisted in this research.

In France, for tenants in arrears, there is an amicable mechanism (Commission de médiation) operated by qualified persons, unions of tenants and landlords, although landlords are not obliged to use this mechanism. Landlords seeking to recover possession and/or arrears of rent must instruct a bailiff to deliver an order to pay (commandement de payer), then and if arrears are not paid, and at least two months before the court date, must notify the administrative local authority (le préfet), who notifies social services, who in turn write to tenants to offer support. Court proceedings can then begin.

During the court stage, the Court of First Instance (Tribunal d'instance) is responsible for eviction decisions, including evictions from public properties. In illegal occupancies, there is a possibility for the landlord to request an accelerated procedure (référé).

At post-court stage, for all types of tenure, referrals can be requested to another procedure, to a specific judge (le Judge de l'Exécution). Where an order to evict has been granted, a bailiff delivers an order to leave (commandement de payer) within two months. After that time, the landlord is entitled to ask the administrative authority (le préfet) for support from the police force (demande de concours de la force publique). The administrative authority then requests the police to make a social enquiry, after which it decides whether or not to send the police and/or to activate a rehousing mechanism.

5. EVICTIONS FROM MORTGAGED PROPERTY

The competent court for the enforcement procedure for evictions from mortgaged property is the court of first instance of the territory where the mortgaged property is located.[66] Article 2191 of Ordinance no 2006-461 states that 'any creditor [créancier], possessing an executor title stating a due claim may proceed to a seizure of property in conditions fixed by this law.' There is no minimum amount stipulated.

When the defaulting borrower fails to respond to a formal notice or reminder by letter, a notice to pay is sent by a bailiff, mandated by the creditor. This formal notice initiates the enforcement procedure and amounts to a claim for seizure of the property.[67] If the borrower does not pay within eight days, a bailiff goes to the dwelling/property to establish a statement of fact. Under penalty of being declared void, the order to

---

[66] Ordinance no 2006-461 (21 April 2006) reforming the seizure of property (saisie immobilière).

[67] CPCE (n 32) R.321-1, R.321-3 and R.321-5.

pay has to be published by the mortgage office (bureau des hypothèques) within two months.[68] The debtor then receives a summons to attend court for an 'orientation hearing'.[69] Here the court verifies that all the conditions of the civil procedure are fulfilled, and in particular, that the creditor possesses an 'executory title'; that is, a title of a debt – in this case, a mortgage loan.[70] At this point, the debtor can request an amicable sale, and the judge can authorize this together with a minimum price, under which the property cannot be sold. If this takes place, then the enforcement procedure is suspended.

The process also allows for the forced sale of the property, and the conditions of the sale contract must be filed before the court. If for any reason an amicable sale has not been made, the court may grant an extension of three months for the debtor to pay his or her debt, or it may order a 'forced sale'. It should be noted that if the borrower (or his or her legal representative) does not attend the hearing, the judge will automatically order a forced sale. This is a sale by auction and requires the creditor to advertise the sale and to comply with other obligations.[71] When a forced sale is made, a judgment 'of adjudication' gives a 'title of sale' to the new owner, which is the equivalent of an eviction decision for the borrower-in-occupation. If the borrower, who is now the previous owner, refuses to quit the property, she or he is considered an illegal occupant, and can be evicted through that process.

There is insufficient data collated in France to give a reliable estimate of the numbers of these procedures.

6. RISK FACTORS LEADING TO EVICTION

Various studies identify a number of risk factors leading to eviction, including households characterized by a wide spectrum of simultaneous difficulties, involving low income, health problems, unstable families and difficulties dealing with administrative issues. The trigger element can often be attributed to a recent decrease of income (including in numerous cases, moving from wage/salary income to retirement pension), combined with the non take-up of various potential solutions. Since there are extensive social welfare allowances, a large social housing stock, and many supportive measures for those at risk of eviction, the causes of

---

[68]   CPCE (n 32) R. 321-6–R.321-10.
[69]   Ibid R.322-4 and R.322-5.
[70]   Ibid R.322-15 et seq.
[71]   Ibid R.322-30 et seq.

eviction cannot be entirely income related. Similarly, there is little research showing that evictions are leading to homelessness. However, anthropological work undertaken with a small number of former homeless people with multiple needs, demonstrates that such persons have been confronted with at least one, and more likely, several evictions in their lifetimes, beginning when they were children.[72]

7. BEST PRACTICE MODELS FOR PREVENTING, TACKLING AND REACTING TO EVICTIONS

While there is no major case law with regard to evictions in the period 2010–2016 in France, there are many examples of good practice. One example is the GIP Charente Solidarités, which coordinates all the actions for the prevention of eviction in the department of Charente. The GIP manages the Housing Solidarity Fund (Fonds de Solidarité Logement [FSL]) and allocates 15 per cent of the fund to the prevention of non-payment of rent. A social assistance (personalized support service) is automatically proposed to any household involved in a procedure of eviction. The GIP systematically prepares a social report for the préfet, at all stages of the procedure. The préfet regularly consults GIP social workers before taking any decision concerning the intervention of the police in relation to evictions. Some 80 per cent of households who engaged with GIP have attended the court hearing, and 72 per cent received extensions of time limits for rent payment. Conversely, some 88 per cent of the households who did not meet the GIP and did not attend the court hearing had their leases terminated without any extensions. In 2013, 65 per cent (295) of the households involved in this process found a 'concrete housing solution', and this figure is increasing every year. Some 40 per cent were tenants (three-quarters in private renting) while a quarter had their debts cleared.

Another example of best practice with regard to preventing, tackling and reacting to evictions is the more informal partnership in Lyon, where an NGO (Alpil) provides professional advice on the legal and social aspects of eviction. This practice takes place in court, at the same time as the eviction hearing. The judge can then refer those at risk of eviction, especially those who are underprepared and particularly vulnerable, to the support services Alpil provides. Various local allocation committees

---

[72] Atlantide Merlat, *Résidents de la République* (Lyon, Faculty of Sociology 2016).

are bringing together all local housing associations, social services agencies, municipalities and NGOs, both to prevent situations of eviction, and to rehouse those who are being evicted. There is also a possibility of moving directly to supported housing without going through the ordeal of the court-directed eviction. In terms of the private rental sector, estate agents and landlords' unions have agreed on a protocol to facilitate alternative solutions to eviction – although this is only based on goodwill.

Having regard to its personal, social and financial costs, the appropriateness of the process of eviction can be questioned. The eviction process is frequently a very traumatic experience for households, where they are removed from stable and active participation in social life. A more universal analysis of the costs of eviction could contribute to the debate on reconsideration of prevention mechanisms and the inefficiency of the actual system, which leads to different forms of homelessness and assumes that in all cases those evicted will find another housing solution. Comparing the costs associated with the preventive mechanisms currently in place and those that would be incurred as a result of stabilizing the household in its tenure would certainly bring much needed clarity on the impact of current eviction processes.

8. CONCLUSION

France has a good systemic prevention approach to evictions, both for tenants and homeowners. However, despite a wide range of instruments, evictions are still high, and most households vanish before the execution of evictions orders by police – avoiding physical eviction can be a significant life-changing issue. The absence of follow-up studies on evicted households is particularly problematic. People with multiple needs, especially those suffering from psychiatric disorders; appear to be particularly susceptible to eviction as a result of rent arrears, although further research is needed to support this conjecture.

The lack of data concerning squatting and slums does not rule out the increasing number of evictions in these occupancies, as ever-growing numbers of homeless people and migrants are forced to find more and more informal solutions to their predicament, *despite* France having a large and sophisticated homeless shelter system. This underlines the paradox that is evident in all aspects of the existing system of housing support in France: the services that are available do not appear to be reaching the households who need them.

3. Evictions in Germany

Christoph U Schmid and Sofija Nikolic

1. INTRODUCTION

Germany is a federal republic consisting of sixteen federal states. Most of the legislative and administrative powers related to housing were transferred from the federation to the federal states in the 2007 constitutional reform. As to the tenure structure, more than half of the whole housing stock is rented (among which about 5 per cent is social rented housing), while owner-occupied housing represents only 42.3 per cent. Although the right to housing is not an individually enforceable right, persons threatened with eviction may resort to various protection mechanisms, and there are administrative precautions for the prevention of homelessness after an eviction. On the one hand, the court is obliged to inform the local social authority responsible for housing homeless people about the start of eviction proceedings. The same obligation falls on a bailiff before the execution of an eviction order. On the other hand, according to the police, security and regulatory laws of the federal states, municipalities have a duty to provide temporary accommodation for evicted people.

2. POLICY BACKGROUND

2.1 General Housing Policy Related to Evictions

Germany is a federal republic consisting of sixteen federal states (*Bundesländer*). In the reform of the federal system in 2007 (*Föderalismusreform*), most legislative competences and government responsibilities for housing policies were transferred from the federation to the federal states. Only the legislation on housing subsidies (*Wohnraumförderungsgesetz*, WoFG), the control of rents and tenancy protection in the private rented sector, both of which are regulated in the German Civil Code (*Bürgerliches Gesetzbuch*, BGB), remained at the national level.[1]

Apart from Switzerland, Germany is the country with the highest percentage of rented dwellings in Europe. More than half of the housing stock is rented, while about 45 per cent of all households live in self-owned residential property.[2] The high level of legal tenant protection seems to contribute to the wide diffusion of rental housing.[3] Indeed, private renting is dominant in Germany, as compared to social rented housing, which in 2017 represented only about 5 per cent of the overall stock of rented dwellings.[4] Moreover, the number of available social dwellings has decreased over the last years due to the privatization of public housing stocks by municipalities and state governments.[5] Between 1999 and 2011, approximately 917 000 flats have been sold by public entities.[6] This trend is reflected in a growing number of homeless people.[7] Even though the right to housing is not considered an individually enforceable right, there is a system of protection against eviction and

---

[1]   Volker Busch-Geertsema, 'National eviction profile Germany' in P Kenna, L Benjaminsen, V Busch-Geertsema and S Nasarre-Aznar, *Pilot Project – Promoting Protection of the Right to Housing – Homelessness Prevention in the Context of Evictions* (VT/2013/056) *Final report* (European Union, European Commission, Directorate-General Employment, Social Affairs and Inclusion 2016) 5.

[2]   Michael Voigtländer, 'Wohneigentum in Deutschland' in Michael Voigtländer and Otto Depenheuer (Hrsg), *Wohneigentum, Herausforderungen und Perspektiven* (Berlin Heidelberg, Springer-Verlag 2014) 61.

[3]   Annika Klopp and Christoph U Schmid, 'The role of tenancy law in the "tenant countries" Switzerland, Austria and Germany – macroeconomic benefits through a balanced legal infrastructure?' in Christoph U Schmid (ed), *Tenancy Law and Housing Policy in Europe* (Cheltenham, Edward Elgar Publishing 2018).

[4]   See 'German Government Statement on Social Housing 2017' <http://dipbt.bundestag.de/doc/btd/18/114/1811403.pdf>.

[5]   Julia Cornelius and Joanna Rzeznik, 'TENLAW: Tenancy Law and Housing Policy in Multi-level Europe: National Report for Germany' (2014) 16 <http://www.tenlaw.uni-bremen.de/reports/GermanyReport_09052014.pdf>.

[6]   Transactions of major housing stock, Federal Institute for Research on Building, Urban Affairs and Spatial Development (BBSR) within the Federal Office for Building and Regional Planning (BBR), Bonn (2013) 6 <http://www.bbsr.bund.de/BBSR/EN/Publications/AnalysenKompakt/Issues/DL_1_2013.pdf?__blob=publicationFile&v=3>.

[7]   See 'Report of the National Coalition of Services Working with the Homeless' (2015) (*BundesarbeitsgemeinschaftWohnungslosenhilfe e.V.*) 2 <http://www.bagw.de/de/themen/zahl_der_wohnungslosen/261.html>.

of organized support if eviction from owner-occupied housing, private or social rented housing leads to homelessness.

2.2 Structural and Societal Factors Related to Evictions

Eviction is in most cases a consequence of rent or mortgage arrears. The main factors for default in payment include unemployment, domestic violence, substance abuse, severe illness and divorce.[8] The results of research conducted in 2012, in the state of North Rhine-Westphalia, confirm these factors. Specifically, two-thirds of all households threatened with eviction were dependent on some kind of transfer payments, usually for long term unemployment.[9]

2.3 Specific Policies Related to Evictions

The basic policy orientation of the legislator towards evictions is twofold. On the one hand, evictions are regulated in civil procedure law in a way that guarantees their swift and effective execution. This is to protect the huge number of private landlords (most of whom are amateur landlords renting out only one or two dwellings), upon whom the German housing system, with its low number of social dwellings, crucially relies for the provision of rental housing to wealthy and vulnerable people alike. The main fear of private landlords is the difficulties associated with the expulsion of tenants who do not pay the rent, damage the dwelling and whose behaviour leads to complaints and rent deductions by other tenants. This orientation is reflected, inter alia, in the priority accorded to evictions over other civil procedures (Article 272 (4) ZPO[10]), and the limited availability of defences against evictions, which are basically confined to cases of 'immoral hardship due to the very particular circumstances of individual cases' (Article 765a ZPO).

On the other hand, the social state principle laid down in Art. 20 (3) Basic Law (*Grundgesetz*), requires that evictions be carried out as *ultima ratio* only and that, if unavoidable, their consequences be mitigated, and the most serious of them, homelessness, be avoided as far as possible. This orientation is reflected in local authorities' duty to provide temporary accommodation (typically in shelters), their power to take over rent arrears and to temporarily seize private dwellings to grant the tenant at risk of eviction an occupancy right under public law, the availability of

---

8 Kenna et al (n 1) 8, 26.
9 Ibid 25.
10 ZPO is the abbreviation for *Zivilprozessordnung* (Code of Civil Procedure).

need-based housing allowances (*Wohngeld*), and the availability of general social benefits (*Sozialhilfe*) for people whose income is below the minimum threshold, which extend to housing costs as well. Regarding the actors entrusted with the prevention of evictions, social authorities and local job centres are most relevant whereas NGOs do not have a significant role, unlike in some other European countries.[11]

3. LEGAL AND CONSTITUTIONAL BACKGROUND TO PROTECTION AGAINST EVICTIONS

3.1 Housing as a Fundamental Right

German law does not guarantee an individually enforceable right to housing.[12] The inviolability of the home is enshrined in Art. 13 Basic Law, but the protection it affords extends only to already existing homes, leaving the access to housing unregulated. The same is true for Art. 14, which protects the freedom of property.[13] Some state constitutions foresee a more developed protection of the home. According to Art. 14 (I) of the Constitution of the Free Hanseatic City of Bremen, 'Every citizen of the *Hansestadt Bremen* has the right to an adequate dwelling. It is a duty of the State and the municipalities to facilitate the realisation of this right.'[14] There are similar provisions in the constitutions of Bavaria and Berlin. Although their wording might lend to a contrary interpretation, these provisions have been construed as not containing subjective and enforceable fundamental rights; thus, unlike in other EU states such as France, an individual has no right to be provided with adequate housing. Instead, these provisions only constitute obligations for states and municipalities to promote an adequate supply of housing.[15] These obligations may become very significant at a political level and justify public expenditure in the sector, but they must not be directly relied upon before courts.

---

[11]   Ibid 17.
[12]   Cornelius and Rzeznik (n 5) 40–41.
[13]   Ibid.
[14]   Constitution of the Free Hanseatic City of Bremen of 21 October 1947.
[15]   Cornelius and Rzeznik (n 5) 41, 90.

3.2 Legislation Relating to Owner-occupiers

Eviction from owner-occupied housing is typically related to the enforcement of a defaulted mortgage. Protective action may take a preventive and a corrective or at least mitigating form. Preventive measures need to be adopted by banks at the stage of setting up a mortgage and later whenever the risk of arrears or default arises. In particular, banks need to provide detailed information on possible risks (such as the risks of a variable interest rate), before the conclusion of a mortgage loan contract. As laid down in § 237 of the Introductory Act to the Civil Code (*Einführungsgesetz zum Bürgerlichen Gesetzbuch*, EGBGB),[16] such information must be based on the European Standardised Information Sheet (ESIS). Another preventive measure is the conservative assessment of the hypothecary value of a property and determination of its mortgage lending value (which is lower than the market value), though these measures will of course decrease the borrowers' ability to buy a house with mortgage financing in the first place.[17] Long-term mortgages with fixed interest rates are also useful to protect the mortgagor and to avoid eviction as a possible consequence of mortgage arrears.[18] If payment difficulties appear, preventive measures include the temporary deferral of payments and the restructuring of debts if the creditor agrees.

If, nevertheless, the mortgagor goes into default, the eviction procedure may be started. Compulsory auction of a house or apartment is regulated in the Act on Compulsory Auction of Immovable Property (*Zwangsversteigerungsgesetz*, ZVG)[19] and the Code of Civil Procedure (*Zivilprozessordnung*, ZPO).[20] Prior to the determination of the auction date, a property valuation report needs to be completed by an independent expert.[21] This is an essential step as a minimum amount based on the valuation is fixed for bids at the auction.[22] Pursuant to § 30 a ZVG,

---

[16] Introduction Act to the Civil Code (*Einführungsgesetz zum BGB*, EGBGB) in the version promulgated on 21 September 1994, *Federal Law Gazette* (*Bundesgesetzblatt*, BGBl.) I 2494.

[17] See the Regulation on the Determination of the Mortgage Lending Value (*Beleihungswertermittlungsverordnung*, BelWertV) of 12 May 2006 (BGBl. I 1175).

[18] Kenna et al (n 1) 8.

[19] Act on Compulsory Auctions (*Zwangsversteigerungsgesetz*, ZVG) of 20 May 1898 (Reichsgesetzblatt, 713).

[20] *Zivilprozessordnung*, ZPO in its version of 5 December 2005 (BGBl. I 3202; corr. 2006, 431; 2007, 1781).

[21] Kenna et al (n 1) 10.

[22] See §§ 74a, 85a, ZVG.

a debtor may request, within two weeks after the start of the proceedings, their temporary suspension for up to six months if there is a chance of him or her paying off the debts. This is, in most cases, achieved by the sale of the property on the market.[23] If the sale of the property in the compulsory auction cannot be avoided, the court will issue a repossession order, which allows the new owner to instruct the bailiff to execute the eviction.[24] According to civil procedure law, the bailiff needs to announce the eviction date at least three weeks in advance, ie before the execution of the eviction. The bailiff is obliged to inform the administrative authority responsible for housing homeless people about the planned eviction, so as to enable the authority to intervene to prevent homelessness.[25]

During the eviction process, the debtor may, under § 765 a ZPO, further delay or avoid the execution of the court order by making a 'hardship request' at least two weeks before the scheduled eviction date.[26] If the competent court responsible finds that the eviction entails 'a hardship that due to the very particular circumstances is immoral (*contra bonos mores*)', it is entitled to reverse, prohibit or temporarily stay the execution of the eviction.[27] This is a cautiously worded formula, which the courts construe narrowly. For example, a serious illness that may deteriorate after the execution of the eviction is one of the circumstances where this provision may be applied. Consequently, the eviction may either be prohibited or it may be carried out when the illness is controlled effectively through medication.[28] A serious risk of suicide, not mere psychological burdens, confirmed by a medical expert appointed by the court, may be another valid reason.[29] However, if the court holds that psychiatric treatment may exclude the risk of suicide, the eviction may

---

[23]   Ibid.

[24]   Ibid. The compulsory auction of a property can also affect the tenant as, according to § 57a ZVG, the new owner is entitled to terminate the rental agreement. The principle *emptio non tollit locatum* does not apply in this context.

[25]   Federal regulations for bailiffs (*Geschäftsanweisung für Gerichtsvollzieher* – GVGA) Art. 130.

[26]   'Unless the grounds on which the petition is based came about only after this time or the debtor was prevented from filing the petition in due time through no fault of his own' (Art. 765a (3) ZPO).

[27]   § 765a (1) ZPO.

[28]   Schmidt-Futterer, Lehmann-Richter, Mietrecht, Großkommentar des Wohn- und Gewerberaummietrechts, 12. Aufl, Beck, München, 2015, ZPO § 765a Rn. 23-24.

[29]   Ibid Rn. 17-18.

go ahead.[30] Moreover, where suicidal tendencies are found to persist, the court may still decide that the eviction may be executed in the presence of a physician or a social worker of the competent regulatory authority, if their intervention is deemed sufficient to eliminate the risk.[31] The hardship defence may also apply on other social grounds: for instance, if the household includes children attending school, an eviction order scheduled for execution during term time may be suspended until the start of school holidays; if eviction would result in children with disabilities becoming homeless, the order may be suspended until alternative accommodation has been found. The same may happen if the landlord defames the tenant, thus preventing him or her from finding new accommodation.[32]

Generally, according to the police, security and regulatory laws of the states, it is a duty of municipalities to provide temporary accommodation, which has to meet minimum standards, for people who would otherwise be homeless. Involuntary homelessness is considered to be a serious threat to public safety; accordingly, it needs to be prevented and counteracted by public measures.[33]

3.3 Legislation Relating to Private Renting

General tenancy law is regulated in the German Civil Code (*Bürgerliches Gesetzbuch*, BGB).[34] Tenancy contracts can be concluded as open-ended contracts, which is mostly the case, or as fixed-term contracts. However, pursuant to § 575 (1) BGB, a fixed-term contract is only allowed if one of the following conditions is met: 1) The landlord wants to use the rented place as a dwelling for himself, members of his family or his household after a certain period; 2) the landlord would like to destroy, change or repair the premises substantially, which would be significantly more difficult if the lease were not terminated; 3) the landlord would like

---

[30] See BGH, decision of 6.12.2012, Az. V ZB 8012.

[31] Schmidt-Futterer, 12. Aufl. 2015, ZPO § 765a Rn. 22.

[32] See Michel Vols, Marvin Kiehl and Julian Sidoli del Ceno, 'Human rights and protection against eviction, in anti-social behaviour cases in the Netherlands and Germany' (2015) 2 (2) *European Journal of Comparative Law and Governance* 179.

[33] See Karl-Heinz Ruder, Grundsätze der polizei- und ordnungsrechtlichen Unterbringung von (unfreiwillig) obdachlosen Menschen unter besonderer Berücksichtigung obdachloser Unionsbürger www.bagw.de.

[34] German Civil Code (*Bürgerliches Gesetzbuch-* BGB), in the version promulgated on 2.1.2002, BGBl. I 42, 2909; 2003 I page 738), last amended by § 4 (5) of the Act of 1.10.2013, BGBl. I 3719.

to lease the premises to a person who is obliged to perform services, eg a guardian or nurse providing services for the landlord. The landlord needs to inform the tenant in writing about the reasons for the fixed-term tenancy when concluding the contract. If no valid condition is fulfilled or if the landlord fails to inform the tenant about the conditions, the tenancy contract is presumed to be open-ended.

Tenancy contracts can be terminated by ordinary notice or, in the case of fixed-term contracts, without notice through the expiry of the contractual period.[35] There are also some special rights of termination regulated in the BGB (eg regarding succession upon death of the tenant) and the ZVG (eg when the dwelling is auctioned off, as mentioned).[36] However, the landlord is prohibited from giving a notice of termination in order to increase the rent.[37]

In open-ended contracts, a notice of the landlord requires a justified interest. According to § 573 BGB, this can be a serious violation of contractual duties by the tenant,[38] the personal need of the premises by the landlord, members of her family or her household, or the frustration of a planned economic use of the property if the tenancy were to be continued. No justified interest needs to be invoked in the following cases: if the rented dwelling is furnished, inhabited by the landlord as well, or if it forms part of a building which is inhabited by the landlord himself and has not more than two dwellings;[39] if it is rented for short-term use only; if it serves for student accommodation; if it is rented by a legal person under public law or a recognized private welfare work organization to host persons in urgent need of shelter.[40] The default period for an ordinary notice is three months, but it is gradually extended in relation to the length of time the tenant has already lived in the dwelling.[41]

---

[35]   § 542 BGB.

[36]   Cornelius and Rzeznik (n 5) 92–93.

[37]   § 573 (1) BGB.

[38]   Qualification of breach of contractual duties as justified interest for termination of tenancy contract depends not only on the number and frequency of breaches, but also on its importance, consequences and likelihood of its repetition. Sometimes only one breach of contractual duties is determined and sufficient reason for termination. See Vols et al (n 32) 170.

[39]   § 573 a (1) BGB.

[40]   § 549 BGB.

[41]   § 573 c BGB; Kenna et al (n 1) 15. According to §§ 568, 569 (4), 573 (3) BGB, a termination notice needs to be in writing and indicate the reasons on which it is based; also, it should inform about a possible objection ex Arts 574–574b BGB.

The tenant may object to the termination by alleging that it constitutes an unjustified hardship for her, her family or members of her household, which prevails over the interests of the landlord (§ 574 (1) BGB).[42] Hardship may also intervene if appropriate substitute residential space cannot be procured on reasonable terms (§ 574 (2) BGB). At the discretion of the court, the tenancy may then be continued for a limited or unlimited time span.[43]

An extraordinary termination of both open-ended and fixed-term contracts without a notice period is only possible with a compelling reason. Pursuant to Articles 543 and 569 BGB, the landlord is entitled to terminate the contract immediately if the tenant violates an important contractual duty, in particular, in case of default of payment of the whole or of a significant part of the rent for two months or in case of rent arrears of at least two monthly rents spread over a period of more than two months. The same applies if the tenant did not pay a security deposit corresponding to at least two monthly rents.[44] However, the termination is rendered invalid if the tenant pays off all rent arrears, which may be done up to two months after the start of the eviction proceedings, though only once in a time span of two years.[45] Termination without a notice period is also possible if the tenant endangers the integrity of the rented property by failing to take necessary care, or if she sublets the property without the landlord's agreement.[46] Another compelling reason for termination exists if one party to the contract permanently and seriously disturbs the domestic peace.[47] Even though the termination of the tenancy has an immediate effect in all these cases, the tenant will be assigned a certain period of time, often two weeks, to vacate the premises.[48]

---

[42] § 574 BGB. Reasons for the extraordinary continuation of a tenancy agreement can be health problems of tenant (or members of her family living in the dwelling) and lack of suitable substitute accommodation. For example, in the case AG Berlin-Mitte, 20.11.2013 – 19 C 77/12, the tenant, suffering from several diseases, had lived in the apartment for 45 years and developed an intense psychic bond to the home and its surroundings. He was not able to obtain an adequate alternative flat due to his financial situation and state of physical health. Therefore, the tenancy was continued for an indefinite period of time.

[43] See § 574a BGB.

[44] § 569 (2a) BGB.

[45] This possibility must not be resorted to if it was already used in the last two years (§ 569 (3) 2 BGB).

[46] § 543 (2) BGB.

[47] § 569 (2) BGB.

[48] Cornelius and Rzeznik (n 5) 93.

If after valid termination the tenant does not vacate the dwelling voluntarily, the landlord can make a request for eviction to the competent court. In principle, evictions of tenants and owner-occupiers are governed by the same rules which include the hardship defence pursuant to §765a (1) ZPO, and the duty of authorities to provide temporary accommodation to avoid homelessness. Yet there are additional protective measures for the tenant. First, during the court proceedings, the tenant may apply for an extension of the eviction deadline (*Räumungsfrist*) (§ 721 ZPO), which must not be longer than one year in total.[49] Pursuant to Article 22 (8) and (9) of the Social Code vol. 2 (*Sozialgesetzbuch*, SGB) and § 36 Social Code vol. 12 (SGB XII),[50] the court is obliged to inform the local social authorities about the start of eviction proceedings, so as to enable the authority to take over rent arrears or to provide temporary accommodation.[51] If temporary accommodation is not available, public authorities may also order that the tenant may be temporarily assigned the same dwelling (where she may stay) if otherwise she were to become homeless after eviction. The private tenancy is then substituted by an occupation right under public law. Under this regime, the full coverage of rental costs is guaranteed to the landlord by the municipality, which renders this solution expensive and rarely applied.[52] Moreover, social authorities may take over the rent to prevent eviction (eg § 22 (7) SGB II). This support usually takes the form of a loan to be paid back by the tenant in instalments.

As regards the execution of a tenant's eviction, there are further differences to owner-occupiers: Movable objects found in the premises which belong to the tenant and are not subject to compulsory enforcement must be returned to the tenant.[53] If none of the household members are present at the time of the execution, or if they do not want to accept these objects, the bailiff can deposit them in a storage office for attached objects at the cost of the evicted tenant.[54] If the tenant does not redeem her belongings within a period of one month after the vacation of the premises, the bailiff is allowed to sell them and lodge the proceeds.[55] Moreover, a recent reform introduced a new provision in § 885a ZPO, which endorsed the practice from Berlin ('Berliner Modell'), according

---

[49]   §§ 721 (1) 1, 794a (1) 1 ZPO.
[50]   *Sozialgesetzbuch*, SGB, BGBl. I Nr. 40/2004 of 31.07.2004.
[51]   Kenna et al (n 1) 12–13.
[52]   Ibid 6.
[53]   Cornelius and Rzeznik (n 5) 174.
[54]   § 885 (3) ZPO.
[55]   § 885 (4) ZPO.

to which the landlord only requests the vacation of the premises and simultaneously exercises a right of lien for rent arrears over all distrainable movable objects of the tenant according to § 562 BGB. In that way, the owner may save removal and deposit costs; however, the tenant's risk of losing her movable property, which will subsequently be auctioned off or dumped, is higher.

3.4   Legislation Relating to Social Renting

The percentage of social rented housing has further decreased over recent years and currently amounts to about 5 per cent only.[56] The transfer of legislative competencies to the states in the 2007 constitutional reform has entailed a diversification of housing policies, as states have adopted their own housing promotion acts.[57] Although the adequate funding of the sector is under the responsibility of the states, financial support of the Federal State will continue to be awarded until the end of 2019.[58] At the municipal level, housing offices are responsible for all issues related to social housing.[59] Significantly, the system of social housing does not only consist of public housing in a strict sense (ie dwellings owned by the municipalities or the state), but also extends to public-private arrangements according to which landlord-investors receive bricks-and-mortar subsidies when committing themselves to charge only lower, typically cost-based rents for a period of 15 years.[60] In order to provide a sufficient amount of dwellings for households with a low income, some municipalities with a severe housing shortage, such as Munich, have prescribed

---

[56]   See Joachim Kirchner, 'The declining social rental sector in Germany' (2007) 7 (1) *European Journal of Housing Policy* 85–101; Heinz Sautter, *Auswirkungen des Wegfalls von Sozialbindungen und des Verkaufs öffentlicher Wohnungsbestände auf die Wohnungsversorgung unterstützungsbedürftiger Haushalte*, Teilabschlussbericht im Rahmen des vom BMBF geförderten Forschungsverbundes, 'Wohnungslosigkeit und Hilfen in Wohnungsnotfällen', Institut Wohnen und Umwelt GmbH, 2005, 17–18; see also the statement of the German Parliament on social housing: <http://dipbt.bundestag.de/doc/btd/18/114/1811403.pdf>.

[57]   Cornelius and Rzeznik (n 5) 45.

[58]   Christiane Droste and Thomas Knorr-Siedow, 'Social housing in Germany' in K Scanlon, C Whitehead and M F Arrigoitia (eds) *Social Housing in Europe* (Chichester, Wiley & Sons 2014) 189.

[59]   Cornelius and Rzeznik (n 5) 47.

[60]   Kenna et al (n 1) 3.

that investors must devote a certain percentage of new housing construction projects to social housing.[61] Low income households that have been issued a public housing certificate are eligible to apply for housing benefits.[62] Landlords are also entitled to apply for subsidies for social housing when making their property available to the municipality for social tenancies.[63] In that way, too, municipalities may fulfil their obligation to prevent homelessness.

At the level of contract law, the same rules applying to private renting also apply to social renting in principle, but there are some exceptions. In particular, social renting has a time-limited character, and the landlord is not obliged to prove a justified interest for the termination of the contract, as in the case of private renting. Some provisions for preventing hardship, such as § 574 BGB and § 721 ZPO, do not apply in the case of social renting.[64] Conversely, eviction from social housing is regulated in the same way as eviction in the private rental sector.[65]

3.5 Legislation Relating to Unauthorized Occupancy

Unauthorized occupancy ('squatting') is not very common in Germany nowadays. There used to be a significant number of squatted houses, especially in Berlin and other major cities in the 1980s,[66] but that trend has decreased over the years.[67] § 123 of the Criminal Code (*Strafgesetzbuch*, StGB),[68] which deals with trespassing in general, also extends to squatting. Squatting is therefore punishable by imprisonment of up to one year or a monetary fine, the latter sanction constituting the rule. In the case of private property, trespass is prosecuted upon the owners' request only, whereas when squatting affects public property, or when squatters endanger public health and safety, public authorities can act *ex officio*.[69]

---

[61]   Cornelius and Rzeznik (n 5) 47.

[62]   Ibid 74.

[63]   Ibid 55, 74.

[64]   Kenna et al (n 1) 19–20. Cornelius and Rzeznik (n 5) 66.

[65]   Ibid.

[66]   For more about squatting movements in Germany and Berlin see Andrej Holm and Armin Kuhn, 'Squatting and urban renewal: the interaction of squatter movements and strategies of urban restructuring in Berlin' (2011) 35 (3) *International Journal of Urban and Regional Research* 644–658.

[67]   Cornelius and Rzeznik (n 5) 37.

[68]   German Criminal Code (*Strafgesetzbuch*, StGB), in the version promulgated on 13 November 1998, BGBl. I 3322, last amended by § 1 of the Law of 24.9.2013, BGBl. I 3671.

[69]   Cornelius and Rzeznik (n 5) 37; Kenna et al (n 1) 20.

The eviction of squatters may not always be easy under civil procedure law. Indeed, if the owner wants to submit a request for eviction to the local court, he is obliged to explicitly name the addressee of the order. Compulsory enforcement is possible, according to § 750 (1) ZPO, 'only if the persons for and against whom it is to be performed have been designated by name ...'. In practice, owners may have a problem in identifying squatters as these are usually unknown. Sometimes owners may even be unaware of the illegal occupation of their property, for example when an occupied house is a second home where the owners stay only occasionally.

3.6 Legislation Relating to Temporary Dispossession (Domestic Violence, Urban Development, Family Law Issues)

Divorce may entail the temporary dispossession of one or both former spouses from a home. Pursuant to § 1568a BGB, in the case of divorce or the dissolution of civil partnership, one of the spouses may request the right to continue to use the rented matrimonial home. In cases of urgent need, the same request is possible already at the stage of separation (§ 1361 b BGB).[70] This request may be granted if one party is more dependent on using the house considering all circumstances, especially the interests of the children. If the tenancy contract has been concluded with the other spouse, the contracting parties will be exchanged by judicial decree, and if both spouses have signed the contract with the landlord, the remaining spouse will continue to use the rented property as a single contracting party. The landlord is entitled to terminate the tenancy contract only if there is a compelling reason, in particular a prohibitive personal characteristic of the spouse entering into the contract.[71]

Domestic violence can also be a reason for temporary dispossession. Specifically, pursuant to § 1 of the Law on Civil Protection Against Violent Acts and Prosecutions (*Gesetz zum zivilrechtlichen Schutz vor*

---

[70] § 1361b BGB, title: matrimonial home when spouses are living apart – (1) If the spouses are living apart or if one of them wishes to live apart, one spouse may demand that the other permit him the sole use of the matrimonial home or of part of the matrimonial home, to the extent that this is necessary, taking account of the concerns of the other spouse, in order to avoid an inequitable hardship.

[71] § 563 (4) BGB.

Gewalttaten und Nachstellungen, Gewaltschutzgesetz, GewSchG),[72] the court may order that the perpetrator be no longer allowed to enter the victim's dwelling. That period may last up to six months and may be extended if the victim is unable to find appropriate alternative accommodation. According to the police laws of the federal states, the police are authorized to evict a violent person, even before court proceedings, from a dwelling in cases of acute danger. This aims to protect the victim and to allow her to obtain a court protection order in the meantime.[73] The validity of a police barring order may extend up to 14 days.[74]

Finally, the implementation of urban development plans can result in temporary or permanent home dispossession. According to § 179 of the Federal Building Code (*Baugesetzbuch*, BauGB),[75] the municipality can order the owner to tolerate the partial or total removal of building structures including dwellings incompatible with the specifications of the urban development plan in force; or when the defects of such structures cannot be remedied in any other way. However, in these cases, the availability of adequate alternative accommodation for the residents needs to be ensured. Pursuant to § 182 BauGB, a municipality is also entitled to terminate a tenancy contract if necessary for the implementation of urban redevelopment measures. The termination notice must be given at least six months in advance. Here, too, alternative accommodation for the tenant and her household members needs to be ensured. Moreover, landlord and tenant may be granted financial compensation when dispossessed due to the premature termination of a tenancy.[76] The municipality can develop a social plan to address changing living

---

[72]   Act on civil law protection against violence (*Gesetz zum zivilrechtlichen Schutz vor Gewalttaten und Nachstellungen – Gewaltschutzgesetz – GewSchG*), in version of 22.12.2001 (BGBl. I 3513).

[73]   Greater Protection in Cases of Domestic Violence, Information on the Act on Protection against Violence, Federal Ministry for Family Affairs, Senior Citizens, Women and Youth, Federal Ministry of Justice and Consumer Protection, 2015 <http://www.bmjv.de/SharedDocs/Downloads/DE/Formulare/Anlagen/Mehr_Schutz_bei_haeuslicher_Gewalt_ENG.pdf__blob=publicationFile&v=5> 9–10.

[74]   Domestic violence: Your rights, protection provided by the police, criminal law, and civil law, BIG Koordinierung, Berlin, 2013, 6 <http://www.big-berlin.info/sites/default/files/medien/330_IhrRecht_en.pdf>.

[75]   Federal Building Code (*Baugesetzbuch, BauGB*) in the version amended by the Act to Amend the Federal Building Code and to Reorder Spatial Planning Law [BauROG], issued on 18.8.1997 (BGBl. I 2081).

[76]   § 185 (1) BauGB.

conditions of the people affected by urban redevelopment measures. Such a plan may extend to assistance in finding new accommodation.[77]

3.7 Soft Law/Codes and their Effectiveness

Recommendations of state governments, the Association of German Cities and other bodies make up a type of soft law for the prevention of evictions.[78] The German Association for the Prevention of Homelessness (*Verein zur Prävention von Wohnungslosigkeit*)[79] recommends the cooperation between municipal administrations and NGOs to achieve a more effective prevention of eviction and homelessness; in particular, establishing special common local offices cooperating with job centres and other social services, institutions and the construction industry.[80] Effective prevention presupposes, first and foremost, timely information of potential eviction measures; then, the competent offices may in most cases provide for adequate alternative accommodation.[81] Centralized special offices are more common in bigger cities than in smaller cities or rural areas. According to a survey conducted in North Rhine-Westphalia in 2014, only 19.4 per cent of the municipalities possessed specialized offices for the prevention of homelessness, while in the rest of the state, responsibilities were divided among different bodies, which entails less effective coordination and longer delays for support action.[82]

---

[77] § 180 BauGB.

[78] Kenna et al (n 1) 21.

[79] Empfehlungen des Deutschen Vereins zur Prävention von Wohnungslosig-keit durch Kooperation von kommunalen und freien Trägern, Deutscher Verein für öffentliche und private Fürsorge e.V., DV 17/13 AF III, 11. September 2013.

[80] See Empfehlungen des Deutschen Vereins zur Prävention von Woh-nungslosigkeit durch Kooperation von kommunalen und freien Trägern, 9-16; See also Zentrale Fachstellen zur Vermeidung von Wohnungslosigkeit und Sicherung dauerhafter Wohnverhältnisse, Ein Praxisleitfaden für Kommunen, Kommunale Gemeinschaftsstelle für Verwaltungsvereinfachung, Ministerium für Arbeit, Soziales und Stadtentwicklung, Kultur und Sport des Landes Nordrhein-Westfalen, Köln 1999.

[81] Kenna et al (n 1) 18.

[82] Ibid.

4. EXTENT OF EVICTIONS FOR THE PERIOD 2010–2015

4.1 Definition of Eviction

The process of eviction as physical expulsion of a person from a property can be divided into three phases: pre-court, court and post-court. These can differ to some extent depending on the type of tenure affected. As cases of eviction belong to the field of private law, they are usually under the jurisdiction of first instance courts (*Amtsgerichte* – AG). Appeals can then be made to district courts (*Landgerichte* – LG). Further appeals on legal grounds (*Revision*) can be made to the Federal Court of Justice (*Bundesgerichtshof* – BGH), the highest federal court for the area of private law.[83] However, these are subject to admission in the appeal decision of the district court or to acceptance by the BGH in a separate admission procedure. In all cases, the admission requires the amount in dispute to be over €20 000, as well as the presence of a qualified reason (such as the fundamental importance of the case or divergence with standing case law).

The pre-court phase for evictions from owner-occupied housing starts with a notice from the bank to the debtor who is in default of mortgage payment. If a settlement cannot be reached, the mortgagee can request the repossession of the mortgaged property before the court, which will usually result in a forced auction.[84] As explained, prior to the determination of an auction date, an independent expert must assess the value of the property. The date of auction must be publicly announced at least six weeks in advance.[85] According to the ZVG, it is possible to conduct several auctions before the property is finally sold. The property may only be auctioned off if the highest bid exceeds 50 per cent of its estimated value.[86] If the highest bid is less than 70 per cent of the estimated value, the creditor is entitled to refuse the bid in the first auction. Then, the court will *ex officio* determine the date for the next auction, which should not be conducted later than six months after the first auction. The 70 per cent rule no longer applies in the second

---

[83]   Courts Constitution Act (*Gerichtsverfassungsgesetz*), in the version published on 9 May 1975 (BGBl. I 1077), last amended by § 1 of the Act of 2.7.2013 (BGBl. I 1938) §12 and § 13.

[84]   Kenna et al (n 1) 9.

[85]   Ibid.

[86]   § 85 a ZVG.

auction.[87] After the sale of the property, the court will issue a repossession order, which provides the legal basis for the new owner to request the bailiff to execute the eviction, thereby activating the post-court phase. The pre-court phase for eviction from private and social rented housing begins with the termination of the contract as described above, the main reason being rent default. If the tenant does not vacate the dwelling voluntarily, the landlord can submit the case for eviction to the local court in whose district the property is located.

Evictions as a consequence of a divorce differ from the previous cases. Sometimes, former spouses reach an agreement about who is going to live in the matrimonial home. Otherwise, it is the responsibility of family courts to make decisions on divorce and its implications, also as regards the assignment of the matrimonial home (§ 1568a BGB). If one spouse is the owner of the home, he or she is entitled to stay in it in principle, and the other spouse may only request to remain in the dwelling if moving out is likely to entail an inequitable hardship for him or her. In all other cases, the court should take its decision in the light of all relevant factual circumstances, paying particular attention to the best interests of the children living in the household.[88]

In the case of domestic violence, the eviction can be executed by the police already in the pre-court phase if there is an acute danger. The period of removal and prohibition of re-entering the dwelling ordered by the police can last up to a maximum of 14 days.[89] A victim of domestic violence should therefore apply for a judicial protection order. According to § 1 of the Act of Protection against Violence (*Gewaltschutzgesetz*), the court may set forth the prohibition of up to six months for a perpetrator to enter the dwelling where the victim lives, order him to respect a certain minimum distance from the home of the victim, and ban him from visiting places where the victim is regularly present.

4.2 Evictions from Mortgaged Property

There are no official statistics on evictions from various types of housing at national level. Some data about eviction from mortgaged property can be obtained through statistics on cases of compulsory auctions. The following table shows the number of cases of real estate repossessions

---

[87]   § 74a ZVG.

[88]   § 1568a (1) BGB.

[89]   See for example § 29a of Allgemeines Gesetz zum Schutz der öffentlichen Sicherheit und Ordnung in Berlin (*Allgemeines Sicherheits- und Ordnungsgesetz – ASOG Bln*) of 14.4.1992.

(for all types of immovable property) from 2010 to 2015, according to the Federal Statistical Office report on Civil Courts juridical statistics:

Table 3.1   Court cases of real estate repossessions

The number of court cases of real estate repossessions	2010	2011	2012	2013	2014	2015
	68 723	62 690	57 013	51 650	48 380	42 670

Data on the number of compulsory auctions can be obtained from commercial companies, but generally without being able to distinguish between various types of property.[90] Sometimes, several auctions will be necessary in order to sell one and the same property, which can lead to imprecise results when counting dates of auctions regardless of the property at issue. The following table shows the number of court dates for compulsory auctions according to Argetra yearly reports from 2010 to 2013:[91]

Table 3.2   Court dates for compulsory auctions

The number of court dates for compulsory auctions	2010	2011	2012	2013
	82 208	73 038	61 500	47 617

The next table shows the number of objects offered at compulsory auctions according to data collected by UNIKA GmbH[92] from 2010 to 2014:

Table 3.3   Objects offered at compulsory auctions

The number of objects offered at compulsory auctions	2010	2011	2012	2013	2014
	49 295	44 377	38 131	34 491	31 000

---

[90]   See Kenna et al (n 1) 22.

[91]   Argetra <https://www.argetra.de/home/argetra/downloads~ae23f6bb38cb1 0bf0138ed167ac3125d.de.html>.

[92]   UNIKA GmbH <https://www.zwangsversteigerung.de/Statistik>.

4.3 Evictions From Private/Social Rented Housing

Official statistics on the number of evictions from private and social rented housing do not exist either at national level.[93] Some data can however be found at local level, though these are usually not collected on a regular basis. According to a statement of the Saxonian Parliament (*Sächsischer Landtag*, 2013), based on the number of eviction cases brought before higher regional courts (*Oberlandesgericht*), there were 3037 cases in 2010 and 3313 cases in 2011.[94] Pursuant to a 2014 statement, there were 3813 eviction cases in 2012 and 3710 in 2013. According to a similar statement from 2016, the number of eviction cases was 5531 in 2014 and 4762 in 2015.[95]

The following table[96] shows the number of eviction cases in the city of Leipzig brought before the district courts as well as the number of cases of executed evictions according to an annual report of the Leipzig Social Service for 2011 to 2014:

Table 3.4   Eviction cases in Leipzig

Evictions in Leipzig	2011	2012	2013	2014
Number of eviction cases before the court	1210	1306	1300	1073
Number of eviction cases according to bailiffs' report	897	876	896	918

Information about the number of eviction cases can also be found in the state of Hamburg. The following table shows the number of eviction

---

[93]   Kenna et al (n 1) 23.

[94]   Sächsischer Landtag, 2013, Räumungsklagen und Zwangsräumungen in Sachsen (Court decisions on and enforcement of evictions in Saxony), Antwort auf die Kleine Anfrage der Abgeordneten Kallenbach. Drucksache 5/11803.

[95]   Sächsischer Landtag, 2016, Wohnungsräumungen in Sachsen im Jahr 2015, Antwort auf die Kleine Anfrage der Abgeordneten Schaper, Drucksache 6/6046.

[96]   Annual report of the Leipzig Social Service for 2013 (Geschäftsbericht 2013, Sozialamt Leipzig), Stadt Leipzig – Der Oberbürgermeister, 18; and the analoguous report for 2014, 17.

applications before the court and the number of executed evictions according to the statements of the regional parliament in Hamburg in 2013 and 2014:[97]

Table 3.5   Evictions in Hamburg

Evictions in Hamburg	2013	2014
Total number of applications for eviction before the court	2501	2051
Number of executed evictions	1451	1108

According to an analogous statement from the Berlin Regional Parliament from 2012, there were 9934 eviction cases before Berlin courts in 2010. The number of eviction notices according to the bailiffs' report was 5603, but there is no official data on the number of executed evictions.[98] In 2011, the number of eviction notices rose to 6777.[99] Pursuant to a report of the Berlin Advisory Body for Family Matters (*Berliner Beirat für Familienfragen*), in 2015 the number of evictions further increased. There are around 10 000 eviction cases per year in Berlin, making it the city with the highest number of evicted people in the whole of Germany.[100] From these, between 5000 and 7000 evictions are executed per year:[101]

---

[97]   Schriftliche Kleine Anfrage der Abgeordneten Özdemir und Antwort des Senats, Wie haben sich die Zwangsräumungen in Hamburg entwickelt?, Bürgerschaft der Freien und Hansestadt Hamburg, 21. Wahlperiode, Drucksache 21/951, 07 July 2015, 2.

[98]   Berlin Parliament (Abgeordnetenhaus Berlin) 2012, Räumungsklagen und Wohnungsräumungen (Eviction Cases and Evictions of Private Residencies). Kleine Anfrage des Abgeordneten Andreas Otto und Antwort, Drucksache 17/10 269, Berlin.

[99]   Berlin Parliament (Abgeordnetenhaus Berlin) 2013, Entwicklung von und Umgang mit Zwangsräumungen von Wohnungen (Development of, and Reaction to, Evictions from Dwellings). Kleine Anfrage der Abgeordneten Elke Breitenbach und Katrin Lompscher, Drucksache 17/12 200, Berlin, 1, 2.

[100]   Dazugehören, Mitgestalten – Familien in der Stadtgesellschaft, Berliner Familienbericht 2015, Berliner Beirat für Familienfragen, pp. 153, 154 <http://www.familienbeirat-berlin.de/fileadmin/Familienbericht/ BBFF_FB_2015_web_final.pdf>.

[101]   Laura Berner, Andrej Holm, Inga Jensen, Zwangsräumungen und die Krise des Hilfesystems, Eine Fallstudie in Berlin, Humboldt-Universität zu Berlin, Institut für Sozialwissenschaften Stadt- und Regionalsoziologie, Berlin,

Table 3.6 Eviction notices in Berlin

Number of eviction notices in Berlin according to bailiffs' report	2010	2011
	5603	6777

4.4 Evictions from Unauthorized Occupancies

As unauthorized occupancy ('squatting') is not common in Germany nowadays, the number of evictions in this sector is negligible though no official data exist.

4.5 Evictions Related to Family Issues

There is also a lack of data on the number of eviction cases related to family issues. Yet an insight can be gained from consulting the reports of the National Coalition of Services Working with the Homeless (*Bundesarbeitsgemeinschaft Wohnungslosenhilfe e. V.*, hereafter BAG report(s)). According to a BAG report from 2010,[102] divorce or separation accounted for 22.82 per cent (men 22.33 per cent, women 24.47 per cent) of the total number of people who lost their homes and ended up homeless. In 2011, the figure was 19.6 per cent (men 20.12 per cent, women 19.39 per cent), and in 2012 it was 19.0 per cent (men 18.9 per cent, women 19.4 per cent). In 2013, the figure declined to 18.1 per cent (men 17.6 per cent, women 19.5 per cent) and in 2014 to 17.2 per cent (men 17.2 per cent, women 17.4 per cent). In court cases involving domestic violence, the number of persons becoming homeless as a result of an eviction order is low. According to the statistics to be found in the BAG reports, 0.93 per cent of the whole number of persons who lost their home during 2010 became homeless as a consequence of eviction due to domestic violence. In 2011 the number was also around 0.9 per cent, whereas in 2013 it dropped to 0.8 per cent. The downward trend continued in 2014 when the number of people who lost their home as a consequence of domestic violence dropped to 0.7 per cent.

2015, 3 <https://www.sowi.hu-berlin.de/de/lehrbereiche/stadtsoz/forschung/projekte/studie-zr-web.pdf>.
[102] Bundesarbeitsgemeinschaft Wohnungslosenhilfe e. V., Statistikbericht 2010, 10, 9, 7 <http://www.bagw.de/de/themen/statistik_und_dokumentation/statistikberichte/statistikberichte_1.html>.

Commentary on the statistics

The lack of official statistics at a national level on the number of evictions from different types of housing tenure constrains scientific analysis. The limited data collected at a local level is incomplete, which makes it difficult to draw precise conclusions on the number and extent of evictions. However, from the information presented above, it is possible to detect a downward trend in evictions from mortgaged property in recent years, and a slight increase in the number of evictions affecting private and social rented housing. Evictions related to family issues have become somewhat less significant in recent years.

4.6   Profile of Those Evicted

Complete sets of data on the profile of evicted persons can be found in research on the prevention of homelessness in North Rhine-Westphalia.[103] In a survey on households threatened with homelessness after eviction undertaken in 2012, single persons without children made up the largest share of 57.1 per cent (men 41.2 per cent, women 15.9 per cent); couples without children represented 9.6 per cent, while couples with one or more children accounted for 16.7 per cent; single mothers accounted for 12.3 per cent, whereas single fathers had a smaller share of just 1.7 per cent.[104] As regards the age of people threatened with eviction, the largest group was the one between 25 and 60 years (between 25 and 35 years: 29.7 per cent; between 35 and 60 years: 44.0 per cent); least represented was the group of people under 18 years (0.3 per cent), followed by the group of persons over 60 years (5.8 per cent), whereas persons between 18 and 25 years accounted for 20.2 per cent of the overall number of threatened people.[105] The share of people with a migrant background was 22.0 per cent.[106] Most of the persons threatened with eviction were dependent on transfer payments (usually unemployment benefits), while only 10.4 per cent had an income from employment.[107]

---

[103]   Jürgen Evers, Ekke-Ulf Ruhstrat, Prävention von Wohnungslosigkeit in Nordrhein-Westfalen (Prevention of Homelessness in North Rhine-Westphalia), Ministerium für Arbeit, Integration und Soziales des Landes Nordrhein-Westfalen, Düsseldorf, Mai 2014.
[104]   Ibid 51.
[105]   Ibid 51–52.
[106]   Ibid 53.
[107]   Ibid.

5. RISK FACTORS IDENTIFIED LEADING TO EVICTIONS

As stated, the main risk factors leading to eviction are unemployment, divorce, domestic violence, severe illness/invalidity and drug abuse. These factors usually account for rent and mortgage arrears, which can result in a judicial eviction order. Often, a combination of two or more risk factors may be present. Unemployed households and households with a low income and substance abuse are more likely to be threatened with eviction than other vulnerable households.[108] A major factor accounting for default in mortgage repayment is the incorrect estimation of low income households of their financial capacities and the overall costs related to a property purchase.[109] Decreases in household income and unexpected increases in household expenses are also common factors that contribute to default in mortgage repayment.[110]

A study of 2625 households threatened with eviction gives an insight into key risk factors. Specifically, 60 per cent of the surveyed households had only financial problems, typically mortgage or rent arrears. The remaining 40 per cent needed further support, 20 per cent on account of mental health problems and addiction, and 18.2 per cent due to specific social difficulties.[111]

6. LINKS BETWEEN EVICTIONS AND HOMELESSNESS

According to the BAG reports, the number of people without housing has been increasing since 2015. In 2014, approximately 335 000 people were homeless, indicating an increase of 18 per cent as compared to 2012; almost one-third of them had a migrant background. The BAG reports further estimate that in the period between 2015 and 2018, the number of

---

[108] Kenna et al (n 1) 26.
[109] Melanie Kolth, 'Payment difficulties of home owners in Germany' in Peter Boelhouwer, John Doling and Marja Elsinga (eds) *Home Ownership: Getting In, Getting From, Getting Out. Part I* (The Netherlands, DUP Science, Delft 2005) 195; Kenna et al (n 1) 8.
[110] Kolth (n 109) 195.
[111] Kenna et al (n 1) 26; BG Volker, J Evers and EU Ruhstrat, *Wirksamkeit persönlicher und wirtschaftlicher Hilfen bei der Prävention von Wohnungslosigkeit* (Bremen, Effectiveness of Personal and Financial Support for the Prevention of Homelessness (GISS) 2005) 30.

homeless people will reach 536 000.[112] According to data from 2014, 71 per cent of homeless people were living alone, whereas 29 per cent lived with a partner and/or children; the share of men in the total number was 72 per cent. There is a direct link between the threat of homelessness and eviction in many cases. The three phases of eviction (pre-court, court and post-court phase) may also be documented in statistical data: In 2014, 172 000 households were threatened with the possibility of losing their homes. In around 50 per cent of these cases, it was possible to solve problems and avoid homelessness through preventive measures. In 86 000 cases, the home was actually lost, with 33 000 cases (38 per cent) of these losses being caused by eviction; 53 000 cases were tenancies in which the tenants left their dwellings before the start of eviction proceedings (or before the scheduled date for the execution of the eviction). In most cases, these were single person households.[113] According to 2014 statistics from BAG, another major reason for the loss of home was the termination of the tenancy contract by the landlord (27.9 per cent). In 2.8 per cent of the cases, people left their dwelling after a court case for eviction had been initiated.[114] Overall, evictions were a driving force for homelessness, although in half of the cases, prevention measures were successfully applied.

7. SUMMARY OF SIGNIFICANT CASES AND REPORTS RELATED TO EVICTIONS FOR THE PERIOD 2010–2015

As explained, eviction may be postponed or avoided through application of the hardship defence laid down in § 765a (1) ZPO, which has been at the centre of a number of interesting cases. In general, when applying this provision to protect the debtor, courts need to balance the interests of the parties. According to a decision of the Federal Constitutional Court (*Bundesverfassungsgericht* – *BVerfG*, 29. 07. 2014 – 2 BvR 1400/14), which dealt with the eviction of an 81-year-old man with medical problems and suicidal tendencies and his wife, courts are obliged under

---

[112]   Bundesarbeitsgemeinschaft Wohnungslosenhilfe e. V., Zahl der Wohnungslosen in Deutschland auf neuem Höchststand, 2015, 1 <http://www.bagw.de/de/themen/zahl_der_wohnungslosen/261.html>.

[113]   Ibid 1–2.

[114]   Bundesarbeitsgemeinschaft Wohnungslosenhilfe e. V., Statistikbericht 2014, 6 <http://www.bagw.de/de/themen/statistik_und_dokumentation/statistik berichte/statistikberichte_1.html>.

Art. 2 (2) of the Basic Law to assess 'if the preservation of life and health interests of the debtor rank higher than the interests which the enforcement measure is intended to preserve'. The intervention which takes place has to be carried out in accordance with the principle of proportionality and the basic right of the debtor under Art. 2 (2) GG, Basic Law. The fact that a debtor in the process of forced auction and eviction asserts that his fundamental right to life and physical integrity is infringed due to eviction, is not sufficient (BGH of 7. 10. 2010 – V ZB 82/10). Similarly, in BGH, 09. 10. 2013 – I ZB 15/13, the court stated that a permanent suspension of an eviction must not be ordered if contrary to the creditor's fundamental rights of property (Art. 14 (1), Basic Law), and effective legal protection (Art. 19 (4), Basic Law).[115] According to this case law, the suspension of an eviction order needs to be time-limited and impose efforts to improve the health of the debtor, as 'in the interest of the creditor, the debtor can be expected to act on the improvement of his state of health'. This decision was confirmed in BGH, 12. 11. 2014 – V ZB 99/14, regarding the eviction from property after compulsory auction.[116]

In BGH, 6. 12. 2012 – V ZB 80/12, the debtor also alleged the risk of suicide and asked for protection under § 765a ZPO. The court obtained an expert opinion of a hospital for psychiatry and neurology, which attested a moderate to severe depressive episode. Under the terms of the court's temporary suspension order, the debtor was required to undergo medical treatment with a view to 'reducing the importance of the house to a reasonable degree and allowing the debtor to settle for a loss of the house', but shortly after that, the debtor interrupted the treatment. The court then decided that she was no longer entitled to protection under Article 765a ZPO as she 'did not take an initiative to treat her mental illness' and 'she considered a treatment not to be necessary, and she stated she was well as long as she did not think of the imminent loss of the house'.

---

[115] For a balance between the interests of both parties and application of Arts 2 (2) on protection of life, 14 (1) on protection of property and 19 (4) on effective legal protection under the Basic Law, see also: BGH, 20. 1. 2011 – I ZB 27/10 (LG Ulm); BVerfG (2. Kammer des Zweiten Senats), 21. 11. 2012 – 2 BvR 1858/12.

[116] For further cases on § 765a ZPO see: BGH, 20.1.2011 – I ZB 27/10 (LG Ulm); LG Braunschweig, 06.03. 2013 – 4 T 116/13 (11); AG Neukölln, 24.07.2013 – 70 K 100/12.

Another eviction case that attracted the attention of the German public took place in Berlin in 2013.[117] The tenant had not paid the rent from August 2012 to March 2013. Before the court, she invoked the hardship defence under § 765a ZPO, stating that eviction would be incompatible with good morals due to her poor health, psychological stress and the threat of homelessness after the eviction, as she was not able to find a new apartment. The court found the report of a general practitioner from the pre-litigation procedure insufficient to justify the application of § 765a ZPO and asked her to submit a certificate of a specialist confirming her health conditions and the potential risk of deterioration after the execution of the eviction, which she did not produce within the fixed deadline. The court stated that 'the imminent homelessness does not in itself constitute particular hardship as a normal consequence of an eviction' and that 'the mere presence of a mental or physical disorder does not justify the protection against eviction' and therefore ruled out the application of the hardship defence.

Regarding the unavailability of alternative accommodation, the decision of LG Kleve of 23. 01. 2013 – 4 T 295/12, shows the usual judicial approach: A *short* postponement of the eviction is possible if alternative accommodation has been shown not to be available immediately or if the debtor cannot be expected to move or accommodated in an emergency shelter in the interval period.[118] In the Berlin case cited above, the first decision dated from 29 October 2012, whereas the eviction was executed only on the 9 April 2013, which gave the debtor more than a short period of time for finding new accommodation.[119] However, the court's approach met with public disapproval and led to demonstrations in support of tenants, when the affected person died in an emergency shelter two days after the execution of the eviction.

Pregnancy can also be a reason for suspending an eviction due to rent arrears. According to Art. 6 (4) of the Basic Law, every mother shall be entitled to the protection and care of the community. The execution of the eviction is, in the case of pregnancy, considered to be an immoral hardship in the sense of § 765a ZPO. Such a suspension may be granted as laid down in § 3 (2) and § 6 (1) of the Law for the Protection of

---

[117]   AG Wedding, 05.04.2013 – 32 M 8038/13.

[118]   In this case the court considered that postponement of eviction for two months was not a short period as the debtor had already avoided execution of eviction which had been scheduled for December and there were no other justifying reasons for further delay. See LG Kleve, 23.01.2013 – 4 T 295/12.

[119]   The entire process from the application to the execution of the eviction took almost 10 months.

Employed Mothers (*Gesetz zum Schutze der erwerbstätigen Mutter, Mutterschutzgesetz* – MuSchG), which grants maternity leave six weeks before and eight weeks after childbirth.

Besides the mentioned cases, further judicially recognized cases of suspension have been illness, physical afflictions and old age.[120] Though § 765a ZPO gives much leeway for interpretation, it can be concluded from the case law that courts generally act in a careful and prudent manner, considering all available facts, evidence, medical documentation and prognostics on the future development of diseases and psychological disorders. When debtors refer to § 765a ZPO, the process between the submission of the request for eviction and its execution is usually long from the creditors' point of view, as in most cases the state of the debtors' health and the duration of medical treatments and other relevant circumstances will be taken into account.[121]

8. BEST PRACTICE MODELS FOR PREVENTING, TACKLING AND REACTING TO EVICTIONS

As regards the eviction of owner-occupiers, German policy measures do not include anything particularly innovative: detailed pre-contractual information (based on the European Standardised Information Sheet) and advice on the consequences of potential mortgage arrears, payment deferral and debt restructuring are not regulated and practised in any particularly attractive way. What may be highlighted, though, is the strictly regulated duty of bailiffs to inform local social authorities about imminent evictions, thus giving them the chance to adopt protective measures, though in some cases time is not sufficient. Similarly, the establishment of 'one stop shop' public-private homelessness prevention centres may be viewed as a recommendable practice, although such centres have yet to be established outside of larger cities.

When it comes to the eviction of tenants, courts are responsible for alerting local social authorities and this may be regarded as a best

---

[120]   See Winfried Schuschke, Die Einstellung der Räumungsvollstreckung, 17. Deutscher Mietgerichtstag 2015, 6 <http://db.mietgerichtstag.de/tl_files/Dateien/Mietgerichtstage/2015/Schuschke%20Einstellung%20Raeumungsvollstreckung.pdf>.

[121]   Evictions after the sale of the property may even take longer. For example, in LG Braunschweig, 06.03. 2013 – 4 T 116/13 (11), the first scheduled date for forced auction was on 17 February 2012 and the last decision upon postponement of the process due to suicide risk was on 6 March 2013.

practice. Conversely, the options of the judicial grace period for vacation of the premises ex § 721 ZPO and the hardship defence ex § 765a ZPO are minimum standards which do not constitute best practices. However, more attention may be paid to § 569 (3) BGB, whereby the tenant can avoid the execution of the eviction based on rent arrears if he or she pays off all rent debts at the latest by the end of two months after the eviction claim is pending. This solution can also be used by a public authority when taking over the rent debt of the tenant to prevent his or her eviction.[122] Additionally, social authorities can assign a defaulting tenant the rented apartment (or other dwelling) under a public law occupation right. However, this is an expensive option, and therefore rarely applied, because the social authorities need to pay the rent to the landlord, which suggests that this course of action does not constitute a best practice.

9. CONCLUSION

All in all, the eviction and homelessness prevention system in Germany is working reasonably well, though mostly through conventional, seldom innovative measures. At the same time, there is considerable room for improvement, especially regarding the faster transmission of information by bailiffs and courts to the competent social authorities. The spread and better development of private-public prevention centres, where expertise and contacts to public authorities and courts, social support groups and credit institutions are assembled, and integrative solutions can be designed and executed in the individual case, would seem to constitute the most important way forward.

---

[122]   § 569 (3) 2 BGB.

4. Social context, evictions and prevention measures in Hungary

Nóra Teller and Eszter Somogyi, with the contribution of Nóra Tosics

1. INTRODUCTION

The financial crisis of 2008 greatly increased the vulnerability of many households in Hungary. Beyond the growth of poverty risk in general, there has also been a dramatic increase in the number of severely materially deprived people. Austerity measures have increased the level of poverty, as has the shift to workfare. There are also substantial affordability problems: in 2013, the share of those who had fallen behind with utility or loan repayments was approximately 26 per cent of the total population. The increase in eviction figures also points to growing housing insecurity in general: in 2012, the Central Statistical Office (CSO) reported 966 evictions from municipal rentals[1] and the judicial executors performed approximately 500 evictions in the same year. In 2016, the figure of evictions grew to over 1700. Eviction processes based on execution procedures for outstanding payments are quasi-automated, which leaves less room for indebted households to react and to turn the process around. The social protection system seems to work only limitedly for vulnerable households; housing allowance is not high enough to prevent the accumulation of housing-related debts. The arrears management system also fails to prevent evictions even in the case of relatively low amounts of arrears, and the central programme was ceased in 2015. Social work is not proactive and there is a lack of cooperation between social workers and private and public landlords. Indebted households, with foreign currency based mortgage loans, have received assistance through various grants and schemes, but the general housing affordability challenge still prevails. These phenomena seem to have

---

[1] Data provided by the CSO housing department in an email exchange.

exacerbated in the past few years and there is a lack of policy change in 2017. All of these factors bring about an increase in housing insecurity for the most vulnerable.

2. POLICY BACKGROUND

The tenure structure in Hungary, based on the last census and expert estimates, shows an overwhelming majority of homeowners. Around 88 per cent of all dwellings are in private ownership; 3–4 per cent are social rentals, and 8–9 per cent represent private rentals including rent-free arrangements with a private landlord. Approximately 20 per cent of all housing in private ownership is with mortgage.[2]

The poverty risk in Hungary has changed in the last decade. According to Eurostat data, the share of the population at risk of poverty increased from 28.2 per cent to 33.5 per cent (2.79 million to 3.29 million) from 2008 to 2013, with a decline to 26.6 per cent in 2016. Social transfers were unable to mitigate the increasing risk of poverty. Moreover, the share of people at risk of poverty after social transfers also increased: from 12.4 per cent in 2008, with a peak in 2015 of 15.6 per cent, and a slight decrease to 14.8 per cent in 2016. There has also been a dramatic increase in the number of severely materially deprived people. In 2008, 17.9 per cent of the population belonged to this group, whereas their share increased to 26.8 per cent in 2013. The increase between 2008 and 2013 was 10 per cent. This trend continued in 2016, when the rate grew further to 29.6 per cent. The share of severely materially deprived people increased very fast and by 2013, the number grew by 50 per cent and reached an overall figure of 26.8 per cent. Since then, there has been a decrease in this respect: in 2016, the figure decreased by approximately 10 per cent which means that despite the reduction in the number of the poorest, the general pauperization of the population is still ongoing.[3] Austerity measures in the social benefit system have increased the level of poverty, as has the shift to workfare (in 2017, over 300 000 people

---

    [2] József Hegedüs, Vera Horváth, Nóra Teller and Nóra Tosics, *Tenancy Law and Housing Policy in Multi-level Europe. National Report for Hungary* (TEN-LAW, 2014) <http://www.tenlaw.uni-bremen.de/reports/HungaryReport_090520 14.pdf> (hereafter TENLAW).

    [3] See Eurostat newsrelease 168/2014 of 4 November 2014 <http://ec. europa.eu/eurostat/documents/2995521/6035076/3-04112014-BP-EN.pdf/62f94e 70-e43a-471f-a466-2e84d1029860> and the yearly available statistics on the Eurostat website: <http:// http://ec.europa.eu/eurostat>.

were employed in obligatory public employment schemes in unproductive jobs for reduced wages and often working part-time).

There are also substantial affordability problems. In 2013, the share of those who had fallen behind with utility or loan repayments was approximately 26 per cent of the total population. A total of 23 per cent had arrears on housing costs and approximately 7 per cent had arrears on loan repayments. Among those living below the poverty line, 63 per cent had problems with arrears.[4] Only among the upper two deciles do housing costs represent less than 20 per cent of monthly income. Increased loan repayment obligations have hit households to a large extent and data from 2011 reveals that the interest rate could have reached up to 47 per cent of the total household income.[5] Other research indicated that in 2009, while 20 per cent of all households were not able to fully heat their home, this share had risen to 27 per cent in 2012.[6]

Indebtedness related to housing costs also increased considerably after the financial crisis of 2008. Between 2009 and 2013, the number of people who were more than 12 months behind on electricity bill payments rose by 37 per cent and the number of gas users with overdue payments rose by 10 per cent. In addition, 72 per cent more district heating customers were more than 12 months behind with their payments. Overall, arrears in utility bill payments accounted for 170 000 households having unpaid bills for over 12 months with more than 400 000 households having unpaid bills of over 3 months. In 2012, a total of 37 000 households had their electricity cut off and a further 100 000 households had their gas cut off, three times more than in 2009. Since indebtedness is the main cause of evictions in Hungary, the growing figures point to the lack of efficient state policies in this respect. Details of prevention and other welfare programmes and their main challenges are discussed in Section 8.

---

[4] Habitat for Humanity Hungary, 'Éves jelentés a lakhatási szegénységröl 2013' ('Annual report on housing poverty 2013') (Habitat for Humanity Hungary 2014) <http://www.habitat.hu/files/Lakhatasi_Jelentes_2013_hosszu.pdf>.

[5] Metropolitan Research Institute, 'Piacfeltáró háttértanulmány az alacsony státuszú többlakásos lakóépületek müszaki felújításait és fejlesztéseit támogató pénzügyi és egyéb termékek kifejlesztéséhez 2011' ['Market research for the development of renovation and development schemes for low status multi-unit buildings 2011']: Manuscript.

[6] TÁRKI, *Monitor Jelentések 2012*, 'Egyenlötlenség és polarizálódás a magyar társadalomban' (TÁRKI Monitoring Report 2012, 'Inequality and Polarisation in Hungarian Society) (Tarki Social Research Institute 2013) <http://www.tarki.hu/hu/research/hm/monitor2012_teljes.pdf>.

3. LEGAL AND CONSTITUTIONAL BACKGROUND TO PROTECTION AGAINST EVICTIONS

Due to the socialist legacy, the housing right regulation in Hungary seems to be different from that of many western European countries. Research published by the authors in 2014,[7] proffered that tenancy regulation is not directly influenced by fundamental rights. Rather, tenancy relationships were considered as a tool to control resources and the provision of housing. After the transition, in 1993, the Housing Act aimed principally to restore market driven tenancy relationships and contractual freedom. It was also the peak period of privatization, when only a small fraction of the dwellings (5 per cent) remained in municipal ownership. Further issues stem from the regulations in the Hungarian Constitution: whereas 'housing' is not a fundamental right in Hungary, there is no explicit obligation on the state enshrined in the Hungarian Constitution to provide housing. However, the new Fundamental Law of Hungary, which took effect on 1 January 2012, takes a step in this direction, declaring that 'Hungary shall strive to ensure decent housing conditions and access to public services for everyone' (Article 22 of the Constitution). As a rather controversial measure, this article was later completed by two more paragraphs, on the state and local municipalities' contribution to decent housing conditions; by ensuring accommodation to 'persons without a dwelling'; and on banning said persons from using public spaces as a dwelling: According to Article 22 (3), 'in order to protect public policy, public security, public health and cultural values, an Act or a local government decree may, with respect to a specific part of public space, provide that staying in public space as a habitual dwelling shall be illegal.'[8] At the municipal level, local authorities, numbering approximately 3200, are obliged to protect people who are without a roof; for example, through services for the homeless. Thus, there is no legal or constitutional duty to provide housing or shelter for homeless people. At the same time, the Fundamental Law criminalizes homelessness (sleeping rough).[9]

The mortgage law grounds for eviction derive from regulations that are included in the Civil Law. The main characteristic of mortgages is that

---

[7] TENLAW (n 2).

[8] Ibid 81. As of October 15, 2018, the regulation has been amended, with an additional emphasis of the enforcement of the prohibition of rough sleeping.

[9] R Bence and T Udvarhelyi, 'The growing criminalization of homelessness in Hungary – a brief overview' (2013) 7 (2) *European Journal of Homelessness* 133.

they ensure the priority of the lender with mortgage right over other lenders. Thus, in cases of non-payment, the lender with mortgage right will be the first in line for loan repayment in the event of foreclosure. Hence, the grounds for eviction are firmly connected with the right to foreclosure based on mortgage non-repayment.

The Chamber of Judicial Executors is responsible for executing mortgage foreclosure procedures (beyond many other execution procedures based on other types of outstanding debts). Defaulted mortgages in Hungary account for approximately 20 per cent of the total outstanding loans (over 900 000 in 2016), and it is submitted that evictions only concern a minimal fraction of the defaulted mortgagees. The loan contracts' structure has been designed in a way that it includes an execution clause issued by a notary public, which means that in the case of non-compliance with the contractual obligations (that is, regular payment), a foreclosure procedure may be started,[10] which makes the foreclosure process practically automatic,[11] even in the case of small debts.[12] This is one of the key issues in the mortgage system that is related to the process of evictions. There is an eviction moratorium for the winter months each year to counteract evictions in the most problematic months. The moratorium is not valid for squatters but is valid in the rented sector. Furthermore, there have been several government interventions to reduce outstanding mortgage debts and therefore the chance of foreclosure and evictions for families with outstanding mortgage payments.[13]

Having regard to the private rental sector, Hungarian laws ensure the protection of possession of the sitting tenants over other stakeholders' rights, which means that if a tenant will not leave a rented dwelling, even if he or she does not comply with the rules set out in the contract, there is a strict execution/eviction procedure to make him or her leave, which might take up to 2–3 years. The private rented sector is severely under-regulated and underreported, mainly due to tax evasion. Accordingly, there are very few court cases relating to this tenure type. It is much more widespread in the private rental sector that seized contracts (if there was a contract at all for the rental) are enforced 'illegally'. Such

---

[10] See Act XLI of 1991 on civil law notaries ('the Notaries Act').

[11] Courts (judges) only get involved if the debtor issues an appeal against the enforcement procedure.

[12] Such cases were mentioned as the most problematic ones in interviews with the judge, the National Office of Judges, and the Chamber of Judicial Executors.

[13] See Section 8 below for further details.

enforcement includes: sending stern reminders to pay, exercising pressure on the tenant to leave the home, and in extreme cases, by shutting down public utility services. A phenomenon closely linked with the unregulated nature of the sector is the lack of registration of the tenants in the private rentals. Frequently, the tenants do not have a direct contract with the public utility service providers, hence they have no personal 'responsibility' for paying the bills (they do not become registered customers of the given utility service). Consequently, the utility companies may launch execution processes against the real estate, and thus, against the private landlord. Hence, in cases of non-paying (unregistered) tenants, it is the landlord who gets into difficulties and may face execution and 'eviction' in cases where he or she cannot regulate the debt in a timely manner.

The basic eviction procedure for the private rental sector is essentially the same as the procedure for owner-occupied housing with a mortgage; the difference being that the eviction process is launched by the landlord. In cases where the rental contract contains an execution clause (because the contract was verified by a notary public); a relatively quick execution procedure may be launched, which may be followed by an eviction process.[14] There are no mandatory grounds for eviction. Discretionary rights for eviction stem from breaching the rental contract and the details of the rental contract are regulated under contract law, whereas the minimum contents of the contract are regulated by the Housing Act. Eviction procedures are launched in a fraction of cases by landlords, and they are launched usually because the tenant does not leave the dwelling after the termination of the contract.

In Hungary, social housing is regulated under the Housing Act, supplemented by important provisions in the Act on Local Governments (as the Local Governments are the owners of social housing), and the Civil Code (for contractual relations in general). Compared to other tenures, it is the municipal sector that initiates the least enforcement and eviction processes, despite the fact that this sector has a large over-representation of non-paying tenants; who have low payment ability rather than low payment morale. Based on data published by the Central Statistics Office (CSO),[15] outstanding rent payments account for 36 per cent of the total potential rent revenue, whereas only a very small fraction of the tenants get evicted on an annual basis.

---

[14]   Process for emptying the flat by the tenant.
[15]   CSO, *Social Statistics* (Budapest, CSO 2012); CSO, *Social Statistics* (Budapest, CSO 2013).

The legal procedure leading to evictions is based on several legal sources. Pursuant to the Housing Act, the municipality notifies the tenant that he or she has outstanding rent payments to be repaid. If there is no response from the tenant after the second or third notice, the municipality launches the termination of the contract based on non-payment. The termination of the contract is issued by the notary of the municipality and the tenant receives a notice that his or her title to the rental has been terminated. In effect this means that the tenant should leave the apartment. More commonly, municipalities will request the tenant to pay a higher fee for usage. In cases where the tenant does not cooperate in settling the debts, the municipality launches an execution procedure to make the tenant pay. In instances where the tenant does not leave voluntarily, the municipality may launch a vacating procedure based on the Judicial Execution Act. Tenants may appeal against the procedure on the basis of the general execution regulation. In cases where the tenant has a contract with an undetermined time, the municipality is obliged to offer another public rental to move to, in order to ensure the family does not become homeless.

As stated, the municipal rental sector is considered the most secure and tolerant tenure type as regards non-payment. However, tenants in the public sector often fail to realize that non-payment of rent may lead to eviction. Furthermore, a tenant who has been evicted from public housing on a number of occasions will be prohibited from seeking this form of tenure for at least five years.[16] This means that losing a public tenancy may result in a longer period of extreme housing insecurity (because for example, transitory homes only take up clients for 1+1 years).

Unauthorized occupancy exists both in the private and the social rented sector. Often, the termination of a rental contract brings about 'unauthorized occupancy' situations, which can be a ground for evictions from the municipal stock. As described above, however, only a fraction of such tenancy situations are sanctioned with eviction procedures. Overall, based on data published by the CSO in 2010, approximately 10 per cent of all evictions from public housing occur because of illegal/unauthorized occupancy (mostly performed by former 'regular' tenants who lose their title to the dwelling). In the case of squatting in private housing or self-build tents on private land, there is very limited information regarding the scale of the problem, and there is no comprehensive data on evictions either. The main issue leading to evictions in this sector is that

---

[16] The length of the ban is determined by each local municipality and thus may vary from one municipality to another.

unauthorized occupancy violates the right to the protection of property. Therefore, private or public owners can easily sue illegal occupants.

Squatters who have been residing in the given housing unit for less than one year can be evicted based on a decision issued by the concerned municipality's notary.[17] The requestor has to deliver well founded arguments and also has to ensure that the movables of the evicted persons are stored adequately within the timeframe determined by law (30 days). In cases where the residents can prove that they have been occupying the land/dwelling for more than one year, an execution process in court must be launched. In cases of units for housing purposes, the court issues a decision within five working days. Should the family remain at the property, a court case for vacating the property has to be launched under the Civil Code.

The procedure has well-defined steps (including several stages of notification). However, in contrast to the cases related to other tenancies, challenging the procedure does not result in suspension of the procedure and the eviction must be executed, unless the parties are able to reach an agreement.

There is no data regarding the extent of unauthorized occupancy and informal housing solutions in general. Moreover, there is no information on the extent of evictions. The data available reports at aggregate level only about the so-called 'defined action' based execution and eviction processes, which include evictions based on termination of rental contracts also. Although there are purportedly many unregulated titles (formally unauthorized occupancies), to very low standard living conditions, similar to housing in segregated Roma neighbourhoods, pocket contracts 'ensure' more or less clear rental or ownership arrangements and situations. In cases where there is no public interest to clear the titles in such neighbourhoods, for example where there is no investment or Roma housing integration programmes, residents are seldom committed to resolve the titles.

Regulations concerning temporary dispossession relate to issues arising from domestic violence. Nevertheless, barring orders only last for 30 days in Hungary, and such orders are disconnected from any sort of execution procedure or eviction procedure in the Hungarian legal system. There may be cases when a divorce ends with the division of property, and in some cases, these are connected with the execution of the property or part of the property; if the party that remains in the dwelling cannot compensate the party who leaves.

---

[17]   Based on Government Decree 228/2009 (X. 16.).

There are no soft-law arrangements utilized by courts and/or other parties that directly influence the extent of evictions. It is asserted that the small number of evictions due to mortgage arrears is linked to the banks' objective of mitigating the risk of large-scale foreclosures that would affect the banks' financial stability. Nevertheless, in 2009, the State Control Agency for Financial Institutions (currently merged with the Hungarian National Bank), launched a 'Code of Conduct' for all financial lending institutions ('Magatartási kódex a lakosság részére hitelt nyújtó pénzügyi szervezetek ügyfelekkel szembeni tisztességes magatartásáról'). The circle group of signing financial institutions is quite large, and by mid 2010, over 275 institutions joined the supporters' group (including 13 banks).[18] The supporters covered approximately 95 per cent of the volume of all residential loans at that time.[19] The Codex was enacted in early 2010 and updated in 2015.[20] The Codex states that beyond providing the best possible symmetry of information and the least possible burdening of the mortgagors with increased costs, the banks should undertake several steps to handle the risk of non-payment and foreclosure (for example, by providing at least 90 days for the indebted household to sell its property before the foreclosure process is launched).

4. EXTENT OF EVICTIONS FOR THE PERIOD 2010–2017

Due to the general lack of data, only limited quantitative information is available on the extent of evictions, for example, for selected parts of the country or parts of Budapest. The lack of data stems from a severely underdeveloped reporting system of the main actor in the domain of evictions, the Judicial Executor's Chamber. The collection of data is regulated by the Act on Judicial Execution;[21] however, it is constrained to collecting aggregate data on the number of procedures and executions

---

18   See the list available at <https://www.mnb.hu/letoltes/alairok-1301129.xlsx>.
19   See   <http://felugyelet.mnb.hu/topmenu/sajto/pszafhu_sajtokozlemenyek/10_01_14-mag_kodex.html>.
20   'Magatartási kódex a lakosság részére hitelt nyújtó pénzügyi szervezetek ügyfelekkel szembeni tisztességes magatartásáról' (9 September 2009) <http://felugyelet.mnb.hu/data/cms2043084/magatartasi_kodex.pdf>; <https://www.mnb.hu/letoltes/aktualizalt-magatartasi-kodex-szovege-1.pdf>.
21   Act on Judicial Execution, Act LIII of 1994, para 250.

relating to real estate property. Other statistical data was collated based on interviews and general statistical sources as cited.[22]

There is no information concerning regional differences on evictions. Nevertheless, taking into account the levels of economic hardship faced by the population in the different parts of Hungary, it can be assumed that evictions based on non-payment of utility bills and loans might be more frequent in less developed regions on the one hand (mainly North-Hungary, Northern Great Plain and South-West Hungary), and in urban areas on the other hand, where the majority of social and private rental housing is, the first comprising the bulk of the most vulnerable population, the second being a very insecure tenure in Hungary.[23] Conversely, the de facto eviction and execution processes are two distinct actions.

Execution processes against real estate, immovable property in general, including land, other types of buildings, industrial premises etc., have been launched in many more cases (over 40 000 in 2013) than what has led to actual evictions and vacating of dwellings. In many instances, for example, the indebted household sells the dwelling and compensates the outstanding debt before the 'end' of the procedure; or the property cannot be sold because the property market is down and the creditor terminates the procedure etc. The number of housing units designated for sale in the framework of an execution process was approximately 2500 in 2013, out of which 517 ended with eviction.[24] In 2016, the figure grew to over 3100, with over 1734 evictions during the year.[25] 2017 saw an increase to over 3600, with approximately 2300 evictions during the year.[26]

The official statistics on evictions is produced by the Hungarian Chamber of Court Bailiffs (Magyar Bírósági Végrehajtó Kamara). The

---

[22]   A major resource of findings in this analysis is the Hungarian report delivered in the framework of the TENLAW project, one of the authors of which, Nóra Tosics, has contributed to both pieces of research and was the legal expert involved in both studies. The TENLAW project's full title is: Tenancy Law and Housing Policy in Multi-level Europe. The project has received funding from the European Union's Seventh Framework Programme for research, technological development and demonstration under grant agreement no 290694.

[23]   TENLAW (n 2).

[24]   We may claim that the difference is a figure which corresponds with the project's aim to uncover forced sales that are categorized as a process of becoming homeless. In the rest of the cases, it is not possible to claim this.

[25]   See <https://www.mbvk.hu/info.php> and <https://mno.hu/belfold/rekordot-dontott-iden-a-kilakoltatasok-szama-1377471>.

[26]   See <https://mno.hu/belfold/csaknem-hetezer-kilakoltatas-tortent-ket-ev-alatt-2432653>.

organization registers all procedures launched, including confiscation of movables and immovables of various types (for example, agricultural land), and evictions of private households, in addition to data on the type of outstanding debts that lead to the execution of the activities of bailiffs. The public statistics, however, do not include data on the composition or circumstances of affected households, nor do they offer any opportunities to follow up on the families that have been evicted. Further detailed data is available on evictions due to defaulted mortgages (mainly foreign exchange), via the Hungarian Financial Supervisory Authority,[27] since the end of 2011, when the regulation on the quota for forced sales was enacted. Banks committed themselves to put a maximum 2 per cent in 2011, 3 per cent in 2012, and 4 per cent in 2013 of all homes on sale out of the defaulted households' housing stock per year. The banks, however, do not make use of the full quota. Thus, since the end of 2011, overall approximately 20 000 homes (2000 to 3000 per quarter year) were included in the execution phase (out of over 115 000 defaulted mortgages).[28] The quota was lifted in 2015.

The data on launched procedures and enacted evictions[29] show the following trend:

In general, in 2011, over 430 000 procedures were launched and only 20 per cent of them were due to outstanding loan repayments (the remainder were due to outstanding housing cost payments such as rent, electricity, gas, water, etc. or parking fines), and close to 40 000 cases were to be executed as auctions. Approximately 9 per cent of all auctions affected diverse real estate including agricultural or industrial land (the remainder of the auctions were not executed because the owners and lenders found other solutions or because it was impossible to sell the immovable property. The total figure on effective auctions, which has been fluctuating around 3000 generally for various types of real estate in the years around 2014, has not increased compared to pre-crisis years.[30]

---

[27] The Authority (in Hungarian 'Pénzügyi Szervezetek Állami Felügyelete') was merged with the Hungarian National Bank in 2013.

[28] See <http://index.hu/gazdasag/2013/07/01/kikakoltatas_ami_eddig_vot_meg_semmi/>.

[29] The procedure itself may take 1–4 years. The annual moratorium on evictions runs from 1 December to the end of spring the following year, and has been running since 2010.

[30] See <http://www.origo.hu/gazdasag/20130222-napi-gazdasag-nem-a-bankok-eroltetik-a-kilakoltatasokat.html>

The annual figure of effective evictions of families from their homes was around 300 per year, despite increasing mortgage defaults and despite having grown by over 50 per cent between 2011 and 2012;[31] a massive increase occurred after 2015. The figure was approximately 200 in 2011, and 300 in 2012 and 2013.[32] Between 2015 and 2016, a dramatic increase occurred from 626 to over 1730 and to 2017 to over 3000. The Hungarian Chamber of Court Bailiffs estimated that 80 per cent of those whose homes were auctioned, moved to residences of family and friends or to private rentals, which indicates that those who were evicted to the streets, represent about 20 per cent of all cases.[33] Even in such cases, it was estimated in 2014 that within a couple of days, the belongings of those evicted were moved from the storage location used in the course of the eviction process to a new location.

It must be added that the majority of completed evictions take place two to three years after the launch of the initial eviction process. The exception concerns the dozen or so cases involving squatters, where the eviction process is much shorter and can lead to eviction in less than a year. Official evictions from the private rental sector are less than a dozen per year within the figures indicated in Table 4.1. Evictions from the social rental sector (that can reach even up to 500–1000 per year, according to the interviews conducted in the framework of the preparation of the Hungarian Report for the National Eviction study[34]), are not indicated in Table 4.1.

Regarding evictions from the public rented sector, a more recent study on the housing management of Hungarian municipalities, who are exclusive landlords in the social rented sector, points to the fact that two out of three landlords (among towns in their survey), have outstanding rent payments amounting to over 20 per cent of the total rent, which makes the sector unsustainable. The number of evictions, accordingly, can be directly linked with sanctioning non-payment to achieve a more manageable pool of tenants. In the course of 2007–2013, for every 1000 flats, the number of evictions increased from 5 to 9.2, with some ups and downs across the period.[35]

---

[31]   See <http://hvg.hu/itthon/20120301_kilakoltatasi_moratorium_kormany>.

[32]   See <http://hvg.hu/itthon/20130307_Indulhatnak_a_kilakoltatasok>.

[33]   See <http://www.origo.hu/jog/lakossagi/20121108-a-remhirek-ellenere-az-idei-kilakoltatasok-szama-250-alatt-maradt.html>.

[34]   See <http://ec.europa.eu/social/BlobServlet?docId=15544&langId=en>.

[35]   M Czirfusz and Z Pósfai, 'Kritikus ponton? Önkormányzati lakásgaz-dálkodás a gazdasági világválság után' ('At a critical point? Municipal housing

Table 4.1 Number of evictions in Hungary 2007–2017

Year	Number of evictions
2007	248
2008	247
2009	367
2010	moratorium
2011	199
2012*	234
2013**	517
2014	moratorium
2015	626**
2016	1734**
2017	over 2300***

Notes:
* Hungarian Chamber of Court Bailiffs quoted in <http://www.napi.hu/ingatlan/nem_tudjak_elarverezni_az_kenyszerertekesitett_ingatlanokat_.553344.html>.
** Hungarian Chamber of Court Bailiffs.

Source: Hungarian Chamber of Court Bailiffs quoted in <http://www.napi.hu/magyar_gazdasag/igy_bukjak_el_lakasukat_az_adosok_meglepo_tenyek_az_arveresekrol.546015.html>.
*** Hungarian Chamber of Court Bailiffs quoted in <https://mno.hu/belfold/csaknem-hetezer-kilakoltatas-tortent-ket-ev-alatt-2432653>.

5. RISK FACTORS IDENTIFIED LEADING TO EVICTIONS

The main risk factor for the initiation of execution/foreclosure procedure(s) in the owner-occupied sector concerns defaulted mortgage loans secured by the debtor's dwelling (or other person's dwelling). Falling into arrears with mortgage payments is often connected to the break-up of the household and the subsequent decrease in household income. Among mortgage loans, foreign exchange loans would appear to indicate the highest risk in terms of falling into arrears. The scale of the potential risk, based on the share of owner-occupied housing with mortgage in Hungary, is approximately 20 per cent, which is close to 23 per cent of all

management after the great financial crisis') (2015) 55 (5) *Területi Statisztika [Territorial Statistics]* 484–504.

dwellings in homeownership. There are, however, relatively few fore-closures actioned on the basis of a defaulted mortgage loan. This is because banks usually try to resolve the matter through negotiating with the homeowner in default to achieve some other solution, such as selling the property on the open market in advance of foreclosure.

For tenants in public rentals, falling behind in rent and/or other utility fee payments are the main risk factors, and the same is true for tenants in the private rental sector; however, the latter are more at risk of being illegally evicted (forced to leave) since the private rental sector mostly operates as a black market economy. Tenancy fraud in the social rental sector may also result in eviction for those convicted.

There is no data on the relative importance of the various risk factors linked to evictions. There is only qualitative information such as inter-views with judges, lawyers and municipalities, summarized in daily media, on the causes leading to execution procedures. According to the experiences of some homeless service providers, most homeless persons are former tenants in the private rental sector who were evicted for being unable to pay the rent, usually because they have lost their job in the informal sector.

It should be pointed out that while the number of initiated execution procedures is high (although the exact number is unknown); those resulting in the auction of the dwelling is much lower, and those resulting in actual eviction lower again. These observations apply only to the public rental sector since data is not available for the private rental sector, as discussed above.

It is suggested that the main risk factors for execution procedures are mainly due to adverse economic circumstances that have worsened on account of the long-lasting effects of the economic crisis such as unemployment, decrease of income and, in the case of mortgage loans, the increased monthly repayments. Increased loan repayments are espe-cially relevant not only in cases involving foreign exchange loans but also in cases where people have taken out several loans. Some people are simply uneducated on the possible consequences of taking out multiple loans. Others often use subsequent loans to pay off their defaults. The negligence of debtors regarding legal procedures can also play an important role in cases reaching ultimate phases (auction/eviction). For example, debtors (owners and tenants) may fail to cooperate with claimants or respond to their warnings (letters, telephone calls etc.), or fail to make use of the legal and social protection tools that are available to them and which may help them to alleviate their financial situation. This is often the case when people see their situation as hopeless, which typically applies to isolated, poorly educated individuals who are experiencing psychological problems. Economic reasons by themselves seldom lead to homelessness, even in cases of eviction; but only when related to other mental and psychological problems.[36]

6. LINKS BETWEEN EVICTIONS AND HOMELESSNESS

The so-called 'February 3' annual homeless surveys include data on the reasons for becoming homeless. According to the survey conducted in 2011, 43.5 per cent of homeless people surveyed indicated that losing their housing had been the direct reason for becoming homeless. The survey also revealed that 6.3 per cent were evicted, 15 per cent could no longer pay their rent (in private and public rentals), 7.7 per cent were homeless following eviction from accommodation provided by a former employer, 6.5 per cent were expelled from their home, 4.8 per cent were victims of housing fraud or misbehaviour, and 3.2 per cent had become homeless because their home was no longer inhabitable. However, only 37.7 per cent of the respondents lived in a home to which they had legal title (either as a tenant or an owner), 21.4 per cent were owners (or had usufructuary rights), and 16.3 per cent were public or private tenants. The survey also revealed that half of the respondents had experienced a gradual home loss process ('housing slope'), and the other half had never enjoyed a stable, secure housing situation. Furthermore, 12 per cent of the respondents became homeless after being released from an institution such as prison or a hospital.[37]

Information on the various types of homelessness occurring after an eviction is sporadic. The above survey, and the interviews that were conducted as part of the survey, indicate that homelessness is often the

---

[36] The so called 'February 3' homeless count indicates that by 2012 the number of people having lost their home as a direct result of an uncertain housing situation and worsening economic circumstances had increased. Gyorsjelentés a 2013. évi Február Harmadika felvételröl: <http://nonprofit.hu/sites/default/files/article/2013/3/gyorsjelent%C3%A9s-hajl%C3%A9ktalan-emberek-2013-febru%C3%A1r-3-i-k%C3%A9rd%C5%91%C3%ADves-adatfelv%C3%A9tel%C3%A9r%C5%91l/hajlektalan_gyorsjelentes_2013feb3.doc>.

[37] Péter Breitner, 'A hajléktalanság lakástörténeti elözményei' ('Antecendents in the housing pathways of homeless') in Györi Péter and Vida Judith (eds) *Változó és változatlan arcú hajléktalanság. Otthontalanul ... Tégy az emberért!* (Budapest, Menhely Alapítvány and BMSZKI 2013).

final stage of a process in which people get into more and more insecure forms of housing, which are often of inferior quality.

The 2011 survey indicates that it is only the most vulnerable who end up sleeping rough directly after eviction, while others find places to live with their family or friends.[38] However, there is no information available on how stable and secure such solutions would be (eg what percentage of the concerned people enjoy it as long-term solution, whereas according to ETHOS,[39] it would also mean a form of homelessness).

The qualitative information also suggests that eviction or other forms of home loss, such as voluntary sale in the event of mortgage default, do not lead directly to homelessness (in the ETHOS typology: roofless, houseless); more often, those affected will either move to their relatives or friends or, if they are former owner-occupiers, to the private rental market.[40]

In cases where people remain homeless after being evicted, it is more likely that they first go to night shelters, as temporary shelters are of low capacity. The study also indicated that people who have no social relationships or friends are more likely to end up on the street, while those who still have contact with social workers and neighbours, for example, are more likely to go to a shelter.

Groups at higher risk of homelessness following an eviction are single elderly people without family; people who have lost their income or have a very low income; isolated people, often with some mental and physical problems; and divorced people, among them mainly men, all of whom very commonly having been evicted from private rentals.[41] Furthermore, less educated people with less stable family backgrounds, among them young people, are more at risk of homelessness, especially if other factors such as mental illness or instability and substance abuse accompany the other factors.[42]

The study also indicated that the number of homeless people with some form of disability or long-term illness is increasing. In percentage

---

[38] For example, the President of the Chamber of Judicial Executors claimed that the movables of evicted families never stay longer than two to three days in the storage facility used to hold possessions before they are transferred to the next place of accommodation.

[39] European Typology of Homelessness and Housing Exclusion (ETHOS).

[40] One of the practising judges interviewed stated that out of 250 execution procedures in a Budapest district that houses low-income families, one person became homeless.

[41] Breitner (n 37).

[42] These figures also indicate a weakening social protection system.

terms, this group comprised 53 per cent of the homeless population of Budapest, and 47 per cent of the homeless population of other cities and towns in Hungary in 2012.[43]

7. BEST PRACTICE MODELS FOR PREVENTING, TACKLING AND REACTING TO EVICTIONS

Anti-eviction and early intervention measures are part of the general social transfer system to promote housing affordability. The system has been changed several times in the past fifteen years. In more recent years, the coverage of the housing allowance scheme was approximately 500 000 households,[44] covering 10–15 per cent of the normative housing costs, depending on the household income level; and hence providing only very limited help with covering housing expenses. In March 2015, the housing allowance in its then current form was stopped and local governments now define the eligibility criteria and fund this benefit themselves. In 2013, the state launched a housing cost compensation programme. Under this scheme, utility service providers have to give customers a 3 to 10 per cent reduction in utility costs based on a national level regulation.[45] This subsidy is regressive, however: the scheme is designed in such a way that households who are able to finance larger housing consumption actually receive a larger grant.

A central housing costs arrears management scheme was in place between 2003 and 2015, with very limited coverage compared to the number of indebted households. It was available mainly in larger towns and cities and compensated 75 per cent of a limited amount of debt for very low-income households. After a peak in 2011, when the number of participating households reached approximately 19 000, the number for 2013 showed a considerable reduction to 7000. Some municipalities, including Budapest, run additional local arrears management schemes. However, due to the fact that private sector tenancies are not reported or registered, tenants seldom had access to the scheme (similar to the

---

[43] Február Harmadika Munkacsoport: Gyorsjelentés a hajléktalan emberek 2013. február 3-i kérdőíves adatfelvételéröl. Összefoglaló, elöadás. (February 3rd Working Group: Preliminary results on homeless survey on 3rd of February, 2013) <http://www.menhely.hu/index.php/hajlektalansagrol/februar-3>.
[44] Hungarian Central Statistics Office data for 2012, for a total of approximately 3.8 million households.
[45] See Act LIV of 2013 on Reduction of housing costs [Törvény a rezsicsökkentések végrehajtásáról].

housing allowance scheme, which is also tied to clear title). There are also a number of NGO programmes that are based on counselling and facilitating negotiations between indebted households and service providers (including private landlords); again, however, the coverage is low and only a couple of hundred households benefit from these programmes. In Budapest, for example, the so called 'Crisis Subsidy' programme has been working for more than a decade in order to prevent the evictions of those whose tenancy contract is to be (or has been) terminated because of rent arrears. The programme, which provides financial support to pay off the debts (rent and public utility fees), is financed by the publicly owned public utility companies and operated by the Hálózat Alapítvány (Network Foundation). The subsidy can be claimed through a social service organization; for instance, the district family social service centres. In some other municipalities, smaller dwellings (with lower maintenance costs) are provided for indebted public rental tenants. In Szombathely (a medium-sized city), there is a special programme (Social Accommodation) for public sector tenants who have accumulated arrears. In addition to being accommodated in smaller and cheaper dwellings, they participate in a special arrears management programme and closely cooperate with the social service centre and make an agreement on how to pay off their debt (or a part of it). On this condition, the municipality writes off the same amount of debt as they paid in case of rent arrears, while setting a minimum level of rent (which can be as low €3 per month). The Municipality of District IV in Budapest also makes it possible for tenants to downscale to a smaller apartment even after their rental contract has been terminated provided that they can make an agreement to pay off their debts.

In 2012, the question of indebted households facing hardship paying back foreign currency loans became a political priority and the government launched several further programmes to 'rescue' the mortgagors. Beyond supporting several financial schemes, the government established the National Asset Management Company (NAMC), which takes over the ownership of to-be-foreclosed dwellings (enforced mortgages),[46] and concludes a rental contract with the sitting tenants to avoid evictions that would be connected to outstanding repayment of foreign currency mortgage loans. By 2016, the total number of properties taken over and operated by the NAMC as rentals was more than 25 000. The NAMC

---

[46]   Only those households whose housing was included in a foreclosure procedure before 1 January 2013, with over 180 days of delayed mortgage loan repayments, were eligible to be taken over by the NAMC.

takes over the foreclosed housing units from the banks at 55 per cent of the value given in the original mortgage contract in Budapest, 50 per cent in rural areas and 35 per cent in other areas.[47] In this way it serves as a 'get-out clause' for indebted households (in terms of their mortgage loans), and the scheme is also attractive for banks that would otherwise not be able to sell/auction the real estate properties at a reasonable price. As of the end of 2014, the NAMC had purchased some 22 500 dwellings, and approximately 100 tenants had fallen behind with payments and were to be steered into the newly launched NAMC arrears management programme. It was expected that the figure might rise to close to 1500 within a year. The arrears management programme is run by the Hungarian Charity Service of the Order of Malta and the Hungarian Reformed Church, both faith-based organizations. The public family help centres that administer the national arrears management scheme have not been included in the programme.

Although the loan underwriting system is also regulated more rigorously as a result of the mortgage crisis (the share of defaulted mortgages is approximately 20 per cent of the total outstanding loans over 900 000 in Hungary), there is still insufficient information available about the exact content of contracts, contractors' obligations in general and, more specifically, their obligations in the event of default. The new law on 'fair banks' (regulation on macro-prudential regulators) was enacted only in January 2015.[48]

Beyond government-funded subsidy programmes, each year there is an eviction moratorium in the winter months (the moratorium does not apply to squatters).[49] However, there is also a downside to this, since it seems that households' repayment motivation falls back in the moratorium phase of the year, which results in an increasing accumulation of debt, reflected in the yearly figures of started execution procedures and evictions. Beyond these measures, some NGOs provide leaflets and free information and counselling services for families in trouble. Ongoing eviction procedures can be postponed only based on procedural regulations; for example, by challenging the municipality's request for payment at a higher rate.

In summary, there are only very few and ineffective preventative measures for eviction. Moreover, landlords are not obliged to inform any

---

[47] See Government Decree 72/2012. (IV.12.).

[48] See <http://www.jogiforum.hu/hirek/32381> and <https://www.mnb.hu/letoltes/baracsi-lorant-grosz-gabriella-faykiss-peter-jegybanki-szabalyozoi-eszko zokkel-megakadalyozhato-a-tulzott-lakossagi-eladosodas.pdf>.

[49] See Act LIII of 1994 on Judicial Enforcement, para 182/A.

housing or other social services agencies about the threat of an eviction, except when minors are affected. In such cases, child welfare services must ensure that children are placed in child welfare centres (based on the Act on Judicial Enforcement, which ensures that the protection of children is in line with the goals set out in the Act on the Protection of Children).

8. CONCLUSION

To date, there has been little research, and consequently minimal statistical data, on the process of foreclosure and execution procedures. The growing number of households in arrears with housing costs, the failure and closure of arrears management programmes and reduction of housing allowance schemes, the procedures of municipal landlords toward tenants without legal title, and the legal and operational deficiencies of the rental sector (public and private) demonstrate the relevance of the issue in Hungary. The problem is framed by high insecurity in several sub-sectors of the housing market. The uncertain regulation of the private rental sector results in the sector operating largely in the black economy, which means that in a large portion of cases there is either no contract or only a legally unsatisfactory one between the parties. Thus, this tenure form includes high risks for both sides (landlords and tenants), and among them the practice of illegal evictions prevails. According to the municipalities, the Housing Act still contains provisions which disproportionately protect tenants' rights in the case of the public rental sector. Therefore, most of the municipalities use only short-term contracts, which often last only for one year and have to be renewed annually. This way, municipalities can avoid long and expensive court procedures to terminate the contract, but the public tenants' security is reduced because they cannot plan for their housing solutions in the longer run.

An accelerated method of debt collection, the 'payment notice procedure', has been in place for a number of years (the relevant legislation being the Judicial Execution Act of 1991 and the Notaries Act of 1991). The payment notice procedure is the most common way of collecting outstanding payments and it has been placed in the competence of public notaries from the court. Accordingly, no court hearings are organized to discover the most appropriate ways of settling outstanding payments. Although the underwriting system of providing loans has been regulated more rigorously as a result of the mortgage crisis, there is still insufficient information available about the exact content of the contract, the contractors' obligations in general and, more specifically, their obligations in the event of default.

Best practices for combating evictions include providing information to affected households on the main risk factors leading to eviction and homelessness, and contacting social service organizations at the earliest opportunity so that they can provide counselling and other support to at-risk tenants, and develop an arrears management programme with them. A number of municipalities and NGOs engage in these types of practices at a local level. At a national level, however, a more effective cooperation system between social service providers, landlords, local authorities, public utility companies and banks needs to be developed.

5. Evictions in Ireland

Padraic Kenna

---

1. INTRODUCTION

Evictions in Ireland are a socially and politically emotive issue. Ireland experienced a major banking and economic crisis following a period of reckless lending between 1997 and 2007. The consequent banking collapse and associated unemployment led to a steep rise in mortgage arrears, and actions for possessions, which peaked in 2014. Some 20 000 households with arrears over two years face the possibility of eviction. Irish constitutional law requires that any eviction be in accordance with the law on mortgage, rental and other repossessions, although human rights issues are not often considered. Most evictions are from private rented housing, with a six-fold increase in eviction-related cases between 2010–2015/16. There is a small social rented sector in Ireland, where some evictions take place. Overall, a shortage of housing for rent, or purchase, results in fierce competition for any available housing, and homelessness is consistently increasing, largely among those evicted from private rented housing. Properly addressing the extent of mortgage arrears and the position of households in long-term arrears has presented challenges for legislators, policy makers and Irish courts.

2. POLICY BACKGROUND

2.1 General Housing Policy Related to Evictions

Housing policy in Ireland has generally promoted owner-occupation, with a range of state supports and subsidies. The state also provides some means-tested social housing support, through direct provision, or rent support for those renting privately.[1] The structure of the Irish housing system of 1.7 million occupied homes in 2016 was as follows: owner-occupier without mortgage/loan (31.5 per cent); owner-occupier with mortgage/loan (27.7 per cent); renting from a private landlord (18.5 per cent); local authority (state) tenants (12 per cent); voluntary/cooperative housing body tenants (1 per cent).[2]

2.2 Structural/Societal Factors Related to Evictions

Between 1998 and 2008, Ireland's residential mortgage lending increased four-fold, as the number of lenders and mortgage products expanded.[3] National house prices quadrupled in this period.[4] After the financial crisis in 2007–2008, there was a collapse, not just of house prices by 50 per cent, but of the main lending institutions in the State; and later, following a State guarantee of these lenders' liabilities, to a collapse in the State finances, and a general recession with high levels of unemployment. Banking debt had become sovereign debt, and in 2010, the Irish Government agreed to a Programme of Financial Support and Memorandum of Understanding with the European Union (EU) and the International Monetary Fund (IMF). This required that the banking system be restructured and recapitalized, and €67.5 billion was conditionally made

[1] See Department of Housing, Planning and Local Government, 'Housing Policy' <http://www.housing.gov.ie/housing/housing-policy>.

[2] Central Statistics Office (CSO), Census 2016 (Dublin, Stationery Office 2016) <http://www.cso.ie/en/media/csoie/newsevents/documents/census2016 summaryresultspart1/Census2016SummaryPart1.pdf>.

[3] See Houses of the Oireachtas, 'Report of the Joint Committee of Inquiry into the Banking Crisis' (2016) Vols 1 & 2; P Honohan, *The Irish Banking Crisis – Regulatory and Financial Stability Policy 2003–2008 – A Report to the Minister for Finance by the Governor of the Central Bank* (Dublin, Central Bank 2010) <http://www.bankinginquiry.gov.ie/Background.aspx>; Commission of Investigation into the Banking Sector in Ireland, *Misjudging Risk: Causes of the Systemic Banking Crisis in Ireland* (Dublin, Stationery Office 2011) (The Nyberg Report); K Regling and M Watson, *A Preliminary Report into the Sources of Ireland's Banking Crisis* (Dublin, The Stationery Office 2010); 'The Cost of Reckless Lending' *The Irish Times* 24 January 2014, <https://www.irishtimes.com/business/financial-services/the-cost-of-reckless-lending-1.1665936>.

[4] See M Norris and D Coates, 'How housing killed the Celtic Tiger: anatomy and consequences of Ireland's housing boom and bust' (2014) 29 (2) *Journal of Housing and the Built Environment* 299–315. The State currently owns 70% of Allied Irish Banks, 75% of Permanent TSB, and 14% of Bank of Ireland, having provided a bail-out of €30bn to these lenders and a further €35bn to other insolvent banks who were involved in property related lending.

available through the European Financial Stability Facility (EFSF), the European Financial Stabilisation Mechanism (EFSM) and the IMF, with bilateral loans from the United Kingdom, Sweden and Denmark. Ireland exited this arrangement in December 2013, but the level of government (and private) debt remains relatively high.

Unemployment rates rose dramatically to 15.2 per cent in 2012, followed by mortgage arrears.[5] By December 2015, of the 750 000 mortgage accounts, some 12 per cent were in arrears, with almost half of these in arrears over two years, amounting to 80 per cent of outstanding balances.[6] There were also 120 000 situations where mortgage lenders had restructured mortgages to avoid repossessions, through a switch to interest-only payments, reduction in payment amount, extension of the mortgage term, capitalizing arrears and related interest, and other measures.[7] Significant numbers of these accounts are with non-bank entities often referred to as 'vulture funds', who have purchased these loans at a significant discount to the nominal loan figure.[8] These adopt a more aggressive repossession approach and a significant proportion of mortgage repossession cases involve these non-bank entities.

2.3 Specific Policies Related to Evictions

Following a change in government after the banking collapse of 2007–2008, the 'Housing Policy Statement' in 2011 stated that the Government was 'acutely conscious of the difficulties faced by households in arrears on mortgage repayments and potentially at risk of losing their homes. A modern and compassionate State must seek to assist such households in a

---

[5] CSO, 'Seasonally Adjusted Monthly Unemployment Rates 2008–2017', <http://www.cso.ie/multiquicktables/quickTables.aspx?id=mum01>.

[6] These figures are supplied by the Central Bank of Ireland. Section 3(a) of the CCMA states that: 'a mortgage arrears problem arises as soon as the borrower fails to make a mortgage repayment by the due date.' Mortgage accounts are loans to individuals for house or apartment purchase, renovation, improvement or own construction of housing fully or completely secured by a mortgage on the residential property which is or will be occupied by the borrower as his/her principal private residence. 'Top up' of existing mortgages are also included.

[7] See <http://www.centralbank.ie/polstats/stats/mortgagearrears/Pages/releases. asp>.

[8] According to the Central Bank of Ireland, non-bank entities comprise regulated retail credit firms and unregulated loan owners. Unregulated loan owners include owners of mortgages not regulated by the Central Bank of Ireland that have purchased mortgage loans secured on Irish residential properties.

measured and proportionate way.'[9] In relation to mortgage arrears the need to enhance State supports to keep people in their homes has been acknowledged. These measures include the Code of Conduct on Mortgage Arrears (CCMA), reform of the conveyancing and insolvency legislation, funding for advice agencies, such as the Money Advice and Budgeting Service (MABS), and a Mortgage To Rent (MTR) scheme.[10]

The CCMA is a 'soft law' code, introduced by the Central Bank setting out the arrangements by lenders for dealing with mortgage arrears.[11] Significant numbers of distressed borrowers avoid losing their homes through these approaches, although these are primarily based on the commercial decisions of the lender and not subject to judicial review.[12]

The law relating to mortgage related evictions was updated in 2009, and requires lenders to obtain a possession order from the courts prior to repossession, unless there is consent.[13] This legislation obliges lenders to use the local Circuit Courts for enforcing the security on 'housing loans',[14] and there are clear rules for the process of repossession.[15] For mortgages created after 2009, courts can adjourn, postpone or suspend possession orders to enable an arrangement for the mortgagor in arrears

---

[9] Department of Environment, Community and Local Government, *Housing Policy Statement* (Dublin, Department of Environment 2011) <http://www.environ. ie/en/DevelopmentHousing/Housing/PublicationsDocuments/FileDownLoad,268 67,en.pdf>.

[10] Department of Environment, Community and Local Government, *Rebuilding Ireland: Action Plan for Housing and Homelessness* (Dublin, Department of Environment 2016) 33.

[11] See Section 3.7 below.

[12] See P Joyce and S Stamp, *Redressing the Imbalance: A Study of Legal Protections Available for Consumers of Credit and Other Financial Services in Ireland* (Dublin, Free Legal Advice Centres – FLAC 2014).

[13] See s 97 LCLRA 2009; *Irish Life and Permanent PLC v Duff* [2013] IEHC 43.

[14] In Pt 12 of Sch 3 to the Central Bank and Financial Services Authority of Ireland Act 2004, a 'housing loan' is defined as an agreement for provision of credit on security of a mortgage of a freehold or leasehold estate or interest in land: for purposes of constructing, improving existing house or buying a house as principal residence of that person or their dependents, or refinancing credit for any of these purposes. The borrower must be a 'consumer' ie a natural person acting outside the person's business.

[15] SI No 264 of 2009, Circuit Court Rules (Actions for Possession and Well-Charging Relief) 2009; SI No 358 of 2012, Circuit Court Rules (Actions For Possession and Well-Charging Relief) 2012; SI No 346 of 2015, Circuit Court Rules (Actions For Possession and Well-Charging Relief) 2015; SI No 171 of 2016, Circuit Court Rules (Actions For Possession, Sale and Well-Charging Relief) 2016.

to repay.[16] The Personal Insolvency Act 2012 introduced the Personal Insolvency Arrangement (PIA) for mortgage and unsecured debt. The Insolvency Service of Ireland (ISI) established 'Guidelines on a reasonable standard of living and reasonable living expenses'.[17] The Guidelines safeguard a minimum standard of living, so as to protect debtors while facilitating creditors in recovering all, or at least a portion, of the debts due to them under the insolvency and bankruptcy laws in Ireland. Legislation enacted in 2013 enables a court to adjourn the proceedings in order to facilitate a PIA as an alternative to repossession.[18] Legislation enacted in 2015 allows a Personal Insolvency Practitioner to request a review by a court on behalf of a debtor where a PIA is rejected by creditors.[19] The duration of personal bankruptcy has also been reduced from twelve years to one year.[20]

A MTR scheme was introduced for those whose mortgages were deemed unsustainable and who agreed to voluntarily surrender their homes. It applies to those without significant equity in the mortgaged property, and whose low income qualifies them for social housing support. These debtors can apply to remain in their homes as local authority or Approved Housing Body (AHB) tenants. There are maximum values on the properties which are eligible, and commercial lenders must agree to each application. A review of the scheme in 2017 showed that of the 2723 applications between 2013 and 2016, only 217 MTR schemes were completed with AHBs.[21]

The emphasis in Government policy since the banking collapse has been on avoiding mortgage related evictions. Yet rents in the private

---

[16]   s 101 LCLRA 2009.

[17]   See ISI, *Guidelines on a reasonable standard of living and reasonable living expenses* (Dublin, ISI 2017) 6. 'Reasonable living expenses' are set out to cover fifteen categories, comprising food, clothing, personal care, health, household goods, household services, communications, education, transport, household energy, savings and contingencies, social inclusion and participation, housing and childcare   <https://www.isi.gov.ie/en/ISI/RLEs_Guidelines_July_2017.pdf/Files/RLEs_Guidelines_July_2017.pdf>.

[18]   s 3 LCLRA 2013. See Section 3.7 below.

[19]   The Personal Insolvency (Amendment) Act 2015.

[20]   Bankruptcy (Amendment) Act 2015.

[21]   See Department of Housing, Planning and Local Government (DHPLG), *Review of the Mortgage to Rent Scheme for borrowers of commercial lending institutions* (Dublin, DHPLG 2017) <http://rebuildingireland.ie/install/wp-content/uploads/2017/02/Review-of-the-Mortgage-to-Rent-Scheme-February-2017.pdf>.

rented sector (unregulated until 2017) have become unaffordable for many low income and benefit-dependent households.[22] Landlords have sought rent increases and low-income tenants have been unable to pay, leaving them open to eviction. Almost all family homelessness arises from private rented sector evictions, largely due to rent increases.[23]

However, there are significant levels of State rent support for private sector tenants to prevent evictions, as well as funding for a tenancy sustainment service. Between 2010 and 2015, some €300 million has been paid by the State to support private renters unable to pay rents, with local authorities taking a more active role in arranging tenancies and undertaking to make payments from the Department of Social Protection (see Table 5.1).

Table 5.1   State supports for mortgages and rents

	2010 €million	2015 €million
Mortgage Interest Supplement	17.6	2.9
Rent Supplement paid by Department of Social Protection[24]	516.5	311.0
Rental Accommodation Scheme[25] payments by local authorities	100.0	136.6
Housing Assistance Payment[26] by local authorities	0.4	15.6
Social Housing Leasing Initiative[27]	3.7	42.2
Total support payments	638.2	508.3

[22] The Census 2016 shows that the average weekly rent across the country increased by 16.8% between 2011 and 2016. A form of rent controls in 'Rent Pressure Zones', with increases capped at 4% per annum, was introduced in the Planning and Development (Housing) and Residential Tenancies Act 2016, ss 34 and 36.

[23] See below Section 4.3.1; Focus Ireland, *Housing – Insights into Family Homelessness* <https://www.focusireland.ie/resource-hub/research/>.

[24] In addition, some €550 000 was paid in 2015, as rent allowance for eighty eligible persons in rent-controlled properties. Clare Daly TD, Written Answers, Tuesday 27 September 2016, Ref No. 31606/16. See also Annual SWS Statistical Information Reports.

[25] This scheme involves rent support payments being paid by local authorities and is in addition to the rent supplement figures paid by the Department of Social Protection.

[26] In this scheme, the local authority undertakes to make payments to a private landlord, for a tenant who is unable to pay the rent.

[27] In this scheme, local authorities lease privately owned properties and allocate these to applicants for social housing.

3. LEGAL AND CONSTITUTIONAL BACKGROUND TO PROTECTION AGAINST EVICTIONS

3.1 Housing as a Fundamental Right

There is no fundamental right to housing in Ireland. Article 40.5 of the Irish Constitution (*Bunreacht na hEireann* 1937) states: 'The dwelling of every citizen is inviolable and shall not be forcibly entered save in accordance with law.'[28] There is no statutory obligation to provide housing, but local authorities are empowered to do so in relation to homelessness under the Housing Act 1988, and generally, for those in housing need under the Housing (Miscellaneous) Provisions Act 2009.

3.2 Law Relating to Owner-occupation

The Registrar of the Circuit Court may grant a possession order in cases of mortgage arrears, although not on the first hearing, unless the borrower consents. A borrower intending to defend the proceedings must enter an 'appearance' within ten days of service of the Civil Bill. There are limited defences, such as technical issues on service of proceedings, *non est factum*, or that the mortgage was made on a 'family home' without the consent of the spouse or civil partner.[29] The case of *AIB v Counihan*[30] established the obligation on Irish courts to carry out an own

---

[28]   In *Irish Life and Permanent PLC v Duff* [2013] IEHC 43, para 50, Hogan J stated: 'It is, however, to say that those elements of formal notice, foreseeability and an independent determination of the objective necessity for possession of the dwelling are presupposed by the guarantee of inviolability and these protections cannot be assured outside the judicial process or, at least, something akin to the judicial process'. See also *Fagan v ACC Loan Management* [2016] IEHC 233.

[29]   s 3 Family Home Protection Act 1976 (as amended) and s 28 and s 32 Civil Partnership and Certain Rights and Obligations of Cohabitants Act 2010. In *Irish Life and Permanent v Dunne* [2015] IESC 64, para 5.23, the Irish Supreme Court reiterated this general lack of a defence where the monies have become due: 'In the absence of there being some legal basis on which it can be said that the right to possession has not been established or does not arise, then the only role which the Court may have is, occasionally, to adjourn a case to afford an opportunity for some accommodation to be reached.'

[30]   *AIB v Counihan* [2016] IEHC 752; See European Communities (Unfair Terms in Consumer Contracts) Regulations 1995, SI 1995/27 as amended.

motion assessment for unfair terms in mortgage loans.[31] The revised Circuit Court Rules of 2016[32] state that: 'the failure of a defendant in a home loan mortgage arrears case to enter an Appearance following the Civil Bill issued by the lenders can result in a summary judgment, involving loss of home without any court consideration of the circumstances of the debtor, or their household members situation.'[33]

Where a defence has been filed, a judge will hear the case, and if a possession order is granted, the lender may obtain an execution order directing the County Registrar or Sheriff (in Dublin or Cork), to put the lender in possession of the property without delay. Courts often suspend the possession order or the enforcement of a possession order to enable those being evicted to secure alternative accommodation. The Sheriff or Registrar is required to execute the order within a reasonable period from the date of receipt and may use reasonable force to gain access to the property.

3.3 Law Relating to Private Rented Dwellings

The law on private rented housing is set out in the Residential Tenancies Act 2004 (as amended).[34] This creates a range of binding statutory tenancy provisions which cannot be contracted out of, or avoided, unless the property is part of the landlord's dwelling. Protections include a recurring six year cycle of tenancy (after six months), where possession can only be obtained on a number of prescribed grounds. While there is a theoretical security of tenure, a landlord can terminate a tenancy for many reasons, and there is really no long-term security of tenure.[35] There

---

[31] This obligation arises from Joined Cases C–240/98 and C–244/98 *Océano Grupo Editorial SA v Rocío Murciano Qunitero; Salvat Editores SA v Prades* [2000] ECR I–4941 and followed in Case C–415/11 *Aziz v Catalunyacaix* Judgment of the Court (First Chamber) 14 March 2013.

[32] SI No 171 of 2016: Circuit Court Rules (Actions for Possession, Sale and Well-Charging Relief) 2016.

[33] Ibid 5. 'PLEASE NOTE that unless you file an Appearance with the County Registrar and file the replying affidavit as set out above, you will be held to have admitted the said claim, and the Plaintiff may proceed with the claim against you and judgment may be given against you in your absence without further notice.'

[34] Residential Tenancies (Amendment) Act 2015; Planning and Development (Housing) and Residential Tenancies Act 2016.

[35] The grounds for repossession are: that there has been a failure to comply with the tenancy obligations; the dwelling is no longer suited to the needs of the tenant(s); the landlord intends to sell the property within three months, or

must be a valid written notice of termination, in writing, signed by the landlord (or agent), specifying the date and reasons for termination and other matters, including notice that any issue as to its validity must be referred to the Residential Tenancies Board (RTB) within 28 days.[36] There is a three-step procedure for the termination of a tenancy for rent arrears.[37]

The notice period depends on the duration of the existing tenancy, and ranges from 28 days in tenancies of less than six months, to 224 days in tenancies of eight or more years duration. If the tenant does not vacate, then a dispute resolution application can be submitted to the RTB. The RTB Tribunal may grant a 'Determination Order' approving the eviction, usually after an informal hearing. The party in whose favour a 'Determination Order' has been made (or the RTB on their behalf) may commence enforcement proceedings through the courts, where there has been non-compliance. Thus, the courts exercise important oversight of the eviction process in the private rented sector, although few tenants defend proceedings to the court stage.

An unlawful termination of tenancy, or illegal eviction, is deemed to have taken place where a landlord, through force, intimidation or otherwise, prevents a tenant from accessing the rented dwelling or removes their belongings from a dwelling.[38] A landlord deemed by the RTB to have carried out an unlawful termination of tenancy, may be

---

requires it for their own or family use; vacant possession is required for substantial refurbishment; or the landlord intends to change the use of the dwelling.

[36] s 62 Residential Tenancies Act 2006. The Residential Tenancies Board (RTB), formerly the Private Residential Tenancies Board, was established by the Residential Tenancies Act (RTA) 2004, as an agency of Government with statutory powers. The central role of the RTB is to support the rental housing market and to resolve cheaply and speedily disputes between landlords and tenants, affording protection to both parties without having to resort to the courts. As a statutory body, the RTB is responsible for the operation of a national registration system for all private residential tenancies and for all tenancies provided in the Approved Housing Body Sector. These are generally social rented tenancies provided by not-for-profit housing providers, often referred to as housing associations. One of the core functions of the RTB is also to provide for both tenants and landlords, a timely and cost-effective dispute resolution service. In addition, the RTB publishes the rent index for private rented accommodation, disseminates information, carries out research and offers policy advice regarding the rental housing sector.

[37] *Canty v Private Residential Tenancies Board* [2007] IEHC 243.

[38] See Residential Tenancies Board, 'What is an illegal eviction?' <https:// onestopshop.rtb.ie/ending-a-tenancy/what-is-an-illegal-eviction/>. The definition

directed to allow the tenant re-entry into the dwelling, and required to pay damages to the tenant. In 2015, the RTB received 320 complaints of alleged illegal eviction (up from 79 in 2011), amounting to 8 per cent of dispute applications, and made awards ranging from €200 to €10 000.[39]

Following the banking collapse, many Buy-To-Let (BTL) landlords were unable to service mortgages, with arrears amounting to some 25 per cent of 137 500 BTL mortgage accounts at December 2015. Some 6000 accounts were in the hands of receivers, who were managing the property and arranging for sale in some cases. The position of tenants in these situations is precarious and there have been reports of large scale repossessions of tenants in these tenanted properties.[40] In 2016, a measure was introduced to prevent purchasers (such as 'vulture funds') of distressed loans from large-scale eviction of tenants in those properties.[41]

3.4 Social Housing Tenancies

Social housing tenancies in Ireland are provided by local authorities and approved housing bodies (AHBs). The legislation on local authority evictions was updated in 2014, when the Housing (Miscellaneous Provisions) Act 2014 replaced parts of the Housing Act 1966. This followed a 'Declaration of Incompatibility' issued by the Supreme Court in *Donegan v Dublin City Council* [2012] IESC 18, where it was held that the existing summary procedure for evictions was not compatible with Article 8 of the European Convention on Human Rights (ECHR). There had been no opportunity for a court to examine the proportionality of making the possession order. The new legislation requires a local authority to issue a tenancy warning for a breach of tenancy conditions.

---

of 'tenant' includes a person who has ceased to be entitled to that occupation by reason of the termination of his or her tenancy.

[39] RTB, *Annual Report 2015* (Dublin, RTB 2015) 28. Some 12% of awards were between €5000 and €10 000.

[40] Threshold, 'Threshold–Statement to the Oireachtas Committee on Housing and Homelessness 2016' <https://www.threshold.ie/download/pdf/threshold_opening_statement19th_may_2016.pdf?issuusl=ignore>.

[41] See <https://www.rt.com/news/335561-goldman-vulture-fund-evictions/>. The 'Tyrellstown' Amendment (s 40 Planning and Development (Housing) and Residential Tenancies Act 2016) confirms that a tenancy cannot be terminated on the grounds of an intention to sell where the landlord is seeking to sell 10 or more dwellings within a development during the relevant time. 'Relevant time' means any period of six months within the period beginning with the offer for sale of the first dwelling and ending with the offer for sale in the development of the last dwelling.

The warning must set out the nature and time of the breach, requiring the tenant to address the issue or warning that possession proceedings may be commenced. In cases of arrears, the warning must state the amount of arrears. A tenant can request a review of the warning within 20 days, and the review must be carried out by a local authority official who was not involved in the initial warning. If the warning is upheld and the tenant does not respond appropriately, the local authority may apply to the District Court for possession; the tenant would normally receive 10 days' notice of the application, except in cases of anti-social behaviour. The application must give grounds for possession and other details, including the tenancy warnings. The possession order will give a date (between two and nine months from the date of the order) when the local authority can repossess the dwelling.

The Residential Tenancies (Amendment) Act 2015 applies to all AHB tenancies, introducing similar tenancy terms to private rented sector tenancies. The legislation also gives the RTB supervisory control of the AHB eviction process – replacing the previous uncertain law dating from the 1860s.

3.5   Law Relating to Unauthorized Occupancy

There are a number of laws relating to eviction from unauthorized sites. Those affected are mainly Travellers, who occupy land, from which they are evicted regularly. Legislation was passed in 2002 in order to facilitate the eviction of persons 'entering and occupying land without consent', making it a criminal offence to trespass on land with an 'object,' such as a caravan.[42] The legislation permits the police (Gardaí) to direct individuals to immediately leave land and remove all objects they have brought onto the land. In these situations, no written notice is served, and if the trespasser does not leave, the police can confiscate and impound caravans, or arrest the person without warrant. While earlier housing legislation had restricted evictions if no alternative accommodation was available, such conditions are not included in the Criminal Justice (Public Order) Act 1994.[43]

---

[42]   s 24 of the Housing (Miscellaneous Provisions) Act 2002 inserted amendments to the Criminal Justice (Public Order) Act 1994, creating what is known as the 'trespass legislation'.

[43]   Travellers can also be evicted from temporary sites under other legislative provisions. See Irish Traveller Movement, *Report in Response to Ireland's Third examination under the International Covenant on Economic, Social and Cultural Rights* (2014) <http://itmtrav.ie/wp-content/uploads/2016/11/ICESCR-Report.pdf>.

There are a limited number of unauthorized occupations of dwellings (known as squatting), but no reliable data exists on this or on the number of enforcement actions taken by the police or property owners.

3.6 Law Relating to Temporary Dispossession (Domestic Violence, Urban Development, Family Law Issues)

There is legislation which permits a person to be 'barred' from a home, in situations where there is any form of physical, sexual and/or psychological violence which threatens the safety or welfare of family members and certain persons in domestic relationships. An 'interim Barring Order' can be awarded by a court where it is of the opinion that there are reasonable grounds for believing that there is an immediate risk of significant harm to the applicant or any dependent person, if the order is not made immediately. Under the Domestic Violence Act 2002, a full court hearing must take place within eight working days of the granting of an Interim Barring Order, and a full Barring Order can then be granted. A Barring Order (of either type) requires the named person to leave, and to stay away from, the family/shared home.

In divorce cases, a court can make property adjustment orders involving division of assets, permitting one party only to live in the home, to the exclusion of the other party. In cases where there are children, the spouse with whom the children live will often be given the right to live in the family home until the youngest child reaches the age of 18 years or 23 years. These provisions are not mirrored in the civil partnership legislation.

3.7 Soft Law/Codes and Their Effectiveness

The Code of Conduct on Mortgage Arrears (CCMA), introduced in February 2009, has been revised three times, with the current CCMA effective from 1 July 2013. Banks, retail credit firms and firms servicing loans on behalf of unregulated loan owners, are all required to 'comply' with the CCMA. It sets out the Mortgage Arrears Resolution Process (MARP), a four-step process that regulated entities must follow.[44] At the end of the MARP, regulated entities are required to provide a three-month notice period to allow cooperating borrowers time to consider their options, such as voluntary surrender or a Personal Insolvency Arrangement (PIA). However, in *Irish Life and Permanent v Dunne and*

---

[44] Step 1: Communicate with borrower; Step 2: Gather financial information; Step 3: Assess the borrower's circumstances; and Step 4: Propose a resolution.

Irish Life and Permanent v Dunphy,[45] the Irish Supreme Court held that the CCMA (2013) did not create any new legal rights for mortgagors. An *affadavit* by the lending institution, to the effect that proceedings were commenced after the three month moratorium period had expired, is sufficient to establish lender compliance with the CCMA.

4.　EXTENT OF EVICTIONS OVER THE PERIOD 2010–2015[46]

4.1　Definition of Eviction – Three Phases as per Evictions Report – Pre-Court, Court and Post Court

The EU Pilot Project Report on homelessness prevention in the context of evictions 2016[47] has identified three phases in the repossession/eviction process: pre-court; court; and the phase from court decision to actual eviction. The pre-court phase begins from the moment of issuance of the formal instruction to leave. The second phase involves the court process itself. The third phase encompasses the period between the court order for possession and the actual physical eviction (if it indeed takes place). The EU Pilot Project Report identified a possible link with homelessness at every stage of this process, and people may become homeless even at the first stage, as they may leave on receiving a notice to quit.

Research from the Central Bank of Ireland shows that, in 2015, some 40 per cent of mortgage-related court proceedings for mortgage arrears resulted in an order for possession.[48] There is a major variation where the loans are held by non-bank entities (64 per cent resulted in an order for possession), and unregulated loan owners (70 per cent resulted in an order for possession). Clearly, the 'vulture funds' are more likely to

---

[45]　*Irish Life and Permanent v Dunne and Irish Life and Permanent v Dunphy* [2015] IESC 64.

[46]　See Table 5.3 below.

[47]　P Kenna, L Benjaminsen, V Busch-Geertsema and S Nasarre-Aznar, *Pilot Project – Promoting Protection of the Right to Housing – Homelessness Prevention in the Context of Evictions* (VT/2013-/056) *Final report* (2016) (European Union: European Commission, Directorate-General Employment, Social Affairs and Inclusion 2016) <http://ec.europa.eu/social/main.jsp?catId=738&langId=en&pubId=7892&type=2&furtherPubs=yes>.

[48]　Department of Finance/Central Bank, *Report on Mortgage Arrears* (Dublin, Central Bank of Ireland 2016) 40.

repossess homes than main bank lenders. However, borrowers are actually more likely to voluntarily surrender or abandon their homes before the conclusion of court proceedings than be forcibly repossessed. Of the dwellings repossessed by lenders between 2009 and 2016, some 66 per cent were repossessed after voluntary surrender or abandonment.[49]

For private tenants, the pre-court phase involves a lengthy process which may include a determination by the RTB, although research and anecdotal evidence suggests that most evictions arise from the first phase (pre-court) of the eviction process. Private tenants do not now rely on the courts to defend possession actions. For social housing tenants, there is normally a full utilization of the three phases, with almost all evictions taking place after the court or third phase.

4.2 Evictions from Mortgaged Property

While new possession proceedings on principal dwelling houses (PDH) may have peaked in 2014, there is a growing number of cases before the courts, with regular adjournments, as shown in this Courts Service data (see Table 5.2):

Table 5.2   Mortgage possession cases in Irish courts[50]

	2010	2011	2012	2013	2014	2015	2016
Circuit Court proceedings for PDH possession order					8164	5021	3679
Circuit Court order for possession of PDH granted	306	353	258	363	1063	1284	1088

There are no figures available on the numbers of possession orders executed, but the numbers of properties repossessed give an indication. At least 100 households were repossessed by Irish mortgage lenders due to being overcharged on their mortgages.[51] Borrowers who took out tracker mortgages (linked to the European Central Bank rate) were

---

[49]   Ibid 33. The small proportion of evictions recorded by the Central Bank do not reflect the true numbers of eviction procedures underway in the courts system.

[50]   Courts Service of Ireland, Statistics and Annual Reports 2010–2016 <http://www.courts.ie/Courts.ie/Library3.nsf/pagecurrent/D171C224DF0083D18 0257FB10043BD33?opendocument&l=en>.

[51]   *The Irish Times* 29 September 2017.

overcharged by many years, which resulted in arrears and subsequent repossession in some cases.[52]

Table 5.3   Summary of evictions in Ireland 2010–2015

	2010	2011	2012	2013	2014	2015
PRTB* – Eviction-related cases referred	580	709	2162	2483	3020	3182
PRTB – Illegal evictions		79	202	228	263	320
LA** Initiated evictions rented housing	1564	1549	1738	1840		
LA Actual evictions rented housing	44	70	83	22		
LA Low cost home ownership schemes – repossessions[53]	89	103	129	111	68	80
Housing Associations Notice Issued	76	85	112	101	106	113
Housing Associations Court Action	21	23	3	22	18	18
Admissions to Shelters for Domestic Violence (women)	1545	1686	1875	2052	1969	1623
Admissions to Shelters for Domestic Violence (children)	2355	2142	2892	2787	2484	2263
Interim Barring Orders in District Court	431	569	520	522	569	563
Permanent Barring Orders in District Court	1064	1043	1165	1167	877	859

Notes:
* Private Residential Tenancies Board.
** Local Authority.

[52]   The Central Bank is now undertaking a review of lenders' approach to tracker mortgages between 2008 and 2015, with 100 000 being examined. Some 9900 accounts have been identified as impacted by these lenders and €78m has been paid in redress to 2600 customers. Ciaran Hancock, 'Lenders pay €78m for denying tracker rates to 2,600 customers' *The Irish Times* 23 March 2017 <https://www.irishtimes.com/business/financial-services/lenders-pay-78m-for-denying-tracker-rates-to-2-600-customers-1.3021675>.
[53]   <http://www.housing.gov.ie/housing/statistics/house-prices-loans-and-profile-borrowers/local-authority-loan- activity>.

4.3 Evictions from Private/Social Rented Housing

4.3.1 Evictions from private rented housing

The data shows an increasing number of eviction related cases referred to the RTB, in addition to an increasing number of illegal evictions between 2010 and 2015, which are much greater than the increase in numbers of tenancies registered.[54] Eviction related cases increased five-fold in the five years, while illegal evictions quadrupled. Thus, the private rented sector remains the primary source of evictions, including illegal eviction. Threshold offers nationwide advice and advocacy to private sector tenants, and its data offers a very good illustration of the extent of eviction related cases over the period under study, as shown in Table 5.4.

Table 5.4   Threshold national housing agency – advice and advocacy statistics 2010–2016

	2010	2011	2012	2013	2014	2015	2016
Illegal eviction threatened	300	299	360	329	280	253	202
Illegal eviction actual	237	247	258	318	181	198	185
Given invalid notice	957	999	761	1127	1218	1195	1109
Rent arrears	431	514	420	580	499	475	368

4.3.2 Evictions from social housing

Evictions from local authority properties remain at a much lower level, despite significant numbers of proceedings initiated by local authorities. The level of repossessions from the various low-cost home ownership schemes reflects general unemployment patterns, and has remained constant over the period.

Approved Housing Bodies (AHBs) had much lower levels of proceedings initiated over the period than local authorities. However, the eviction rate for AHBs, at approximately 20 cases per annum, is proportionally higher than that for local authorities.

---

[54] The number of tenancies registered with the P(RTB) increased from 231 818 in 2010 to 319 600 in 2015.

4.3.3 Other evictions

While those who are admitted to shelters for domestic violence are not counted as homeless, these figures nevertheless relate to exclusion from home, albeit in a non-legal setting. In many cases, there are children involved and any comprehensive examination of evictions must include these. Over the period examined, there was a consistent pattern of use, with some small increases in 2013 and 2014.

The Courts Service collates data on temporary and permanent barring orders issued under the domestic violence legislation.[55] Here, the data shows a small decrease from a peak in 2012 and 2013.

5. RISK FACTORS IDENTIFIED LEADING TO EVICTIONS

The extent of homelessness arising from evictions is not entirely linear. Studies show that evicted people rely on family or friends initially to avoid homelessness. It is only after these resources and supports have been exhausted that actual homelessness takes place. As such, the official recorded figures are likely to underestimate the numbers made homeless by evictions, including those who are 'couch surfing', living in unauthorized occupancies or literally overcrowding family (parents') homes. Irish census data records the numbers of homeless persons, and the comparisons between Census 2011 and Census 2016 are indicated in Table 5.5.[56]

---

[55] Relevant legislation is the Family Law (Maintenance of Spouses and Children) Act 1976; Family Law (Protection of Spouses and Children) Act 1981; Domestic Violence Act 1996; Non-Fatal Offences Against the Person Act 1997; Family Law (Miscellaneous Provisions) Act 1997; Domestic Violence (Amendment) Act 2002; Civil Partnership and Certain Rights and Obligations of Cohabitants Act 2010.

[56] See CSO, *Census 2011: Homeless Persons in Ireland* (Dublin, Stationery Office 2011) <http://www.cso.ie/en/media/csoie/census/documents/homeless personsinireland/Homeless_persons_in_Ireland_A_special_Census_report.pdf> and CSO, *Census 2016, Profile 5 Homeless Persons in Ireland* (Dublin, CSO 2016) <http://www.cso.ie/en/csolatestnews/presspages/2017/census2016profile5-homelesspersonsinireland/>.

Table 5.5   Homelessness data from Census 2011 and Census 2016

	Census 2011	Census 2016
Total homeless persons	3808	6906
Male	2539	4018
Female	1269	2888
Families with one child	114	326
Families with two children	71	261
Families with three children	35	131
Families with four or more children	29	111
Total homeless children in family units	498	1594

The Irish State regularly publishes administrative (non-legally binding) 'Strategies' and 'Action Plans' on homelessness.[57] The 'Homelessness Policy Statement 2013', states in relation to 'Prevention' that: 'Effective action is required to prevent, as far as possible, the occurrence or recurrence of homelessness. This will require a range of measures from identifying households at risk, to working with people who are losing tenancies and ensuring that adequate advice, advocacy and sustainment measures are in place in the context of overall social housing policy as set out in the Government's Housing Policy Statement.'[58]

5.1   Risk Factors for Mortgagors

A study of 21 000 households in 2015,[59] based on the Central Bank of Ireland loan-level data and borrowers Standard Financial Statements, showed that those with long-term mortgage arrears (LTMA) (over one year), who are most at risk of repossession, are significantly more likely to have the following characteristics: lower income, higher mortgage burdens relative to income, larger mortgage affordability shocks, unemployment shocks and divorce since origination. They are also more likely to have accumulated large stocks of non-mortgage debts, such as Buy-to-Let mortgages, credit card, car loans and other consumer debt.

---

[57]   There is a statutory obligation on local authorities under Pt 2, Ch 6 of the Housing (Miscellaneous Provisions) Act 2009, to create a local 'Homeless Strategy', but this is not a statutory obligation to provide housing.

[58]   See <http://www.housing.gov.ie/housing/homelessness/policy/homelessness>.

[59]   R Kelly and F McCann, 'Some defaults are deeper than others: understanding long-term mortgage arrears' (Research Technical Papers 16/RT/04, Central Bank of Ireland 2015) <http://www.centralbank.ie/publications/Documents/05RT15.pdf>.

LTMA borrowers face higher interest rates, and LTMA are more prevalent among more vulnerable family types, such as single borrowers with
multiple children.[60]

A detailed study by MABS of 50 households in a rural area in the West
of Ireland indicated that, of those in mortgage arrears in 2016, the
average age of distressed mortgage clients was fifty years.[61] Family sizes
were also larger than average, and household income was relatively low,
with poverty rates and unemployment rates relatively high. Some form of
assistance scheme, pension or welfare payment was the main source of
household income for most, with only very few having any 'realizable
asset' whatsoever to fall back on. Significantly, most encountered payments difficulties in the early years of the loan, often where brokers,
sub-prime lenders and subsequently, wound-up institutions were
involved. Most borrowers in the study had been offered loans based on
'precarious' income related to construction or services industry work.
The research also showed that although there was a willingness by
lenders to restructure the mortgage, this only applied where lenders
expected to recoup the full amount of capital and interest, and in no case
was a write-off of debt proposed. In a follow-up study 18 months later,
some arrears had been settled and repayments commenced. However, in
addition to the households who had lost their homes in the earlier study,
loss of family home was identified as 'imminent or likely outcome for
20 per cent of cases, in the foreseeable future.'[62]

The risks factors for evictions and homelessness in the private rented
sector have been examined by Focus Ireland and are detailed in Section 6
following.

---

[60]   R Kelly and F McCann, 'Households in long-term mortgage arrears:
lessons from economic research' (Central Bank of Ireland, Economic Letter
Series, No. 11, 2015) 2 <http://www.centralbank.ie/publications/Documents/
Economic%20Letter%20-%20Vol%202015,%20No.%2011.pdf>.

[61]   S Stamp and P Joyce, *Analysis of Mortgage Arrears Among South Mayo
MABS' Clients* (2016) (South Mayo MABS) <https://www.mabs.ie/downloads/
news_press/South_Mayo_MABS_Mortgage_Research_August2016.pdf>.

[62]   S Stamp and P Joyce, *Analysis of Mortgage Arrears Among South Mayo
MABS' Clients, April 2016 v September 2017* (2017) (South Mayo MABS)
<http://www.citizensinformationboard.ie/en/news/2017/news20171212_1.html>.

6. LINKS BETWEEN EVICTIONS AND HOMELESSNESS

The availability of local authority and other social housing for those evicted has not kept pace with requirements.

The Assessment of Social Housing Need and Homelessness in 2016 showed that those who were homeless, living in an institution, emergency accommodation or hostel increased from 2808 in 2013 to 5401 in 2016 (see Table 5.6). Households who sought social housing assistance due to their mortgage being deemed unsustainable under the Mortgage Arrears Resolution Process increased from 154 to 657 in the period, while the overall numbers of households in need of social housing support increased from 89 872 to 91 600.[63]

Table 5.6 Local authority assessments of housing need and homelessness

	2011	2013	2016
Homeless	2348	2499	5159
Travellers	1824	1632	1778
Unfit accommodation	1708	647	2304
Overcrowded accommodation	4594	2896	3517
Involuntary sharing	8534	9587	11 476
Institutional care/homeless	538	2808	5401
Medical/compassionate reasons	9548	2909	2096
Older persons	2266	1844	2327
Disabled/handicapped	1315	3938	5753
Unable to afford	65 643	66 983[64]	60 396
Unsustainable mortgage		154	657
Total	98 318[65]	89 872*	91 600*

[63] The Housing Agency, *Summary of Social Housing Assessments 2016 Key Findings.* The Social Housing (Assessment) (Amendment) (No.2) Regulations 2011, allow for a borrower whose mortgage has been deemed unsustainable under the Mortgage Arrears Resolution Process (MARP) to be assessed for social housing.

[64] From 2013, new guidelines were applied to this category, 'dependent on rent supplement', and 'unsuitable accommodation due to particular household circumstances', the latter, 'populated by households not in receipt of rent supplement, but with a difficulty in affording private accommodation'.

[65] The 2011 Assessment was a snapshot of those registered with housing authorities as in housing need at that time, but authorities were not required to

Note: * For 2013, those in Rental Accommodation Scheme rented housing were not counted and in 2016 those in accommodation provided under the Housing Assistance Payment (HAP) scheme, Rental Accommodation Scheme (RAS), and Social Housing Current Expenditure Programme (SHCEP) were not included. For 2013 and 2016, there seems to be some overlap between 'main need for social housing support' and 'breakdown of accommodation requirements'. In line with earlier years, the total figures would have resulted in 95 897 for 2013 and 100 864 for 2016.

The reasons for households becoming homeless are not published by Irish local authorities or the State. However, the Minister for Housing, Planning, Community and Local Government has stated that:

> Recent housing authority analysis into reasons for homeless presentations by families identifies two broad categories: departure from private rented accommodation, primarily following receipt of a 'notice to quit', and family circumstances which includes both relationship breakdown and overcrowding. As noted, it is overly simplistic to classify presentation by a single causative factor and it is likely in many cases that underlying reasons overlap. This analysis corresponds with recent independent surveys carried out by homeless service providers.[66]

Indeed, there has been a rapid increase in recent years of families becoming homeless. Focus Ireland has tracked this increase,[67] and has examined the reasons why so many families are losing their homes.[68] According to Focus Ireland research and analysis, the overwhelming number of families becoming homeless had their last stable home in the private rented sector, and the crisis in this sector is the immediate cause of their homelessness – landlords selling up or being repossessed, shortage of properties to rent, scarcity of landlords accepting rent supplement, and high rents. Most of the families becoming homeless have never experienced homelessness before. Thousands more families are struggling on very low incomes or social welfare, and many are falling into serious housing difficulties as rents continue to rise. Some families are becoming homeless as rent supplement payments fail to cover the rent. They fall into arrears and end up losing their home.

---

reassess applicants for that Assessment to confirm that those on the list were still seeking and in need of social housing support.

[66]   See Parliamentary Question No 454, Written Answer, 2 May 2017.

[67]   See Focus Ireland, <https://www.focusireland.ie/resource-hub/latest-figures-homelessness-ireland/>.

[68]   See Focus Ireland, 'Housing – Insights into Family Homelessness' <https://www.focusireland.ie/resource-hub/research/>.

From our front-line work, Focus Ireland know that the single largest cause of homelessnes [sic] is now property being taken out of the rental market, either by the landlord selling up, or using the property for their own family. Other families can't find anywhere to rent as payments are too low and many landlords do not accept rent supplement ...[69]

Homelessness among families and children has increased dramatically since 2014 (when data was first collated nationally). Table 5.7 shows the trends of increasing family and child homelessness arising mainly from 'evictions' from rented housing.[70]

Table 5.7   Rising homelessness since 2014

	July 2014	July 2015	July 2016	July 2017
Adults	2509	3285	4177	5187
Children	749	1383	2348	2973
Families	344	657	1030	1429

7. SUMMARY OF SIGNIFICANT CASES AND REPORTS RELATED TO EVICTIONS IN THE PERIOD 2010–2015

There were three significant eviction related cases in the period. In *Donegan and others v Dublin City Council*,[71] the Irish Supreme Court held that the local authority summary eviction procedure under the Housing Act 1966 was incompatible with Article 8 ECHR, as there was no opportunity for a court to examine the proportionality of making the possession order. A new procedure, set out in the Housing (Miscellaneous Provisions) Act 2014, provides for warnings and reviews in the process, but also requires a court to have regard to whether 'in the circumstances it is just and equitable to make the order', and 'the proportionality of making a possession order under this section, having

---

[69]   See Focus Ireland, 'About Homelessness' <https://www.focusireland.ie/resource-hub/about-homelessness/>.

[70]   Department of Housing, Planning and Local Government, 'Data on homelessness' <http://www.housing.gov.ie/housing/homelessness/other/homelessness-data>. I am grateful to Wayne Stanley, Research and Policy Analyst at Focus Ireland, for compiling this table.

[71]   *Donegan and others v Dublin City Council* [2012] IESC 18.

regard to the grounds for the possession application.'[72] In *Irish Life and Permanent v Dunne and Irish Life and Permanent v Dunphy* [2015] IESC 64, the Supreme Court held that the CCMA did not impact on mortgage law on repossessions, beyond requiring an undertaking by the lender that the moratorium period had been respected. The case of *Start Mortgages & Ors v Gunn & Ors*[73] exposed a *lacuna* in the law on repossessions created by the Land and Conveyancing Law Reform Act 2009 (hereafter LCLRA). This led to a temporary slowdown in court orders, until the passing of the LCLRA 2013, which restored the situation.

8.   BEST PRACTICE MODELS FOR PREVENTING, TACKLING AND REACTING TO EVICTIONS

8.1   Tenancy Protection Service

In response to the growing number of tenants presenting to homeless services, in 2014, Threshold established the Tenancy Protection Service in Dublin. The organization had identified that many tenants were leaving private rented accommodation due to unaffordable rent increases, or because they had received a notice of termination from their landlord. Due to the shortage of affordable rental accommodation, a growing number of these households were ending up in homeless services. Others became homeless due to the fact that many landlords were not willing to accept rent supplement.

The Tenancy Protection Service intervenes to prevent tenancy breakdown and the occurrence of homelessness. It advocates with landlords and letting agents to find solutions to housing issues that threaten tenancies. The main issues dealt with by the service to date have been invalid notices of termination and threats of eviction, rent reviews both valid and invalid, as well as issues relating to social housing supports such as Rent Supplement and the Housing Assistance Payment.[74] As part of the service, a protocol was put in place with the Department of Social Protection, which allows the payment of an enhanced rent supplement payment where a rent increase threatens the viability of a tenancy. The service was extended nationally in 2017 and has had considerable success in the prevention of homelessness, with services provided in 4000 cases in 2016.

---

[72]   s 12 (9) Housing (Miscellaneous Provisions) Act 2014.
[73]   [2011] IEHC 275.
[74]   <https://www.threshold.ie/housing-supports/>.

8.2 Landlord Cannot Penalize Tenants for Referring Cases to the RTB

The Residential Tenancies Act 2004 seeks to ensure a landlord shall not penalize a tenant for referring a dispute to the RTB.[75] Section 14 (2) of the Act states that '... a tenant is penalised if the tenant is subjected to any action that adversely affects his or her enjoying peaceful occupation of the dwelling concerned.'[76]

The RTB also carries out extensive publication of data relating to evictions on its website. It collates and publishes data on cases referred to it, commissions' research on residential tenancies,[77] provides policy advice and guidance and also publishes the results of its Determination Orders and court decisions. Putting this information into the public domain in this open and transparent manner provides a valuable resource for tenants and helps monitor the processes that can lead to eviction in private rented housing.

8.3 Other Organizations and Measures Supporting Those at Risk of Eviction

8.3.1 Organizations

The Free Legal Advice Centres (FLAC) is an organization that operates a free and non-means tested telephone information and referral line that offers basic information on all areas of law to the public, as well as a countrywide network of legal advice centres where people can get confidential, basic legal advice for free from volunteer lawyers. The FLAC can take strategic cases to test and possibly change the law or practice in significant areas, such as debt.[78] The FLAC also produces legal guides and information sheets on a variety of topics, including 'A Guide to Possession Proceedings in the Circuit Court'.

The role of the Money Advice and Budgeting Service (MABS) has been enhanced to include a Dedicated Mortgage Arrears service and a Court Mentor service, to assist debtors faced with court proceedings.

---

[75] s 14 (1) (a) and s 14 (2) Residential Tenancies Act 2004. The tenant shall not be penalized for giving evidence in any proceedings under the legislation to which the landlord is a party, or for making a complaint to the *Garda Síochána* (Police) or a public authority in such matters.

[76] Proceedings in relation to an offence under this Act may be brought and prosecuted by the RTB and this constitutes a limitation.

[77] See <http://www.prtb.ie/media-research>.

[78] See <http://www.flac.ie/>.

MABS is also centrally involved in a new aid and advice scheme for people in serious mortgage arrears as part of *Abhaile*, the national Mortgage Arrears Resolution Service, established in 2016.[79] The Irish Mortgage Holders Organisation (IMHO) has arrangements with two banking organizations, namely AIB Group and KBC Bank Ireland, whereby customers can contact the IMHO for direct assistance (free of charge) regarding their mortgage arrears with these banks. In Ireland, there are also a number of social movements that seek to challenge and publicize evictions from homes, as part of peaceful protest, such as the Anti-Eviction Taskforce[80] and The Hub-Ireland.[81]

8.3.2 Legal measures

The Consumer Protection (Regulation of Credit Servicing Firms) Act 2015 provides that people whose mortgages have been transferred to unregulated entities will have the same protection that they had before the loan was sold. The Central Bank's Consumer Protection Code 2012 was updated in 2015 by an addendum making it clear that the Code now applies to credit servicing firms, which are firms that manage loans on behalf of unregulated entities, such as 'vulture funds'.

8.3.3 Measures that could work but that are not implemented

There have been suggestions that newly formed housing agencies could purchase tranches of distressed mortgages and act as social housing landlord to the occupiers. Cluid HA[82] and Oaklee Housing Association offers a mortgage to rent (MTR) scheme.[83] iCare Housing (an AHB) has

---

[79]   <http://www.keepingyourhome.ie/en/mortgage_arrears_aid_and_advice_scheme.html>.

[80]   See Anti-Eviction Taskforce, <https://www.facebook.com/pg/AntiEviction Taskforce/about/?ref=page_internal>. This group's website states: 'Recession or no recession, there is no moral reason why any individual or family should be threatened with eviction from their home. Yet it is happening with increasing frequency, not only in Ireland but in numerous countries across the world. The reason given is almost always a monetary one. Someone has fallen behind on their mortgage payments or has hit rock bottom through no fault of their own.' The aim of the Anti-Eviction Taskforce is to bring the injustice of forced eviction into the mainstream and prevent any more homes being seized by financial institutions.

[81]   See <https://www.thehub-ireland.com/>.

[82]   See <https://www.cluid.ie/what-we-do/case-studies/mortgage-to-rent-scheme/>.

[83]   See <https://www.oaklee.ie/media/2102/guide-to-the-mortgage-to-rent-scheme.pdf>.

6. Evictions in Italy

Elena Bargelli and Giulia Donadio[1]

1. INTRODUCTION

Evictions in Italy have recently acquired primary importance on the political agenda and in public debate due to a dramatic surge in ouster proceedings from rented and privately owned residential tenures. This chapter starts with an overview of the eviction policy in the Italian legal system. It focuses on the socioeconomic factors related to evictions and the measures designed to prevent arrears, cease evictions from owned primary residences, as well as measures that postpone evictions from rented primary residences. Against this backdrop, the chapter then focuses on the right to housing as a fundamental right, as articulated as an expression of the Italian constitutional principles of social solidarity (Article 2) and equality (Article 3). The chapter subsequently examines the procedures leading to eviction in particular areas (mortgaged properties, rented housing, unauthorized occupancies), and clarifies their respective procedural phases. The chapter then identifies various common risk factors for evictions and provides a brief case-law summary in order to highlight the existence of best practices in response to increasing eviction proceedings in Italy.

2. POLICY BACKGROUND

2.1 General Housing Policy Related to Evictions

Since the economic crisis, evictions in Italy in both owner-occupied and private rental tenures have soared, which is discussed further in

---

[1]   Although this chapter is the result of the authors' joint efforts, paragraphs 1, 2, 3.1, 3.3, 3.4, 3.5, 3.6, 5.2, 8.2, 9 were written by Elena Bargelli, and paragraphs 3.2, 3.7, 4, 5.1, 5.3, 5.4, 5.5, 6, 7, 8.1 were written by Giulia Donadio.

Section 4. Simultaneously, squatting and unauthorized occupancy have significantly increased.[2] In order to prevent the eviction of debtors from the weakest segments of the population and the consequent risk of homelessness in both the owner-occupied and rental sectors, best practice measures have been adopted by various governments. While the delay and suspension of evictions had already been in force in private tenancies well before the onset of the crisis, measures to prevent the foreclosure of immovable goods are quite new.

2.2 Structural/Societal Factors Related to Evictions

The (single) most influential factor for the increase in evictions in the Italian mortgage system is the current economic crisis. The mortgage market in Italy was not profoundly affected by the speculative bubble that exploded in other European countries in the last decade, since 2008.[3] This is mainly due to the conservative attitude of the Italian banks, which usually acted responsibly in providing loans and were reluctant to overestimate the value of the immovable goods given as securities.[4] Furthermore, the debt accumulated by households did not raise concern, as, according to the most recent Eurispes data, Italy has the highest rate of savings in Europe.[5] However, Italy was hit by the deepest economic crisis since the country's unification in 1861, fuelled by high national debt and weak economic growth, resulting in an extensive labour market crisis. It is hardly surprising that tenants and home buyers in arrears have become a social and political issue.

---

[2] See Section 3.5; European Network for Housing Research (ENHR), 'The tip of the iceberg. Squatting of public tenures and rental unaffordability in Italy' (2014) (4) *ENHR-Newsletter*

[3] For an overview, see E Arroyo Amayuelas, 'Crisis? What crisis?' in M Anderson and E Arroyo Amayuelas (eds) *The Impact of the Mortgage Directive in Europe. Contrasting Views from Member States* (Europa Law Publishing 2017) 4 ff. As to Spain, see M Anderson and HS Moreno, 'The Spanish crisis and the Mortgage Credit Directive. Few changes in sight' in M Anderson and E Arroyo Amayuelas (eds) (ibid) 50–103.

[4] *Linee guida per la valutazione degli immobili in garanzia delle esposizioni creditizie*, 14 December 2015, <https://www.abi.it>.

[5] <http://www.repubblica.it/economia/2015/01/30/news/un_italiano_su_due_non_arriva_a_fine_mese_e_il_55_per_cento_vorrebbe_tornare_alla_lira1061271 96/?ref=HREC1-1>.

2.3 Specific Policies Related to Evictions

Since 2013, the Italian legal system has introduced moratoria, financial support and other measures aimed at the weakest categories of debtors at risk of eviction from their primary residence(s). In the sector of owner-occupied tenures, the main welfare measures introduced are the Credit Fund for the Purchase of the Primary Home and the House Guarantee Fund. Furthermore, the ABI (Italian Bank Association) signed an agreement on 31 March 2015, with ten leading consumer associations,[6] regulating the area of family credit.[7] Finally, several measures have recently been taken with the implementation of Directive 2014/17/EU on Mortgage Credit,[8] which was transposed into Italian law by the adoption of the Legislative Decree (Decreto Legislativo) no. 72/2016 and entered into force on 4 June 2016. All these measures will be discussed below in Section 8.

In the private rental sector, a national Fund to support tenants in arrears due to economic hardship or force majeure arose in 2013, which is also outlined in Section 8. Further preventive measures apply to non-professional debtors, regardless of whether the reason for defaulting lies in the payments for the primary residence. The settlement Procedure of Overindebtedness (Procedura di composizione di crisi da sovraindebitamento) is aimed at promoting a debt restructuring plan agreed between creditors and debtors, including consumers.

In 2014, the Early Termination of Eviction Procedure (Chiusura anticipata della procedura esecutiva) was introduced by Law decree no. 132/2014 (Article 164 bis of the preliminary provisions in the Civil Procedural Code [hereinafter CPC]). This provision mitigates the effects of eviction by explicitly allowing the court to stop the eviction procedure before its natural ending, when it is highly probable that creditors will not be satisfied by the auction of debtors' assets, regardless of whether the creditor agrees.

---

[6] *Acu, Adiconsum, Adoc, Cittadinanzattiva, Confconsumatori, Lega Consumatori, Movimento Consumatori, Movimento difesa del cittadino and Unione nazionale consumatori.*

[7] <https://www.abi.it/Pagine/news/Raggiunta-intesa-su-nuova-moratoria-famiglie.aspx>.

[8] Directive 2014/17/EU of The European Parliament and of the Council of 4 February 2014 on Credit Agreements for Consumers Relating to Residential Immovable Property and Amending Directives 2008/48/EC and 2013/36/EU and Regulation (EU) No 1093/2010 OJ L 60, 28.2.2014. For further details about its implementation in Italy, see E Bargelli and G Donadio, 'The impact of Directive 2014/17/EU in Italy' in M Anderson and E Arroyo Amayuelas (eds) (n 3) 304 ff.

3. LEGAL AND CONSTITUTIONAL BACKGROUND TO PROTECTION AGAINST EVICTIONS

3.1 Housing as a Fundamental Right

The right to housing is recognized as a fundamental right in the Italian legal system.[9] Although the Italian Constitution does not expressly mention the right to housing, its recognition was affirmed by the Constitutional Court in 1988, as a consequence of the principles of social solidarity[10] and equality,[11] as acknowledged in the Italian Constitutional Court judgment no. 404 of 1988.[12] This judgment indirectly concerned eviction, as the court amended the rule of residential tenancy law,[13] insofar as it did not recognize the right of an unmarried partner to stay in the dwelling after the death of the partner tenant.

Since then, the right to housing has been considered not only as a constitutional goal to be enacted by the legislator, but also as a human right with horizontal effects among private parties. This trend has been more recently reinforced by the reference to Article 8 ECHR (the right to respect for private and family life). According to this constitutional basis, Italian courts are keen to acknowledge non-pecuniary damages in cases of an infringement of the peaceful enjoyment of the home by third parties.[14] Courts are more restrictive in recognizing the horizontal impact of the right to housing on contracts. The only case was one in 2009, when the Italian Supreme Court held that a clause that prohibited a tenant from accommodating people, other than family members, for longer than a certain period of time was void, as it opposed the 'mandatory duties of social solidarity imposed by Article 2 of the Constitution.'[15]

---

[9]   See Bargelli, Abitazione (diritto all'), *Enciclopedia del diritto*, Annali, 2013, 1 ff.

[10]   Art 2 Italian Constitution.

[11]   Art 3 Italian Constitution.

[12]   Constitutional Court, 7 April 1988, no. 404, in *Giustizia civile (GC)* 1988, I, 1654.

[13]   Art 6 L. no. 392/1978.

[14]   Cass. SS. UU. 1 February 2017, no. 2611, in *Responsabilità Civile e previdenza* (RCP), 2017, 824 ff, with comment of A Dinisi, *Immissioni di rumore e danno non patrimoniale*.

[15]   Cass. 19 June 2009, no. 14343, in *Rassegna diritto civile* (RassDC), 2011, 992, with comment of R Caso, *Fondamento costituzionale del dovere di ospitalità e conformazione dell'autonomia privata*.

Further constitutional dimension of the right to housing stems from the European Convention on Human Rights (ECHR) and the European Social Charter. However, there are not, currently, Italian judgments expressly relating to these sources. Conversely, the European Committee of Social Rights found that Italy infringed Articles 31, 30, 16 and 19 of the European Social Charter in cases concerning discrimination against Roma, Sinti and other nomadic populations, as discussed below (see Section 3.5 on the law related to unauthorized occupancy).

In the past, the European Court of Human Rights (ECtHR) condemned Italy for the violation of property rights protected by Article 1, Protocol 1 (ECHR), in cases of suspension of eviction orders in densely populated municipalities, as well as landlords' prolonged inability to recover possession of their flats due to the lack of police assistance combined with the length of eviction proceedings in Italy.[16] More specifically, the ECtHR has repeatedly found violations of the landlords' right to due process (Article 6 ECHR) and property rights (Article 1, Protocol 1 ECHR), although it did not deny the need to protect weaker tenants. In the case of *Immobiliare Saffi v Italy*, the ECtHR reiterated that 'an interference, particularly one falling to be considered under the second paragraph of Article 1 of Protocol 1 ECHR, had to strike a "fair balance" between the demands of the general interest and the requirements of the protection of the individual's fundamental rights.'[17] In 2004, the Italian Constitutional Court advised the legislator to limit these special measures to a specific period of time and issue them in exceptional situations, in order to avoid a disproportionate burden on the landlords' right to property.[18] In 2007, the Council of Europe recognized that the Italian legal system had enacted several effective remedies for securing compensation for delays in enforcing court eviction orders, particularly through

---

[16] See *Spadea and Scalabrino v Italia*, 28 September 1995, no. 12868/87; *Immobiliare Saffi v Italia*, 28 July 1999, no. 22774/93; *Ghidotti v Italia*, 21 February 2002, no. 28272/95; *Sorrentino Prota v Italia*, 29 January 2004, no. 40465/98; *Bellini v Italia*, 29 January 2004, no. 64258/01; *Fossi Mignolli v Italia*, 4 March 2004, no. 48171/99; *Mascolo v Italia*, 16 December 2004, no. 68792/01; *Lo Tufo v Italia*, 21 April 2005, no. 64663/01; *Stornelli and Sacchi v Italia*, 28 July 2005, no. 68706/01, *Cuccaro Granatelli v Italia*, 8 December 2005, no. 19830/03. For a more detailed analysis see E Bargelli, 'Exploring interfaces between social long-term contracts and European law through tenancy law' in L Nogler and U Reifner (eds) (2014) *Life Time Contracts* (The Hague; Eleven 2014) 627 ff.

[17] *Immobiliare Saffi v Italy*, ECtHR, 28 July 1999 § 49.

[18] See Const. Court, 28 May 2004, n. 155, *Giurisprudenza italiana*, 2005, 1804; Const. Court, 7 October 2003, no. 310, *Giustizia civile*, 2003, I, 2319.

automatic compensation, in the event of legislative suspension, proceedings against tenants, and proceedings against the State for failure of the police to provide assistance and for delays in judicial proceedings and enforcement.[19]

3.2 Law Relating to Owner-occupied Housing

Notwithstanding the emphasis on the constitutional status of the right to housing, until recently there has been no special legal framework targeted at the eviction of owner-occupied primary residences. An eviction follows the rules provided by Article 555 and following of the CPC, regulating forced sales of immovable goods in general.

A special provision to prevent eviction from primary residences was introduced in 2013, by virtue of Legislative Decree no. 69/2013, amending Article 76 of the President of Republic Decree no. 602/1976. The rule prohibits Equitalia (a public company in charge of collecting taxes) from evicting a debtor from their primary residence, provided that certain strict conditions are met.[20] This prohibition, however, does not apply to private creditors.

A limited protective rule is enshrined in the statute on Insolvency Law (Royal Decree 16 March 1942, no. 267), which provides that a bankrupt party's dwelling used as a primary residence cannot be diverted until liquidation has been completed.[21] No further protective measures were established by the reform of insolvency law enacted by Law 6 August 2015 no. 132.

A significant legal framework of measures preventing eviction from mortgaged residential properties has been developed by the implementation of the Mortgage Credit Directive 2014/17 EU. Pursuant to Article 28 of Directive 2014/17/EU, Article 120- quinquiesdecies TUB (the Italian Banking Law Code, Decree no. 385/1993) states that creditors must adopt measures to manage the relationship with debtors in default.

---

[19] Committee of Ministers Final Resolution (2007) 84, in *Council of Europe Committee of Ministers, Supervision of the Execution of Judgments of the European Court of Human Rights*, Council of Europe, 2008, 108 f.

[20] The requirements can be summarized as follows: a) the debtor owns only the immovable property that is used as primary residence; b) the default does not exceed €120 000; c) the value of the immovable, after having deducted the mortgage, is less than €120 000; d) the immovable does not fall under the cadastral categories A8 (villas) or A9 (castles), and, in any case, is not luxurious.

[21] See Art 47 subs. 2 of Insolvency Law (R.D. 16 March 1942, no. 267, *Disciplina del fallimento, del concordato preventivo, dell'amministrazione controllata e della liquidazione coatta amministrativa*).

The new statute generally strengthens the aim of predicting and preventing foreclosures.

3.3 Law Relating to Private Rented Housing

The Civil Procedure Code provides a set of general rules on evictions following the termination of tenancy contracts (Articles 657–658).[22] In addition, procedural rules aimed at protecting tenants at risk of eviction have been provided by Italian residential tenancy law since 1978 (Articles 55–56 L. no. 392/1978). More specifically, residential tenancy law grants the tenant the right to remedy the default, by paying, at the first hearing, the whole amount of the overdue rent and additional expenses plus the interest accrued and the procedural expenses. In cases where the tenant adduces evidence of difficulties faced, the judge can fix a term within 90 days for payment (a 'mercy-deadline', which might be granted to a maximum of three times in four years). In issuing the judicial order, the judge establishes the date of the enforcement within six or, in exceptional circumstances, twelve months.

Suspensions of eviction orders non-related to arrears were provided up to the year 2015. Article 6 L. no. 431/1998, stated that the enforcement of eviction orders in densely populated municipalities were postponed for up to six months from the entering into force of the statute. This limit could be extended to 18 months in case of weakness factors related to age, unemployment and number of children etc. If the eviction order was enforceable after the coming into force of the statute, the tenant could only once request to postpone the eviction order up to six months from the notice. In these cases, however, landlords were compensated by a 20 per cent rent increase (subsection 6). Subsequently, provisions allowing the legal suspension of eviction orders were yearly reiterated in the annual decree, extending the effects of several Government measures (so called Milleproroghe: see, for instance, L. no.14/2012; L. no. 15/2014) up to 2015.

3.4 Law Relating to Social Rented Housing

Since the housing market is unable to satisfy the demand for accommodation, housing is conceived of as a public service whose provision is

---

[22] For a more detailed analysis of the procedure see R Bianchi, *Residential Tenancies and Housing Policy in Italy* (Pisa, Pisa University Press 2017) 265 ff.

integrated at public level.[23] The national legislator defines the principles and criteria to be observed at regional and municipal level(s).[24]

There are two types of tenures with a public purpose:

1. 'Public Housing' (ERP = Edilizia Residenziale Pubblica) was provided by L. no. 865/1971. Regulation is on a regional basis.[25] Dwellings belonging to public entities, such as municipalities, fall under this group.
2. 'Social Housing' (ERS = Edilizia Residenziale Sociale), promoted by the National Housing Plan 2008,[26] comprises various financial projects (including project finance, 'assisted housing' and 'contracted-out housing'). It is addressed to households that do not meet the requirements for a public dwelling and, at the same time, have insufficient income to afford to pay a market rent. It includes dwellings built with public subsidies, on the basis of an agreement between public entities and private investors.

As a whole, housing with public purpose makes up 23 per cent of the total number of tenancies, equal to 4.5 per cent of the country's housing stock.

3.5 Law Relating to Unauthorized Occupancy

Illegal occupancy mainly affects public tenures and, more specifically, vacant dwellings pending restoration or assignment. The economic crisis has contributed to increasing this trend. It is estimated that, on average, 4.6 per cent of public dwellings are illegally occupied.[27] The biggest cities are the most severely hit by illegal occupation. These are estimated to include 93 000 occupied flats in Rome, and 45 000 in Milan. Illegal occupations in Southern and Central Italy outnumber those in Northern

---

[23]   Art 117 Italian Constitution.

[24]   Note that Italy is made up of 20 regions each with its own regional administration, plus two self-governing provinces. Each region is then made up of provinces, which are further divided into municipalities.

[25]   See Leg Decree 31 March 1998, n. 112.

[26]   Decree Law no. 112/2008 converted into Law no. 133/2008.

[27]   Nomisma, *La condizione abitativa in Italia* (2010) 41. Nomisma has been collecting data since 2008.

Italy.[28] Illegal occupancy generates concern especially when it is managed by criminal groups or fosters criminality. Therefore, the legislator has recently introduced measures to discourage this trend.

In 2014, a statute (Law Decree no. 47 of 28 March 2014, the so-called Housing Plan (Piano Casa), Article 5) prevented illegal occupants from benefitting from public services such as energy contracts, telephone lines, or from registering themselves as inhabitants of the occupied dwelling.

In 2017, Law no. 48 ('Urban Security', Article 5) considered prevention of illegal occupancies one of the aims pursued by the 'security agreements' that the mayor and the prefect of police are allowed to conclude. It further provided that every eviction from occupied dwellings shall be managed not only by the courts, but also by the public forces. Therefore, an eviction might be postponed or prioritized, despite a judicial order, when it creates risks to public security. In addition, the mayor might entitle illegal occupants to benefit from public services and get the residence permit where children or persons in need are present (Article 11).

Illegal occupancy also includes the non-authorized encampments of Roma, Sinti and Caminanti. These are occupied by about 40 000 people (0.2 per cent of the Italian population), and are primarily situated in peripheral areas in the immediate outskirts of cities. Most are unauthorized and are subsisting below the minimal standard of living, lacking a regular supply of water, electricity, heating and sewerage system.

Owing to the severe degradation of these areas, in 2008, the Italian government carried out a census of the camps in Lombardy, Lazio and Campania and allocated approximately €30 million to reduce the number of illegal camps and improve living conditions. However, this funding did not include the integration of these populations by providing them with public tenures.[29]

Eviction is a critical issue for these people. In recent years, the European Court of Human Rights has repeatedly issued interim measures to stop the forced eviction of Roma.[30] In addition, Italy was condemned by the European Committee of Social Rights for discrimination and infringement of the right to housing against Roma, Sinti and other

---

[28] <http://www.lastampa.it/2017/08/27/italia/cronache/dossier-occupazioniQz4U3PjnOuTd3xG54ukol/pagina.html>.

[29] Amnesty International, *La risposta sbagliata. Italia: il Piano nomadi viola il diritto di alloggio dei Rom a Roma* (2010).

[30] <https://www.opensocietyfoundations.org/voices/last-minute-court-ruling-could-prevent-future-roma-evictions>; <https://www.amnesty.org.uk/press-releases/italy-cruel-and-callous-roma-eviction-defies-european-court-ruling>.

nomadic populations.[31] More specifically, the eviction of such groups was held to lack any legal basis, and was not accompanied by the availability of alternative accommodation.

3.6 Law Relating to Temporary Dispossession

'Temporary dispossession' covers various categories of people who are evicted in order to protect other family members, or to refurbish inhabitable dwellings.

- **Eviction in the case of separation and divorce (Article 337-sexies of the Civil Code [CC])**
  After separation or divorce, one of the spouses may be allowed to continue living in the family/marital home if she or he has custody of the children. In fact, eviction of children from the family home would infringe their best interests. Therefore, the other spouse will be excluded from his or her own home, regardless of whether he or she is the owner. According to recent data, the right to live in the marital home is granted to former wives living with the children, in the majority of the cases (69 per cent).[32]

- **Eviction of violent spouse or removal of the victim from the family home**
  Cases of domestic violence, harassment, the threat to an individual's moral or physical integrity, in the context of families, fall under the category of victims of 'family abuse'.
  In these cases, pursuant to Articles 342*bis* CC and 736 CPC, the victim may claim for a judicial injunction against the perpetrator of violence or harassment. The court order can ban the guilty party from his or her own home and places where the victim usually frequents, as a precautionary measure. Law no. 119/2013, known as the 'Anti-Femicide Act', reinforced the protection of the victims of family abuse by introducing the intervention of the police force in cases of need, in order to evict the violent spouse. National data on

---

[31]   European Committee of Social Rights, Decision 7 December 2005 (*ERRC v Italy*); European Committee of Social Rights, Decision 25 June 2010 *COHRE v Italy*. For further details see G Guiglia, 'Il diritto all'abitazione nella Carta Sociale Europea: a proposito di una recente condanna dell'Italia da parte del Comitato Europeo dei Diritti Sociali' in *Rivista telematica giuridica dell'Associazione italiana dei costituzionalisti*, 2011, in part. 8 ff <www.associazion edeicostituzionalisti.it>.

[32]   <www.Istat.it> Report issued on 14 November 2016.

the number of eviction orders due to domestic violence are not available. A report published by a judge of the Tribunal of Milan stated that the total number of protection orders issued by the Tribunal was small (less than 31 for the years 2009–2011[33]).

- **The right to inhabit the marital home or family home after the spouse/partner's death**
  The spouse is entitled to inhabit the family home for all her or his life, pursuant to Article 540 CC. This provision is extended to the partner of a civil union (Italian same-sex marriage), according to Law no. 76/2016. Moreover, a cohabitant (who is neither married nor a party to a civil union) has a special temporary right to inhabit the dwelling in which the couple used to live, after a partner's death.

3.7 Soft Law/Codes and Their Effectiveness

There are some non-profit associations and charities that seek to help people facing an eviction.

The ADICO (Association for the Defence of Consumers),[34] for instance, provides a help desk that assists people in cases of default of rent and after they have received a formal notice of eviction from the landlord. In addition, various locally organized 'anti-eviction networks' strive to protest against and prevent evictions when public officers enforce eviction orders. Through the promotion of demonstrations and pickets, these anti-eviction networks highlight the difficult situations faced by those being evicted and capture public attention and opinion. The increase in public attention has led some municipalities to introduce various good practices. Some Italian municipalities, such as Pisa, Pavia and other central-northern cities, have ordered the suspension of all evictions during the winter months, following the model developed by many European countries, including France.

4. EXTENT OF EVICTIONS 2010–2015

Since the beginning of the economic crisis, there has been a general increase in evictions in Italy.

Evictions from owner-occupied dwellings have increased considerably, as a result of the enforcement of mortgages. According to a report by

---

[33] F Roia, *Crimini contro le donne* (Milan, Franco Angeli 2014).
[34] <http://www.associazionedifesaconsumatori.it/sportelli/sfratti-condominio>.

ADUSBEF,[35] between 2008 and 2012, evictions due to non-performing loans increased by almost 97.8 per cent; with an additional 10.3 per cent in 2013. The report shows an average number of 19 evictions per day in Italy. The situation became even worse in 2014, with an overall increase of 161 per cent of eviction procedures from 2008 to 2014. In 2015, there were 225 891 eviction procedures in Italy, and in 2016, the number of evictions is estimated at 267 323 (with an increase of 18.33 per cent).[36]

With regard to private renting in Italy, between 2005 and 2007 there were approximately 44 000 evictions per year.[37] Then, between 2008 and 2014, there was an overall increase of 47.8 per cent, but a huge reduction in 2015 (decreasing 16.6 per cent).[38] A significant risk factor for eviction is the lack of economic resources and subsequent non-payment of rent: from 2007 to 2013, the eviction orders issued for non-payment of rent almost doubled – from 33 959 to 65 302.[39] In the same period (2007–2013), the number of eviction orders for termination by the landlord also had a significant increase (about 300 per cent). It is likely that this is another effect of the crisis.

Evictions from social/public and institutional rented housing are not widespread. Public entities, in fact, prefer not to bring legal actions to evict tenants who breach their contract. Instead, public entities try to break the debt down into smaller instalments or to obtain public subsidies for households in situations of particular difficulty.

Even when eviction represents the main choice, public agencies do not always participate or assist in the process of trying to secure the optimal outcome – often for organizational reasons related to every office. This lack of involvement is usually reflected in the outcome. In addition, social housing tenants associations often promote a strong opposition to dispossession, arguing that the right to housing is a fundamental human right and cannot be violated when the households, following an eviction, do not have any alternative accommodation.

---

[35] ADUSBEF is an Italian association for the protection of bank and financial services clients (*Associazione difesa utenti servizi bancari e finanziari*). See documents at <http://www.adusbef.it/documenti>. In particular, this research has been carried out by ADUSBEF by analysing data emerging from 35 Italian Tribunals and collected until the end of 2013.

[36] Astasy srl and T.S.E.I, 'Italian Report and Data on Evictions', issued in 2016, <www.astasy.it> , which collects data concerning the period 2010–2015.

[37] There were 45 814 evictions in 2005 and 43 869 in 2007 (source: Ministero dell'Interno, 'Evictions from residential dwellings in Italy' (2015) <https://www.cisl.it/attachments/article/2736/sfratti_2015-dati-ministero.pdf>.

[38] Ministero dell'Interno (n 37).

[39] Ibid.

As regards illegal occupancy, evictions are often difficult to carry out. Generally, owners have to go through a long court-based procedure to obtain possession and demonstrate their right to the property. Where the eviction order is issued, intervention of a public force is generally required.

When illegal occupancy concerns public/social dwellings, management companies are entitled to use more effective remedies with a strong intervention of public forces, in order to put an end to the squatting. Reliable data on the eviction of squatters is difficult to obtain.

5. DEFINITION OF EVICTION – THREE PHASES AS PER EVICTION REPORT – PRE-COURT, COURT AND POST-COURT

The term 'eviction' refers to the final act of a complex procedure, which leads to the dispossession of immovable goods after a non-performing loan (mortgaged property), rental termination (tenancy), unauthorized occupancy, or other situations. The Italian legal system also uses the term 'eviction' to cover the complex procedure that leads to dispossession. The following sections consider the three phases of eviction for each specific type of housing tenure.

5.1 Evictions from Mortgaged Properties

The grounds for eviction in terms of mortgage law are outlined in the Civil Code, in the TUB (Italian Banking Law Code), and in the Civil Procedure Code. The Civil Code (CC) provides a general principle, according to which, every breach of contract that may lead to a termination of that contract must be 'non-scarcely significant' (Article 1455 CC).

Pursuant to Article 40 TUB, non-performance is significant when there is a delay of at least 30 days (and up to 180 days) in the payment of an instalment and, more importantly, when a delay occurs at least seven times during the contractual relationship.

Following significant non-performance, there is a pre-court phase where the bank sends the debtor a letter of formal notice, asking for the payment of the due amount. If the debtor does not settle overdue payments, the creditor can initiate the court-based phase. This can lead to a formal payment injunction, called 'Decreto ingiuntivo' (Article 633 ff. Civil Procedure Code), where the creditor reiterates their payment request. The debtor, at this stage, may propose a formal opposition to the injunction within 40 days, before the court.

However, if the opposition is declared unfounded, the injunction becomes enforceable and the creditor notifies a writ of execution and service of an enforcement order. This statute gives the debtor ten days for the payment of the whole capital, interest and expenses, after which the execution and the foreclosure will take place, within the next 90 days. At this point, the debtor still owns the mortgaged property. Accordingly, the court files a case for the forced sale of the property within 90 days. The submission of all the necessary documents follows within 120 days. When the filing is complete, the court appoints an appraiser within 30 days, in order to determine the sale price. The judge can also establish the date and kind of sale (for example an auction sale or a contractual sale). The sale generally takes place two or three years after the first initial notice.

5.2   Evictions From Private/Social Rented Housing

5.2.1   Eviction from private rented housing

Eviction is based on the termination of the tenancy contract due to expiration or non-performance. Any eviction process can start only if the landlord complies with the requirements for termination and withdrawal set out by Law no. 431/1998. Pursuant to Article 657 CPC, the landlord may issue a formal notice, by which the tenant is requested to leave the dwelling within a certain period of time. This notice also contains a summons to appear before a judge. Consequently, the court-based phase starts, and the judge is entitled to validate the order requesting the tenant to leave the property.

If the tenant continually fails to pay the amounts due, the landlord can request both the eviction of the tenant and payment of the whole amount due (Article 658 CPC). Actually, a quick, informal procedure for eviction is available to the landlord under Articles 657 and 658 of the CPC, whereby the court promptly grants the landlord a decision authorizing him or her to evict the tenant in arrears. Only in the event of opposition by the tenant does the procedure revert to an ordinary lawsuit.

The right to evict a tenant may not be immediately enforceable. In accordance with Article 56 Law no. 392/1978, a judge may delay the date for the execution of an eviction (see also Section 3.3 above). Where a tenant does not voluntarily respect an order to leave a dwelling within the terms indicated by a judge, he or she can be issued with a notice (precetto), informing him or her that in the event of non-compliance with the order, a forced execution will be carried out (Articles 605–611 CPC). This last phase may require the intervention of the police.

5.2.2   Eviction from social rented housing

Eviction procedures for social rented housing generally follow a specific set of rules. Each region can however decide both the requirements and the procedures for eviction, which in turn gives rise to a very fragmented national situation.

Eviction can be the consequence of several different reasons, which can be generally grouped within the following categories expressly provided by law: violations of the rules regarding the use of the dwelling, non-regular payment, and original or supervening lack of the necessary requirements to receive the dwelling.

A previous judicial phase is not necessary to enforce dispossession, as the order of the municipality already represents a title empowering forced execution. The date of execution is determined by the order of eviction; generally, it has to comply with the terms set out by regional laws.

Some regional statutes provide both eviction procedures in accordance with private law rules and administrative procedures.[40] Administrative procedures are quicker, as they lead to the automatic loss of the right to stay in a dwelling. In some cases, however, municipalities prefer not to adopt an order of eviction, for instance in cases of non-payment of rent. Accordingly, the entities that manage public dwellings may decide to follow the ordinary private law procedure against defaulting tenants. Judicial control of the legitimacy and fairness of the municipality order of eviction only takes place in cases where the tenant files an opposition to the procedure.

5.2.3   Eviction from unauthorized occupancies

Unauthorized occupancy gives rise to different legal consequences. First, illegal occupancy is a violation of the owner's right to possess the immovable property. In order to terminate the occupancy, the owner can send the occupant a formal notice, asking him or her to leave the property within a reasonable time. Subsequently, a court-based phase may start. If the occupant does not comply with the terms set out by the notice, the owner can file a special action in defence of possession. The action gives rise to a summary legal proceeding, which aims to reinstate the owner with possession of his or her property (Article 1168 CC).

---

[40]   Tuscan Regional Law 20 December 1996, no. 96, arts 16, 30, 33.

Secondly, illegal occupancy is also viewed as a violation of the owner's property right. The occupant may argue that the owner has lost the right to own the dwelling. In this case, the owner must claim that his or her property right is still in place, providing evidence on how he or she is entitled to the ownership (and has not subsequently lost this entitlement).

Thirdly, squatting is a criminal offence under Article 633 of the Criminal Code. After the 'notitia criminis', the occupant is charged with the criminal offence and may or may not be convicted.

Whenever the court decides that there is no legal basis for the occupancy, an order of immediate eviction is issued and managed by the prefect, as explained under Section 3.5. When occupants refuse to leave the dwelling, the intervention of the police is the most frequent outcome to secure possession by the owner.

5.3   Other Evictions

5.3.1   Evictions in the case of separation and divorce
Family home assignment is based on a court judgment, unless the spouses reach an agreement by means of an alternative dispute resolution procedure called 'assisted negotiation', which was introduced by L. legislative decree no. 34/2014.

After the court's decision or the validation of an assisted negotiation agreement concerning the assignment of the family home, the procedure is generally informal. Only if the other former spouse does not comply with the decision, can the one who is entitled to live in the marital home claim an eviction order.

5.3.2   Eviction of violent spouse
In cases of domestic violence, a judge may order the eviction of the violent family member from the family home and determine its duration. The enforcement may require the intervention of the police. The decree is issued in a council chamber and cannot be appealed. A complaint against the decree is permitted, without any prejudice to its enforceability.

5.4   Commentary on the Statistics

This chapter has highlighted the general increase in the number of people evicted, or at risk of eviction, in all types of residential sector. The statistics quoted above show that, in Italy, evictions are primarily the consequence of the economic recession and the deterioration of the financial conditions of many Italian households.

Recent data highlights that the impact of the global economic crisis has led to a collapse in the housing market,[41] with the consequence that residential tenures have become more accessible in both the owner-occupied and rental markets. For instance, since 2012, rent levels have decreased by 25 per cent and sale prices by 15 per cent. From 2010 (the peak of the economic crisis) to the second half of 2015, the devaluation of real estate was on average 15 per cent, and 20 per cent for non-new builds.[42] Notwithstanding this change in the real estate market, the ongoing economic stagnation raises the concern that this critical situation will not be resolved in the near future.

5.5 Profile of Those Evicted

There is insufficient official data available across the country on the numbers of people who are involved at all stages of the eviction process. However, some surveys and research have revealed a fragmented framework, with victims of evictions and housing emergencies coming from different contexts and experiences. The Tuscany Regional Department for Welfare and Housing Policy and a private foundation (Fondazione Michelucci)[43] have investigated the phenomenon by interviewing various people involved. The individuals chosen were representatives of different social categories, such as single parents, young couples, immigrants, and old people living alone. Despite these differences, various common features emerge from the survey: in most cases, families live with only one salary, when only one family member has a job; they also experience eviction problems after a job loss or the death of a family member. The average age of an evicted person appears to be around 55–65 years. This may be due to the fact that job loss during this time of life is becoming increasingly frequent, because of the economic crisis and the collapse of key industrial sectors in Italy, such as the construction industry.

---

[41] E Sgambato, 'Istat e Assofin-Crif-Prometeia: mutui ancora a picco', *Il Sole 24 Ore*, 12 December 2012.

[42] ISTAT, 'I prezzi delle abitazioni', 4 October 2016, 1 <http://www.istat.it/it/files/2016/10/CS-abitazioni-provv-Q22016.pdf?title=Prezzi+delle+abitazioni+-+04%2Fott%2F2016+-+Testo+integrale+e+nota+metodologica.pdf>.

[43] <http://www.fondazionecasalucca.it/assets/Uploads/Pubblicazioni/la-Toscana-degli-sfratti.pdf>.

6. RISK FACTORS IDENTIFIED LEADING TO EVICTIONS FROM EACH HOUSING TENURE

Data shows that the majority of evictions of tenants are the consequence of the non-payment of rent (89 per cent in 2013).[44] This confirms that adverse economic circumstances are clearly the most important risk factor in the field of tenancy.

Economic distress also plays a key role in evictions from mortgaged properties. It is worth noting that, in some cases, banks may be incentivized to promote evictions in order to recover lending debt as a dramatic consequence of a risky over-lending policy they might have carried out in the past. The forced sale of mortgaged dwellings has, however, always been considered as a last resort, owing to the extensive and sometimes unsuccessful procedures involved.[45] Over the last few years, despite the significant increase in the number of evictions, the number of houses sold at auction has been decreasing. In addition, discounts and multiple sales are higher. As a result, there is an increased tendency to avoid eviction procedures and, instead, to find an agreement with the debtor, which often prevents eviction.[46]

The temporal connection with the economic crisis suggests that many of these evictions are due to the effects of the crisis, such as the reduction in income and job loss. Despite some reduction in the amount of rents, their level is still comparatively high (if related to an average income), especially because both the demand for houses to rent and house taxation have increased since the beginning of the crisis.[47]

---

[44]   Scuola Superiore dell'Amministrazione dell'Interno, Ufficio Centrale di Statistica (2014) 7.

[45]   E Sgambato, 'Le aste immobiliari crescono ma spesso vanno deserte' ('Auctions of dwellings increase but they are often not attended') *Il Sole 24 Ore, Casa 24 Plus 2013* (Sgambato (2013) I) <http://www.casa24.ilsole24ore.com/art/mercato-immobiliare/2013-04-10/aste-immobiliari-crescono-spesso-175705.php?uuid=AbQW11lH>.

[46]   Sgambato (2013) I (n 45); Borse.it, *Crisi: nel 2012 nuovo balzo delle esecuzioni immobiliari, +22% dal 2009* (Crisis: in 2012 a further rise in evictions, +22% since 2009) (2014) <http://redazione.borse.it/2014/04/02/crisi-nel-2012-nuovo-balzo-delle-esecuzioni-immobiliari-22-dal-2009/>; Fallimenti.it, *Ancora vendite in calo: le aste immobiliari sono in crisi* (Sales still decreasing: auctions of dwellings are in crisis) (2013) <http://www.fallimenti.it/aste-immobiliari/ancora-vendite-in-calo3a-le-aste-immobiliari-sono-in-crisi-425>.

[47]   E Sgambato, 'Affitti – Canoni in calo e morosità: due spine per i proprietari' ('Tenancies – Decreasing rents and non-payment: two thorns for home owners') *Il Sole 24 Ore, Casa 24 Plus* 2013 (Sgambato (2013) II)

Termination by the landlord before the expiration of the contract is allowed, but only in circumstances expressly provided by the law. Some of these take into account the necessities of the landlord (such as the landlord wanting to use the rented dwelling for him/herself or his/her relatives; or that he/she wants to sell the dwelling) and are therefore highly relevant in a period of economic crisis.

7. LINKS BETWEEN EVICTIONS AND HOMELESSNESS

Although specialist studies concerning the link between eviction and homelessness are not available, newspapers and local sources appear to be reporting, almost on a daily basis, on the homeless emergency affecting many Italian cities.[48] The eviction problem is now considered 'a social bomb',[49] often leading to homelessness.

Homelessness can be linked to evictions from rented dwellings and mortgaged properties. In the most acute circumstances, homelessness occurs immediately after eviction. Sometimes, homelessness results from being unable to find any housing alternative (including staying with a hosting relative or 'co-housing' in hostels). Local associations such as 'Caritas' centres often try to contain the housing emergency in these situations, providing short-term free accommodation. Unfortunately, homelessness affects a wide range of evicted people, regardless of their education or former job.[50] The most worrying issue for evicted people is that where eviction is a consequence of job loss, and despite trying to survive without an income, they find it very difficult to find a permanent solution to their homelessness, insofar as they cannot easily re-enter the job market and therefore cannot afford to pay rent or finance a loan.[51] Accordingly, the highest risk of homelessness after an eviction affects

---

<http://www.casa24.ilsole24ore.com/art/mondo-immobiliare/2013-08-05/affitti-canoni-calo-morosita-104421.php?uuid=AbJrgPKI>.

[48]   'Istat, Report on Homeless People, 2015' <https://www.istat.it/it/files/2015/12/Persone_senza_dimora.pdf?title=Le+persone+senza+dimora+-+10%2Fdic%2F2015+-+Testo+integrale.pdf>.

[49]   See 'L'Italia sotto sfratto' <http://inchieste.repubblica.it/it/repubblica/rep-it/2012/10/19/news/sfratti-44856857/>.

[50]   F Mancosu, 'Sfratti e senza tetto in aument'<http://www.umbria24.it/terni-caritas-sfratti-e-senzatetto-in-aumento-dal-comune-lavoriamo-sul-lungo-termine/219620.html>.

[51]   <http://iltirreno.gelocal.it/pisa/cronaca/2014/08/19/news/costretta-a-chiedere-l-elemosina-in-corso-italia-a-58-anni-1.9782210?ref=fbfti>.

those people who have no means to climb the social/economic ladder (including, for example, immigrants and old people).[52]

8. SUMMARY OF SIGNIFICANT CASES AND REPORTS RELATED TO EVICTIONS FROM 2010–2015

Evictions are widely covered by the media in Italy, and typically focus on two main issues. The first concerns the critical situations in which evicted people are unable to repay loans or to pay the rent and consequently face an eviction order. Dramatic personal stories were collected by an investigative report by *L'Espresso*, at the end of 2015.[53] The report highlighted difficult situations such as the case of a middle-aged woman, Ms M, living with a disabled daughter, who had faced various eviction orders over the years. Ms M finally got the opportunity to live in a public dwelling in Rome owing to her daughter's medical condition. However, the unfortunate fact that Ms M's daughter was disabled was sadly transformed by the media into a 'privilege' in order to obtain the public dwelling. During this time the City of Rome had 50 000 people on a waiting list seeking accommodation and 100 000 people facing a real 'housing emergency'.

The second problem identified in media reports concerns the unauthorized occupancy of public dwellings. For example, following an inquiry led by the public authorities in Rome, 743 people illegally occupying public dwellings were evicted.[54] The inquiry also uncovered an illegal business based on the transfer of the dwellings, promoted by web advertising and performed by criminal organizations.

---

[52]   ST Cambini and N Solimano, 'Sfratti, una questione non prorogabile' 2013 <http://www.fondazionecasalucca.it/assets/Uploads/Pubblicazioni/la-Toscana-degli-sfratti.pdf>.

[53]   <http://espresso.repubblica.it/inchieste/2015/12/18/news/senza-casa-il-dramma-degli-sfratti-in-italia-si-specula-ma-aumenta-chi-non-ha-un-tetto-1.243938>.

[54]   <http://roma.corriere.it/notizie/cronaca/15_luglio_09/sfratto-743-inquilini-abusivi-case-alloggio-popolare-716742d4-2658-11e5-9a08-f80f881ecc8e.shtml>.

9. BEST PRACTICE MODELS FOR PREVENTING, TACKLING AND REACTING TO EVICTIONS

9.1 Owner-occupied Housing

9.1.1 Preventive measures

Preventive measures can be implemented at (1) the pre-contractual stage, and (2) the contractual-performance stage.

1. **Pre-contractual stage: responsible lending and duties of disclosure**

    Directive 2014/17 EU on Mortgage Credit has had a significant impact on the Italian provisions regarding the pre-contractual stage. Italy transposed Directive 2014/17 EU by adopting the Legislative Decree no. 72/2016.[55] The main approach of the transposition of the MCD (Mortgage Credit Directive) into the Italian legal system seems to focus on responsible lending and borrowing. On one hand, in terms of responsible lending, the new legislation aims to stop any kind of 'predatory lending'. New rules on appraisals, set out by Article 120 duodecies TUB, for instance, give a clear example of this approach, by preventing malpractices in terms of credit unworthiness and overindebtedness. On the other hand, responsible borrowing is one of the most important objectives of the new rules on transparency, enacted by the government and the Bank of Italy.[56]

---

[55] The legislation was enacted on 21 April 2016 and entered into force on 4 June 2016.

The Decree introduced a new set of rules in the Italian '*Testo Unico Bancario*' (D.Lgs. no. 385/1993, a sort of *Banking Law Code*), amending Title VI of the statute with a '*Capo I-bis*' (Arts 120 *quinquies* and ff). Following the Italian Parliament's adoption of the Decree, the Bank of Italy developed a prudential regulation in order to ensure the effectiveness of the Directive and amended two Regulations issued by the Bank of Italy (Regulation on Transparency and Fairness of 2009 and Regulations no. 285 and no. 288/2013.

[56] In this framework, Art 120.2 *novies* TUB introduces the ESIS (in Italian known as 'PIES', '*Prospetto europeo standardizzato*'), by which the consumer is provided with all the personalized information needed to compare the credit agreements available on the market and make an informed decision regarding the conclusion of the agreement. The ESIS model for Italy (PIES) is provided by Annex 4 to the Bank of Italy Regulation adopted on 29 July 2009 and amended in 2016. The above-mentioned provisions, therefore, are part of a transparency-oriented legislative technique. The notion of transparency has been extensively analysed by Italian scholars. See S Pagliantini, 'Trasparenza', in *Enc. Dir.*,

2.   Contractual-performance stage: mid-term subsidies granted by the government upon agreement with the mortgage industry

The main initiatives put in place by the Italian government in order to combat the cycle of default on mortgage/eviction/foreclosure addresses temporary economic hardship and access to credit for people under thirty-five with a limited income.

- The Fondo di solidarietà (Solidarity Fund),[57] finances the suspension by the mortgagor of the payment of due instalments (capital and interest) of the loan subscribed for the purchase of the primary (and only) residential home, in cases of
  - (a)   death;
  - (b)   total impairment caused by accident or disease;
  - (c)   non-voluntary termination of an employment contract or an independent contractor agreement, the latter being by far the most common cause of hardship.[58]
- The 2015 agreement between the ABI and ten consumer associations regulates the area of family credit.[59] The agreement allows families experiencing hardship to request the suspension of the payment of the due capital for 12 months, provided they meet certain requirements.[60]

Annali (Milano 2011). Transparency aims to protect the consumer by defining a series of informative duties that banks must perform in the pre-contractual phase. See T Rumi, 'Profili privatistici della nuova disciplina sul credito relativo agli immobili residenziali' (2015) *Contratti* 70; S Pagliantini, 'Statuto dell'informazione e prestito responsabile nella direttiva 17/2014/UE (sui contratti di credito ai consumatori relativi a beni immobili residenzial' (2014) (2) *Contratto e Impresa/Europa* 525.

[57]   The Agreement was established by the Law 24 December 2007, n. 244, as modified by the Law n. 92/2010 and integrated by Ministerial Decree n. 37 of 22 February 2013.

[58]   In order for the Fund to intervene, the capital lent must not exceed €250 000 and the owners' income indicator (ISEE) must not be higher than €30 000 per year.

[59]   <https://www.abi.it/Pagine/news/Raggiunta-intesa-su-nuova-moratoria-famiglie.aspx>.

[60]   The credit agreement must have a duration of at least 24 months and the request can be addressed to the creditor if in the two years prior to the request the debtor died or lost his or her job or became seriously ill (loss of self-sufficiency or disability) or was subject to a reduction in working hours and thus the prerequisites for participating in social programmes such as *cassa integrazione* (unemployment insurance system). If the loan is secured for an immovable residential property, the family can ask for suspension. Between March 2015 and December 2016, 11 338 families obtained the 12-month

- The Guarantee Fund for first home residential mortgages[61] operates by standing surety upon first demand on mortgages or mortgage portfolios, in the amount of up to 50 per cent of the capital loaned.

9.1.2 Tackling measures and reacting measures

The main tackling measure aims to offer the debtor a 'last resort remedy' against dispossession and forced sale (Article 495 CPC). When the court issues the order of forced sale, the debtor may file a request for the 'conversion' of the procedure. If the request is accepted, the court states that the forced execution on the estate may be stopped provided the debtor pays a certain amount of money (entire debt plus interest on arrears, and expenses of the procedure).

Reacting measures are quite weak in the Italian system. This is due to the insufficient supply of social housing and the lack of public investments. In 2013, for example, 650 000 households were still on the social housing waiting list.

A quick re-housing of evicted people is considered the most effective tackling measure; at this stage, however, it is still a privilege. In this framework, the pilot project Housing First aims to provide homeless people with accommodation as the first step in reintegrating them back into society. Tuscany, Sicily and Emilia Romagna have been implementing this project and there are several re-housing projects for Roma and Sinti.

9.2 Private Rented Housing

9.2.1 Preventive measures

The National fund for supporting access to rented housing (Fondo nazionale per il sostegno all'accesso alle abitazioni in locazione: Article 11 L. no. 431/1998) facilitates access to the private rental market for people who cannot afford to pay market rents. In the mid-term perspective, it works as a means of preventing tenants from falling into arrears. However, the resources allocated to the fund have been reduced over the

---

suspension set by the above-mentioned agreement between the ABI and ten leading consumer associations <https://www.abi.it/Pagine/news/Moratoria_rate.aspx>.

[61]   The Fund was established by Law no. 147/2013.

years (minus 41 per cent from 2000 to 2006) and therefore its effectiveness is currently limited.[62]

9.2.2 Tackling measures

Beside the tenant's right to remedy the default in rent payment and the moratoria aimed at protecting the most vulnerable debtors, legislative decree no. 102/2013 established a fund for tenants in arrears due to economic hardship or force majeure (unemployment, a significant reduction in working hours, forced end of an autonomous job and serious diseases affecting the income).[63] The financial support, which cannot exceed €8000 for each household, may either settle overdue rent up to two years or subsidize the payment of rent due up to the postponed eviction, where the landlord agrees.

After the eviction phase, municipal social policies provide special assistance to households or single persons at risk of homelessness. Social services are responsible for tackling homelessness by providing temporary shelter, and primary services such as food, medical care, clothes and personal hygiene facilities.[64]

10. CONCLUSION

In Italy, the problem of housing affordability is far from being solved. In both owner-occupied and private rental tenures, the economic crisis has led to an increase in the number of households having difficulty paying mortgage instalments and rents. Moratoriums and other anti-eviction measures work as stopgaps, but a more consistent, well thought out housing policy is needed. The imbalance between rental and ownership[65]

---

[62]   Sunia, 'Il Fondo Sociale per l'Affitto', (2007) 4 <http://www.sunia.it/documents/10157/4f9ce507-7c1d-46f2-b6bb-1f6b835b5a7f>.

[63]   Ministry of Infrastructure and Transport Decree 14 May 2014.

[64]   See, for instance, the hosting centre in Milan, via Graf, <http://www.comune.milano.it/wps/portal/ist/it/news/primopiano/tutte_notizie/politiche_sociali/accoglienza_senzatetto_cani_30112017>.

[65]   See the Report 'Distribuzione della proprietà e del patrimonio immobiliare e flussi dei redditi delle locazioni' <http://www.finanze.it/export/sites/finanze/it/.content/Documenti/altri/Immobili_2015_3_Distribuzione_della_proprietx_e_del_patrimonio_immobiliare_e_flussi_dei_redditi_delle_locazioni.pdf>. Less than a fifth of the Italian households (18.7 per cent) live in rented apartments. These are mainly single-income families (67 per cent), with a substantial share of workers (39.6 per cent) and retired people (32.9 per cent): those who lost the race to purchase a house during the decade before the crisis. This is an utterly

is not the spontaneous outcome of a natural bent of Italian people for estate property but is encouraged by the institutional framework. The preference for purchasing is the outcome of social policies that channelled the housing demand towards the real estate market, the dismantling of public housing development programmes, and the divestitures of public real estate over the last decade.

Stronger investments in social housing and subsidies for tenants in the private rental market are needed in order to enhance the integration between owner-occupied, private rented and social rented housing tenures.

---

impoverished segment of the population, gliding into social marginalization: the household income is lower than €30 000 for 96.5 per cent, and lower than €20 000 for 76 per cent, which means that the rent takes up on average half of the earnings of a household, and up to two-thirds in major towns.

7. Evictions in the Netherlands

Michel Vols[1]

1. INTRODUCTION

This chapter assesses the number of evictions in the Netherlands as well as the legal protection offered against eviction. Data shows that approximately 20 000 eviction judgments are given in the social rental sector every year. The main reason is rent arrears. The data also shows that approximately one-third of these judgments are actually executed. Evictions do take place in the private rental sector as well, but clear data is lacking. Although private rental tenants enjoyed the same level of tenure security as those in the social rental sector, recent legislation has introduced short-term leases and made the eviction of private rental tenants easier. In the owner-occupied sector, thousands of evictions occur every year, but precise data is lacking. The main reason is mortgage arrears. Another cause of evictions is administrative closures of premises due to drug-related crime. Research has found that local authorities close hundreds of residential properties each year. This chapter shows that Dutch law provides people at risk of eviction with robust legal protection. Under Dutch law, they are entitled to have the proportionality of the eviction assessed by a court. Nonetheless, quantitative analysis of eviction litigation finds that in most cases, proportionality defences do not have a significant impact.

In light of the recent economic and financial crises in various countries throughout the world, it is becoming extremely difficult to ignore the growing numbers of evictions.[2] A considerable literature has grown up around the reasons for evictions, the tense relationship of evictions with human rights such as the right to housing, and the consequences of

[1]   This work was supported by the Netherlands Organization of Scientific Research NWO (Veni grant 451-15-013).
[2]   K Brickell, MF Arrigoitia and A Vasudevan, *Geographies of Forced Evictions* (London, Palgrave 2017).

evictions.[3] However, data about the actual number of evictions and an overview of the legal protection in jurisdictions are often very limited. This lack of data hinders the possibility of comparative (legal) analysis. Therefore, this chapter aims to provide an overview of the number of evictions in the Netherlands in both the owner-occupied sector as well as the rental sector. Furthermore, the chapter assesses the legal protection against eviction offered by Dutch legislation and policy and gives an account of interventions to prevent and address evictions in the Netherlands.

2. POLICY BACKGROUND

2.1 General Housing Policy Related to Evictions

The Dutch housing stock consisted of 7 641 323 premises in 2016.[4] In the last few decades, it has been official government policy to promote home ownership and this policy has been successfully implemented. In 1986, a large minority of premises were owner-occupied (43 per cent), whereas in 2016, a majority of all premises are occupied by the owners (56.2 per cent).[5] The vast majority of the owner-occupied premises are encumbered with a mortgage.[6] The total mortgage debt is more than 100 per cent of the Gross Domestic Product.

One of the government's tools to promote home ownership was the establishment of the Homeownership Guarantee Fund (WEW) in the nineties. The WEW introduced the National Mortgage Guarantee Scheme (NHG), which provides a mortgage guarantee for mortgage loans up to €245 000 from 2015 (in 2014: €260 000). Borrowers pay a fee of 1 per cent of the loan fee of when the mortgage is established. If it is necessary

---

[3] See S Fick and M Vols, 'Best protection against eviction? A comparative analysis of protection against evictions in the European Convention on Human Rights and the South African Constitution' (2016) 3 *European Journal of Comparative Law and Governance* 40–69; P Kenna, L Benjaminsen, V Busch-Geertsema and S Nassare-Aznar, *Pilot Project – Promoting Protection of the Right to Housing. Homelessness Prevention in the Context of Evictions* (VT 2013/056) (European Union: European Commission, Directorate-General Employment, Social Affairs and Inclusion 2016).

[4] Centraal Bureau voor de Statistiek (CBS), Statline (2016) <http://stat line.cbs.nl/>.

[5] I Visser, *De executoriale verkoop van onroerende zaken door de hypotheekhouder* (Boom Juridische uitgevers 2013) 75; CBS 2016 (n 4).

[6] CBS, Statline (2015) 63.

to sell a dwelling and the proceeds are insufficient to redeem the loan, the NHG will, under conditions, take over the remaining debt. In 2015, 78 per cent of the buyers who bought premises of less than €245 000 financed the purchase with a mortgage and an NHG surety.[7]

The other part of the housing market mainly consists of rental premises. Private landlords own 13 per cent of the housing stock, which is roughly 30 per cent of the rental premises. Most of the rental premises in the private rental market are owned by private investors (77 per cent), and the other premises are owned by institutional landlords such as insurance companies.[8] It is estimated that the vast majority of private investors own less than ten premises.[9]

Housing associations rent out the majority of the rental premises: they own 29.5 per cent of the total housing stock, which is nearly 70 per cent of all rental premises. The housing associations are private non-profit organizations that are statutorily obliged to provide affordable housing to the public.[10] According to the Housing Act 2015, the housing associations must rent the vast majority of their premises to people with a relatively low annual income (approximately €36 165 in 2017).[11]

2.2 Structural/Societal Factors Related to Evictions

Evictions do take place in the Netherlands, mainly due to payment arrears. The economic crisis stemming from 2000 to 2010 is said to have had a significant impact on the number of evictions. In the vast majority of cases, the reason for eviction is related to the occupiers' declining income or unemployment due to the economic recession.[12] Moreover, a growing number of evictions has to do with the recent repressive approach of Dutch housing associations and local authorities towards squatting and housing-related crime such as drug dealing and growing cannabis.[13]

---

[7]   Homeownership Guarantee Fund (WEW), *Jaarverslag 2014* (2015) 10.

[8]   M Jonker-Verkaart and F Wassenberg, *Kansen voor particuliere huur in Nederland* (Den Haag, Platform31, 2015) 14.

[9]   Ibid 17.

[10]   K Hermans, 'The Dutch strategy to combat homelessness: from ambition to window dressing' (2012) 6 (2) *European Journal of Homelessness* 103.

[11]   Art 46 of the Housing Act 2015.

[12]   N Boerebach, 'Prevention of evictions by social housing organisations in the Netherlands' (2013) *Homeless in Europe 2013* 12.

[13]   M Vols and S Fick, 'Using eviction to combat housing-related crime and anti-social behaviour in South Africa and the Netherlands' (2017) 134 (2) *South African Law Journal* 327–360.

2.3 Specific Policies Related to Evictions

From 2006 to 2014, the Dutch national government and the four biggest cities established and implemented an action plan to address homelessness and to reduce the number of evictions.[14] The evaluation of this action plan showed that the number of evictions in 2014 had been reduced by 22 per cent compared to 2005.[15] At local level, a number of policies are developed to prevent evictions. In the four big cities, but also in other municipalities, local authorities, housing associations and other stakeholders such as Social Services and Municipal Health Services have established inter-agency cooperation. These stakeholders inform one another about problems such as rent arrears and to take action (eg support with debt management) to prevent evictions.[16]

3. LEGAL AND CONSTITUTIONAL BACKGROUND TO PROTECTION AGAINST EVICTIONS

3.1 Housing as a Fundamental Right

Dutch legislation does not contain a fundamental right to housing as such. However, the Dutch Constitution lays down the obligations for authorities to provide sufficient living accommodation, and holds that the state is responsible for adequate housing and its distribution.[17] Furthermore, the Constitution gives inhabitants the right to respect for his or her private life[18] and the right to the inviolability of the home.[19] These two rights can only be restricted legitimately if an Act of Parliament provides a legal basis for such a limitation. Under Dutch law, it is not a matter of

---

[14]   W de Graaf, L van Doorn, R Kloppenburg and C Akkermans, 'Homeless families in the Netherlands: intervention policies and practices' (2011) 2 (1) *Journal of Social Research & Policy* 8; Hermans (n 10); S Gerull, 'Evictions due to rent arrears: a comparative analysis of evictions in fourteen countries' (2014) 8 (2) *European Journal of Homelessness* 148.

[15]   M Tuynman and K Planije, *Het kán dus!* (Utrecht, Trimbos 2014) 6.

[16]   RTHMK Kloppenburg, WAW De Graaf, M Wewerinke, C Akkermans and L Van Doorn, *Preventie en aanpak van dakloosheid van gezinnen bij vier centrumgemeenten* (Utrecht, HU 2009) 59; De Graaf et al (n 14) 9–11; K Planije, L Hulsebosch and M Tuynman, *Monitor Stedelijk Kompas 2013* (Utrecht, Trimbos 2014) 53.

[17]   Art 22 of the Dutch Constitution.

[18]   Art 10 of the Dutch Constitution.

[19]   Art 12 of the Dutch Constitution.

debate whether eviction can be seen as an interference with these rights. Consequently, various Acts of Parliament contain detailed provisions that stipulate the conditions under which authorities may restrict these rights by, for example, entering someone's home without permission or issuing an eviction order.

Besides that, the Netherlands ratified several international treaties that contain (elements) of the right to housing, such as the International Covenant on Economic Social and Cultural Rights, the European Social Charter and the European Convention on Human Rights (hereafter ECHR). With respect to evictions, Article 8 of the ECHR has the most impact on the eviction practices in the Netherlands.[20] Following the case law of the European Court of Human Rights, the Dutch Supreme Court held that eviction is a very serious interference with the right of the inviolability of the home. According to the Supreme Court, everyone at risk of this interference should in principle be able to have the proportionality of the eviction determined by an independent court before the eviction is carried out.[21]

As a result of these national and international requirements, procedural and substantive safeguards protect evictees. Under Dutch law, all occupiers are entitled to apply to a court to have their right to reside in a property reviewed by the court and request to dismiss an eviction order or to postpone the eviction. A number of tenure-specific eviction procedures and provisions are discussed in detail in the sections following.

3.2 Law Relating to Owner-occupation

The main ground for eviction in the owner-occupied sector is breach of the terms of the mortgage deed. The most common breach is mortgage arrears. Under Dutch law, the mortgagee has the right to summary execution.[22] This means that the mortgagee does not need to obtain a

---

[20]   M Vols, 'Artikel 8 EVRM en de gedwongen ontruiming van de huur-woning vanwege overlast' (2015) 2 *WR Tijdschrift voor huurrecht* 55–62; M Vols, M Kiehl and J Sidoli del Ceno, 'Human rights and protection against eviction in anti-social behaviour cases in the Netherlands and Germany' (2015) 2 *European Journal of Comparative Law and Governance* 156–181.

[21]   Hoge Raad 28-10-2011, *Nederlandse Jurisprudentie* 2013, 153; M Vols, PG Tassenaar and JPAM Jacobs, 'Dutch courts and housing related anti-social behaviour: a first statistical analysis of legal protection against eviction' (2015) *International Journal of Law in the Built Environment* 148–161.

[22]   Art 3:268 (1) of the Civil Code.

court's permission to sell the mortgaged property at a public auction.[23] However, Dutch law allows the parties to sell mortgaged properties by private treaty as well. Both the mortgagee and the mortgagor are entitled to request a court to allow him or her to sell the property by private treaty.[24] If the court allows the private sale, it can also oblige the mortgagor to vacate the property at the moment of the transfer of ownership of the property.[25] However, in the case where the mortgagee and the mortgagor both agree with the private sale of the property, the court's permission is not required.[26]

Since 2016, the mortgagee is not entitled to sell a mortgaged residential property immediately if the mortgagor is in arrears. The Civil Code obliges mortgagees to first contact the mortgagor personally for a consultation concerning the payment problems. The right to summary execution can only be used after such a consultation, and when the mortgagor is in arrears for at least two months, except in cases where these requirements are unreasonable.[27] This provision is the direct result of the implementation of the European Mortgage Credit Directive (2014/17/EU).

3.3 Law Relating to Private Renting

The legal requirements that apply to evictions in the private rental sector are practically the same as those that apply to the social rental sector. Most of the relevant provisions can be found in the Dutch Civil Code. The main ground for eviction in the rental market sector of the housing market is rent arrears. Failure to pay rent will qualify as a violation of the tenant's statutory obligation to behave as a good/prudent tenant and a breach of the lease, as will subletting, disruptive behaviour and involvement in drug-related crime. There are some other statutory grounds for landlords to terminate a lease, but in practice they do not play a significant role.[28]

A key characteristic of Dutch landlord-tenant law is that tenants enjoy robust protection against the termination of the lease. For decades, leases in both the private and social rental sectors were open-ended contracts,

---

[23] Visser (n 5).
[24] Art 3:268 (2) of the Civil Code.
[25] Art 3:268 (2) of the Civil Code.
[26] PA Stein, *Groene Serie Vermogensrecht* (Deventer, Kluwer 2016) sections 5,3,18.
[27] Art 7:128a of the Civil Code.
[28] Art 7:274 of the Civil Code.

even if parties concluded a temporary contract.[29] In addition, if the landlord wishes to terminate the lease unilaterally, this can only be done by a court.[30] There are two different court procedures that can be used to terminate a lease; however, landlords prefer to request the court to terminate the lease because of a breach of the lease.[31] The basic rule of this procedure is strict: every breach of the lease allows the court to terminate the lease and, consequently, issue an eviction order.[32] Accordingly, in cases where the landlord requests an eviction order, the court will first assess whether a breach of the lease has occurred. Furthermore, if a tenant puts forward a proportionality defence the court will need to take that into account as well. The tenant does not have to be legally represented, although this is recommended.

The National Committee of District Courts has laid down in a written recommendation that, in principle, three months of rent arrears will be a sufficient serious breach of the lease to allow a landlord's eviction claim. A recent analysis of case law concerning rent arrears eviction cases found that courts do follow this recommendation and allow most landlords' claims after three months of arrears.[33]

In 2016, the rules in the private rental sector changed. Parliament established the Act on Movement in the Housing Market 2016, which stipulates that new temporary contracts can be terminated unilaterally by a private landlord if the contract period has expired. Private landlords do not need to go to court to terminate the lease. However, if the tenant refuses to vacate the property, the landlord still has to request a court to issue an eviction order. Given the requirements arising from Article 8 ECHR, it is expected that the court will still assess the proportionality of the eviction. Whether the Act on Movement in the Housing Market 2016 really made it easier for private landlords to evict a tenant will be dependent on how intense this proportionality review will be.

---

[29]   There are a number of statutory exceptions. For example, Dutch law recognizes leases regarding the use of residential premises, which use, by its nature, is of short duration (Art 7:232 of the Civil Code). An example of such a lease is a lease regarding the rental of a holiday home. It is easier to terminate these leases, but the landlord still needs to obtain an eviction order if the tenant refuses to vacate the premises voluntarily.

[30]   Arts 7:231 and 7:274 of the Civil Code.

[31]   See Vols et al (n 20).

[32]   Vols (n 20).

[33]   M Vols and N Minkjan, 'Huurachterstand, huisuitzetting en rechterlijke besluitvorming' (2016) 37 (2) *Recht der Werkelijkheid* 9–30.

After the court issues an eviction order, the tenant can appeal the judgment and following that, even appeal to the Supreme Court. If the eviction order has immediate effect, the bailiff will serve the occupier a notice of the court judgment and an eviction date. The actual eviction will usually take place two or three weeks after the bailiff gave the notice. Before the actual eviction takes place, the bailiff must inform the local authority.[34]

3.4 Law Relating to Social Renting

The legal requirements that apply to evictions in the social rental sector are practically the same as those that apply to the private rental sector. However, in the social rental sector, open-ended contracts remain standard and leases can only be terminated unilaterally by court order. As in the private rental sector, tenants are allowed to advance a proportionality defence and argue that the landlord's claim should be dismissed. However, several quantitative analyses of eviction litigation concerning rent arrears, nuisance behaviour and drug-related crime have shown that tenants are not very successful in convincing courts.[35]

3.5 Law Relating to Unauthorized Occupancy

The Netherlands has a long squatting tradition and squatters used to enjoy robust legal protection against eviction.[36] However, in 2010, the Squatting and Vacancy Act was established. Since then, squatting is a criminal offence under Dutch law.[37] The Criminal Code provides a legal basis for the Public Prosecutor to evict squatters. To prevent an eviction based on criminal law, the squatters are entitled to initiate preliminary relief proceedings and request for a ban on the eviction. Besides that, the property owner is entitled to initiate eviction proceedings to have the squatters evicted.

In 2011, the Supreme Court held that the Squatting and Vacancy Act did not constitute a violation of Article 8 ECHR. However, it found that squatters, as any other occupiers at risk of losing their home, should in principle be able to have the proportionality of the eviction determined

---

[34] Art 14 of the Bailiffs Act.
[35] Vols et al (n 21); Vols and Minkjan (n 33).
[36] T Buchholz, *Struggling for Recognition and Affordable Housing in Amsterdam and Hamburg* (Groningen, University of Groningen 2016).
[37] Arts 138, 139 and 429 sexies of the Criminal Code.

by an independent court before the eviction is carried out.[38] Case law shows that squatters regularly try to stop criminal law evictions by advancing proportionality defences. Yet, in most cases the squatters lose their case.[39] Nonetheless, it does happen that courts allow proportionality defences and refuse to issue an eviction order.[40]

There remains a clear incentive for property owners to prevent squatting in their property or the local authorities oblige them to rent out their vacant premises. Dutch law offers a number of options that entitle property owners to protect their property against squatters by allowing so-called property guardians to live in the dwelling, without offering those occupiers the tenure security as provided by Dutch landlord–tenant law.[41] It is estimated that there are more than 50 000 property guardians in the Netherlands.[42] The various contracts between property owners and property guardians all share the same characteristic: they are not considered as a lease, and therefore the strong protection against eviction is not applicable. Nevertheless, Dutch law requires property owners to go to court if a property guardian does not vacate his or her home after the termination of the contract. During the court proceedings, the property guardian is still entitled to advance a proportionality defence and argue that eviction is disproportionate. Case law shows that courts do take into account proportionality issues, but do not always agree with the property guardian.[43]

3.6 Law Relating to Temporary Dispossession

Another reason for eviction is the temporary administrative closure of a property.[44] There are three reasons for such an administrative closure:

---

[38]   Hoge Raad 28-10-2011, *Nederlandse Jurisprudentie* 2013, 153. BQ9880.

[39]   Eg Rechtbank Midden-Nederland 8 April 2015, ECLI:NL:RBMNE:2015: 2623 paras 4.13–4.18.

[40]   Rechtbank Noord-Holland 11 March 2013, ECLI:NL:RBNHO:2013: BZ5008 para 4.7.

[41]   Eg Art 15 of the Squatting and Vacancy Act.

[42]   Buchholz (n 36) 94.

[43]   Rechtbank Midden-Nederland 9 April 2014, ECLI:NL:RBMNE:2014:1309 para 4.12.

[44]   M Vols, *Woonoverlast en het recht op privéleven* (Den Haag, Boom Juridische uitgevers 2013); Vols and Fick (n 13); LM Bruijn, M Vols and JG Brouwer, 'Home closure as a weapon in the Dutch war on drugs: does judicial review function as a safety net?' (2017) *International Journal of Drug Policy* 1–11.

violation of building regulations, severe nuisance behaviour or drug-related crime such as the cultivation and dealing of cannabis. In case of these events, local authorities are entitled to close down a property for up to five years.[45] The local authorities have a statutory obligation to take into account the closure order's consequences for the occupiers and must ensure that the order is not disproportionate.[46] After an administrative closure order is issued, nobody is allowed to enter the property anymore. The occupiers are entitled to challenge the closure order at court, and advance, for example, proportionality defences. However, an analysis of over one hundred judgments shows that occupiers are not very successful in convincing courts that the closure and its consequences violates their rights.[47]

After an administrative closure of a rental property, the landlord is allowed to unilaterally terminate the lease, so that the tenants are not allowed to re-enter the property after the administrative closure period.[48] Nevertheless, if the tenants refuse to vacate the premises, the landlord still needs to request the court to issue an eviction order. Several courts have established that in deciding whether to issue an eviction order or not, Article 8 ECHR obliges judges to take into account the tenants' proportionality defences. Consequently, it is doubtful whether the option to unilaterally terminate the lease is really helpful for landlords.[49]

3.7 Soft Law/Codes and Their Effectiveness

The four largest municipalities and a large number of smaller municipalities have established action plans such as Stedelijk Kompas (Urban Compass) and Plan van Aanpak maatschappelijke opvang (Plan of Approach to Social Care) to reduce the number of evictions.[50] As a result, local authorities, housing associations and other stakeholders have initiated inter-agency cooperation to inform one another about problems

---

[45] Art 17 of the Housing Act, Art 174a of the Municipalities Act and Art 13b of the Opium Act.

[46] Art 3:4 of the General Administrative Law Act.

[47] M Vols and LM Bruijn, 'De strijd van de burgemeester tegen drugscriminaliteit. Een eerste statistische analyse van de toepassing van artikel 13b Opiumwet' (2015) *Netherlands Administrative Law Library (NALL)* October 2015, 1–23; Bruijn, Vols and Brouwer (n 44).

[48] Art 7:231 (2) of the Civil Code.

[49] Vols (n 20).

[50] Planije et al (n 16).

such as rent arrears and to take action to prevent evictions.[51] Evaluations published in 2014 show that these projects have been fairly successful in preventing evictions.[52]

4. EXTENT OF EVICTIONS OVER THE PERIOD 2010–2015

4.1 Definition of Eviction

Kenna et al have distinguished three phases in the eviction process: (i) the pre-court phase, which begins from the moment of issuance of the formal instruction to leave; (ii) the court phase; and (iii) the post-court phases, which refers to the period between the court's eviction judgment and the actual physical eviction. All three phases have a link with homelessness. For example, occupiers may become homeless in the first phase of the eviction process (the pre-court phase) if they decide to vacate their home after receiving a notice to leave the property.[53]

4.2 Evictions from Mortgaged Property

Under Dutch law, the mortgagee does not require the permission of the court to sell the mortgaged property at a public auction.[54] Consequently, most evictions in the mortgaged sector will remain in the pre-court phase, as defined by Kenna et al.[55] There is no central register with systematically collected data concerning evictions in the owner-occupied sector.

Yet, some data concerning mortgage arrears and public auctions are available. As stated above (Section 3.2), mortgage arrears are the main reason for evictions in the owner-occupier sector. Table 7.1 shows the

---

[51] G Schout, G De Jong and I Van Laere, 'Pathways toward evictions: an exploratory study of the inter-relational dynamics between evictees and service providers in the Netherlands' (2015) 30 (2) *Journal of Housing and the Built Environment* 184.

[52] Tuynman and Planije (n 15); Planije et al (n 16).

[53] Kenna et al (n 3) 21–22.

[54] People are entitled to initiate court proceedings to prevent the public auction. The available case law suggests this does not happen frequently. See for example: Rechtbank Den Haag 13 February 2017, ECLI:NL: RBDHA:2017: 1632.

[55] Kenna et al (n 3) 67.

number of consumers in mortgage arrears over the period 2010–2015.[56] The increase is considerable: in 2015, 112 per cent more consumers were in mortgage arrears than in 2010.

Table 7.1   Consumers in mortgage arrears for the period 2010–2015

	Number of consumers in mortgage arrears
2010	52 821
2011	62 453
2012	77 145
2013	94 794
2014	111 284
2015	111 925

Nevertheless, mortgage arrears do not automatically result in eviction from a mortgaged property. According to data collated by the Dutch Land Registry Office, the number of public auctions in recent years averages approximately 2300 per year (see Table 7.2).[57]

Table 7.2   Public auctions with the Land Registry Office

	Public auctions
2010	2086
2011	2811
2012	2488
2013	1863
2014	2178
2015	2309
2016	2114

However, the figures in Table 7.2 include auctions of non-residential premises. Besides that, it excludes the number of properties sold by private treaty. There is no data available on the number of residential mortgaged properties sold by private treaty. Nonetheless, to gain some

---

[56]   Credit registration office BKR, *Maatschappelijk Jaarverslag* (Tiel, BKR 2015) 7.

[57]   Dutch Land Registry Office <www.kadaster.nl/executieveiligen>.

insight on the number of privately sold mortgaged properties, it is interesting to analyse the data published concerning the NHG Mortgage Guarantee. The Home Ownership Guarantee Fund (WEW) publishes data on the number of forced sales of mortgaged premises with NHG guarantee that result in a net loss (see Table 7.3).[58]

Table 7.3   Forced sales of mortgaged premises with NHG guarantee

	Private sale (%)	Public auction (%)	Total
2010	70	30	1335
2011	75	25	2201
2012	87	13	3576
2013	93	7	4580
2014	89	11	4799
2015	86	14	4477

Table 7.3 shows that the number of forced sales in 2015 is considerably higher (335 per cent) than in 2010. It also shows that the vast majority of the forced sales of mortgaged properties with NHG guarantee are completed by private treaty. Therefore, it is safe to assume that the total number of evictions from mortgaged premises each year is considerably higher than the 2000 to 2500 public auctions per year. Given the data in Tables 7.2 and 7.3, a conservative estimate would be that approximately 20 per cent of evictions in the mortgaged sector are the result of public auctions, and 80 per cent the result of forced private sale. This leads to a further conservative estimate of there being 1500 public auctions of residential premises per year,[59] 6000 private forced sales per year and, accordingly, 7500 (pre-court) evictions from mortgaged property per year.

---

[58]   WEW, *Jaarverslag 2011* (2012) 22; WEW, *Jaarverslag 2014* (2015) 29; WEW, *Jaarverslag 2015* (2016) 11.

[59]   The number is considerably lower than the number of auctions presented in Table 7.2, because the data in this table includes public auctions of non-residential premises and dwellings.

4.3   Evictions From Private/Social Rented Housing

No data could be sourced on evictions in the private rented sector.[60] There is data regarding evictions in the social rented sector. Every year, the organization of the housing associations (Aedes) publishes the number of (estimated) eviction judgments and executed eviction judgments as reported by its members. Eviction judgments refer to the number of court judgments that entitled the housing association to evict a tenant. Unfortunately, the data does not show how many eviction claims are lodged with the court, and how many of these claims are dismissed by the court. Therefore, it is unknown how many tenants encounter eviction proceedings in the social rented sector each year.[61]

Still, data on the number of cases won by landlords is available (see Table 7.4). The number of eviction judgments in the social rented sector for the years 2010 to 2016 reached a peak of more than 23 000 during the economic recession years (2012–2014). The figure for 2016, 18 500, represents a 20 per cent drop.[62] The number of executed eviction judgments (in which the tenant remains in the property after the eviction period has expired and the bailiff is required to execute the order of the court) also peaked during the economic crisis years, before declining. In 2016, approximately 30 per cent fewer eviction judgments were executed than in 2013.

The data with regard to executed eviction orders is, however, somewhat misleading, since a closer assessment of the definitions used indicates that the actual number of evicted tenants is higher. In 2016, for example, besides the 4800 eviction orders executed by the bailiff, a further 1700 tenants did not wait for the bailiff and left the property voluntarily. This means that in 2016 the actual number of evictions was 6500. Similarly, the actual number of evictions for 2015 and 2014 is, respectively, 7710 and 8700 when the number of tenants leaving voluntarily (2210 in 2015; 2800 in 2014) is taken into account.[63]

---

[60]   See I Van Laere, M De Witt and N Klazinga, 'Preventing evictions as a potential public health intervention: characteristics and social medical risk factors of households at risk in Amsterdam' (2009) 37 *Scandinavian Journal of Public Health* 700, for some insights on the number of evictions in the private rental sector in Amsterdam. Still, they found that the number of evictions cannot be calculated because of imprecise datasets.

[61]   Vols and Minkjan (n 33).

[62]   Aedes, *Corporatiemonitor* (Den Haag, Ades 2017).

[63]   Ibid.

Table 7.4   Eviction judgments and executed eviction judgments in the social rented sector

	Eviction judgments	Executed eviction judgments	Executed judgments (%)
2010	19 650	5900	30
2011	18 800	6000	31.9
2012	21 700	6480	29.9
2013	23 100	6980	30.2
2014	23 500	5900	25.1
2015	22 000	5550	25
2016	18 500	4800	25.9

This does not automatically mean that the number of actual evictions is on the rise. In the other years, Aedes applied the same definition of executed eviction order and the measurement is, as a result, in all years, the same. Still, until 2013, the 'hidden number' of voluntary executed judgments was not published by Aedes. Therefore, it is reasonable to suggest that the number of evicted persons is somewhat higher than as shown in Table 7.4.

Rent arrears is by far the most important cause of eviction over the last few years. Table 7.5 shows that this type of breach of the lease is, in 80 to 85 per cent of all executed eviction judgments, the main reason.[64] Other breaches of the lease such as nuisance behaviour, illegal subletting and drug-related crime play a less important role. Yet, while interpreting these numbers, it should be taken into account that, in many cases, there are combined breaches of the lease (eg rent arrears and nuisance behaviour) that may only be registered as rent arrears.[65]

Schout et al investigated the decisions housing associations make with regard to which eviction judgments will be executed.[66] Their findings are presented in Table 7.6.

---

[64]   Ibid.
[65]   C Akkermans and M Räkers, *Handreiking voorkomen huisuitzettingen* (Eropaf 2013) 26.
[66]   Schout et al (n 51) 185.

Table 7.5   Reasons for executed judgments in the social rented sector

	Arrears (%)	Nuisance (%)	Subletting (%)	Drugs (%)	Other (%)
2010	78.4	8	4.9	4.6	4.2
2011	78.8	7	7.5	6	0.7
2012	79.3	6.5	7.9	5.6	0.7
2013	88.4	2.9	3.1	4.2	1.4
2014	85	3.8	5.6	4.8	0.6
2015	84.2	5.4	5.1	4.9	0.4
2016	85.1	4.1	6.4	3.6	0.8

Table 7.6   Percentage of executed judgements for each reason

	Total (%)	Arrears (%)	Nuisance (%)	Subletting (%)	Drugs (%)	Other (%)
2006	40	35	91	97	92	91
2007	38	33	80	98	85	45
2008	36.1	30.9	81	89.4	79.8	70.1
2009	31.3	28.6	62.8	63.1	94.1	62.3

The table above shows that in specific rent arrears, approximately 32 per cent of all eviction judgments were executed between 2006 and 2009. This was lower than in the cases involving other reasons for eviction. Unfortunately, there is no more recent data available for the percentage of executed eviction orders per reason.

4.4 Evictions from Unauthorized Occupancies

No data has been collected concerning the number of evicted squatters or property guardians. Yet, some data is available regarding squatting in general. The evaluation report of the Squatting and Vacancy Act was published in 2015. It shows that the Public Prosecution Service dealt with a rising number of cases concerning squatting. Table 7.7 shows 2555 per cent more cases concerning squatting were handled by the Public Prosecution Service in 2014 than in 2010.[67]

---

[67] S Zeelenberg, E van Kessel, I Giesbers and Y Groote, *Van ontruimen naar inruimen* (Amsterdam, RIGO 2015) 16.

Table 7.7   Squatting cases dealt with by the Public Prosecution Service

	Squatting cases
2010	9
2011	71
2012	77
2013	111
2014	239

The evaluation report does not contain any data on evictions of squatted buildings. However, there are some indications that the number of evictions following the criminal ban on squatting in 2010 have peaked during 2010 and 2015. For example, Amsterdam had approximately one thousand squatted buildings in 1981 and was characterized as the squatting capital of the Netherlands. In 2012, only twenty squatted buildings remained in Amsterdam. According to media reports, 724 evictions of squatted buildings took place in Amsterdam between 1 October 2010 and May 2015.[68] Since the number of squatted buildings has declined so significantly, it can be expected that the number of evicted squatted buildings in the future will not be that high.

4.5   Other Evictions

Until 2015, there was no data systematically collected on the number of administrative closures of premises. Based on an analysis of municipal policy documents and case law, Vols and Bruijn estimated that a few hundred residential premises were closed by local authorities because of drug-related crime between 2008 and 2014.[69] The number of drug closure orders, however, has grown significantly in the last two years. Vols et al surveyed fifty local authorities (including the authorities in the forty largest municipalities) concerning the number of drug closure orders issued in 2015 and 2016.[70] As can be seen from the results shown in Table 7.8, the number of local authorities that responded to the survey was the same for both years (39). However, the number of administrative

---

[68]   AT5, 'Politie steeds sneller over tot ontruiming; kraak duurt gemiddeld twee weken' (2015) <http://www.at5.nl>.

[69]   Vols and Bruijn (n 47).

[70]   M Vols, JP Hof and JG Brouwer, *De handhaving van de Woningwet en de aanpak van malafide pandeigenaren* (Den Haag, Boom Juridische uitgevers 2017).

orders reported was significantly higher in 2016. This increase (approximately 53 per cent) indicates an upward trend in the number of residential premises closed and occupiers evicted.

Table 7.8   Administrative closures of residential premises in fifty Dutch municipalities

	Number of respondents	Number of administrative orders
2015	39	325
2016	39	498

4.6   Profile of Those Evicted

There is no clear data concerning the characteristics of evictees in the mortgaged sector. Still, the Credit Registration publishes data concerning the age of people in mortgage arrears. As stated above, mortgage arrears is the most significant reason for eviction in the owner-occupied sector. Data suggests that most of the people in mortgage arrears are between 31 and 50 years old.[71]

With regard to the profile of evictees in the rental sector, there is no data available concerning the private rental market. In the social rental sector, in most cases the housing associations do not record the evictees' type of household or age in the majority of cases (59 per cent in 2016). Table 7.9 shows the available data on the distribution of evictions among several types of households in the social rented sector.[72]

The table shows that among the single households that were evicted, most evictees were between 30 and 60 years old, followed by singles between 18 and 30 years old. According to Aedes, housing associations evict significantly fewer tenants who live with children.[73]

---

[71]   BKR, *Jaaroverzicht* (Tiel, BKR 2013) 18; BKR, *Maatschappelijk Jaarverslag* (Tiel, BKR 2014) 6.

[72]   Aedes (n 62).

[73]   Ibid 2.

Table 7.9   Types of evicted households in the social rental sector

	Single 18–30 years old (%)	Single 30–60 years old (%)	Single 60 years and older (%)	Single parent (%)	Couple without children (%)	Couple with children (%)	Others (%)	Unknown (%)
2013	9	15	2	3	4	2	0	65
2014	7	16	2	2	3	2	X	67
2015	8	22	2	4	2	2	1	60
2016	9	19	4	3	2	2	1	59

Other studies give additional insights into the characteristics of tenants facing eviction. Akkermans' study of persons at risk of eviction in the city of Utrecht found that all of them had financial problems with the housing association and other organizations, such as health care insurance companies and utility companies. A majority of the tenants reported problems with regard to their physical or mental health too. Some tenants reported problems concerning criminal activities, addictions and under-developed language and mathematical skills.[74] Yet, Wewerinke et al's qualitative study of thirty-two households facing eviction from their rental property found that they displayed different characteristics. Their financial situation and problems varied, some had serious mental health problems and others did not, and some of them had a support network and other persons did not. As a result, the researchers concluded that only tailor-made approaches to prevent evictions will be effective.[75]

5.   RISK FACTORS IDENTIFIED LEADING TO EVICTIONS

Research into the risk factors associated with evictions found that evictions are linked to problems concerning unemployment, divorce, neighbour disputes, mental and physical health, addiction, literacy problems and other insufficient skills necessitated for independent living and

[74]   C Akkermans, *Schuldhulpverlening en dreigende huisuitzetting* (Utrecht, HU 2011) 42–43.

[75]   D Wewerinke, W De Graaf, L van Doorn and J Wolf, *Huurders over een dreigende huisuitzetting* (Nijmegen RUMC 2014) 54.

building/maintaining a social network.[76] The absence of assistance and care, a history of unstable housing and the lack of (sufficient) social support also increase the risk of eviction.[77]

Research on evictions in the Dutch context shows that most of the risk factors apply to the Netherlands as well. For example, Van Laere et al's study of homeless adults in Amsterdam, gives some insights into the risk factors in a Dutch context. This research found that for 38 per cent of the adults surveyed, their homelessness was the result of eviction.[78] More often, they belonged to a major migrant group and were generally single and slightly older and had more alcohol and financial problems than the groups of homeless adults that were homeless due to other reasons. In addition, the eviction group reported financial problems (81 per cent) and domestic conflicts (44 per cent). Moreover, the vast majority of the group (78 per cent) reported medical problems such as addiction (59 per cent), mental health problems (63 per cent) and physical problems (17 per cent). Significantly, the eviction group of homeless adults had financial problems more often than adults who had become homeless for other reasons. The main reason for debts, among all recently homeless adults, was the loss of a job or a chronic shortage of income (49 per cent), buying drugs (18 per cent), gambling (10 per cent) and other reasons such as fines or health costs (23 per cent). The main creditors are banks (35 per cent) and landlords (34 per cent).[79]

Another study of Van Laere and his team also assessed characteristics of people living in Amsterdam that had been evicted and people at risk of eviction. This study found that evictees were more likely to be single, of Dutch origin and addicted to drugs than non-evicted people. Financial mismanagement was found to be a risk factor for eviction.[80]

In its analysis of evictions in the social rental sector, Aedes found that tenants in a weak financial position (eg those on social benefits) are at greater risk of being confronted with an eviction. Moreover, the data also shows that tenants with mental health problems are at a greater risk of

---

[76] Schout et al (n 51) 184; M Holl, L van den Dries and JRLM Wolf, 'Interventions to prevent tenant evictions: a systematic review' (2016) 24 (5) *Health and Social Care in the Community* 533.

[77] Holl et al (n 76) 533.

[78] I Van Laere, M De Witt and N Klazinga, 'Pathways into homelessness: recently homeless adults problems and service use before and after becoming homeless in Amsterdam' (2009) 9 (3) *BMC Public Health* 3.

[79] Ibid 7.

[80] Van Laere et al (n 60) 701–702.

eviction too.[81] No data is available with regard to evictees in the mortgaged sector of the housing market. Yet, the NHG Mortgage Guarantee Organisation publishes data concerning the reasons for the forced sale of mortgaged premises with such a guarantee that results in a net loss. Table 7.10 shows that the end of a relationship, unemployment or the involuntary loss of income are the main reasons for forced sale(s) with a net loss.[82]

Table 7.10   Reason for forced sale of mortgaged property with guarantee that ended in a net loss

	End of relationship (%)	Unemployment/ involuntary loss of income (%)	Incapacity for work (%)	Other reason (such as non-payment) (%)
2010	43	19	1	37
2011	50	21	2	27
2012	61	16	2	21
2013	77	18	X	X
2014	68	21	X	X
2015	59	29	5	7

According to the NHG Mortgage Guarantee Organisation, the number of forced sales with a net loss can be strongly linked to the credit crisis. The decline of housing prices means that if couples split up, they have to sell their property at a loss. Furthermore, more people lost their jobs and were unable to pay their excessively high monthly mortgage repayments anymore.[83] Consequently, this data suggests that risk factors identified in the owner-occupied sector of the housing market include financial instability, job insecurity and properties with high and risky mortgages.

---

[81]   Aedes (n 62) 3.
[82]   WEW, *Jaarverslag 2015* (2016).
[83]   WEW, *Jaarverslag 2013* (2014) 39; WEW, *Jaarverslag 2015* (2016) 28.

6. LINKS BETWEEN EVICTIONS AND HOMELESSNESS

A number of studies identify eviction as a significant pathway into homelessness.[84] Research clearly suggests that eviction is a major pathway into homelessness in the Netherlands as well.[85] Van Laere and his research team for example, sampled 120 adults in Amsterdam who had recently become homeless.[86] Before homelessness, two-thirds of the adults were living in a rented property. The three main pathways to losing their home were evictions (38 per cent), relationship problems (35 per cent) and other reasons (28 per cent).

7. BEST PRACTICE MODELS FOR PREVENTING, TACKLING AND REACTING TO EVICTIONS

There is a relatively small, but growing body of knowledge concerning ways to address and prevent evictions.[87] A number of studies have been conducted on how evictions are prevented and addressed in the Netherlands. Van Laere et al found that outreach networks should respond quickly to persistent rent arrears and nuisance. Landlords need to share information with social services. During a home visit by social workers, the underlying problems and unmet support should be assessed. They suggest specifically that low-income single men, with financial, addiction and other health problems should be targeted.[88] Another study concludes that housing associations should report households at risk of eviction to a central organization that handles these reports. The research suggests (i) that a purely administrative, non-personal relationship between tenants and housing association should be avoided (ii) that an active approach should be adopted regarding the provision of assistance and (iii) that outreach support should coordinate the efforts of landlords, social workers and medical workers.[89]

A study of Schout et al gives an overview of promising interventions that aim to prevent and combat evictions in the Dutch context.[90] This

---

84   Holl et al (n 76) 532.
85   Schout et al (n 51).
86   Van Laere et al (n 78).
87   See for a systematic literature review: Holl et al (n 76).
88   Van Laere et al (n 78).
89   Van Laere et al (n 60) 703–704.
90   Schout et al (n 51) 184

study cites debt advice, the monitoring of evictions on municipal level, agreements between housing associations and debt support organizations, and the establishment of community public mental health care networks that respond to signals of vulnerability of households as interventions worth pursuing. Furthermore, conflict escalation between housing association staff and tenants should be avoided and the capability of confronting conflicts constructively should be institutionalized. Housing association staff need to be trained in detecting signs of conflict escalation and develop negotiating skills. In addition, the researchers suggest a reduction of the concentration of people with a combination of social and medical problems in one neighbourhood. Lastly, housing associations and other professional support services involved need to recognize that prevention of eviction is an 'integral assignment that provides opportunities to learn for all actors'.[91]

A number of other studies regarding evictions in the Dutch context produced interesting results too. De Graaf and his research team found that evicted families are offered support in assertive, but also somewhat coercive outreach programmes. The evictees are offered support, but under the threat of losing their home. The researchers found that evicted families managed to keep their home, but that it is very difficult to ascertain the general success rate of the outreach programme with regard to the long-term effects.[92] Akkermans assessed an eviction prevention programme in the city of Utrecht that consisted of two years of housing supervision and debt support. She found that the success factors of the programme were the multidisciplinary cooperation of stakeholders, the active approach in addressing the financial and non-financial problems of the tenants, and clear rules in addition to the obligatory character of participation in the project.[93]

In another recent study in the Dutch context, De Vet et al considered how a relapse into homelessness can be prevented when rehousing people from shelters to community living. They found evidence that the Critical Time Intervention model seems to be suitable for vulnerable people who are going through a transition in their lives. This model aims to facilitate continuity of care and community integration and to ensure that the person has enduring ties to support systems and their community during critical periods.[94]

---

[91]   Ibid 196.

[92]   De Graaf et al (n 14) 12–13.

[93]   Akkermans (n 74) 50.

[94]   R De Vet, DAM Lako, MD Beijersbergen, L Van den Dries, S Conover, AM Van Hemert, DB Herman and JRLM Wolf, 'Critical Time Intervention for

Housing associations and municipalities are using this academic knowledge to address and prevent evictions in daily life.[95] The data published by Aedes concerning the social rental sector indicates that 97 per cent of housing associations reach out to the tenant by telephone, 90 per cent visit the tenant at home, 85 per cent work together with health care or debt help organizations and 71 per cent collaborate with the local authorities, and that 63 per cent of housing associations have intensified their rent collection policy to prevent high rent arrears. According to the housing associations, home visits and a strict rent collection policy are the most effective strategies to prevent arrears and evictions.[96] Other research found that municipalities are also active in preventing and addressing evictions and that the number of evictions has declined in recent years because of these interventions.[97]

8. CONCLUSION

The research findings presented in this chapter show that evictions take place in the Netherlands, in both the rental and owner-occupied sectors. Although data on evictions and homelessness is not systematically collected and the total number of evictions is not known, it is evident that in the Netherlands, several thousand people lose their home on an annual basis. The main reason for eviction in both the rental and the owner-occupied sector is payment arrears. Under Dutch law, people at risk of eviction seem to enjoy robust legal protection against eviction: the Supreme Court has acknowledged the ECHR requirement to entitle residents to have the proportionality of the loss of their home determined by a court. However, several studies found that although courts do assess proportionality issues and balance the parties' interests, proportionality does not result in a large number of refusals of eviction orders. Regarding interventions to prevent and address evictions, the studies presented here suggest that early intervention, a focus on financial and non-financial

---

people leaving shelters in the Netherlands: assessing fidelity and exploring facilitators and barriers' (2017) 44 (1) *Administration and Policy in Mental Health* 67–80.

[95] C Akkermans and M Räkers *Handreiking voorkomen huisuitzettingen* (Eropaf 2013); Wewerinke et al (n 75).

[96] Aedes (n 62).

[97] Planije et al (n 16) 53.

problems, inter-agency cooperation and outreach programmes are effective in tackling the problem of evictions. Encouragingly, it was found that these methods and techniques are now more frequently used by local authorities and housing associations in the Netherlands.

8. Evictions in Poland

Witold Borysiak

1. INTRODUCTION

In Poland, the number of eviction cases resolved by the courts remains at a relatively stable level. According to judgments by the Constitutional Court, eviction without any adequate alternative housing or its adequate replacement ('eviction to nowhere') is prohibited and is considered unconstitutional. The municipality in which the property to be vacated is located, is obliged to identify available temporary lodging, shelters or other places of accommodation where the debtor can stay following eviction. There is also a special form of legal protection for vulnerable groups of tenants, for instance pregnant women or minors. These vulnerable groups have the right to be evicted to a second accommodation. Owners who cannot reclaim their property because of the lack of social housing have a right to compensation.

The main reason for evictions in Poland is adverse economic circumstances, which leads tenants and owners to rent and mortgage arrears. Other reasons for eviction include breaches of tenancy terms, or psychosocial vulnerabilities (such as alcohol or drug addiction). Key structural risk factors leading to eviction are poverty and unemployment. Moreover, Poland lacks a system of solutions to support municipalities that would give adequate access to social housing for those entitled to it. The existing solutions are insufficient in relation to citizens' needs.

2. POLICY BACKGROUND

2.1 General Housing Policy Related to Evictions

The central institution responsible for creating and implementing housing policy in Poland is the Ministry of Infrastructure and Development. The

Ministry recently prepared new official Guidelines for National Development of Housing, which were officially adopted by the Council of Ministers in September 2016.[1]

There are no specific housing policies on evictions. However, the most important rules on evictions (including all of the procedural aspects of evictions) are regulated in the Act on Tenants' Rights and Municipal Housing Stock (AoTR),[2] in the Code of Civil Procedure[3] (Article 1046 CCP), and in the Decree of Ministry of Justice on the procedure of expulsion from premises.[4] Both private and municipal sectors are regulated by the same legal rules.

2.2 Structural/Societal Factors Related to Evictions

Sociological surveys confirm that the key structural risk factors leading to eviction are poverty and unemployment. Furthermore, a certain percentage of those evicted constitute people with addictions (such as alcohol or drug addiction) or psychosocial vulnerabilities (eg mental illness). Sometimes a combination of these factors leads to eviction. In practice, the main reason for cancellation of a contract of lease of premises is a delay in paying rent and utility expenses. In some cases, the reason for the termination of contract may also be due to misbehaviour on the part of the lessee.

---

[1]   The resolution of the Council of Ministers Nr 115/2016 of 27 September 2016 on adopting Guidelines for National Development of Housing (uchwała Rady Ministrów w sprawie przyjęcia Narodowego Programu Mieszkaniowego) <http://mib.bip.gov.pl/budownictwo/programy.html>.

[2]   Ustawa z dnia 21 czerwca 2001 r. o ochronie praw lokatorów, mieszkaniowym zasobie gminy i o zmianie Kodeksu cywilnego [The Act of 21 June 2001 on Tenants' Rights, Municipal Housing Stock and the Civil Code Amendment Act] Dziennik Ustaw [*Journal of Laws*] 2016, item 1610, as amended; referred to as the Act on Tenants' Rights and Municipal Housing Stock or AoTR.

[3]   Ustawa z dnia 17 listopada 1964 r. – Kodeks postępowania cywilnego [The Act of 17 November 1964 – the Code of Civil Procedure of the Republic of Poland] *Journal of Laws* 2016, item 1822, as amended; referred to as the Code of Civil Procedure or CCP.

[4]   Rozporządzenie Ministra Sprawiedliwości z dnia 22 grudnia 2011 r. w sprawie szczegółowego trybu postępowania w sprawach o opróżnienie lokalu lub pomieszczenia albo o wydanie nieruchomości [The Decree of Ministry of Justice of 22 December 2011 on the detailed procedure of expulsion from premises and accommodations or repossession of a real estate] *Journal of Laws* 2012, item 11; referred to as the Decree of Ministry of Justice on the procedure of expulsion from premises or DMJ.

The main problem that occurs in Poland in the context of eviction, is the lack of social housing. In addition, Poland also lacks a system of solutions to support municipalities that would facilitate adequate access to social housing for those entitled to it.

2.3 Specific Policies Related to Evictions

In Poland, housing policy development is created mainly by local governments (usually municipalities). According to Article 4 AoTR, the municipality is responsible for the creation of conditions to provide for the housing needs of local communities. Municipalities should provide social housing for their citizens to meet the housing needs of households with low incomes using municipal housing resources. Under Article 4 AoTR, the municipalities must also provide all their citizens with night shelters and sheltered accommodation. The legal basis for these services is also provided for in the Act of 12 March 2004 on Social Assistance.[5] According to section 1(3) of Article 17 of this Act, a municipality is legally obliged to provide shelter, meals and essential clothing to persons deprived of their property during the process of eviction.[6]

Financial support for establishing social housing, sheltered accommodation and homes for homeless people is regulated by the Act of 8 December 2006 on Financial Support for Establishing Social Premises, Sheltered Accommodation, Night Shelters and Homes for the Homeless.[7]

According to the rule established in Article 16 AoTR, an eviction cannot be enforced in the period from 1 November to 31 March, if the previous owner or tenant did not have the right to social or replacement housing. This so called 'winter-eviction moratorium' will be discussed in further detail in Section 8.

---

[5] Ustawa z dnia 12 marca 2004 r. o pomocy społecznej [The Act of 12 March 2004 on Social Assistance] *Journal of Laws* 2016, item 930, as amended; referred as the Act on Social Assistance.

[6] See Iwona Sierpowska, *Pomoc społeczna. Komentarz* (Warsaw, Wolters Kluwer 2014) 141 et seq.

[7] Ustawa z dnia 8 grudnia 2006 r. o finansowym wsparciu tworzenia lokali socjalnych, mieszkań chronionych, noclegowni i domów dla bezdomnych [The Act of 8 December 2006 on Financial Support for Establishing Social Premises, Sheltered Accommodation, Night Shelters and Homes for the Homeless] *Journal of Laws* 2017, item 1392, as amended; referred as the Act on Financial Support for Establishing Social Premises.

3. LEGAL AND CONSTITUTIONAL BACKGROUND TO PROTECTION AGAINST EVICTIONS

3.1 Housing as a Fundamental Right

The Act of 2 April 1997, the Constitution of the Republic of Poland,[8] guarantees in Article 30, the inviolability of human dignity.[9] According to this article, 'The inherent and inalienable dignity of the person shall constitute the source of freedoms and rights of persons and citizens. It shall be inviolable. The respect and protection thereof shall be the obligation of public authorities.' According to the judgments of the Constitutional Court[10] and commentary in Polish legal literature,[11] the removal from a lodging ('eviction to nowhere') of persons who are not responsible for being unable to satisfy their housing needs with their own resources and who cannot afford to pay the costs associated with their lodgings, infringes this article.

Moreover, Article 75 (1) of the Polish Constitution states that: 'Public authorities shall pursue policies conducive to satisfying the housing needs of citizens, in particular combating homelessness, promoting the development of low-income housing and supporting activities aimed at acquisition of a house by each citizen'. According to Article 75 (2) of the Constitution: 'Protection of the rights of tenants shall be established by statute.'[12] The aforementioned constitutional provisions establish the framework under which the Polish State can regulate housing law. Article

---

[8]   Ustawa z dnia 2 kwietnia 1997 Konstytucja Rzeczpospolitej Polskiej [The Act of 2 April 1997 – the Constitution of the Republic of Poland] *Journal of Laws* No 78, item 483, as amended; referred as the Polish Constitution/the Constitution. The official translation is available at <http://www.sejm.gov.pl/prawo/konst/angielski/kon1.htm>.

[9]   This article is regulated in the first part of Chapter II of the Constitution ('The freedoms, rights and obligations of persons and citizens – the General Principles').

[10]   Judgment of the Constitutional Court of 4 April 2001, K 11/00, OTK-ZU [*Official Journal of the Constitutional Court*] 2001, No 3, item 54 and the decision of the Constitutional Court addressing the legislative deficiencies of 4 April 2001, S 2/01, OTK-ZU 2001, No 3, item 58.

[11]   Ewa Bończak-Kucharczyk, *Ochrona praw lokatorów i najem lokali mieszkalnych. Komentarz* (Warsaw, Wolters Kluwer 2013) 24–26; Zenon Knypl, *Eksmisja i prawa człowieka – wykonywanie eksmisji z lokali mieszkalnych* (Sopot, Currenda 2015) 163–164.

[12]   This article is regulated in first part of Chapter II of the Constitution ('Economic Social and Cultural Freedoms and Rights').

75 of the Constitution does not provide individuals with a direct legal claim against other entities (for example municipalities or cooperatives).[13] The legal doctrine of constitutional law emphasizes that this article creates a legal basis for a special Act that will protect tenants.[14] Furthermore, according to this article, satisfying the housing needs of citizens should be treated as a general constitutional value assigning limits of creation and interpretation of established laws.[15] The state shall support activities aimed at the acquisition of a house by each citizen; however, according to the judgments of the Constitutional Court, it not only means an acquisition of the ownership of such a house, but also means the acquisition of any right to such a house that grants a person stability over time and is protected by law.[16]

It should be added that according to Article 76 of the Polish Constitution, 'Public authorities shall protect consumers, customers, hirers or lessees against activities threatening their health, privacy and safety, as well as against dishonest market practices. The scope of such protection shall be specified by a statute.' This article has only vertical effect and establishes the framework under which the Polish legislator can regulate the protection of consumers in housing law.[17] For example, Article 76 is recognized as a legal basis for the protection of tenants. The Constitutional Court in one of its judgments ruled that Article 76 should be treated as the basis for protection against excessively high rents, as far as combating unfair market practices is concerned.[18] The Court stated that this basis further constitutes grounds for the introduction of statutory

---

[13] Leszek Garlicki, *Konstytucja Rzeczypospolitej Polskiej. Komentarz. Tom III* (Warsaw, Wydawnictwo Sejmowe 2003) Art 75, 2–3; Przemysław Mikłaszewicz, *Konstytucja Rzeczypospolitej Polskiej. Komentarz. Tom I. Komentarz do art. 1–86* (Warsaw, CH Beck 2016) 1711–1712.

[14] Garlicki (n 13) Art 75, 5–6; Małgorzata Bednarek, *Prawo do mieszkania w konstytucji i ustawodawstwie* (Warsaw, Wolters Kluwer 2007) 531 et seq; Bończak-Kucharczyk (n 11) 24; Zenon Knypl, *Eksmisja – prawo i praktyka* (Sopot, Currenda 2009) 54–59. In Polish law the statute, which fulfilled the constitutional duty laid down in Art 75 (2) of the Polish Constitution to establish protection for tenants, is the Act on Tenants' Rights and Municipal Housing Stock.

[15] Garlicki (n 13) Art 75, 2–3; Mikłaszewicz (n 13) 1712; Bednarek (n 14) 531–534.

[16] See Judgment of the Constitutional Court of 29 May 2001, K 5/01, OTK-ZU 2001, No 4, item 87.

[17] Garlicki (n 13) Art 75, 2–3; Bednarek (n 14) 583 et seq.

[18] Judgment of the Constitutional Court of 12 January 2000, P 11/98, OTK-ZU 2000, No 1, item 3.

protection against owners who may abuse their dominant position by setting unfair or arbitrary rents. In practice, this means that the state can, for example, determine in a statute, the maximum annual increase of rent in the private market or maximum limits of rent in the sector of renting houses from public entities.

In the doctrine, it is stated that the constitutional requirement to protect tenants' rights should be balanced with other protections guaranteed in the Polish Constitution, such as, for example, the requirement of protection of property, contained in Article 21 (1) and Article 64 (1) and (2) of the Constitution. The Constitutional Court in the judgment of 4 April 2001, K 11/00, stated that this protection of tenants who cannot afford to pay rent and other associated costs for their accommodation owing to their poor financial situation, cannot deprive owners of their ownership right. Otherwise it would be a violation of the essence of this right and would conflict with Article 31 (3) of the Polish Constitution (the so called 'Principle of proportionality').

3.2 Law Relating to Owner-occupation

There is no single 'housing law' in the Polish legal system. Provisions on housing that are relevant to the right to housing in the eviction process are dispersed in a variety of different legal acts. The protection of the house-owner and the discretionary grounds of eviction can be found mainly in the Act of 23 April 1964, the Civil Code of the Republic of Poland[19] and the Act of 24 June 1994 on the Ownership of Premises.[20]

The most common ground of eviction from premises that are owned by occupants is Article 16 of the Act on the Ownership of Premises. This article establishes the so-called forced sale of premises. According to section 1 of this article, the occupier can be evicted if he or she: (1) is in long-term arrears; (2) flagrantly or persistently acts against the applicable rules of home community; (3) by his or her inappropriate or antisocial behaviour affecting other occupiers.

A residential community that encompasses the owners of apartments in a building (Polish *wspólnota mieszkaniowa*)[21] has the right to sue for the

---

[19] Ustawa z 23 kwietnia 1964 r. Kodeks cywilny [The Act of 23 April 1964 – the Civil Code of the Republic of Poland] *Journal of Laws* 2017, item 459, as amended; referred as the Civil Code or CC.

[20] Ustawa z 24 czerwca 1994 r. o własności lokali [The Act of 24 June 1994 on the Ownership of Premises] *Journal of Laws* 2015, item 1892, as amended; referred as the Act on the Ownership of Premises.

[21] This decision is taken in the form of resolution by the majority of votes.

sale of the property and the eviction of the owner. In such a case, the owner of the property does not have the right to social or replacement housing.[22]

Also, in every other situation, a creditor, for instance a bank in the cases of mortgage enforcement, may require the sale of the owner's property at auction in the expulsion procedure.[23] The attached immovable property is sold at public auction.[24] The person who successfully buys the property can acquire the right to be awarded ownership (Polish *przysądzenie własności*) of the immovable property. From that moment, the new owner may require the previous owner to leave the property. This eviction procedure applies under the rules established in Article 1046 CCP and in the Decree of Ministry of Justice on the procedure of expulsion from premises. It means that if the previous owner, after the end of the eviction procedure, does not have alternative accommodation, a municipality is obliged to provide him with a shelter.

3.3 Law Relating to Private Renting

The contract of lease is subject to the Civil Code of the Republic of Poland. The Code provides special provisions on the lease of premises.[25] However, the most important act regulating the protection of tenants is the Act on Tenants' Rights and Municipal Housing Stock. This Act protects tenants from the most sensitive issues connected with evictions; for example, it protects an occupant against unfavourable terms and conditions of a contract, sudden or unfounded termination of a contract, and sudden and excessive rent increase and other similar fees.[26] Some of these rules are outlined in Section 8 below.

Eviction from private rented premises requires a court order. The case proceedings can be omitted only in exceptional circumstances. For example, where the debtor or tenant previously willingly signed a notary deed, submitting to execution, such a notary deed can serve as an enforcement instrument.[27] In practice, such situations occur only in cases of the so-called 'occasional lease', which is regulated as a specific form

---

[22] See Art 16 (2) of the Act on the Ownership of Premises.
[23] See Art 922 ff CCP.
[24] Art 952 ff CCP.
[25] Arts 680–692 CC.
[26] See further Bończak-Kucharczyk (n 11) 26–29; Bednarek (n 14) 531 et seq; Roman Dziczek, *Ochrona praw lokatorów, dodatki mieszkaniowe- Komentarz, wzory pozwów* (Warsaw, LexisNexis 2012) 9 et seq.
[27] Art 777 (1) CCP.

of lease in AoTR.[28] This form of a lease requires a notary deed and further notification of the agreement to the tax office.[29] Such a contract must also indicate the accommodation to which the tenant will be able to move after the termination of the lease.[30] However, due to its formalities, the contract of 'occasional lease' is very rare in practice.[31] In 2017 the Polish legislator added another exception from the rule that eviction from private rented premises requires a court order. This exception is the so-called 'institutional lease' and is similar to the 'occasional lease' due to the fact that the tenant needs to sign a notary deed, submitting to execution. In such a contract the landlord must be a business entity who professionally rent premises. Also signing such contracts is currently very rare in practice.

3.4 Law Relating to Social Renting

According to Article 4 (2) AoTR, a municipality provides dwellings for persons or families who are unable to secure housing for themselves and meets the housing needs of households on low incomes. The municipality is also required to provide social dwellings to persons who have a right to social housing according to the judgment of a court. According to Article 22 AoTR, part of the municipality housing stock shall be reserved for social housing. The tenancy agreement of such premises must be concluded for a limited period of time only with a person who does not have legal title to other premises and whose household income does not exceed the amount specified in the resolution of the municipal council.[32] The rate of rent of such a dwelling may not exceed half of the lowest rental rates in force for municipal housing stock.[33] The increase of such rates is also strictly regulated in Articles 8a and 9 AoTR. It is worth noting that the law does not differentiate between private and social

---

[28]   See Art 19a s 2 AoTR. See Bończak-Kucharczyk (n 11) 284; Katarzyna Zdun-Załęska, *Ustawa o ochronie praw lokatorów, mieszkaniowym zasobie gminy i zmianie Kodeksu cywilnego – Komentarz* (Warsaw, Wolters Kluwer 2014) 139; Roman Dziczek, *Prawo mieszkaniowe w praktyce* (Warsaw, Lexis-Nexis, 2012) 401–402.

[29]   See Bończak-Kucharczyk (n 11) 285; Zdun-Załęska (n 28) 139.

[30]   See Bończak-Kucharczyk (n 11) 285–286; Zdun-Załęska (n 28) 139–140; Jacek Chaciński, *Ochrona praw lokatorów Komentarz* (Warsaw, CH Beck 2013) 152–154; Dziczek (n 28) 403.

[31]   See Bończak-Kucharczyk (n 11) 282 et seq and Dziczek (n 28) 401 et seq.

[32]   Art 23 (1-2) AoTR.

[33]   Ibid.

dwellings in the context of lease contracts. Lease relationships in the municipal sector are almost identical to those in the private sector.

In light of Article 2 AoTR,[34] Polish law likewise does not differentiate standards of protection between people living in public rented premises and social rented premises and does not differentiate eviction procedures between evictions from social or public housing and from institutional accommodation.[35] According to the judgment of the Polish Supreme Court of 5 April 2013, III CZP 11/13[36] (described in Section 7), if the person being evicted from social housing is listed in Article 14 section 4 AoTR, he or she must be rehoused to other accommodation (even when this person had not paid the rent). This also means that the eviction should be suspended until the municipality offers the family new accommodation according to general rules.[37]

3.5 Law Relating to Unauthorized Occupancy

Domestic trespass in Poland is punishable under Article 193 of the Criminal Code. According to this article, any person who forces their way into another person's house, apartment, premises, quarters, or a fenced plot of land, or who does not leave such a place despite a demand from an authorized person, is liable to a fine, the restriction of liberty or imprisonment for up to one year. However, there is no more specific information available as to the number of cases that have been resolved on the basis of this article in situations of unauthorized occupancy (eg when the perpetrator does not leave the house or apartment on request).

In Polish law, there is no obligation to offer social accommodation (social premises or temporary premises) to a person who is evicted, when this person was living in the accommodation without any legal right (for example squatters).[38] Moreover such persons can also be evicted between 1 November and 31 March.[39] However, according to Article 24 AoTR, persons living in accommodation without the legal right to do so may

---

[34] Art 2 (1) and Art 2 (2) AoTR.
[35] See Bończak-Kucharczyk (n 11) 299 ff and Chaciński (n 30) 37 ff.
[36] OSNC [*Official Journal of the Polish Supreme Court – Civil Chamber*] 2013, No 11, item 121.
[37] This issue is discussed further in Section 8 below.
[38] See Art 17 and Art 25d AoTR.
[39] This was confirmed by the Supreme Court Judgment of 20 May 2005, III CZP 6/05, OSNC 2006, No 1, item 1.

during the eviction process request the court for social housing, when this is justified, on the basis of the principles of social coexistence (rules of equity).

3.6   Law Relating to Temporary Dispossession

According to Article 11a section 1 of the Act of 29 July 2005 on Combating Domestic Violence,[40] if one of the family members, who occupies an apartment together with other members, uses violence toward other family members, making cohabitation impossible, the person affected by violence may request a court order for the eviction of the perpetrator from the accommodation. The court should give its verdict within one month of the request being made. Before deciding upon an eviction, the court can impose a barring order on the offender requiring him or her to leave the family home or prohibiting him or her being near to his previous home.[41] In exceptional cases, for example when the perpetrator of domestic violence threatens other family members, he can be temporarily arrested.[42] According to Article 11a section 3 of the Act, in such a situation, the general rules of eviction enforcement apply, which are described in Article 1046 CCP and in the Decree of Ministry of Justice on the procedure of expulsion from premises. In Polish law there is no obligation to offer such a person social housing or temporary accommodation.[43] This means that the perpetrator of domestic violence will usually be evicted by a bailiff into a shelter.

Temporary exclusion from accommodation is possible in the case of a restraining order (barring order). This restraining order may be imposed only by the court on the grounds of Polish criminal law.[44] Restriction orders are, *inter alia*, a prohibition on contacting certain individuals (Article 39 point 2b of the Polish Penal Code), and an order to leave the premises jointly occupied with the other person (Article 39 point 2e of

---

[40]   Ustawa z 29 lipca 2005 r. o przeciwdziałaniu przemocy w rodzinie [The Act of 29 July 2005 on Combating Domestic Violence] *Journal of Laws* 2015, item 1390, as amended; referred as the Act on Combating Domestic Violence.

[41]   Arts 39 and 41a of the Polish Penal Code.

[42]   See Art 258 § 3 of the Act of 6 June 1997, the Code of Criminal Procedure of the Republic of Poland, *Journal of Laws* 2016, item 1749, as amended; referred as the Code of Criminal Procedure.

[43]   See Arts 17 and 25d (1) AoTR.

[44]   See Arts 39 and 41a of the Polish Penal Code.

the Polish Penal Code). Such orders last for a period of between one year and 15 years, the specific time is defined in the verdict of the court.[45]

According to Article 58 § 2 of the Act of 25 February 1964, Family and Guardianship Code (FGC),[46] if the spouses occupy shared accommodation, in the event of a divorce the court must also rule on the use of the residence. Following a joint motion of the parties, the court may, in its ruling on divorce, also grant the accommodation to one of the spouses, if the other spouse consents to leave the premises without alternative accommodation being provided. The court ruling considers primarily the needs of the children and the spouse entrusted with the exercise of parental authority (Article 58 § 4 FGC). In exceptional cases, where the grossly reprehensible conduct of one spouse makes cohabitation impossible, the court may order his or her eviction under Article 58 § 2 FGC.

3.7 Other Relevant Laws

In Poland, measures exist to prevent unfair duress being placed on tenants with respect to payment of rent, and to prevent the illegal eviction of tenants. Illegal eviction is punishable under Article 191 of the Criminal Code. According to this article, anyone who uses violence or an illegal threat to force another person to conduct himself or herself in a specified manner (for example to enforce a claim or to force a person to leave the accommodation) is liable to imprisonment for a period of between three months and five years. Moreover, domestic trespass in Poland is punishable under Article 193 of the Criminal Code.

3.8 Soft Law/Codes and Their Effectiveness

There are no distinct soft law measures (non-legally binding policies and protocols) used by courts, municipalities, landlords or lenders in the process of evictions. This is due to the AoTR, which establishes a

---

[45] See Art 43 § 1 of the Polish Penal Code. The internal statistical system of the Ministry of Justice indicates in the position 'Judgments of District and County Courts on criminal restrictions' the following number of orders granted on Art 39 point 2e of the Polish Penal Code: 2010 (20 orders); 2011 (110 orders); 2012 (167 orders); 2013 (288 orders); 2014 (948 orders); 2015 (1452 orders).

[46] Ustawa z 25 lutego 1964 r. – Kodeks rodzinny i opiekuńczy [The Act of 25 February 1964 – Family and Guardianship Code] *Journal of Laws* 2017, item 682, as amended; referred as the Family and Guardianship Code or FGC.

minimum level of protection for tenants renting social or public premises. It should also be added that AoTR provisions are mandatory.

In Poland, examples of good practice in such cases are rare and are not systematized. Their existence is dependent on the goodwill of a particular creditor or bailiff. For example, up until November 2011, in the cases where the subject of an eviction was a minor, the bailiff was enabled to apply to the Family Court to issue appropriate orders on the basis of Article 109 FGC.[47] According to the court's order, the minor could be placed in a foster family, the child's family home or institutional care. Most of the bailiffs still retain this practice, which is generally a favourable solution for minors – however, there is no one singular practice established in such a situation.[48] Moreover, sometimes bailiffs prolonged the eviction proceedings in such a way that they could not be ended before the beginning of the period of protection established in Article 16 AoTR.

4. EXTENT OF EVICTIONS OVER THE PERIOD 2010–2015

4.1 Definition and Phases of Eviction

In Poland, only the Ministry of Justice collects general information about the number of evictions. The data collected by the Department of Statistical Management Information of the Ministry of Justice does not distinguish between certain types of tenures being evicted and phases of the eviction. There are only two types of statistical data collected by the Department: (i) the number of eviction cases (in statistics – *opróżnienie lokalu mieszkalnego*) proceed every year mainly by the District Courts[49] (which from 2013 included the number of cases in which the court was obliged to decide about the right to social housing and the number of

---

[47] According to Art 109 § 1 FGC, if the child's welfare is endangered, the guardianship court must issue a relevant order. See old version of Art 1046 § 8 CCP; See also Krystyna Krzekotowska, *Eksmisja z lokali mieszkalnych* (Bielsko-Biała, Studio Sto 1999) 112–113.

[48] In practice this means that it depends mainly on the bailiff or the court if the child is evicted into a shelter with other members of his or her family or whether he or she is separated and placed in the foster family, the child's family home or institutional care.

[49] The signature in the internal statistical system of the Ministry of Justice – C010m.

social premises granted in the judgments); (ii) the number of bailiffs' actions during the process of eviction.[50] The number of eviction cases in the District Courts[51] for the period 2010–2015 is shown below in Table 8.1 and the number of bailiffs' actions is shown in Table 8.2.

Table 8.1   Eviction cases in District Courts

Year	The number of cases submitted	The number of cases resolved[52]
2010	34 510	32 863
2011	34 494	34 792
2012	34 077	34 052
2013	30 794	30 411, including: a) 23 662 cases in which the suit was granted in whole or in part, comprising: cases on eviction in which the court was obliged to decide about the right to social housing: • judgments in which the right to social housing was granted: 12 507 • judgments in which the right to social housing was not granted: 7 639 • cases in which court **was not obliged** to decide about the right to social housing: 1516 • The number of social premises granted in the judgments on eviction: 15 730 b) 1539 cases in which the suit was dismissed

[50]   Wydział Statystycznej Informacji Zarządczej, 'Czynności komornika w zakresie eksmisji, 1999-2016' [Department of Statistical Management Information – 'Actions of Bailiff during the process of eviction – 1999-2016'] document dated 14.2.2017 <http://isws.ms.gov.pl/pl/baza-statystyczna/opracowania-wieloletnie/>.

[51]   Eviction cases are seldom heard by the Regional Courts, due to the value of the matter at issue, to be in the jurisdiction of this courts. For example, in 2015, there were only 28 cases submitted and 29 cases resolved (including three cases in which the suit was granted in whole or in part, and two cases in which the suit was dismissed).

[52]   For the years 2010–2012, the 'Number of cases resolved' denotes the civil actions that were granted in whole or in part, dismissed, returned or rejected, or the proceeding terminated or adjusted in some other way.

Table 8.1 (continued)

Year	The number of cases submitted	The number of cases resolved
2014	28 231	27 920, including:
		a)19 337 cases in which the suit was granted in whole or in part, comprising:
		cases on eviction in which the court **was obliged** to decide about the right to social housing: • judgments in which the right to social housing was granted: 11 050 • judgments in which the right to social housing was not granted: 7106 • cases in which court **was not obliged** to decide about the right to social housing: 1180 • The number of social premises granted in the judgments on eviction: 13 643
		b) 1314 cases in which the suit was dismissed
2015	26 486	27 019, including:
		a) 19 177 cases in which the suit was granted in whole or in part, comprising:
		• cases on eviction in which the court **was obliged** to decide about the right to social housing: • judgments in which the right to social housing was granted: 10 853 • judgments in which the right to social housing was not granted: 7225 • cases in which court **was not obliged** to decide about the right to social housing: 1099 • The number of social premises granted in the judgments on eviction: 13 317
		b) 1202 cases in which the suit was dismissed

Table 8.2   Number of bailiffs' actions during the process of eviction

Year	The number of cases submitted Divided for cases when enforcement title (A) does not provide the right to social housing or (B) does provide the right to social housing	The number of cases resolved Divided for cases when enforcement title (A) does not provide the right to social housing or (B) does provide the right to social housing
2010	6569 (A) 1997 (B) 4572	7014 (A) 2369 (B) 4645
2011	7198 (A) 2177 (B) 5021	7260 (A) 2311 (B) 4949
2012	9070 (A) 3002 (B) 6068	7812 (A) 2504 (B) 5308
2013	8557 (A) 2506 (B) 6051	8665 (A) 2774 (B) 5891
2014	8538 (A) 2889 (B) 5649	8679 (A) 2770 (B) 5909
2015	8879 (A) 2903 (B) 5976	8671 (A) 2939 (B) 5732

4.2 Evictions From Mortgaged Property

There is no exact data on how many of the evictions from owner-occupied residences are a result of mortgage enforcement. Furthermore, there is no precise data on the number of previous owners who received a repossession order or an eviction order. The observations show that the number of such evictions is very low.[53]

In the internal statistical system of the Ministry of Justice, there is only one summary position 'Judgments of District Courts on restitution of

[53]   In practice, failure to pay mortgage fees will not necessarily lead to eviction (in many, if not most cases, people leave the premises voluntarily). It is also worth noting that the money from a public auction is returned to the former owner, who usually is enabled to purchase or rent another apartment.

property/repossessions' (*wydanie nieruchomości*).[54] Those statistics apply to Article 921 CCP, which regulates any cases of evictions from immovable property or premises. Therefore, this group may include cases of eviction from commercial premises, second homes etc.[55]

4.3 Evictions From Private/Social Rented Housing

There is no accurate data on the extent of evictions from private or social rented principal primary residences in general. As stated, the data collected by the Department of Statistical Management Information of Ministry of Justice does not distinguish between the certain types of tenures being evicted.

4.4 Evictions From Unauthorized Occupancies

There is no relevant data or even estimations on the number of either legal or illegal evictions from accommodations that are occupied by unauthorized people (independently from whether it is squatting, self-build without permission or unauthorized encampments). Research shows that the number of such evictions is fairly low. However, it is worth noting that the illegal seizure or occupation of condemned or abandoned buildings is not often practised.

4.5 Other Evictions

In Poland, illegal evictions from a leased property are exceptional and usually take place when people lease premises without formal con-tracts.[56] There are no statistics showing the number of illegal evictions that take place every year. The only existing information refers to the total number of crimes under Article 191, in which, in 2015, the number of proceedings initiated amounted to 2065 and the number of crimes recorded (after taking into account the backlog cases) amounted to

---

[54] The signature in the internal statistical system of the Ministry of Justice – C011.

[55] For example, in 2015, in the District Courts, the number of cases on restitution of property/repossessions amounted to 2432 cases submitted and 2325 cases resolved.

[56] It should be noted that in Poland, there is no precise estimation of how many owner-occupied dwellings are illegally rented because both parties try to avoid taxes imposed by the state.

1551.[57] There are no official statistics on the number of landlords convicted for illegal evictions; however, those cases are rare in practice. According to information from the press, convicted landlords are not usually imprisoned and are usually fined or given a deferred sentence.

Table 8.3 indicates the number of cases based on Article 11a section 1 of the Act on Combating Domestic Violence for 2011–2015[58] as recorded by the internal statistical system of the Ministry of Justice.

Table 8.3   *Cases based on Article 11a s.1 of the Act on Combating Domestic Violence 2011–2015*

Year	Number of cases submitted	Number of cases resolved (eviction cases resolved)
2011	197	105 (49)
2012	730	620 (268)
2013	1114	879 (387)
2014	1152	1134 (487)
2015	1406	1301 (571)

There is no precise data regarding the number of evictions decided in divorce judgments. In the internal statistical system of the Ministry of Justice, there is only one summary position 'Judgments on the matters of divorce decided on the ground of Article 58 § 2 FGC without first sentence.'[59] The data includes cases where the court (1) ordered that common accommodation be shared between former spouses, (2) granted the accommodation to one of the spouses, (3) evicted one of the spouses (primarily for domestic violence).[60]

4.6   Commentary on the Statistics

As stated, only the Ministry of Justice collects general information about the number of evictions and the collated data does not distinguish

---

[57] Statistics available at <http://statystyka.policja.pl/st/kodeks-karny/przestepstwa-przeciwko-4/63486,Zmuszanie-art-191.html>.

[58] There is no data for 2010 because Art 11a (1) was not in force at that time.

[59] The signature in the internal statistical system of the Ministry of Justice – C004a.

[60] In 2015, for example, in the Regional Courts, the number of cases on divorce decided on the ground of Art 58 § 2 FGC (without first sentence), amounted to 2155 cases submitted and 2221 cases resolved.

between the different types of tenures being evicted. The number of eviction cases resolved by the courts has remained at a fairly stable level. In addition, there is no available summarized data regarding the characteristics of the households involved in the process of eviction, even when divided into geographical regions. Nonetheless the vast majority of eviction cases take place in the major Polish cities, mainly Warsaw, Katowice, Wrocław and Gdańsk.[61] Accordingly, the development of an independent, regular, comprehensive and detailed monitoring and reporting system, covering household composition, the age and labour status of people being evicted or other characteristics of those who are subject to initiated and executed evictions, in all housing tenures in Poland is urgently required.

There are no detailed studies or data determining the exact number of people evicted to shelters, which makes it difficult to estimate the number of people who subsequently become homeless. Similarly, there is no precise information on how eviction to a shelter affects those involved or on the consequences of choosing to leave voluntarily, before eviction occurs.

There is no available detailed statistical data on the average time of evictions; that is, the time between initiated and executed evictions. Accordingly, the average periods of time between initiated and executed evictions cannot be addressed.

4.7 Profile of Those Evicted

In Poland, there is no available data on the characteristics of the households involved in the process of eviction. This data is not collected by the Ministry of Justice or by the Polish Institute of Justice and the municipalities. Moreover, in cases of eviction there is no available official information in relation to the income of households being evicted. However, sociological surveys confirm that evictions are mainly due to adverse economic circumstances connected with addictions or psychosocial vulnerabilities (such as mental illness etc).[62]

---

[61]   According to an April 2013 survey carried out by the *Dziennik Gazeta Prawna* (*Daily Legal Newspaper*), among the 11 cities' inhabitants questioned in the survey, the vast number of evictions were in Warsaw. The survey also revealed that eviction density is highest in the city of Szczecin (one eviction notice per 194 inhabitants).

[62]   See Section 2; Danuta M Piekut-Brodzka, *Bezdomność* (Warsaw, Chrześcijańska Akademia Teologiczna 2006) 100 et seq; Iwona Grabarczyk, *System wsparcia i pomocy bezdomnym* (Olsztyn, Wydawnictwo UWM 2007) 18;

5. RISK FACTORS IDENTIFIED LEADING TO EVICTIONS

Polish literature primarily cites economic and social factors as the causes of evictions (eg unemployment, poverty) and social pathologies (eg alcoholism, domestic violence). Research conducted among homeless people shows that the most frequent chains of events leading to eviction are:[63]

- Unemployment → poverty → dwelling rent debts → eviction
- Misuse of alcohol → poverty → dwelling rent debts or inappropriate use of apartment → eviction
- Alcohol abuse (→ sometimes domestic violence) → end of family life or cohabitation → loss of housing → eviction
- Release from prisons → failure to find a job → failure to lease housing due to lack of income → eviction
- Risky financial behaviour → loss of employment or income → loss of housing → eviction.

The interviews frequently indicate poverty as the main cause of eviction. The reason for poverty is usually a lack of education or the unstable family situations of Polish citizens (including alcoholism). According to the Central Statistical Office, 7.4 per cent of people in Poland live in households where incomes are below the poverty level (minimum subsistence level). The relative level of poverty is 16.2 per cent.[64] In the case of poverty, it is easy to fall into rent arrears, which results in the procedure for eviction.

Unemployment is usually associated with poverty.[65] In Poland, the level of unemployment is equal to 11.7 per cent of the economically

---

Franciszek Głód, *Bezdomni* (Wrocław, PWT we Wrocławiu 2008) 70 et seq; Andrzej Przymeński, 'Aktualny stan problemu bezdomności w Polsce. Aspekt polityczno-społeczny' in M Dębski and K Stachura (eds) *Oblicza bezdomności* (2008) 26 et seq.

[63] Marcin J Sochocki, 'Skala i charakter bezdomności w Polsce' in M Dębski (ed) *Problem bezdomności w Polsce. Wybrane aspekty* (2010) 96 et seq; See also Piekut-Brodzka (n 62) 116 et seq.

[64] Główny Urząd Statystyczny, 'Ubóstwo w Polsce w latach 2013-2014' <http://stat.gov.pl/obszary-tematyczne/warunki-zycia/ubostwo-pomoc-spoleczna/ubostwo-w-polsce-w-latach-2013-i-2014,1,6.html>.

[65] Andrzej Przymeński, *Bezdomność jako kwestia społeczna w Polsce współczesnej* (Poznań, Wydawnictwo Akademii Ekonomicznej 2001) 72–73;

active population, although it is claimed that this value is under-estimated.[66] Unemployment was the main cause of homelessness in Poland in the nineties.[67] This was due to the changes caused by the transition from a socialist economy to a capitalist economy. Another common cause of poverty leading to eviction is alcoholism.[68] Alcohol abuse strongly affects family ties and often causes the separation of its members. The studies indicate that it also leads to destruction of the movables in the occupied apartment.

Homelessness is also the result of the municipalities' inadequate housing policies.

Reprivatization is a further factor. During the socialist era, many people had their property expropriated by the state but were able to recover it following the transition to a free market economy. Recovery often entailed the eviction of sitting tenants, usually because the owners wished to convert the existing building to another one (such as a shop or hotel). Consequently, people residing in a house or an apartment that has been returned to previous owners often face eviction proceedings.

6. LINKS BETWEEN EVICTIONS AND HOMELESSNESS

Most of the information on risk factors for eviction and on evictions leading to homelessness derives from sociological studies and interviews. Sociological research shows that there is no single reason for homeless-ness; rather, homelessness is a consequence of many different reasons.[69] Moreover, homeless people indicate more than one cause of their situation. Some of the factors interact with each other.[70] As a result, in the Polish literature most authors share the view that the factors leading

---

Maciej Dębski, 'Homelessness in Poland: an analysis of the Pomeranian Province' (2011) 5 (1) *European Journal of Homelessness* 86.

[66]   Główny Urząd Statystyczny, 'Zarejestrowane bezrobocie – pierwszy kwartał 2015' <http://stat.gov.pl/obszary-tematyczne/rynek-pracy/bezrobocie-rejestrowane/bezrobocie-rejestrowane-i-kwartal-2015-r-,3,19.html>.

[67]   Dębski (n 65) 87. See also Przymeński (n 65) 26.

[68]   Głód (n 62) 72–73; Przymeński (n 65) 120; Dębski (n 65) 73.

[69]   Grabarczyk (n 62) 18 et seq; Piekut-Brodzka (n 62) 100 et seq; Przymeński (n 65) 122 et seq; Dębski (n 65) 52 et seq.

[70]   For example, in the case of women, domestic violence is usually combined with the disintegration of family ties. Similar effects arise when one of the family members is addicted to alcohol or drugs.

to homelessness overlap and cannot be examined separately.[71] According to the literature, the most common reasons for homelessness are eviction and unemployment.[72] The poor situation both on the housing and labour market in Poland affects people economically and as a consequence, they are unable to pay rent.[73] In addition, such factors as poverty, psychosocial vulnerabilities, addictions and the failure of the social assistance system lead to homelessness.[74]

7. SUMMARY OF SIGNIFICANT CASES AND REPORTS RELATED TO EVICTIONS IN THE PERIOD 2010–2015

In the judgment of 8 of April 2010, P 1/08,[75] the Constitutional Court confirmed the constitutionality of Article 18 section 5 AoTR, which establishes the right to claim compensation from the municipality if it does not designate a temporary lodging for a person being evicted.[76] The judgment confirmed the broad possibility of claiming compensation from the municipality by the owners of the estate, if the municipality does not comply with its obligations.

In the judgment of 4 November 2010, K 19/06,[77] the Constitutional Court stated that the first version of Article 1046 § 4 CCP, which did not establish the term for the municipality to designate a temporary lodging during the process of eviction, did not conform to the requirement of protection of property (Article 64 section 1 of the Polish Constitution), in connection with the rule of proportionality (Article 31 section 3 of the Polish Constitution). In the same judgment, the Constitutional Court decided that the impossibility of evicting a perpetrator of domestic

---

[71] Maciej Dębski, 'Przyczyny bezdomności i powody pozostawania w niej. Typologie i kwestie sporne' in M Dębski (ed) *Problem bezdomności w Polsce. Wybrane aspekty* (2010) 198.

[72] Głód (n 62) 70–71; Przymeński (n 65) 150–153.

[73] As stated in the literature, the lack of funds for rent combined with long-term unemployment are the major causes of eviction or the main reason to leave the occupied accommodation due to its high degree of devastation. See Przymeński (n 65) 26–31; Dębski (n 65) 86.

[74] Głód (n 62) 72 et seq; Dębski (n 65) 57–58.

[75] OTK-ZU 2010, No 4, item 33.

[76] In this case, heard by the court in Grudziadz, an association of property owners claimed compensation from the municipality following the municipality's refusal to provide social housing to people evicted.

[77] OTK-ZU 2010, No 9, item 96.

violence does not conform to the requirements of Article 71 section 1 of the Polish Constitution. The judgment was issued at the request of the Polish Ombudsman, who reacted after receiving a significant number of complaints from creditors and owners. The Polish Ombudsman pointed out that, in practice, it is not possible to carry out the eviction of a person for whom the court does not grant social accommodation. According to Article 1046 §4 CCP, the court and the bailiff have to delay the eviction of such a person until the municipality designates him or her a temporary lodging. This is also the case for a perpetrator of domestic violence facing eviction. The effect of the judgment resulted in changes to Article 1046 CCP in the Act on Combating Domestic Violence, and the announcement of the Decree of the Ministry of Justice on the procedure of expulsion from premises. In this judgment, the Polish Constitutional Court referred to Article 8 of the European Convention on Human Rights (ECHR) and was of the opinion that an eviction without any adequate alternative housing or adequate housing replacement violates this Article.[78] The Polish Constitutional Court also adopted the view that Article 30 of the Polish Constitution, in connection with Article 8 ECHR, requires that persons in special personal or family circumstances should be granted at least the minimum safeguards intended to satisfy their housing needs. In order to achieve this aim, Polish law should establish a procedure by which such persons will be relocated to other premises (social housing accommodation or temporary premises).

In the judgment of 18 October 2017, K 27/15,[79] the Polish Constitutional Tribunal stated that so called 'evictions to nowhere' based on the Article 144 of the act of 17 June 1966 on Administrative Enforcement Proceedings[80] infringed Articles 30 (the protection of the human dignity), Article 71 (the protection of the family life) and Article 75 (the right to housing) of the Polish Constitution. Article 144 permits the removal of the tenant from a premises without designation of temporary lodging, when the tenancy relationship was based on the administrative decision (eg when the tenant was a policeman or a secret services officer).

---

[78]　The Constitutional Court also cited, in the context of protection of the people being evicted, three verdicts of the European Court of Human Rights – the Judgments of 24 May 2007 Tuleshov against Russia (Case No 32718/02), the Judgments of 9 October 2007 Stanková against Slovakia (Case No 7205/02) and the Judgments of 15 January 2009 Ćosić against Croatia (Case No 28261/06).

[79]　OTK-ZU 2017, item 74.

[80]　The Act of 17 June 1966 on Administrative Enforcement Proceedings, Journal of Laws 2017, item 1201, as amended.

There are two other highly important judgments of the Supreme Court of 21 January 2011, signature III CZP 116/10[81] and signature III CZP 120/10.[82] In both cases, the landlord made a claim against the municipality for loss of profits on the grounds that they could not benefit from their property because of the municipality's failure to designate temporary lodgings for the defaulting tenant. The Supreme Court expressed the opinion that the municipality could be held liable to the landlord (pursuant to Article 417 § 1 CC, in connection with Article 1046 §4 CCP) for the damage caused by the lack of designation of a temporary lodging, to which the debtor should be evicted. The right to claim full compensation in such a situation is also established clearly in Article 18 section 5 AoTR. Damages are calculated on the basis of the general provisions contained in the Civil Code (Article 361 CC). This means that the compensation awarded covers both the losses that the owner has suffered, as well as the profits that he or she would have obtained if no losses had been sustained. In practice, damages are calculated on the basis of the rent that the owner would receive from another tenant if it were not for the fact that the existing tenant cannot be evicted due to the municipality's failure to designate temporary lodgings.

In the context of evictions from social housing, another important judgment is that of the Supreme Court of 5 April 2013, III CZP 11/13.[83] This judgment confirms the rule that the protection of tenants established in Article 14 section 4 AoTR also applies to evictions from social housing. This means that a household being evicted from one social housing unit has the right to be rehoused in another, and that the eviction should be suspended until the municipality offers the family new accommodation. According to the municipal authorities, this judgment could mean that residents of social housing would no longer be under an obligation to pay rent to their local municipality – eviction thus becomes a fiction.

---

[81]   OSNC-ZD [Official Journal of the Polish Supreme Court – Civil Chamber. Supplementary Collection] 2011, No C, item 54.

[82]   OSNC-ZD 2011, No C, item 55.

[83]   OSNC 2013, No 11, item 121. In this case the woman lived in the social premises for which she had not paid a small rent. The municipality of Szczecin city started eviction proceedings against her. The court decided that the Art 14 (4) AoTR does not differentiate standards of protection between people living in publically rented premises and socially rented premises.

8. BEST PRACTICE MODELS FOR PREVENTING, TACKLING AND REACTING TO EVICTIONS

8.1 Most Effective Measures for Preventing Evictions

In Poland, it is the state that determines the maximum increase of rent on the private market (Article 8a AoTR and Article 9 AoTR). The legal basis of this protection is Article 76 of the Polish Constitution.[84] The Act on Tenants' Rights and Municipal Housing Stock establishes a minimum level of protection for the majority of tenants.[85] These provisions are mandatory and cannot be exempted from, even in the event of an agreement between the parties.[86] The same Act protects tenants from excessive rent increases and other similar fees.

According to Article 8a sections 1 and 3 AoTR, a property owner may increase the rent or other charges for the use of the premises, sending the tenant written notice of cancellation, which is in effect by the end of the calendar month. The term of the notice of cancellation is three months. The legislator regulates two types of rent increases.[87] When the amount of rent for the use of the premises in a year exceeds or follows a level higher than 3 per cent of the replacement value of the premises, then the increase is possible only in justified situations described in Article 8a section 4a AoTR or Article 8a section 4e AoTR. Moreover, at the written request of the tenant, the landlord is obliged within 14 days to submit in writing the reasons for the increase of rent and its calculation.[88]

The increase of the rent above the limit is possible only in extra-ordinary situations, such as inflation (Article 8a section 4e AoTR) or the situation where previously the rent did not cover expenses related to the maintenance of the premises (Article 8a section 4a AoTR).[89]

---

[84]   Judgment of the Constitutional Court of 12 January 2000, P 11/98, OTK-ZU 2000, No 1, item 3.

[85]   With some exceptions, when the legal relationship is grounded on the special provisions of administrative law.

[86]   See Bednarek (n 14) 623 et seq; Dziczek (n 26) 117–123.

[87]   See Bednarek (n 14) 627 et seq; Zdun-Załęska (n 28) 86–87; Dziczek (n 26) 90–91; Chaciński (n 30) 98–99.

[88]   Art 8a (4) AoTR.

[89]   See further Bednarek (n 14) 636–640; Zdun-Załęska (n 28) 87–88; Chaciński (n 30) 100.

The tenant may challenge the increase of the rent or other charges.[90] The tenant can claim that the increase is unjustified or that it is justified, but at a different rate. The tenant is required to pay rent or other charges for the use of the premises in the previous amount until the verdict of the court is achieved.[91] The burden of proof of the accuracy of the increase is on the landlord (Article 8a section 5 point 2 AoTR). The increase of the rent, or of other charges for the use of the premises, cannot be made more often than every six months.[92]

The aforementioned measures are useful in preventing evictions and consequently in preventing homelessness. They introduce statutory protection against owners who may misuse their dominant position by setting unfair or arbitrary rents.[93] In this detailed regulation, the legislator tried to establish a balance between landlords' and tenants' rights.

The most effective measures for better prevention of evictions are timelines and triggers for eviction process stages necessary to initiate an eviction.[94] The timelines, which enable the owner to start a procedure against the tenant, are regulated in the Act on Tenants' Rights and Municipal Housing Stock. The landlord can send the tenant a notice to quit usually after a period of three full months' rent arrears.[95] During this procedure, the tenant may request a time extension. Only in exceptional cases is it possible to send a notice to quit without giving a notice period (see for example Article 13 AoTR). Tenants are also protected from sudden or ungrounded termination of a contract.

8.2 Most Effective Measures for Tackling Evictions

According to the rule established in Article 16 AoTR, eviction cannot be enforced in the period from 1 November to 31 March if the previous owner or tenant did not have the right to social or replacement housing. This is one of the most important measures tackling eviction in Poland.[96] This regulation is fully effective because it secures the poorest people from eviction to a shelter during the autumn or winter. However,

---

[90] Art 8a (5) point 2 AoTR. See Bednarek (n 14) 640–642; Zdun-Załęska (n 28) 87–89.

[91] Art 8a (6a) point 2 AoTR.

[92] Art 9 (1b) AoTR.

[93] Judgment of the Constitutional Court of 12 January 2000, P 11/98, OTK-ZU 2000, No 1, item 3.

[94] See further Bednarek (n 14) 557 et seq; Zdun-Załęska (n 28) 100–109.

[95] Art 11 (2) point 2 of AoTR.

[96] See more Zdun-Załęska (n 28) 126–127.

sometimes this regulation is subject to debate in Polish literature, because the landlords are unprotected during the time stipulated in the Act on Tenants' Rights and Municipal Housing Stock.[97] It is worth noting that this rule does not afford protection to: perpetrators of domestic violence; persons who flagrantly or persistently act against the applicable home order; people who by their inappropriate behaviour make use of other units or the common property burdensome; people who occupy the accommodation without any legal right.[98]

When a debtor and his family have to vacate premises and they have the right to social housing, the bailiff cannot enforce eviction until the competent municipality proposes such accommodation. The municipality has the responsibility to ensure the accommodation for the debtor (and his family) and the eviction procedure is postponed until the municipality redeems its obligation. The time when a municipality offers a debtor social housing depends on many factors; for example, whether or not at the time of eviction such accommodation exists. This measure is very effective and in practice, the process of eviction is usually postponed (in exceptional cases even for 2–4 years).[99] Before moving the debtor to the social housing proposed by the competent municipality, the bailiff shall hear out the debtor pursuant to Article 6 of the Decree of Ministry of Justice on the procedure of expulsion from premises (or 'DMJ'). The debtor is heard in the presence of a bailiff and the hearing is recorded in protocol.[100] The debtor is entitled to legal representation at the hearing; however, it is very exceptional in practice. This hearing postpones the procedure of eviction and sometimes fulfils the role of quasi-mediation. First, after the process of hearing executed by the bailiff, the debtor is given an order to perform voluntarily the obligation to return the immovable property or vacate the premises. Secondly, the bailiff must afford the debtor a prescribed time limit to do so, the length of which is determined according to the circumstances of the case.[101]

---

[97]   Bończak-Kucharczyk (n 11) 343 et seq.

[98]   See Art 17 AoTR in connection with Art 16 AoTR.

[99]   However, it could be argued that the above-mentioned eviction protection measures could also discourage new renting. Most owners do not want to rent housing to the poor or unemployed people for fear that they will not be able to remove those persons from the premises. The result is a situation in which owners of apartments in the private housing sector, bearing in mind the provisions of the AoTR, avoid signing new contracts or start to rent them non-contractually.

[100]   See Art 760 §2 CCP.

[101]   See Art 1046 §1 CCP.

In Polish law, when an enforcement title against the debtor ordering him to vacate the premises does not provide the debtor's right to social or replacement housing, the bailiff must first hear out the debtor and request him to voluntarily give back the immovable property or vacate the premises. Secondly, the bailiff designates the debtor a prescribed time limit, the length of which is determined according to the circumstances of the case.[102] After the expiry of this period, the bailiff assesses whether the debtor is legally entitled to another property and determines his family situation (Article 1 section 1 DMJ). This assessment procedure also tackles and postpones the eviction procedure. Having taken these steps, the bailiff then sends a notice to the appropriate municipality (that is, the municipality with jurisdiction over the property from which the debtor is to be evicted) for the designation of temporary accommodation.[103] The bailiff then suspends the eviction procedure until the competent municipality proposes temporary lodging for the debtor,[104] in accordance with the prohibition in Polish law of the so called 'eviction to nowhere'. Suspension of the eviction procedure may last up to six months. Only after this period can the bailiff relocate the debtor to a shelter or other institution that provides places to sleep.

8.3 Most Effective Measures for Reacting to Evictions

In Poland there exists special legal protection for vulnerable groups.[105] According to the AoTR, there is a group of tenants who are more sufficiently protected in the process of eviction and must be evicted to the secondary accommodation.[106] In such cases, it is obligatory for a court to provide them with this accommodation or another place to live. Article 14 section 4 AoTR lists the categories of tenants included in this group, namely

---

[102] Ibid.

[103] Art 2 (1) DMJ.

[104] Art 1046 § 4 sentence 2 CCP. The only exception to this rule is where the creditor or a third party proposes accommodation that complies with the requirements of a temporary lodging (see Art 1046 § 5 CCP); in which case the bailiff may not suspend the eviction procedure.

[105] See Bończak-Kucharczyk (n 11) 343 et seq; Bednarek (n 14) 695–699; Zdun-Załęska (n 28) 115–121; Dziczek (n 28) 382–386; Chaciński (n 30) 135–142.

[106] The exception to this rule is where the above-mentioned tenants are entitled to reside in another property or premises.

- pregnant women
- minors
- disabled people and their carers who live jointly with them
- incapacitated people and their carers who live jointly with them
- incapacitated patients
- pensioners eligible for social assistance benefits
- the unemployed
- persons who meet the conditions designated by the resolution of a municipal council.[107]

This provision does not apply to persons who have lost legal title to their premises which are not in the public housing stock,[108] if such a legal title results from an agreement which was concluded after 1 January 2005.[109] However, in such situations, the right to be accommodated in social housing may result from the decision of the court.[110] In practice, courts often apply this provision: in approximately 60–65 per cent of the cases, the courts have granted the tenant secondary accommodation (see Section 4).

Persons listed in Article 14 section 4 AoTR must be rehoused to other accommodation even when they have already rented it from the municipality.[111] In practice, this means that the person being evicted from such a house has at least the right to a social housing unit and the eviction must be suspended until the municipality offers new accommodation according to the general rules described above. Therefore, even in the event of non-payment of rent, a person listed in Article 14 section 1 AoTR cannot be evicted to a shelter and must be rehoused in social housing.

This rule does not apply to the following: perpetrators of domestic violence; persons who flagrantly or persistently act against the applicable home order; people who by their inappropriate behaviour make use of

---

[107]   In Poland, the resolution of a municipal council can designate special conditions, the fulfilment of which would grant the tenants the right to be evicted to secondary accommodation (Art 14 (4) point 6 AoTR). The court is obliged to grant (in the sentence of the verdict) the tenant secondary accommodation. In such a situation, the court is obliged to provide the tenant with another place to live.

[108]   Art 14 (7) AoTR.

[109]   Dziczek (n 28) 385–387.

[110]   See Art 14 (1) AoTR.

[111]   See Bończak-Kucharczyk (n 11) 351 et seq.

other units or the common property burdensome; people who occupy the accommodation without any legal right.[112]

Tenants not belonging to one of the groups listed in Article 14 section 4 AoTR can be evicted to secondary accommodation if the court decides that in the sentence of the verdict. During an eviction hearing the court *ex officio* examines whether special conditions exist, according to which the tenant may be granted secondary accommodation. The court takes into account the reasons for eviction, the previous use of the premises by the tenant, and the financial situation of the tenant and his or her family.[113] If the court decides not to grant the tenant secondary accommodation, he or she is evicted into temporary premises proposed by the competent municipality or into a shelter. This measure is effective in preventing homelessness because, in practice, it prevents or postpones the evictions.[114]

8.4 Measures that Could Work but that Are Not Implemented

In Poland it is possible to initiate an alternative to the judicial process of dispute resolution, such as arbitration, conciliation or mediation. However, there is no obligatory mediation between landlords and tenants or creditors and borrowers. Additionally, the parties are not formally obliged to undertake mediation before the enforcement of the eviction. Because of this, mediation is not common in Poland; and neither is conciliation, since public institutions are not obliged to provide services of this nature, although conciliation could precede court proceedings. Furthermore, lease agreements do not usually contain an arbitration clause. Finally, there is no legally established formal association of tenants, which could also act as a tenants' plenipotentiary.

Consequently, there should be a formal obligation to **start mediation procedures** between the parties before the enforcement of the eviction, in which they try to reach agreement on an arrears repayment plan and prevent eviction. Mandatory mediation should also be provided in cases involving the eviction of a spouse from premises jointly occupied by both spouses. The parties should be encouraged at every stage of their conflict to submit their case to arbitration. Moreover, a public institution that represents tenants' interests in these circumstances should be established.

---

[112] See Art 17 AoTR in connection with Art 14 AoTR.

[113] Art 14 (1) AoTR in connection with Art 14 (3) AoTR.

[114] However, sometimes it could also discourage new renting because some owners do not want to rent housing to the aforementioned groups of people for fear that they will not be able to remove those persons from the premises.

Similarly, a legally established tenants' association would provide valuable balance in policy-making arrangements relating to evictions.

In Poland, there is no legal obligation on landlords or bailiffs to inform social services of the threat of eviction before the beginning of the procedure. Outreach services should be warned *ex officio* about planned evictions and courts should automatically inform them about the eviction procedures. It is probable that the landlords would be obliged to send a written notice to the local social welfare organizations before they formally terminate the lease contract. Timely contact with tenants when they are starting to encounter problems is usually crucial to successfully preventing evictions.[115] It is also worth noting that in Poland, a significant number of people do not possess adequate knowledge on the law of property. Hence, they do not know how to act during the procedure of eviction.

9. CONCLUSION

In theory, Polish law provides sufficient protection against arbitrary and illegal eviction. The so-called 'eviction to nowhere' has been deemed unconstitutional. Moreover, courts are obliged to assess the situation of the person being evicted using formal criteria established in the AoTR. Vulnerable people and people with disabilities receive substantial protection in the process of eviction. They must always be evicted to secondary accommodation and it is obligatory to offer them any kind of accommodation or another place to live (see article 14 section 4 AoTR). The only exception to this rule exists when those tenants are legally entitled to reside in another property or premises.

However, in practice the most common situations are when evictions lead to homelessness due to the deficit in social housing. Currently, a municipality has to provide replacement housing for evicted tenants. It frequently happens that, in practice, such accommodations do not exist. As a matter of fact, the deficit in social housing makes the eviction procedure time-consuming. In addition, it often happens that a municipality does not secure the proper accommodation for the person who is being evicted. Moreover, in many cases the replacement accommodation,

---

[115]   For example, Arts 36 ff of the Act on Social Assistance established that there could be a standard social assistance provided for those who face the threat of eviction. See Sierpowska (n 6) 183 et seq.

if available, is unsuitable and the municipality officers do not respect current regulation by refusing to offer housing below minimum standards.

As stated in the Introduction, Poland lacks a system of solutions to support municipalities that would give adequate access to social housing for those entitled to it.[116] The existing implemented solutions are insufficient in relation to the citizens' needs. The main problem is that the housing deficit remains at a high level, estimated at around 1.5 million accommodations.[117] Solving this problem requires the creation of a state aid system that will accelerate the development of housing.[118]

---

[116] Najwyższa Izba Kontroli, 'Realizacja zadań w zakresie gospodarki mieszkaniowej przez organy administracji rządowej i jednostki samorządu terytorialnego' (2012) 11 <http://www.nik.gov.pl/plik/id,3581,vp,4565.pdf>.

[117] Ibid 11.

[118] Ibid 9 et seq.

9. Evictions in Slovenia: legal aspects, data limitations and good practices

Maša Filipovič Hrast

1. INTRODUCTION

Housing is one of the key pillars when discerning people's welfare and well-being, despite being often labelled as the unstable pillar of the welfare state. The right to housing is embedded in several international documents, including the Universal Declaration of Human Rights (UDHR), the International Covenant on Economic, Social and Cultural Rights (ICESCR), the European Social Charter, the EU Charter of Fundamental Rights, and the Habitat Agenda. These documents emphasize the importance of security of tenure, as well as the affordability, habitability, accessibility, location and cultural adequacy of housing. Therefore, understanding the way countries prevent eviction or address housing needs after eviction and the protection of people's right to housing is of great relevance.

Slovenia is a society of homeowners, yet one with markedly low levels of indebtedness of households. Despite having a low number of owners with mortgages, in comparison to the EU average, there has been a significant increase in the share of owners with a mortgage in the last decade. This increase also potentially means a higher share of the population at risk of eviction. The risks have also increased due to the economic crisis, which has affected Slovenia quite significantly and was marked with high unemployment rates and an increase in poverty levels.

In this chapter, the issue of housing and eviction in Slovenia is addressed. Slovenia, similar to other Central and Eastern European countries, is marked with high home ownership rates, and due to the specific development of the housing market (ie large-scale privatization, large share of self-build[1]), it also has lower indebtedness of households.

---

[1] See Sma Mandič, *Stanovanje in država* (Ljubljana, Znanstveno in publicistično središče 1996).

First, the general housing policy context and main structural factors that define housing risks such as the small social rented sector, the small private rental sector and the increasing unemployment and poverty rates due to the economic crisis, will be outlined. Following from that, a summary of Slovenia's legislation related to evictions which illustrates the level of protection of homeowners and renters against eviction is provided, and the main data on eviction in Slovenia is described. Gaps in the data are also identified. The final section of the chapter presents a selected number of good practice measures with reflections on their limitations. In conclusion, the chapter discusses the findings and addresses the gaps in the knowledge and research in this area.

2. POLICY BACKGROUND

2.1 General Housing Policy Related to Evictions

The housing policy in Slovenia is fragmented and underdeveloped.[2] Following from the independence and large-scale privatization of public housing, the development of the social rented sector was slow, and the municipalities responsible for its development have faced various problems in financing and the advancement of this sector. Strategic documents at national level were often adopted quite late, with several years in between. The National Housing Programme 2000–2009, for instance, has been succeeded by the Resolution on National Housing Programme 2015–2025, which is the most recent document setting the priorities in housing policy in Slovenia. These priorities are primarily aimed at reaching a balance between demand and supply, improving the accessibility of dwellings and mobility, supporting housing renovation and strengthening the rental sector. From the perspective of the prevention of housing exclusion and evictions, an important objective of this document is also increasing security in and the growth of the rental sector, by reducing illegal renting and stimulating owners into renting out non-used dwellings. This can be achieved by introducing public service for rental housing management that would function as an intermediary between owners and renters. However, another new instrument is also mentioned which could potentially be introduced which would enable swifter evictions from rental dwellings. Additionally, one of the stated new instruments are rents linked to costs, however it is unclear how this will

---

[2] R Sendi, *Stanovanjska reforma: pričakovanja, potrebe in realizacija* (Ljubljana, Urbanistični inštitut Republike Slovenije 2007).

affect the vulnerability of renters, despite the envisioned introduction of a new more uniform housing subsidy. The most recent policy changes therefore might affect eviction rates; however, the direction of this effect is unclear.

2.2 Structural and Societal Factors Related to Evictions

Slovenia is a society of homeowners, as 76.7 per cent of households were homeowners in 2014 (see Table 9.1 below). This share has slightly decreased when compared to 2006, when the figure represented 84.5 per cent. This decrease is primarily due to the increase in the share of renters in social dwellings or users, which increased from 11.3 per cent to 17.4 per cent. The increase in the share of renters in social dwellings and users is mainly due to the increased number of users of dwellings (rent free) and indicates the importance of family assistance in ensuring housing. The share of households with a mortgage is relatively small. Despite having a low number of owners with mortgage in comparison to the EU average, there was a significant increase in the share of owners with a mortgage from 1.5 per cent in 2006 to 10.3 per cent in 2014 (see Table 9.1). The increase of households with a mortgage potentially indicates a higher share of population at risk of eviction due to arears.

The 2008 economic crisis worsened the situation and increased risks, as unemployment rates and poverty rates have increased and the accessibility of housing loans has also diminished. Since 2008, the unemployment rates in Slovenia increased to 10.1 per cent in 2013; however, they decreased to 7.9 per cent in 2016.[3] Along with rising unemployment there was rising poverty, especially among the group of unemployed, as access to unemployment benefit is limited. The at-risk-of-poverty rate also increased from 9.1 per cent in 2009 to 14.3 per cent in 2015.[4] Among the unemployed, the at-risk-of-poverty rate is much higher, and has risen from 25 per cent in 2005 to 44.9 per cent in 2015.[5] The rise in the number of financially vulnerable households implies a possible higher risk of eviction due to arrears (mortgage, rent or in payment of other housing costs). This is also indicated with a slight increase in the

---

[3] Eurostat, 'Total Unemployment Rate' 2016 <http://epp.eurostat.ec.europa.eu/tgm/table.do?tab=table&init=1&language=en&pcode=tsdec450&plugin=1>.

[4] Eurostat, 'At-risk-of-poverty rate by poverty threshold and household type – EU-SILC survey' 2016 <http://appsso.eurostat.ec.europa.eu/nui/show.do?dataset=ilc_li03&lang=en>.

[5] Ibid.

housing cost overburden rate (from 3 per cent in 2006 to 6.1 per cent in 2015[6]), which is still however, below the EU average (11.3 per cent in 2015).

Table 9.1   Ownership status 2006–2014; Slovenia and EU (in %)

	2006 %	2007 %	2008 %	2009 %	2010 %	2011 %	2012 %	2013 %	2014 %
Slovenia									
Owner	84.5	81.3	81.3	81.3	78.1	77.5	76.2	76.6	76.7
Owner, with mortgage or loan	1.5	4.3	5.5	6.9	7.7	7.7	8.4	9.6	10.3
Tenant, rent at market price	4.2	5.5	4.9	4.1	5.0	5.5	5.5	5.7	5.9
Tenant, rent at reduced price or free	11.3	13.2	13.8	14.5	16.9	17.0	18.3	17.7	17.4
EU-28									
Owner	:	:	:	:	70.7	70.6	70.6	70.1	70.1
Owner, with mortgage or loan	:	:	:	:	27.7	27.3	27.1	27.4	27.1
Tenant, rent at market price	:	:	:	:	17.3	17.6	18.2	18.9	19.0
Tenant, rent at reduced price or free	:	:	:	:	12.0	11.8	11.2	11.0	10.9

Source: Eurostat, 'Housing Data' (2014) <www.eurostat.silc>.

2.3   Specific Policies Related to Evictions

In general, several social protection instruments are relevant for decreasing the housing and eviction risks. Rent subsidies are available to those in the rental sector, which can be seen as an important measure that can prevent eviction due to rent arrears. In cases of eviction, evicted households can receive aid from Social Work Centres (slo. Centri za

[6]   Eurostat, 'Housing cost overburden rate by sex – EU-SILC survey' 2014 <http://ec.europa.eu/eurostat/tgm/table.do?tab=table&init=1&language=en&pcode =tessi160&plugin=>.

socialno delo) (financial aid, advice), and can apply for emergency dwellings if these exist in the municipality (only in larger cities), or for social housing. However, it should also be noted that several changes have been implemented in social policy. In 2012, a new Financial Social Assistance Act,[7] and the Exercise of Rights to Public Funds Act 2010, came into force, defining the rights to financial social assistance and to supplementary allowance.[8] Important was the new regulation that introduced a specific order of application for the social transfers, which can lead to reduced transfers. This new legal framework has increased vulnerabilities of certain groups, such as single-parent households, households with children aged 15–18 years, large families and elderly people. However, the position of those without income, savings or any means has slightly improved,[9] indicating a mixed effect of the legislative changes on the well-being of households.

3. LEGAL AND CONSTITUTIONAL BACKGROUND TO PROTECTION AGAINST EVICTIONS

3.1 Housing as a Fundamental Right

Housing in Slovenia is not defined as a fundamental right per se. The Constitution of the Republic of Slovenia[10] declares that the state shall create opportunities for citizens to obtain proper housing.[11] What constitutes a proper or suitable dwelling is defined in Article 10 of the Housing

---

[7] Financial Social Assistance Act (Official Gazette 61/2010) <http://zakonodaja.gov.si/rpsi/r09/predpis_ZAKO5609.html>.

[8] The Financial Social Assistance Act 2012 is targeted at ensuring a minimum income for living. Supplementary allowance contributes to the long-term costs of living (such as the upkeep of the dwelling). The right to social assistance is limited by the income and property status of a person, while the right to supplementary allowance is intended for those who are long-term unemployed or incapable of working or elderly (for women, the age limit is 63 years and for men, 65).

[9] P Dremelj, S Smolej, R Boškić, T Narat, L Rihter, N Kovač and Tomc B Kobal, *Ocena učinkov izvajanja nove socialne zakonodaje. Končnoporočilo* (Ljubljana, IRSSV 2013).

[10] Hereinafter 'the Constitution'.

[11] Art 78 of the Constitution.

Act.[12] Additionally, Article 36 of the Constitution guarantees the inviolability of the dwelling. Limitations of enforcement and security of a debtor's existence and dignity arise from the constitutional principle of the social state and the constitutional right to personal dignity and safety.[13] In particular, a housing right and protection from eviction is pronounced within the social rental sector. Pursuant to Article 104 of the Housing Act, it is not possible to terminate a tenancy contract, even though a tenant fails to cover the rent price or the price of other running costs, in cases where tenants are faced with extraordinary circumstances beyond their control, due to which they are unable to cover the expenses (eg death in the family, unforeseen loss of employment, serious illness, natural disasters, etc).[14]

3.2 Law Relating to Owner-occupation

A major risk factor for the eviction of an owner-occupier is missed payments of debts and mortgage. On the basis of the Consumer Credit Act,[15] the mortgage contract must be made in the form of a notary agreement and the notary has to inform the debtor of the legal consequences in cases of breach of contract. The creditor can, on the basis of a directly enforceable claim in enforcement proceedings, demand repayment of the claim and the process of eviction is quick.[16] Furthermore, the

---

[12]   A suitable dwelling is a dwelling in a one- or multi-dwelling building constructed in accordance with the minimum technical conditions for the construction of residential buildings and dwellings and for which a permit for use has been issued in compliance with the regulations on the construction of objects. A dwelling must have separate sleeping and living parts (except in the case of a bedsit) and must satisfy the housing needs of the owner or tenant and immediate family members who live with the owner or tenant in a common household, and must correspond to the spatial standards described under Art 87 of the Housing Act.

[13]   Arts 79 and 117 Enforcement and Securing of Civil Claims Act.

[14]   S Mežnar and T Petrovič, 'National Report for Slovenia' in TENLAW, *Tenancy Law and Housing Policy in Multi-level Europe* (Celje, International School for Social and Business Studies 2014). The condition for enforcing this provision is that the tenant initiates proceedings for obtaining subsidy of the rent price and exceptional assistance for the expenses with the dwelling. The deadline for initiating the proceedings is thirty days from the emergence of the circumstances.

[15]   Consumer Credit Act (Official Gazette 59/2010).

[16]   Dida Volk, *Izvršba: izterjava denarnih terjatev in vse kar morate vedeti o sodnem postopku: priročnik* (Enforcement of financial claims and all you need to know about legal procedure) (Ljubljana, DZS 2003) 351.

Enforcement and Securing Civil Claims Act[17] stipulates that in the event of the sale of the immovable property that represents the debtor's dwelling, the debtor is protected so that he or she can exercise a right of residence in the sold dwelling. This right is limited to three years. However, exempt from this right are those evicted due to repayment of the claim arising from a loan for construction or the purchase of this immovable property or debt-claims secured by mortgage on immovable property.[18]

The Enforcement and Securing of Civil Claims Act specifically takes into account the interest of the creditor to ensure the effectiveness of enforcement and the final realization of the creditor's human right to judicial protection.[19] The creditor has, according to Enforcement and Securing of Civil Claims Act, free choice[20] of means that he or she can propose in order to obtain the repayment of his or her claim.

Important also are the limitations of the enforcement procedure, which protect the existence of the debtor. According to Article 101 of the Enforcement and Securing of Civil Claims Act, the following incomes cannot be subjected to enforcement: social transfers, scholarships, child support and other similar sources of income. Furthermore, the debtor is entitled to retain a minimum wage.[21]

---

[17]   Art 210 Enforcement and Securing of Civil Claims Act.

[18]   See also Volk (n 16) 140.

[19]   Judicial decision of the Constitutional Court of the Republic of Slovenia, No. U-I-339/98 of 21 1.1999).

[20]   Since the Act Amending the Enforcement and Securing of Civil Claims Act in 2002, it is no longer provided that the court *ex officio* limits enforcement only on limited execution measures. The debtor may therefore achieve the result that the execution on the immovable property does not take place if there are sufficient other execution measures to cover claims. In addition, the debtor has always, during the enforcement proceeding (and of course before that), the possibility to settle the claims so as to prevent the execution. If the debtor does not want to settle the debt, then the selling of the immovable property in necessary interference with the right of property of the debtor so that the creditor receives the repayment of his claim (pursuant to the Ministry of Justice and Public Administration Act 2012) takes place; See also Art 169 of the Act Amending the Enforcement and Securing of Civil Claims Act.

[21]   Art 102 Enforcement and Securing of Civil Claims Act.

3.3 Law Relating to Private Renting

The termination of a contract in the private rental sector is regulated in the Housing Act 2003.[22] The grounds for termination and eviction are the same for the private and non-profit sectors. However, the law also indicates that additional reasons are viable for the termination of the contract provided they are listed in the tenancy contract, which may be defined quite broadly and encompass different situations.[23] However, it seems that in practice, contracts do not usually include these additional reasons and legally regulated reasons are of utmost importance.[24] Since these are clearly specified in the Housing Act, this could be presented as good practice for regulation of termination and grounds for eviction in the private rental sector.

Conversely, despite clear regulation on termination, legal experts note that market rentals are neglected in the 2003 Housing Act and accompanying legislation. This is especially observed in reference to the provisions on maintenance and repairs and the rigid legislation for the landlord, for example, they may end the contract only in a court procedure. An additional problem is the poor protection afforded to tenants after the tenancy agreement has expired, as they can be evicted at any time despite perhaps paying the rent and living in the dwelling with the consent of the landlord.[25]

3.4 Law Relating to Social Renting

The protection of tenants in the social rented sector is the most robust and is clearly defined in the Housing Act 2003. The rental contract must be concluded for an indefinite period of time, and it may be terminated only due to reasons listed in the Housing Act, including: causing major damage or changes to the housing; performing an activity in the housing without a permit; non-payment of rent or costs; violating the house rules; subletting without the agreement of the owner; and communicating false data to obtain the dwelling. The legal conditions for termination of

---

[22] Art 103 Housing Act 2003.

[23] See A Vlahek, 'Odpoved Stanovanjske Najemne Pogodbe' ('Cancellation of rental contract') (2006) 7 *Podjetje in Delo* 1222–1235; Mežnar and Petrovič (n 14).

[24] S Mežnar and T Petrovič, 'Termination of tenancy contract in Slovenia: Time for a change. LeXonomica' (2013) 5 (2) *Journal of Law and Economics* 111, 117.

[25] Ibid 111.

tenancy contracts are predominately mandatory in order to protect the tenants' weaker position, while being more lenient for the tenant, who can terminate the contract without any valid reason at any time.[26] Moreover, the process of termination of a contract is highly regulated, and a written warning must be submitted by the landlord and the method of rectifying the reason for termination must be listed; in addition to the requirement of a suitable time limit for rectifying the reason for termination.[27]

When a decision of a claim to vacate a dwelling becomes final (the court issues the judgment), the person must move out in 60–90 days.[28] If the owner or tenant does not comply with the deadline set by the court in the decision for vacating the premises, the landlord may file an application for enforcement of the court's decision. Pursuant to Article 71 of the 1998 Enforcement and Securing of Civil Claims Act, the tenant may propose to the court the partial or complete postponement of the enforcement. However, in this case the tenant must plausibly demonstrate that in the case of immediate enforcement, he would suffer significant damage/harm and, furthermore, this harm must be greater than the damage which is to be inflicted to the landlord.[29]

3.5 Law Relating to Unauthorized Occupancy

Regarding illegal building in general, a court may impose an order on a builder to demolish the building and restore the immovable property to its previous situation.[30] Illegal constructions are a matter of administrative procedure. An inspector or administrative authority issues as a rule a decision that it is necessary to demolish an illegal construction. The property right on the immovable property extends to the building built on the immovable property (Law of Property Code, Article 56).

The illegal occupation of land and illegal building in Slovenia is commonly linked to Roma settlements. The main deficiency in this area is the lack of integrated measures to deal with the problem. There are no holistic plans on how to deal with Roma settlements and no integrated approach exists on legalization of these settlements, or on their relocation

---

26 Mežnar and Petrović (n 14).
27 Art 103 Housing Act 2003.
28 According to Art 112 Housing Act 2003.
29 Mežnar and Petrović (n 14).
30 Art 47 Law of Property Code (Official Journal of the Republic of Slovenia, number 91/2013).

and even exact data on the number of these settlements.[31] However, municipalities often try to apply specific solutions, specifically through the law on the Roma community,[32] which asserts that the state and local authorities must regulate the problems of Roma settlements. The government can intercede in local spatial regulations with official acts, if the legal and spatial disorganization of Roma settlements has severe effects on health, continuous environmental risk and public order.[33] The National Programme of Measures for Roma of the Government of the Republic of Slovenia 2010–2015[34] has left this problem in the jurisdiction of municipalities and their spatial plans. These usually have temporary solutions where current settlements are tolerated. There are also examples of good practices, where municipalities (eg Municipality Murska Sobota and Municipality Krško) have first tolerated illegal building on agricultural land and later legalized the buildings and enabled purchase of the land.[35]

3.6 Law Relating to Temporary Dispossession

According to the Family Violence Prevention Act 2008, a victim of domestic violence can ask the court to prevent the perpetrator of violence from doing the following: entering the living premises of the victim; being within a defined distance of the living premises of the victim; approaching places where the victim usually stays (workplace, kindergarten, school, etc); contacting the victim in any way; meeting the victim in any way. The above court orders can be applied for six months, and on the request of the victim, extended for a further six months. In addition, Article 21 of the Act enables the court to transfer accommodation in common use to the exclusive use of the victim upon his or her request, for a period of six months. This period may be extended for a further six months in the event that the victim cannot secure alternative accommodation in the time provided.

---

[31] Jernej ur Zupančič, 'Prostorski problemi romskih naselij v Sloveniji – elaborat' ('Spatial problems of Roma settlements') (Ljubljana, Ministrstvo RS za okolje in prostor 2010) <http://www.mzip.gov.si/fileadmin/mzip.gov.si/page uploads/publikacije/prostorski_problemi_romskih_naselij_elaborat.pdf>.

[32] ZromS, OG RS, no 33/07.

[33] Art 5, ZromS, OG RS, no 33/07.

[34] Government of RS, 2010.

[35] Zupančič (n 31).

3.7 Other Relevant Laws

In Slovenia, those living in denationalized dwellings (ie dwellings nation-alized under socialism that have been restituted to their original owners) have a special protected tenancy. A rental contract between the housing right holder and the previous holders of ownership rights is still valid, regardless of the restitution of the ownership right to the denationalization claimant. These rental agreements are for non-profit rent and of a permanent nature, which means that the new owners have no use of the returned property and potentially are therefore not interested in the continuation of the contract, which can produce conflicts between renters and tenants.[36] The tenancy in the denationalized apartments is regulated under the Housing Act 2003. However, the status of the tenants in denationalized dwellings has been deteriorating, with changes in legislation and a decrease in protection of tenants (the lease is not permanent due to the possibility of moving the tenant to another dwelling, nor inheritable) along with significant rent increases (a 613 per cent increase in the rent ceiling in 12 years).[37] Feantsa filed a complaint against Slovenia, which targeted the destabilized housing security of 13 000 tenants in denationalized dwellings.[38] The decision of the European Committee of Social Rights (ECSR) in February 2010 held that Slovenia was in violation of the law in respect to the rights of tenants in denationalized dwellings, and emphasized the precarious position of sitting tenants.

3.8 Soft Law/Codes and Their Effectiveness

The possibility of alternative dispute resolution is available, although there are no specific procedures developed precisely for tenancy matters. Instead, a court-annexed mediation is usually offered to the parties.[39] There are two Acts used in Slovenia for alternative dispute resolution: the Mediation in Civil and Commercial Matters Act, 2008, and the Act on Alternative Dispute Resolution in Judicial Matters, 2009.

---

[36]   J Debevec, 'Najemniki denacionaliziranih stanovanj' ('Renters in denation-alized dwellings') in S Mandič and M Filipovič (eds) *Stanovanjske študije* (Ljubljana, FDV 2002).

[37]   See Feantsa complaint and decision: <http://www.feantsa.org/spip.php?article676&lang=en>; J Murgel, 'Slovenija je kršila pravice najemnikov de-nacionaliziranih stanovanj' ('Slovenia has violated the rights of renters in denationalized dwellings') 2010 15 *Pravna praksa* 21–22.

[38]   (CC53/2008).

[39]   Mežnar and Petrovič (n 14).

4. EXTENT OF EVICTIONS OVER THE PERIOD 2010–2015

4.1 Evictions from Mortgaged Property

The available data on evictions does not indicate the reasons for eviction for the different types of housing tenure. However, the data from the Ministry of Justice indicates the number of enforcement procedures on immovable property; that is, procedures where a debt has to be repaid and the lender/party to whom the debt is owed has claimed for this immovable property, which includes not only mortgages but also all other debts. Unfortunately, the statistics as currently recorded do not distinguish between primary homes, second homes and commercial premises. According to the data from the Ministry (see Table 9.2), the number of closed cases in 2012 was 10 424, and in 2015, the figure was 11 477,[40] more than 22 000 unsolved cases in each year remaining. The average time in court was 29.5 months in 2015 (ie real time of procedures). The number of cases received has been falling from 2010, when it was 10 960 cases, to 7866 cases in 2015.

Table 9.2   Enforcement procedure on immovable property

	Unfinished cases (in the beginning of observed period)	Received cases	Cases in proceedings	Solved/ closed cases	Average real time of procedure in months
2010	21 158	10 960	32 118	9274	n.a.
2011	22 876	10 510	33 386	9311	n.a.
2012	24 121	10 311	34 432	10 424	28.6
2013	24 129	11 482	35 611	10 608	28.5
2014	25 409	9659	35 068	12 970	26.5
2015	22 247	7866	30 113	11 477	29.5

Source: Ministry of Justice, personal inquiry (21.3.2017).[41]

[40]   For 2013, the data is preliminary. The closed cases/solved cases are all cases in which the court has given a decision.

[41]   See also: Court statistics. <http://www.mp.gov.si/si/obrazci_evidence_mnenja_storitve/uporabni_seznami_imeniki_in_evidence/sodna_statistika/>.

In addition to the information collated by the Ministry of Justice, further data on eviction procedures is available from the Supreme Court of the Republic of Slovenia, which is based on an electronic database ('vpisnik') and includes data for the whole of Slovenia. The Supreme Court collects the data on a number of court decisions for vacating the premises (evictions).[42] The data does not distinguish between private and commercial properties. However, the data presented here includes only those procedures where at least one of the debtors was a physical person, the intention being to exclude as many businesses/companies as possible. There are several methodological constraints: the data does not indicate whether objections have been filed regarding these court decisions, or whether these decisions have been implemented (or the claim to vacate has been withdrawn). The data provided shows (see Table 9.3) that the number of court decisions for vacating the premises (evictions) has been decreasing slightly from 2010 onward, from 352 decisions down to 247 decisions in 2015.

Table 9.3   Court decisions for eviction/vacating the premises[43]

Year	Number
2010	352
2011	321
2012	313
2013	283
2014	228
2015	247

Source: Supreme Court of the Republic of Slovenia, personal inquiry, 14 February 2017.

4.2   Evictions from Private/Social Rented Housing

The data on evictions in social housing is included in the above data; as previously noted, there is no distinction made regarding the type of housing in enforcement proceedings. Unfortunately, there is no central evidence on evictions in social housing in Slovenia in total. However, to present at least an illustrative example on the issue of eviction in social

---

[42]   The methodological notice here relates to the number of cases where the court has made a decision; however, it does not necessarily mean an eviction was carried out.

[43]   Slo. Sklepi o izvršbi – deložacija.

rented housing, the above data is supplemented by data on evictions from the Municipal Housing Fund of Ljubljana. Since this is the largest housing fund in Slovenia that provides social housing, it is also one of the most relevant case studies. This data is therefore descriptive, yet indicates the trends in evictions and differences between eviction processes initiated and actual evictions executed. As the data shows (see Table 9.4), the number of actual evictions is much smaller than the number of claims made for termination of a tenancy contract, eviction and repayment of debt. The number of filed court cases for eviction in each year (see Table 9.3), has slowly decreased only from 2013. The increase in court decisions in the same years can be linked to previously initiated procedures. The number of evictions actually carried out is usually smaller than the number of court orders for eviction, either due to voluntary vacating of the premises or through reaching an agreement with the Housing Fund and finding alternative (emergency) dwelling.

The problems of eviction have been recognized in the Housing Programme of the Municipality of Ljubljana for 2017–2018.[44] In this programme, anti-eviction measures are elaborated, such as preparedness to reach out of court settlements for repayment of debts, offering smaller and cheaper dwellings to indebted households, offering counselling for gaining financial assistance, offering emergency units to the evicted and offering free mediation services. The programme also emphasizes cooperation with other actors in preventing evictions, such as the Social Work Centres (see Section 2.3) and non-governmental organizations (NGOs) that carry out preventive work with renters.

There is no data that offers information on evictions in the private rental sector. However, one important fact is that most vulnerable households often rent unofficially, and are therefore unprotected against eviction by law. Recent research has found that approximately 11 per cent of landlords in the private rental market in the Municipality of Ljubljana wish to rent without a contract, however this number might be underestimated.[45] The significant incentive to rent unofficially is the high tax burden. Slovenia has one of the highest tax rates for tenancies in

---

[44] Housing programme of Municipality of Ljubljana for 2017 and 2018 (2016). No: 014-140/2016. Ljubljana: Municipality of Ljubljana. Adopted on 17. 11. 2016.

[45] R Sendi, 'Major characteristics of Slovenia's silent private rented sector' Paper presented at ENHR Conference, Tarragona 2013 <http://www.enhr.net/documents/Papers%20Spain/Papers/WS22/Sendi%20ENHR%202013.pdf>.

Table 9.4   Evictions from non-profit housing in the Municipality of Ljubljana

	Court cases for termination of tenancy contract (filed in that year)	Court order for eviction**	Provision of emergency housing in lieu of eviction	Voluntary vacating of premises after court decision and before commence-ment of enforcement proceedings
2004	Na.	30	2	2
2005	Na.	39	7	7
2006	Na.	43	4	4
2007	Na.	31	5	5
2008	Na.	25	1	1
2009	Na.	19	5	5
2010	27	14 (17**)	6	6
2011	40	16	6	7
2012	33	19 (22**)	7	7
2013	34	8 (16**)	4	8
2014	14	18	3	3
2015	10	20	11	7
2016	9	10	3	0

Note: ** Housing programme of Municipality of Ljubljana for 2017 and 2018 (2016).

Source: Municipal Housing Fund, personal inquiry, 27 January 2017.

Europe, ie 25 per cent of the rent price with only 10 per cent of acknowledged costs.[46]

4.3   Commentary on the Statistics

In Slovenia there is a lack of data on evictions. The most important available sources of data stem from the Ministry of Justice and the Supreme Court; both gathering data from all courts on the enforcement proceedings. However, the main problem is that the data from the Ministry of Justice refers to the number of cases in proceedings or closed

---

[46]   Mežnar and Petrovič (n 14).

cases without distinction of primary homes, second homes and commercial premises and therefore does not enable a realistic estimate of evictions of households to be made. More detailed data on evictions is available from the Supreme Court, where the eviction procedures have been limited to those where the debtor is a physical person. But in addition, the Supreme Court data does not enable a distinction to be made between evictions in ownership and the rental sector, nor does it provide any information on evicted households. This means there is a significant lack of precise information for a more detailed and thorough understanding of eviction trends and characteristics in Slovenia.

4.4 Profile of Those Evicted and Risk Factors Leading to Eviction

As this chapter has shown, the data on evictions and dispossessions from official sources does not identify the characteristics of different households.[47] Even at a local level, for instance through the Housing Fund of the Municipality of Ljubljana, there is no data on the profiles of the evicted households or risk factors leading to eviction.

5. LINKS BETWEEN EVICTIONS AND HOMELESSNESS

In Slovenia, there are no specific studies on evicted households or general studies on the reasons for homelessness; furthermore, studies on specific risk factors are rare. However, a recent study from 2012 dealing with applicants for social housing and emergency units in the Ljubljana Municipality[48] addresses the issue of evictions. Emergency units are units offered by the Municipal Housing Fund to address the most urgent housing needs. However, due to the small number of available dwellings, there is a waiting list. The survey, carried out among those living in these emergency dwellings and the applicants for these dwellings,[49] specifically asked participants to detail the reasons for their current housing

---

[47] Ministry of Justice, Supreme Court of RS.
[48] S Mandič, Maša Filipovič Hrast, M Mrzel and T Rozman, 'Kako izboljšati ponudbo najemnih stanovanj v MO' ('How to improve the supply of rental dwellings in Municipality of Ljubljana- Final Report') (Ljubljana, FDV 2012).
[49] The sample group was 39 (N =139). However, with this question more than half of the sample group did not respond to all the questions. We are reporting valid per cent.

circumstances (looking back over five years). Eviction due to non-payment of rent was indicated by 19.4 per cent of the respondents and loss of dwelling due to mortgage arrears was indicated as a cause by 4.5 per cent; 11.9 per cent of the respondents indicated that they lost their housing due to inappropriate living/dwelling conditions (eg demolition). Moreover, the most common reasons cited were loss of job (75.5 per cent), grave illness (57.5 per cent), divorce or death of a partner (47 per cent) and domestic violence (43.9 per cent).[50]

A study on the homeless in the city of Ljubljana, undertaken by Dekleva and Razpotnik in 2007,[51] interviewed homeless persons on the reasons for their homeless status and 54 per cent revealed that eviction was the cause. This was the third most common justification given by the interviewees, falling behind only 'financial troubles' and 'individual decision'. However, eviction here must be understood in a wider sense and not as a specific official act prescribed by the court. The authors of the cited study view the individual decision and eviction as two sides of the same coin, as individual decision precedes the eviction, people leave their place of living before they are actually evicted. Other common problems were: loss of job (49 per cent); ending of relationship (33 per cent); conflict with parents (31 per cent); mental health problems (individuals 27 per cent, family members 20 per cent); alcohol abuse (family members 25 per cent, individuals 22 per cent); drug abuse (individuals 18 per cent, family members 7 per cent); and domestic violence (23 per cent).[52]

6. SUMMARY OF SIGNIFICANT CASES AND REPORTS RELATED TO EVICTIONS IN THE PERIOD 2010–2015

In 2012, the media reported on a case where a debtor had lost his dwelling due to a minor debt, which gained a lot of public attention. This was due to the fact that a creditor has, according to the Enforcement and Securing of Civil Claims Act, free choice of means that he or she can propose to secure repayment of his or her claim (see also Section 3.2

---

[50]   Mandič et al (n 48).

[51]   B Dekleva and Š Razpotnik, *Brezdomstvo v Ljubljani* (Ljubljana, Pedagoška fakulteta 2007). The homeless were defined as rough sleepers, those sleeping in shelters and other places and not having a permanent place to live and no home.

[52]   Ibid 54.

above). Therefore, execution upon immovable property may be the first and only execution measure in the enforcement proceeding. The Human Rights Ombudsman of the Republic of Slovenia challenged this state of affairs, arguing that the law as it stood did not offer sufficient protection to households at risk of eviction and, furthermore, that the relevant provisions of the Enforcement and Securing of Civil Claims Act were not in accordance with the principle of proportionality, as stipulated in Article 3 of the same Act. The Slovenian Government ordered[53] the Ministry of Justice to examine the existing legal instruments and look into the protection of the principle of proportionality. However, following the analysis, it was concluded that the existing legal means ensure sufficient legal protection of the debtor. Consequently, only minor changes to the legislation were proposed and adopted by the government in July 2014.

Evictions, especially from the social housing sector, have received significant attention from civil society organizations. In the period following 2010, NGOs have become more active in supporting people threatened with eviction. Free legal aid has been criticized as being too inaccessible to vulnerable groups, as not only income but also posses-sions are taken into account in determining entitlement to such aid. Civil society has started to offer additional free legal aid organized on a voluntary basis. An important example of best practice in this regard is Botrstvo – brezplačna pravna pomoč (Godfathers – free legal aid, organized by Association Zveza prijateljsvo mladine). This project aims to supply free legal aid to those in need, and as stated by one of volunteers in a media article: 'Free legal aid is intended for helping with existential and housing problems, as many people are incapable of paying rent and high housing costs in non-profit dwellings. Their debts accumu-late and we help them to arrange instalment repayment of debt and to receive a smaller non-profit dwelling or emergency housing unit, that they are capable of paying'.[54] Activists have claimed that the non-profit housing sector is failing to uphold its basic purpose of offering housing to the most vulnerable and that changes to legislation are needed, including: additional financial aid; more flexibility from the municipality that would enable the tenant to move to another dwelling or emergency

---

[53] Decision of Government of RS no. 06000-1/2012/4. 15. 3. 2012.
[54] Nina Zidar Klemenčič, rtvslo.si, 30.1.2014 <http://www.rtvslo.si/slovenija/revezem-rubijo-tri-role-wc-papirja-sluzijo-pa-rubezniki-in-odvetniki/328653>.

housing where he or she would be able to pay the costs; lowering some of the elements of non-profit rent and also lowering of additional housing costs.

7. BEST PRACTICE MODELS FOR PREVENTING, TACKLING AND REACTING TO EVICTIONS

7.1 Effective Measures for Preventing Evictions

An effective measure for preventing evictions is the strong protection of tenants' rights with limited reasons for eviction and clear procedures to be followed in cases involving evictions from the social rented sector. Especially important in this regard is the protection from eviction afforded by Article 104 of the Housing Act 2003, which lists the extraordinary circumstances[55] in which it is not possible to terminate a tenancy contract, even though the tenant fails to cover the rent price or the price of other running costs. Consequently, this measure was evaluated by experts as being very effective in preventing evictions from this sector.[56]

Another preventive measure of best practice from the foregoing analysis is implemented through cooperation between the local Municipal Housing Fund (Municipality of Ljubljana (JSS MOL)) and the NGO, Kralji Ulice. Working with the homeless, JSS MOL has recognized that problems involving tenants, such as non-payment of bills and misuse of dwellings, need to be addressed before they escalate into potential evictions from dwellings. For this purpose, the JSS MOL began co-operating with Kralji Ulice, a Ljubljana-based homelessness prevention service. The programme has included offering support to tenants that have problems and are at risk of being evicted. The programme is presented as a very open process; offering help to individuals, being open to the needs of tenants, and not in any way prescriptive.

7.2 Effective Measures for Tackling Evictions

Article 71 of the 1998 Enforcement and Securing of Civil Claims Act provides that during the eviction process, the tenant can propose to the court the partial or complete postponement of the enforcement. If the

---

[55] For example, a death in the family, unforeseen loss of employment, serious illness, natural disaster.

[56] See Mežnar and Petrovič (n 14).

tenant's circumstances are particularly dire, the court can decide to postpone eviction for three months, but only once. Furthermore, the effectiveness of the Article 71 measure is restricted due to the strict conditions attached (see Section 3.4).

7.3 Effective Measures for Reacting to Evictions

The provision of 'emergency' housing can be seen as an effective measure for reacting to evictions. However, there is no evidence that this measure is cost effective.

As the various Housing First[57] projects indicate, the provision of emergency temporary accommodation (such as shelters) and other support services can cost more than rehousing homeless people in permanent accommodation at the first opportunity.

In Slovenia, Article 88 of Housing Act 2003 stipulates that those in dire housing need, such as families facing eviction, must be offered emergency units. The Housing Fund of the Municipality of Ljubljana specifically states that an emergency housing unit can be rented in cases of eviction of a household that could become homeless, and the data already presented indicates the use of this measure. However, the disadvantage of this measure is that the provision of emergency units is not obligatory and therefore they exist only in larger municipalities. Moreover, another current and significant disadvantage of the measure is the long waiting list[58] and the temporary nature of the emergency units, as well as, in some cases, the lower housing standard.

7.4 Measures that Could Work But that Are Not Implemented

Financial support schemes can be an effective way to prevent evictions, and means-tested targeted housing allowances have proven to be useful instruments for improving housing outcomes.[59] In Slovenia, the housing

[57] N Pleace and J Bretherton, 'The case for Housing First in the European Union: a Critical Evaluation of Concerns about Effectiveness' (2013) 7(2) *European Journal of Homelessness*, 21–42; Busch-Geertsema, 'Results of a European Social Experimentation Project' (2014) 8(1) *European Journal of Homelessness*, 13–28.

[58] It can take several years for applicants to receive such a unit. However, evicted households may have priority over others on the waiting list, depending on the circumstances.

[59] European Commission, 'Social investment package', Commission Staff Working Document 'Confronting homelessness in the European Union' Brussels (SWD 2013) 42.

costs overburden rate has increased for poor households from 14.7 per
cent in 2005 to 26.3 per cent in 2013.[60] Also, as noted by the Association
of Tenants, the payment of housing costs can often lead to conflict
between tenant and landlord, as the landlord can demand higher payment
than the actual costs (and the companies are not obliged to show the costs
in the building and their division to the tenant, but only to the owner).
Consequently, a measure that would support the payment of these costs
and potentially indirectly also impose some control regarding their
amount, would help those in the private rental sector.

Another possible measure that could work, but is not implemented, is
mediation and/or the provision of intermediary agents in the private
rental market, which would promote renting by private landlords but also
offer more protection to the renters in the private sector. More vulnerable
groups need support in renting the dwelling in the private rental market
and also need support in cases of conflict between them and the landlord.
An intermediary, mediation service between landlords and tenants is
needed to prevent potential conflicts from escalating to eviction. Specialized institutions such as social rental agencies (which currently do not
exist in Slovenia) could take on a mediation role. Such an intermediary
organization is envisaged in the new Resolution on National Housing
Programme 2015–2025, in the form of public service for rental housing
management, under the remit of the current Housing Fund of the
Republic of Slovenia.

8. CONCLUSION

The structural characteristics of the Slovenian housing stock, with high
shares of home ownership and low indebtedness, present a comparatively
low risk factor for eviction. The existing legal procedures linked to
evictions allow for a relatively high level of legal protection for renters in
the non-profit rental sector. In addition, the whole court procedure is
quite long. Despite the increase in risk factors due to the economic crisis
and higher unemployment and poverty rates, the number of evictions, as
the limited available data shows, has not been increasing, but has even
slightly decreased since 2010. Consequently, evictions do not represent a
major social problem and are not addressed by policy measures as a
specific priority at national level; for example, within the Resolution on
the National Housing Programme 2015. At a local level, there has been

---

[60]   Eurostat 2014 (n 6).

policy attention to the problem of evictions in the social rented sector. In the Municipality of Ljubljana, for example, the local housing programme for 2017–2018 contains a specific section on anti-eviction measures and tries to address this issue.

In cases of owners facing eviction, the Ombudsman has already in 2012 argued for some changes to the legislation regarding the principle of proportionality. This was subsequently confirmed by the European Court of Human Rights in *Vaskrsić v Slovenia* (App No 31371/12), a 2017 case in which the claimant complained that the sale of his home at public auction had involved a disproportionate interference with his property rights, as the property had been sold for 50 per cent of its market value in the course of debt enforcement proceedings arising from a principal debt of only €124.[61] Following this, in 2018, Parliament adopted the Act Amending the Enforcement and Securing of Civil Claims Act, which includes new provisions on limiting eviction from housing in which the owners are living, and where the household debt is small.[62] The court would be obliged to include Social Work Centres and enable postponement of eviction in cases where the debt is highly disproportional to the value of property.

In addition, it is vital to point out the significant lack of research in this area. Further research would enable a better and more comprehensive understanding of the trends in the number of evictions and, specifically, in the number of evictions due to mortgage arrears, as well as the factors leading to eviction and the consequences of evictions, such as the potential link between eviction and homelessness. National changes are necessitated and increased consideration of the policies concerning evictions, and more generally, housing exclusion issues and the improvement of data collection methods that would facilitate informed policy making. The main shortcoming of the present system seems to be the lack of more proactive preventive measures and support, such as measures that would actively identify those in housing distress and with rent/housing costs/mortgage arrears. In particular, such practices could be not only part of informal practices but also part of formal and institutionalized procedures.

---

[61] EHRM, 25-04-2017, no. 31371/12: also Poročilo o zadevi Vaskrsić (2012) <http://beta1.finance.si//files/2012-03-16/120315_Vaskrsic.pdf>.

[62] Ministry of Justice, News on adopted *Act Amending the Enforcement and Securing of Civil Claims Act* <http://www.mp.gov.si/si/medijsko_sredisce/novica/7523/>.

10. Evictions and homelessness in Spain 2010–2017[1]

Sergio Nasarre-Aznar and Rosa Maria Garcia-Teruel

1. INTRODUCTION

The present chapter examines the phenomenon of evictions and its relationship with homelessness in Spain from 2010–2017. The causes that have led to evictions are analysed, principally the lack of a functional diversified range of housing tenures and the negative consequences of the 2007 crisis that have led many households to overindebtedness, default, eviction and, in some cases, ultimately to homelessness. The chapter also covers the delayed response of the legislator to prevent, tackle and react to evictions primarily through transitory measures that have had limited success. The narrow scope of the 'right to housing' in Spain has contributed to this. Best practices and the need for continued development are also discussed. In addition, available data on evictions from mortgaged and rented property is provided for the period 2010–2015, which coexists with cases of home forced-removal such as dispossessions arising from divorces and domestic violence. Finally, the main causes for homelessness are analysed, and the relationship with evictions is outlined.

[1] This chapter has been possible thanks to the participation of both authors in (a) the Project of the Spanish Ministry of Economy 'Collaborative housing' (DER2017-84726-C3-1-P); b) and at the Tenlaw Project (2012–2015) of the 7th Framework Program of the European Commission, led by Prof C Schmid, University of Bremen. Prof Nasarre-Aznar is an ICREA Fellow 2016–2020 and one of the four co-coordinators of the 'Pilot project – Promoting protection of the right to housing – Homelessness prevention in the context of evictions', VT/2013/056 (delivered to the EU Commission in March 2016).

2. POLICY BACKGROUND

2.1 General Housing Policy Related to Evictions

The situation of Spain in relation to evictions during the period 2010–2017 can be considered, to some extent, as a consequence of not having developed a proper alternative to full homeownership for decades.[2] The vast majority of households, normally, have been compelled to buy their dwellings, which has resulted in many of them becoming overindebted[3] due to the negative economic consequences of the 2007 crisis. As a consequence of this overindebtedness, many of them were evicted and, in some cases, some have ended up homeless.

In this vein, Cuerpo et al[4] for the EU Commission assert that: 'the state of development of rental markets as a genuine alternative to home-ownership stands out as a particularly relevant institutional factor shaping the outcome of the housing market and playing a balancing role and alleviating house price pressures.' The negative consequences of not having genuine and diverse alternative housing tenures, such as a functional tenancy market or intermediate housing tenures, have been pointed out by the United Nations New Urban Agenda of Habitat III 2016 (sections 35 and 107).[5]

Consequently, this has resulted in Spain being a country with a small rental market (around 14.4 per cent in 2017), with 41.4 per cent of the

---

[2] This has been pointed out by the OECD, *Recommendations for Spain* (2014), 94 and the International Monetary Fund (IMF), *Art. IV. Recommendations* (2011) Spain.

[3] The rate of non-performing loans (98 per cent of them guaranteed with a mortgage; NPL are those defaulted in their payments by more than 90 days) to buy dwellings in June 2006 was only of 0.39 per cent, around 3 per cent in September 2009 and of 4.6 per cent in September 2016, according to the Asociación Hipotecaria Española, *Tasas de dudosidad del crédito inmobiliario* (Sep 2016) 2, 6.

[4] Carlos Cuerpo, Sona Kalantaryan and Peter Pontuch, *Rental Market Regulation in the European Union* (EU Commission, DG-Economic and Financial Affairs, Economic Papers 515, April 2014) 1.

[5] See also DG Blanchflower and AJ Oswald, 'Does high home-ownership impair the labor market?', in *Peterson Institute for International Economics* (May 2012, Working Paper 13-3) <http://www.piie.com/publications/wp/wp13-3.pdf>.

rental black market in 2015,[6] with only 20 per cent of current tenants happy to remain as such if they had the possibility to buy[7] and with unaffordable rents in the private tenancy market sector: in March 2017, in only three out of 50 Spanish provinces was home renting more affordable than home buying.[8] Table 10.1 evidences some reasons for this.

Table 10.1   *Legal framework and policies for homeownership and leased homes in Spain*

	Homeownership	Rented home
Incentives	Tax incentives for many years (some since 1960s).	Since 2010 (deductible expenses for the landlord within the personal income tax, VAT exemption, etc). Tax incentives for the tenant are no longer applicable for contracts agreed after 1 January 2015, but some Autonomous Regions have their own.[9]
	Housing Public Plans oriented (including incentives of all sorts for developers, buyers, financial institutions, etc.) to house building and house buying.	The National Plan 2013–2016 is the first one in recent Spanish history that only gives incentives to leases and rehabilitation. However, the Housing Plan 2018–2021 again offers grants up to more than €10 000 to young people to buy properties in small villages.[10]

---

[6]   El Mundo, 'Cuatro de cada diez alquileres de vivienda no se declara a Hacienda' <http://www.elmundo.es/economia/2016/04/19/571600d722601dd3048b45ba.html>.

[7]   Fotocasa, *Los españoles y su relación con la vivienda* (2015). <http://prensa.fotocasa.es/wp-content/uploads/2016/06/Los-espanoles-y-su-relacion-con-la-vivienda-en-2015.pdf>.

[8]   <http://www.elconfidencial.com/vivienda/2017-01-29/si-pagases-lo-mismo-de-alquiler-que-de-hipoteca-comprarias-casa_1315309/>.

[9]   See Transitional Provision 15th Act 35/2006 (BOE no. 285, 29.11.2006) and art 1 Catalan Act 31/2002 (DOGC no. 3791, 31.12.2002).

[10]   El Mundo, 'El Gobierno dará una ayuda de hasta 10.800€ a los jóvenes para la compra de vivienda', <http://www.elmundo.es/economia/vivienda/2017/05/04/590af00a268e3ecd3a8b45b9.html>.

	Homeownership	Rented home
Affordability	Structured and professional finance market (Mortgage Act + Mortgage Market Act = modern system of land credit), at least since 1981.	Absence of any professional or structured market. Failure of financial vehicles since 2003 originally intended to promote leases. Spanish REITs' (2009) positive impact on tenancies is under discussion.[11]
	Mature re-finance system (mortgage securitization), since 1872 and, especially, 1981. Affordable mortgage loans.[12]	Leases securitization possible since RD 926/2008, but rarely used. Underdeveloped market.
Safety and transparency of the markets	Clear cut rules for rights and obligations of buyers and for financial institutions.	Historical pendulum and inefficient distribution of rights and obligations between landlord and tenant. This is especially evident in the decrease of tenants' protection in Act 4/2013 and, because of this, leases bubbles in Barcelona, Madrid and other key cities in Spain since end-2016.[13]

---

[11] The first Act on Spanish REITs (11/2009) foresaw a tax rate of 19 per cent and the rental had to last at least seven years, when the REIT was the developer of these properties too. After the amendment of Act 11/2009 through Act 16/2012, the new tax rate for REITs is 0 per cent and the duration of the contracts is three years. The increased number of REITs in Spain is thought to be promoted thanks to the law amendments in 2012. See Noelia Fernández and María Romero, 'Las socimi y el mercado inmobiliario' (2016) 253 *Cuadernos de información económica*.

[12] Now their cost is increasing due to legal instability (new laws, constant challenges to mortgage law by national and international courts, increase in consumers' protection), but they are still considered the most affordable mortgage loans in Europe. The average mortgage rate in Spain is 1.98%. See El Mundo, 'Son tan malas nuestras hipotecas?' <http://www.elmundo.es/economia/vivienda/2017/05/05/590b4bd5268e3e89708b4598.html>.

[13] Sergio Nasarre-Aznar and Elga Molina Roig, 'A legal perspective of current challenges of the Spanish residential rental market' (2017) 9(2) *International Journal of Law in the Built Environment* 10–11; Sergio Nasarre-Aznar and Elga Molina Roig, 'Parámetros para un nuevo marco de los arrendamientos urbanos, tras la Agenda Urbana de Habitat III 2016', in Esther Muñiz Espada,

Table 10.1 (continued)

	Homeownership	Rented home
	Fast mortgage foreclosure (but less since case *Aziz v CatalunyaCaixa*, explained below), even in insolvency processes.	Inefficient system of eviction and continuously reformed (last reforms at Act 4/2013 and Act 42/2015).
	Transfer of all home risks and home expenses to the buyer.	Landlords usually transfer many risks and costs to tenants. Quite often, landlords have little incentive to take care of the property due to low returns (4%).
	Transactions and financial arrangements usually controlled by notary publics and land registrars (gatekeepers).	Leases black market of 41.4%. Many undocumented transactions; unstructured and uncontrolled market. There is some improvement of this aspect with Act 4/2013.

Source: Adapted and updated from S Nasarre-Aznar, MO Garcia and K Xerri, 'Puede ser el alquiler una alternativa real al dominio como forma de acceso a la vivienda? Una comparativa legal Portugal-España-Malta', in *Teoría y Derecho*, núm. 16/2014, 195.

To fully frame the lack of attractiveness of tenancies in Spain, this must be combined with the relative weak welfare state. For instance, Spain has recently raised the retirement age to 67;[14] public health[15] and

---

Sergio Nasarre-Aznar, Estela Rivas Nieto and Ángel Urquizu Cavallé (coord), *Reformando las tenencias de la vivienda* (2018) 19.

[14] By Art 4 Act 27/2011, 1 August, *sobre actualización, adecuación y modernización del sistema de Seguridad Social* (BOE 02/08/2011 no. 184, 87495).

[15] By RDL 16/2012, 20 April, *de medidas urgentes para garantizar la sostenibilidad del Sistema Nacional de Salud y mejorar la calidad y seguridad de sus prestaciones* (BOE 24/04/2012 no. 98 p. 31278). See European Foundation for Improvement of Living and Working Conditions (Eurofound), *Access to Healthcare in Times of Crisis*, Publications Office of the European Union (Luxemburg, 2014) 23, where it is stated that health protection for undocumented immigrants has been reduced in 2012 due to the crisis; see also 38 and 61 where a case study of shortcuts affecting mental health assistance is presented. At 12 it is affirmed that: 'One indicator of reduced availability of healthcare services as a

education[16] services have suffered recent cutbacks; while retirement pensions are constantly under scrutiny in the media.[17] According to Eurostat,[18] in 2015, Spain ranked among those Western European countries (Greece, Italy, Ireland, Cyprus, Portugal) with the highest rate of at-risk-of poverty or social exclusion.

Recent legal reforms in the law of leases have partially improved the situation of landlords. However, Act 4/2013, following OECD recommendations to liberalize tenancy agreements to increase their share, has substantially decreased tenants' rights, worsening their stability[19] and do not include rules to increase their affordability or flexibility.

For many families in Spain, then, especially in the context of a 20 per cent unemployment rate (second worst in Europe after Greece, 44 per cent youth unemployment rate in 2016[20]), private rented housing is not a real option. The Housing State Plan 2013–2016 only subsidized part of the rent to households that earn a maximum of less than €1600 a month in 2017. Social rented housing only amounts to 2 per cent of the total, signalling that it is already insufficient to meet demand.[21]

This is also leading to 'generational' negative externalities, namely that Spain is the second country in Europe in which the lack of affordable housing is the most predominant reason for not leaving one's parents'

---

consequence of the crisis is that, after years of steady reduction, average waiting times for some surgical operations in Portugal, Spain, England and Ireland show a small increase (OECD, 2013)'.

[16]   By RDL 14/2012, 20 April, *de medidas urgentes de racionalización del gasto público en el ámbito educativo* (BOE 21/04/2012 no. 96, 30977).

[17]   See <http://www.elmundo.es/espana/2017/01/04/586c0a0de2704e8f4b8b4 5ac.html>.

[18]   <http://epp.eurostat.ec.europa.eu/statistics_explained/index.php/File:At-risk-of_poverty_or_social_exclusion_rate,_2011_and_2012.png>.

[19]   Sergio Nasarre-Aznar, Maria Olinda Garcia and Kurt Xerri, '¿Puede ser el alquiler una alternativa real al dominio como forma de acceso a la vivienda? Una comparativa Portugal-España-Malta' in *Teoría y Derecho* (No. 16/2014) 188–217.

[20]   Instituto Nacional De Estadística, *Encuesta de población activa, trimestre 2/2016*. <http://www.ine.es/dyngs/INEbase/es/operacion.htm?c=Estadistica_C&c id=1254736176918&menu=ultiDatos&idp=1254735976595>.

[21]   Interview with a senior for social housing of a *Comunidades Autónomas* (CA).

house,[22] the first where women have their first child the latest,[23] and in which by 2050, 41.4 per cent of the population will be over 60 years old (compared to 24.4 per cent in 2015).[24]

2.2 Structural/Societal Factors Related to Evictions

The ubiquity of homeownership and the lack of promotion of leases as a type of tenure have been identified as two of the major causes of the 2007 economic, financial and housing crisis.[25] Thus, sub-prime lending for those who do not fulfil ordinary mortgage eligibility criteria results in a high LTV (loan-to-value) ratio, increased interest rates and the demand for a personal guarantor to secure the loan; all of which increases the probability of default and subsequent eviction – the consequences of the latter extending to third parties (such as a relative who has personally guaranteed the loan).[26]

However, the bases of the problem are deeper. A significant factor influencing the high (26 per cent in 2013, but approximately 16 per cent in 2018) unemployment rate is Spain's failing building industry, which had since the mid-1990s been the main driver of the Spanish economy. The number of unemployed men and women has increased from 787 351 and 1 230 012 respectively in 2007, to 2 060 207 and 1 988 286 respectively in 2010[27] (although in 2015 there were again more unemployed women than men[28]).

---

[22]   European Commission, *Flash Eurobarometer, No 202 Young Europeans: A survey among young people aged between 15 and 30 in the European Union* (Analytical Report, 2007).

[23]   At the average age of 31.9. Eurostat, 'Mean age of women at childbirth' 2015. <http://ec.europa.eu/eurostat/web/population-demography-migration-projections/births-fertility-data/main-tables>.

[24]   See <http://www.helpage.org/global-agewatch/population-ageing-data/country-ageing-data/?country=Spain>.

[25]   See Sergio Nasarre-Aznar, 'La vivienda en propiedad como causa y víctima de la crisis hipotecaria' (2014) 16 *Teoría y Derecho* 10–36.

[26]   See the link between accessibility, effort and overindebtedness in Cáritas and Fundación Foessa, *La vivienda en España en el siglo XXI* (2013) 119 ff.

[27]   Servicio Público De Empleo Estatal, *Demandantes de empleo, paro, contratos y prestaciones por desempleo* (October 2010).

[28]   There were 1 943 480 unemployed men and 2 288 652 unemployed women in 2015. Data obtained from the *Servicio Público de Empleo Estatal*, Annual Report (2015) <https://www.sepe.es/contenidos/que_es_el_sepe/publicaciones/pdf/pdf_sobre_el_sepe/informe_anual_2015.pdf>.

Unemployment is also affecting the rise of defaults in the payment of compensation pensions to former spouses and alimony to children,[29] an increase in squatting[30] and more and more condominiums being in a state of disrepair.[31]

Lack of liquidity of lending institutions has been also negatively impacting the recovery of the country, impeding entrepreneurship, increasing the number of broken companies for lack of funding and consumption[32] and hindering the recovery of the property sales market.[33]

Reckless banking practices, such as credit default swaps with consumers, have exacerbated the situation; for example, by increasing the debt owed by borrowers.[34] However, the extent of these practices is still under discussion.[35]

---

[29] According to the Prosecutor General's Office ('Memoria elevada al Gobierno de S.M', 2014, 698), 'the economic crisis has also increased the procedures to modify measures to adapt pensions to the new economic reality of parents, with an increase of enforcement measures to compel their payment' (free translation from the Spanish) <https://www.fiscal.es/fiscal/PA_WebApp_ SGNTJ_NFIS/descarga/MEMFIS14.pdf?idFile=dd3ff8fc-d0c5-472e-84d2-231be 24bc4b2>.

[30] There were 1669 squatting crimes in 2013, while in 2008, only 622 people were convicted for it. Squatting is the criminal offence that increased the most since 2008 (168.3 per cent). See INE, *Estadística de condenados. Adultos.* 2013.

[31] See Sergio Nasarre-Aznar, 'New trends in condominium law and access to housing in post-crisis Spain' in Amnon Lehavi (ed), *Private Communities and Urban Governance* (USA, Springer 2016) 178.

[32] According to data provided by the National Statistics Institute (INE, www.ine.es), the number of debtors that fell into bankruptcy in the full year 2016 was 4754, of which 3248 were limited liability companies and only 674 were natural persons without business activity.

[33] While in 2006 there were 955 186 housing sales, in 2013 there were just 300 349, but the sales increased in 2016 to 457 689 (source Spanish Ministry of Development, data available at <http://www.fomento.es/BE2/?nivel=2&orden= 34000000>).

[34] See Plataforma De Afectados Por La Hipoteca And Desc, *Emergencia habitacional en el estado español* (2013) 11.

[35] One example of this are default interest rates, which are usually high on a typical mortgage loan contract (somewhere between 17 per cent and 25 per cent): first, it is too late to avoid mortgage enforcement hence eviction, as the borrower has already defaulted; second, it is not clear whether it falls within judges' competence to decide if that percentage is too much or it is not (it would depend on the damaged incurred by the bank); third, default interest rate in the renowned CJEU, Aziz case was 18.75%; fourth, interest floor clauses were adopted as part of reckless practices (STS 9-5-2013, RJ 2013\3088 and ECJ 21 December 2016,

Some other factors that have been highlighted as deficiencies of the system are that renegotiation of debt is only voluntary for the lending institution, that the current Spanish system does not allow non-recourse mortgages or *datio in solutum*, that in mortgage enforcement processes, defences by mortgagors are few, that there exists a residual debt after an insufficient mortgage enforcement and that the borrower needs help to negotiate with the lender and to reorganize himself.[36] Some other failings have been added: the mortgage enforcement process is too lender-driven, lack of publicity in auctions, and lack of information about overindebtedness and evictions to take proper measures.[37]

Conversely, all these elements have in some way been addressed by the legislator and other agents both in the past and more recently. Article 140 Mortgage Act allows the parties to arrange a non-recourse mortgage, but nobody availed of this provision before 2007 and it has had limited uptake:[38] a somewhat 'compulsory' (through a Code of Conduct accepted by many lending institutions) renegotiation of the mortgage with those most vulnerable including the *datio in solutum*. The Act 1/2013 allows defence through abusive clauses in contracts and foresees electronic auctions;[39] implementation of several intermediation and housing counselling services in some Autonomous Regions (*Comunidades Autónomas*, CAs); increased activity by charities, consumers' associations and other institutions and social movements.

It would appear that all of these reforms and measures have changed, at least to some extent, the banks' attitude toward eviction in the event of mortgage default. Eviction was a commonly used remedy during the first

---

C 154/15); fifth, under the Spanish system there is a double control of legality of mortgage loan contracts (notaries public and land registrars), which might not have worked well sometimes, but are already existing tools that could be useful (see Sergio Nasarre-Aznar, 'Malas prácticas bancarias en la actividad hipotecaria' in *RCDI* núm. 727/2011, 2665 – 2737).

[36] See 'Paper delivered to the President of the Catalan Parliament by Catalan Ombudsman, TSJC, Bar of Lawyers, Bar of Notaries, Secretary of Housing of Catalan Government and Cáritas Diocesana' 15 December 2011 at Cáritas Diocesana de Barcelona (2013) 146.

[37] CES-EGAB, 'El sobreendeudamiento familiar: un análisis desde la CAPV' (2014), 98, 114–118, 136 and Nasarre-Aznar (n 35) 2723–2724.

[38] Since the introduction of art 140 LH, it must be agreed previously in the mortgage deed, preventing the mortgagor in advance from recovering the entire amount apart from the property value. See Nasarre-Aznar (n 35) 2665–2737.

[39] <https://subastas.boe.es>.

years of the crisis (2007–2009). However, the Spanish Mortgage Association reports that, by December 2012, 8.4 per cent of housing mortgages
were freewill (by agreement of lenders and borrowers) refinanced and/or
restructured (delays, suspension of instalment payments, extension of
mortgage repayment period, modification of interest rates, alternative
forms of repayment and voluntary *datios in solutum*),[40] which translates
to €50 000 million. Thus, renegotiation seems to have been a preference
for banks only in more recent years.

2.3 Specific Policies Related to Evictions

Although the crisis began in 2007, the Spanish government did not
undertake specific legal measures to solve or alleviate its effects,[41]
including mortgage borrowers' overindebtedness and evictions, until
2011. Some of the Autonomous Regions (*Comunidades Autónomas*,
CAs) reacted earlier (eg Catalonia in 2007[42]) and some others later
(Andalusia[43] and Navarre[44] in 2013, the Basque Country[45] in 2015 and
Valencia[46] and Extremadura[47] in 2017). Moreover, this delayed reaction
and the lack of reliable data on the scope of the crisis and its effects, has
been identified as a cause for the start of social movements such as
15-M[48] (2011) and PAH[49] (2009) and the rise of the so-called 'Robin-
prudence' (based on the principle of Robin Hood avenging the poor
against the rich and powerful).

---

[40] See <http://www.elconfidencial.com/empresas/2014-05-09/la-banca-ha-
refinanciado-el-15-del-credito-200-000-millones-y-la-mitad-esta-en-mora_1276
04/>.
[41] Eg The Act 41/2007 (BOE 8-12-2007, no. 294, p. 50593) reformed
Spanish mortgage law and the mortgage market but did not foresee any
provisions in relation to this.
[42] Act 18/2007, of 28th December, on the right to housing. DOGC no. 5044,
of 9.1.2008.
[43] Act 4/2013, of 1st October. BOE no. 263, of 2.11.2013.
[44] Act 24/2013, of 2nd July. *Official Gazzete of Navarre* no. 133, of
12.7.2013.
[45] Act 3/2015, of 18th June, on housing. BOE no. 166, of 13.7.2015.
[46] Act 2/2017, of 3rd February, on the social function of housing. BOE
no. 56, of 7.3.2017.
[47] Act 2/2017, of 17th February, on social emergency of housing. BOE
no. 69, of 22.3.2017.
[48] <http://www.movimiento15m.org>.
[49] <http://afectadosporlahipoteca.com>.

Some of these legal measures can be considered as transitory (that is, to counteract the immediate effects of the crisis), and some others, structural (that is, to stabilize the system to avoid further 2007-type economic crises).

In relation to transitory measures, at Spanish level, a 'Good Banking Practices Code' was passed by Act 6/2012[50] and it includes acquaintances, postponement of payments, reduction of interest rates and, finally, a *datio in solutum*. Though requirements to benefit from these measures were very tough at the beginning, by May 2017 more than 7000 *datios in solutum* had been arranged and 24 000 evictions had been avoided.[51] In its turn, Act 27/2012[52] introduced a moratorium on evictions that now extends to May 2020 and created the 'Social Fund of Dwellings'. However, the Social Fund has achieved only limited success: in 2017 there were only 2116 available dwellings for the whole of Spain. Finally, RDL 8/2011, 1 July,[53] increased the mortgagor's minimum unforeclosability threshold; that is, the part of the monthly income of a mortgagor that cannot be seized by the mortgagee. For example, for 2017, the threshold for a single person was €1061 per month; and for a family of four (two adults plus two minors, where only one adult works), €1697 per month. These are the third highest thresholds in Europe after Belgium and Germany.[54] This, together with the moratorium on evictions, can be included as a good practice, as it assures that vulnerable families retain a decent minimum income that cannot be seized by creditors, and that the most vulnerable households cannot be evicted, even if a court ruling decided so.

At CA level, Catalan Act 18/2007 (further developed by Act 4/2016[55]), Andalusian Act 4/2013, Navarrese Act 24/2013, Act of the Basque Country 3/2015, Act 2/2017 of Extremadura and Act 2/2017 of Valencia impose penalties, tax increases and even forced expropriations on property owners for violation of the social function of ownership; that is, not using their properties as dwellings and keeping them empty. Most of

---

[50]   BOE no. 60, of 10.3.2012.
[51]   <http://www.elmundo.es/economia/2017/02/22/58ad5c7346163f361f8b461b.html>.
[52]   BOE no. 276, of 16.11.2012.
[53]   BOE 7-7-2011, no. 161, 71548.
[54]   P Kenna, L Benjaminsen, V Busch-Geertsema and S Nasarre-Aznar, *Pilot Project – Promoting Protection of the Right to Housing – Homelessness Prevention in the Context of Evictions* (VT/2013/056). Final report (Brussels, European Commission 2016) 182.
[55]   BOE no. 15, of 18.01.2017.

these measures have been challenged before the Spanish Constitutional Court and, overall, their efficiency is at stake. Finally, economic aid is provided to vulnerable households by charities[56] or public administrations, helping those in need to meet their mortgage or rent requirements and to prevent eviction.

In relation to specific housing provision services, occasionally there is a duplicity of two or more services[57] such as state, NGOs, municipalities, CA, etc, trying to reach the same result (prevent eviction, renegotiation of debt, *datio in solutum*, etc), which in turn reduces their efficiency (eg no single negotiator in each lending institution). An additional problem is that in Catalonia, only 4.5 per cent of municipalities have a councilor dedicated only to housing, which is normally shared with planning, environment or youth.[58] Thus, collaboration and coordination among institutions seems to be crucial for their success. One example of this is the creation of commissions to provide urgent shelter (eg Articles 95.6 and 104 h Catalan Housing Act 18/2007). The Catalan 'Emergency Table'[59] provides for cases in which the order of the 'list of applicants' (that is, the regular way to be granted social housing), can be precluded and a person, due to his or her specific needs (validated by social services), can be granted housing. Following the rule of 'housing first', the 'Emergency Table' does not grant rooms or temporary shelter, but a right of use for two years in exchange for an affordable amount of rent.

---

[56] Eg Cáritas Barcelona, which gave €2 million in 2013 as housing aid, while it was €1.1 million in 2010. Cáritas Diocesana de Barcelona, *Llar, habitatge i salut, acció i prevenció* (Col·lecció informes núm. 2, 2013) 73.

[57] See Carme Trilla Bellart, 'L'habitatge en el món local' in Judith Gifreu Font and Josep Ramón Fuentes Gasó (eds) *Règim jurídic dels governs locals de Catalunya* (Valencia, Tirant lo Blanch 2009) 889.

[58] Leonardo Díaz (ed), *Polítiques públiques dels municipis catalans* (Barcelona, Fundació Carles Pi i Sunyer 2014) 165.

[59] The Catalan Emergency Table has its own regulations. Contrast this with the recent case in April 2014 of 22 families that were squatting a building in Seville (called 'corrala Utopía') who were evicted by court order. The Andalusian government, due to the lack of reaction of Seville City Hall, provisionally reallocated them, prioritizing this case above the 'list of applicants' due to the 'social emergency' of this case but with a dubious clear legal backing, creating a full-blown discussion of the measure at national level. See discussion <http://leolo.blogspirit.com/archive/2014/04/11/realojo-temporal-por-motivos-de-urgencia-social-3001560.html>.

An especially sensitive area is energy poverty. The ACA study[60] revealed that since 2014, 15 per cent of families (6.2 million people) have had to use an excessive amount of their economic resources to pay for utilities. The main cause has been the increase in the price of energy (78 per cent between 2008–2014), and the reduction in family income (7.14 per cent between 2008–2016, according to INE). Under Article 6 Act 24/2015,[61] the Catalan Government issued a regulation prohibiting power companies from cutting off vulnerable families' utilities without taking into account the season in which the proposed cut is to take place. The Constitutional Court suspended this Act[62] but Article 6, regulating energy poverty, was not challenged. The Spanish Government has passed RDL 7/2016,[63] by which power companies cannot cut off utilities of vulnerable consumers and it also creates a discount of 25 per cent on the electricity bill.

In relation to the aforementioned structural reforms, Act 1/2013, following the European Court of Justice (ECJ) case of *Aziz v Catalunya-Caixa*,[64] allowed mortgagors to defend themselves against a mortgage enforcement process by raising arguments coming from abusive clauses present in guaranteed loans. Along with this, several amendments to mortgage law and the mortgage process were included. In addition, Spain introduced a limited *fresh start* system (a system of debt forgiveness) for certain insolvency proceedings through Article 21 Act 14/2013,[65] and then with Act 25/2015,[66] to promote entrepreneurship. Finally, Catalonia introduced into the Catalan Civil Code through Act 19/2015,[67] two new types of housing tenures – the shared ownership and the temporal ownership – seeking to combine stability, affordability and flexibility in access to housing.[68]

---

[60] Asociación De Ciencias Ambientales, *Pobreza, vulnerabilidad y desigualdad energética. Nuevos enfoques de análisis.* 2016 <http://www.niunhogarsin energia.org/panel/uploads/documentos/estudio%20pobreza%20energetica_aca_ 2016.pdf>.

[61] BOE no. 216, of 9.9.2015.

[62] ATC no. 160/2016, of 20 September (RTC 2016\160).

[63] BOE no. 310, 24 December 2016.

[64] Case C-415/11.

[65] BOE no. 233, of 28.9.2013.

[66] BOE no. 180, of 29.7.2015.

[67] BOE no. 215, of 8.9.2015.

[68] See Sergio Nasarre-Aznar (dir), *La propiedad compartida y la propiedad temporal (ley 19/2015). Aspectos legales y económicos* (Valencia, Tirant lo Blanch 2017). Rosa Maria Garcia-Teruel, Núria Lambea Llop and Elga Molina Roig, 'The new intermediate tenures in Catalonia to facilitate access to housing'

There is however clear room for improvement, especially with regard to the need for increasing the availability of social housing and the need to improve the repair of the housing stock. According to research, Spain has the lowest share in Europe (after Greece)[69] of available social housing for renting (2 per cent).[70] The insufficiency of the pool of social dwellings created by RDL 27/2012 (discussed above), has forced NGOs and public administrations to try to obtain as many properties as possible to make them available to those in need; for example, through agreements with banks[71] and through compulsory pre-emption rights.[72] The 'intrusive' measures of increased taxation, penalties and expropriation of empty dwellings undertaken by certain CAs and municipalities pursue the same goal. In its turn, the need for housing repairs can be considered the primary reason for properties to remain vacant in Spain, regardless of whether the landlord is private or public. At national level, the State Plans 2013–2016[73] and 2018–2021, focus mainly on promoting reparations and leases, but this last one promotes also homeownership for young people moving to small villages.

All of these developments have impacted the administrations involved, leading to an overload on social services departments, a pressure to create emergency shelters and a pool of enough social housing, new ways of cooperation with the third sector and a need to obtain reliable data on the scope of the evictions.

(2015) 2 *Revue de Droit Bancaire et Financière* 115–118. Héctor Simón Moreno, Núria Lambea Llop and Rosa Maria Garcia-Teruel, 'Shared ownership and temporal ownership in Catalan Law' (2017) 9 (1) *International Journal of Law in the Built Environment* 63–78.

[69]   It amounts to only one dwelling per each 1000 habitants, unlike 120 in Germany and 145 in The Netherlands.

[70]   Housing Europe, *The State of Housing in the EU 2015* (Brussels, 2015) <http://www.housingeurope.eu/resource-468/the-state-of-housing-in-the-eu-2015>.

[71]   For example, the Catalan government arranged with credit institutions such as Catalunya Banc, SL (on 8-10-2013), Bankia, SL (on 21-2-2014), SAREB (on July 2014) and more recently with BBVA (on July 2016, providing more than 1800 dwellings) that they will use a certain number of empty dwellings to social rent them to vulnerable people appointed by social services.

[72]   Art 2 DL 1/2015 (DOGC no. 6839, 26 March 2015).

[73]   BOE 10-4-2013, no. 86, p. 26623.

3. LEGAL AND CONSTITUTIONAL BACKGROUND TO PROTECTION AGAINST EVICTIONS

3.1 Housing as a Fundamental Right

The right to housing under Spanish law is not a fundamental right.[74] According to Article 53.3 of the Spanish Constitution (Constitución Español, CE),[75] the right to housing provided in Article 47 CE ('right to enjoy decent and adequate housing'), is considered only as a programmatic principle; that is, the public authorities, legislation and the judiciary are guided by it,[76] but it cannot be used by itself as a legal ground to ask a judge for a dwelling or as a ground to ask for protection from the Constitutional Court.[77]

Thus, Article 47 CE is considered just sufficient to pass legislation to provide access to housing that is affordable, decent and adequate. This is commonly the purpose of the Spanish Housing Plans[78] that specify public support such as subsidies, etc, for certain groups, including young people,[79] households with an income of less than €1600 per month (this is true for 2017), single-parent families,[80] to buy or to lease, for reparation and regeneration purposes. This Spain-wide legislation is complemented by pieces of legislation in each CA that are also grounded in the Constitution.

---

[74] The right to housing under Spanish law is not a fundamental right (STS 31-1-1984, RJ 1984/495 and STS 19-4-2000, RJ 2000/2963).

[75] 'Recognition, respect and protection of the principles recognised in Chapter 3 shall guide legislation, judicial practice and actions by the public authorities. They may only be invoked before the ordinary courts in accordance with the legal provisions implementing them'.

[76] Eg the legislation must tend to fulfil it.

[77] ATC 20-7-1983 (RTC 1983/359) and ATS 4-7-2006 (JUR 2006/190875).

[78] The current Housing Plan for 2013–2016 (RD 233/2013, 5 April, BOE no 86, 10-4-2013).

[79] The Royal Decree 1472/2007 (BOE no. 267, of 7.11.2007) regulates the basic emancipation income of the youngsters, but was repealed by the Royal Decree Law 20/2011, 30 December 2011, on urgent budget, tax and financial measures to correct the public deficit (BOE no. 315, of 31.12.2011). However, the new Housing Plan 2018–2021 is again expected to help young people to buy a dwelling.

[80] Art 1.2.i. of the National Housing and Rehabilitation Programme 2009–2012. Royal Decree 2066/2008, 12 December (BOE 24-12-2008, no. 309, 51909).

The Spanish Supreme Court has described the concept of 'right to enjoy decent and adequate housing' as an undefined legal concept.[81] Thus, housing is crucial to develop the fundamental rights of freedom,[82] the sanctity of the home/intimacy,[83] and the free development of one's personality.[84]

Consequently, Article 47 CE cannot be used, for example, to prevent eviction resulting from mortgage enforcements,[85] or default in paying the rent under a lease. In effect, these are rights and claims granted to lenders and landlords (respectively), precisely because of the constitutional right to private property (but not fundamental right), and from private law rules included in the Civil Code 1889 (CC), the Mortgage Act 1946 (LH) and the Urban Leases Act 1994 (LAU), in addition to other general principles of law such as *pacta sunt servanda*.

But precisely due to the limited strength of Article 47 CE, some CA legislators[86] and judges/courts have since 2010 gone beyond it and have used other constitutional or supra-national sources or simply general principles of law to strengthen the right to housing to protect those evicted; that is, making it prevail, even if this situation distorts longstanding private law rules and creates a sense of legal uncertainty for real estate stakeholders (lenders, real estate agents, landlords) and (international) investors,[87] with ultimately negative consequences for other households in need of housing. This is the so-called 'Robin-prudence'.[88]

---

[81] STS 17-7-1990 (RJ 1990/6566).

[82] Art 16 CE. See STS 27-11-2000 (RJ 2000/9525).

[83] Art 18.2 CE. See ECHR *Moreno Gómez vs Spain* 16-11-2004, No. 4143/02 and STC 26-4-1999 (RTC 1999/69).

[84] Art 10.1 CE. See STS 7-11-1997 (RJ 1997/8348).

[85] ATC 19-7-2011 (RTC 2011\113).

[86] Eg in the new Basque Country Housing Act, Art 9, granted the right to housing, but it is currently suspended by the Constitutional Court.

[87] As stated by the European Commission-Economic and Financial Affairs, *European Economy. Financial assistance programme for the recapitalisation of financial institutions in Spain* (5th Review, Winter 2014, Occasional Papers 170-January 2014) 26.

[88] See full discussion at Sergio Nasarre-Aznar, 'Robinhoodian' courts' decisions on mortgage law in Spain' (2015) 7 (2) *International Journal of Law in the Built Environment* 27–147. Some of these court decisions are AAP Navarra 17-12-2010 (AC 2011\1), AJPI no. 4 Arrecife 8-4-2013 (CENDOJ 35004420042013200001), SJPI no 7 Collado Villalba (Madrid) 5-9-2013, Order JPI no. 39 Madrid 6-3-2013 (AC 2013\726) and Order of Criminal Court no. 4 Sabadell 8-5-2013 (JUR 2013\242758).

With regard to international courts, the European Court of Human Rights (ECtHR), in the case of *Ceesay Ceesay and Others v Spain*, stopped the eviction of 40 squatters of a building owned by Sareb in the Catalan municipality of Salt. The Court ruled that the Spanish government had not provided enough evidence on the measures it was going to take in relation to the squatters, and especially their children, once they were evicted, to prevent the violation of Article 3 ECHR (prohibiting torture and inhumane or degrading treatment and punishment), and Article 8 ECHR (dealing with respect for one's private and family life). The Catalan government, in accordance with its powers, reacted promptly and granted them social housing. This measure was officially announced in December 2013[89] and it also allowed the eviction to be continued, which took place in mid-December 2013.[90]

Article 16 of the European Social Charter, dealing with the right of the family to social, legal and economic protection, is not generally used by Spanish ordinary courts in relation to housing or evictions. It was quoted indirectly at SAP Alicante 25-6-2010,[91] in relation to the obligation of a developer to guarantee the amounts advanced to him or her prior to the construction of a property.

Similarly, the United Nations International Covenant on Economic, Social and Cultural Rights (ICESR)[92] is scarcely used by Spanish ordinary courts. In Order JPI no. 5 Cartagena 6-2-2013,[93] for example, it was quoted indirectly, but the Order affirms that the existence of a 'right to housing' in international conventions[94] does not mean that a person has 'a universal right to be a homeowner, not even a subjective right to be required directly from public authorities.'[95] The judgment adds that the right to housing is not present in Article 34.3 of the European Charter of Fundamental Rights 2000.

---

[89] ARA, 'La Generalitat ja té a punt pisos de lloguer social per reallotjar les famílies del bloc de Salt ocupat' <http://www.ara.cat/societat/Generalitat-lloguer-reallotjar-families-Salt_0_1013898806.html>.

[90] Nerea Guisasola, 'Cuatro familias del bloque de Salt aún no tienen vivienda social', *La Vanguardia* 10.1.2014, <http://www.lavanguardia.com/local/girona/20140110/54398999407/salt-cuatro-familias-bloque-sin-vivienda-social.html>.

[91] AC 2010\1342.

[92] Ratified by Spain on 27-4-1977 (BOE 30-4-1977, no. 103, 9343).

[93] AC 2013\1033.

[94] Eg in Art 25 UN International Convention of Human Rights and Art 11 UN International Covenant on Economic, Social and Cultural Rights, related to an adequate level of life.

[95] Free translation from Spanish.

Finally, STC 4-11-2013[96] states that the demolition of an illegally built house does not contravene Article 18.2 of the Spanish Constitution[97] or Article 8 of the ECHR as the forced entry of the authorities into the property was necessary and proportionate to evacuate the occupant family in order to undertake the demolition. The Spanish Constitutional Court also refused to apply the precedent set in the ECtHR case of *Yordanova and others v Bulgaria*,[98] on the basis that the *Yordanova* case was based on the violation of the European Convention of Human Rights on ethnic discrimination (Roma), which was not the case here.

However, two members of the Court expressed their dissent with the decision for several reasons, including that the Court does not link Article 18.2 of the Spanish Constitution and Article 8 ECHR with Articles 47 and 39 of the Spanish Constitution, which deal with the protection of family and minors.

3.2 Law Relating to Owner-occupation

As mortgaged households were shocked by evictions in relatively high numbers since the beginning of the 2007 crisis,[99] Spain, since 2011, has been combining a twofold approach to prevent evictions: the free renegotiation of debt,[100] with a sort of 'quasi-compulsory' negotiation through the aforementioned Code of Good Practice, and a *datio in solutum* between lending institutions and vulnerable families.[101]

As stated, the New Urban Agenda of Habitat III (Quito, 2016) supports the need for housing tenure diversification. In this regard, Catalonia introduced into the Catalan Civil Code, through Act 19/2015, two intermediate tenures: shared ownership and temporal ownership, both of which seek to combine stability, affordability and flexibility,[102] while

---

[96] RTC 2013\188.

[97] Art 18.2 CE deals with intimacy and inviolability of domicile fundamental rights.

[98] *Yordanova v Bulgaria* (Application no. 25446/06) ECHR Judgment 29 September 2012.

[99] Kenna et al (n 54) 56, 84.

[100] Which is the base of any private-law system (Art 1255 CC). This renegotiation may include acquittances, postponement of payments and reduction of interest rates.

[101] Through RDL 6/2012 (reformed by Act 1/2013, RDL 1/2015, Act 25/2015 and recently by RDL 1/2017), which can also be done through public and/or social intermediation services.

[102] See Sergio Nasarre-Aznar, 'A legal perspective of the origin and the globalization of the current financial crisis and the resulting reforms in Spain' in

avoiding the overindebtedness of families in accessing homeownership. While shared ownership allows families to gradually buy a property (staircasing), thus paying a rent for the share they do not own yet, temporary ownership allows them to buy a property only for the number of years they need it and not necessarily indefinitely if they do not require so.[103]

The measures to tackle evictions, such as[104] the moratorium on evictions 2012–2020, the *fresh start* for insolvent households and the strengthened defenses against abusive clauses have been addressed above. Complementing these measures, in the field of housing dispossessions due to divorces/separations, it is a judicial practice to decide on the shared custody of children[105] (that is helping to reduce the impact on housing and economic stability of parents) when it is possible, according to the principle *favor filii*. According to INE,[106] 24.6 per cent of all divorces resulted in shared (joint) custody in 2015.

Although there are some protocols to enhance interaction between courts and social services[107] they are not generalized. However, in the case of vulnerable mortgagors (discretionary, appreciated case by case and judge by judge), Article 704 LEC allows a judge to delay the physical removal (*lanzamiento*) for one month and, under special circumstances, an additional month. It is usual to find judges that extend this period of one month for considering it insufficient.[108] In addition, consumers' associations, social movements, charities and public administrations have developed brochures and webpages to inform people what

---

Padraic Kenna (ed) *Contemporary Housing Issues in a Globalized World* (UK, Ashgate 2014) 70–71.

[103]   See further Sergio Nasarre-Aznar and Héctor Simón Moreno, 'Fraccionando el dominio: las tenencias intermedias para facilitar el acceso a la vivienda' (2013) 739 *RCDI* 3063–3122; Garcia-Teruel et al (n 68) 115–118; Simón Moreno et al (n 68).

[104]   See above.

[105]   Foreseen in Art 233-8 Catalan Civil Code.

[106]   INE, *Estadísticas de nulidades, separaciones y divorcios* (2015).

[107]   Eg the multi-protocol in the city of Barcelona 4-3-2013 and the multi-protocol for Catalonia 5-7-2013: *Protocol d'excució de les diligències de llançament als partits judicials de Catalunya*, 5-7-2013. Resolution JUS/1696/2013, 16th July, DOGC no. 6431, 2 August 2013 <http://noticias.juridicas.com/base_datos/CCAA/511082-resolucion-jus-1696-2013-de-16-de-julio-por-la-que-se-hace-publico-el-protocolo.html>.

[108]   Such as in SJPI Madrid de 6-3-2013 (CENDOJ 28079420392013200001).

to do in case of risk of eviction.[109] Finally, in relation to the re-housing support measures, as stated above, there are measures in place to add empty housing stock to the market, to increase the pool of rented social housing,[110] to increase the minimum unforeclosability threshold, and to create emergency housing commissions.

In addition to these measures, there are regular actuations to provide social housing to those evicted. When it is clear that the mortgagor is unable to remain in the property,[111] charities and public authorities[112] offer them a new property (usually as close as possible to the previous one, according to the family needs) or help them to enter into a new one that is privately owned. Financial assistance is also available to those evicted, to help them to start paying the rent in a new dwelling.[113] In Catalonia, in 2016, the financial assistance available (both for mortgage enforcement or rent default) amounted to €200 per month for evicted people under Resolution TES/7/2016[114] and GAH/940/2016.[115] Squatting[116] has been used as an 'informal' rehousing method; PAH claims to

---

[109] See, for example, the brochures issued by the Catalan Government '*Quèferquan*' <http://agenciahabitatge.gencat.cat/wps/wcm/connect/29a7fb14-690d-4a77-b31c-9b9e810eb932/QueferquanWebJunyWeb.pdf?MOD=AJPERES&CACHEID=29a7fb14-690d-4a77-b31c-9b9e810eb932>.

[110] Such as the creation of the 'Social Fund of Dwellings' since 2012.

[111] Either because he is already in the process of being evicted or the bank has not agreed that he can remain, rather than as a homeowner, as a tenant.

[112] The CAs usually have 'registers of applicants' of social housing for renting or buying, such as the ones in Catalonia (Decree 75/2014) and the Basque Country (Order 15/10/12). Municipalities also have their own pool of public housing and also manage those assigned by the CA (eg in Catalonia through arts. 25.2 and 27 Act 7/1985), often used to cover social emergencies in cases of evictions or domestic violence.

[113] Only since February 2013. This is to help the evicted – for mortgages, *datio in solutum*, for leases – to pay for the new dwelling to a maximum €200 per month for 12 months.

[114] DOGC of 14.1.2016.

[115] DOGC of 4.4.2016.

[116] Squatting is considered to be a criminal offence according to Art 245.2 Criminal Code, although there are competing views on the appropriateness of this approach. In any case, the courts apply it only as a ultima ratio measure (if there is no other way of protecting the owner's right), which entails that it is common to perceive that criminal courts refer the aggrieved party to the civil jurisdiction in cases of squatting of clearly abandoned properties. Sometimes, however, squatting causes negative externalities to the neighbourhood. See an example of neighbours' reaction at <http://www.naciodigital.cat/delcamp/reusdiari/noticia/5474/veins/barri/fortuny/contra/ocupacio/pah/reus>.

have promoted the relocation through squatting of more than 2500 people up to September 2015.

Finally, if it is agreed by the Public Administration to perform reparations, renovation or urban regeneration works that affect the usual residence, the occupants have a right to provisional lodging plus a right to return to the home when the work has been completed.[117] If there is a mandatory expropriation by a Public Administration, those people affected have a right to social housing of adequate size, to rent or to buy.[118]

3.3   Law Relating to Private Renting

Since 2012, the number of evictions in the rental sector has been higher than the number of evictions from mortgaged property.[119] In this context, various measures to tackle tenants' evictions (such as protocols between the judiciary and public administration), and the effective blocking of mortgage related evictions by social movements, are discussed here.

In addition, Articles 10 to 13 Spanish Housing Plan 2013–2016 cancelled all subsidies for buying dwellings and instead made the provision of financial assistance, in the form of contributions to rent, to those in need a priority. In some CAs there is special emergency assistance for failure to pay rent for people at risk of eviction;[120] while some other CAs, such as the Basque Country, have organized mediation services between landlords and tenants to resolve payment conflicts. (The Basque Country has provided mediation services since 2007.) Several charities have also introduced a mediation system in the field of tenancies, such as *Cáritas Barcelona*, which from 2011–2014 circumvented 750 evictions.[121]

It is noteworthy, though, that while reform of urban leases by Act 4/2013 has addressed landlords' interests, guarantees for tenants have been reduced at the same time – including reduced minimum duration of contracts and control of rent increases. This contrasts with the position of

---

[117]   Art19.2 RDL 7/2015 (BOE no. 261, of 21.10.2015).

[118]   Art 19.1 RDL 7/2015.

[119]   Kenna et al (n 54) 56, 64.

[120]   Eg in Catalonia (Art 11.2 Decree 75/2014) a maximum of €3000 or 12 months. Resolution TES/7/2016, of 4 January. DOGC no. 7037.

[121]   Cáritas Diocesana de Barcelona (n 56) 19.

tenants in the three countries with the highest share of rented properties in Europe, namely Germany, Austria and Switzerland.[122]

Finally, the rehousing measures discussed above are applicable to both mortgaged home situations and evicted tenants, with the exception of the Social Fund of Dwellings and the minimum unforeclosability threshold. The minimum income that an evicted tenant with remaining debts is entitled to retain is less than that for a mortgagor, as RD 8/2011 increased this minimum amount for mortgagors but not for tenants. The unforeclosability threshold for tenants in 2018 is €735.90 per month (the equivalent to the minimum wage), but it increases proportionally if the perceived salary is higher (Article 607 LEC).

3.4 Law Relating to Social Renting

Generally speaking, social landlords are more tolerant of rent arrears than private landlords.[123] In fact, usually, those in a situation of vulnerability are not evicted from public housing. Moreover, there are various forms of financial assistance available to tenants of rented public housing.[124]

The quality of social rented housing is also an issue. The need for reparations to avoid substandard housing is constant, which was addressed in Article 119 and following of the Spanish Housing Plan 2013–2016 and in Article 47 and following of the Spanish Housing Plan 2018–2021.

There are also accompanying services, such as social workers and mediators, to address problems of coexistence, rent arrears and housing deterioration. In Catalonia, there are special mediation services for public housing led by the public administration, though in practice, it has limitations.[125] NGOs undertake more social tasks, such as finding

---

[122] Sergio Nasarre-Aznar, 'Lease as an alternative to homeownership in Europe. Some key legal aspects' (2014) 6 *European Review of Private Law* 815–846.

[123] The AVS (major association of social housing providers) report does not consider eviction from social housing a serious problem. It is used as a last recourse after applying several financial (postponements of payments, revision of rent) and negotiation (requiring to pay through an attorney, conciliation, arbitration) techniques. AVS, *Diagnóstico 2012. La gestión de la vivienda pública de alquiler* (2012) 78, 108 and 109.

[124] In Catalonia, for example, there exists the so-called 'implicit aid', which entails a discount (maximum amount of €3600 per year) done directly and in advance on the rent. While in 2012, 1272 tenants benefitted, they were 1962 in 2013.

[125] Interview with a senior for social housing of a CA.

employment for social tenants and preparing evictees' curriculum vitaes, etc. Social tenants from *Cáritas Barcelona*[126] are also included in a programme called 'Oikos', which offers high levels of support to facilitate full and autonomous social integration.

Finally, a measure to encourage private landlords to provide a sort of social rented housing is the so-called *avalloguer*. This measure covers three monthly rents (for private rental contracts), or six monthly rents (social rental contracts), to the landlord, in situations where the tenant defaults and is subject to eviction procedures (Decree 75/2014). It applies in the Basque Country (for empty dwellings at Decree 466/2013, and that of intermediation as real estate agent at Decree 43/2012). Co-ordination between social services and housing services has increased since the beginning of the crisis, though there is room for improvement.[127]

3.5   Law Relating to Unauthorized Occupancy

3.5.1   Squatting

Squatting is a criminal offence under Spanish law. However, there is a trend in doctrine and the judiciary to resolve squatting issues through the use of civil law rules instead of criminal rules, as criminal law under Spanish law is considered a law of last resort.

Squatting has in recent years been used by evicted families to force banks to negotiate.[128] The booklet of guidelines on squatting published by PAH points out that squatting's 'main claim is to obtain social rented housing for families'[129] from banks.[130] A similar situation occurs when squatting is used to 'encourage' the Public Administration to rapidly grant social rented housing, such as in the case of the 'Corrala Utopía'.[131]

---

[126]   Cáritas Diocesana de Barcelona (n 56) 43–45.

[127]   Interview with a senior for social housing of a CA.

[128]   As the bank would need to start another judicial process after enforcing the mortgage to remove the squatter, its taking possession of the property will be delayed and will be costly, thus sometimes banks would prefer to negotiate instead of enforcing the mortgage.

[129]   Free translation from Spanish language.

[130]   PAH, *Manual 'Obra social la PAH'* (2013) 4–12 <http://afectados porlahipoteca.com/wp-content/uploads/2013/07/MANUAL-OBRA-SOCIAL-WEB-ALTA.pdf>. See a case of squatting a building pertaining to an inactive builder by several people and for the same goal at <http://www.hoy.es/videos/sociedad/201404/27/madres-okupas-piden-alquiler-3513305835001-mm.html>.

[131]   See <http://sevilla.abc.es/provincia/20131116/sevi-familias-ocupas-esta-dispuestas-201311161052.html>.

Squatting has also been used for other purposes since the beginning of the crisis:

1. By banks. Some cases[132] have been reported of a bank directly offering for sale squatted dwellings with a price reduction of up to 50 per cent. The bank advertised on its webpage 'the property is conveyed illegally squatted by third parties'.[133]
2. By criminal gangs. Criminal gangs squat empty properties, which they illegally 'sell' or 'rent' to third parties. They also make illegal connections to utility supplies (water, gas and electricity), which they include in the price of the transfer.[134]

In reality, the courts rarely accept the defence of 'extreme necessity' as a means of justifying squatting, as there is the possibility of applying for social housing and social assistance or for non-contributory Social Security benefits.[135] Note that the procedure to evict squatters has been recently amended to make it faster through Act 5/2018.[136]

3.5.2 Illegal encampments or self-building

There are 10 000 substandard dwellings in Spain, in which Roma families live, and 4 per cent of these are *chabolas* (illegal constructions).[137] There has not been a clear policy in relation to these illegal encampments during the construction boom times, and they have only been demolished when the space they occupied was needed to expand the city.

The scope and efficacy of the *Estrategia Nacional para la Inclusión Social de la Población Gitana en España* 2012–2020[138] has yet to be seen, the goal of which is to reduce *chabolismo* to 0.5 per cent and substandard dwellings to 3 per cent by 2020. Regarding illegal housing,

---

[132] Here is the example of Bankia: <http://www.elmundo.es/economia/2014/03/07/53190979268e3ef6508b459b.html>.

[133] Free translation from Spanish language.

[134] See <http://ccaa.elpais.com/ccaa/2014/01/22/madrid/1390420420_2967 20.html>.

[135] See SAP Barcelona 12-12-2016 (JUR 2017\39309) and SAP Zaragoza 4-3-2014 (JUR 2014\95152).

[136] BOE No. 142, 12.6.2018.

[137] Cáritas and Fundación Foessa, *La vivienda en España en el siglo XXI* (2013) 233.

[138] Available at <http://www.msssi.gob.es/ssi/familiasInfancia/inclusion Social/poblacionGitana/docs/EstrategiaNacionalEs.pdf>.

the controversial STC 4-11-2013 in relation to the invasion by the police of an illegally built dwelling and the non-application of ECtHR's ruling in the controversial *Yordanova* case, have been discussed above.

3.6   Law Relating to Temporary Dispossession

3.6.1   Divorce

Under Spanish civil law, nullity, separation and divorce usually entail the loss of possession of the family home to one of the spouses.[139] This is also the case for *de facto* or legal partnerships.[140] The general rule is that the spouse who is granted custody of the children gets possession of the family home. In the absence of children, the spouse more in need gets possession. These two rules apply regardless of who is the owner or is entitled to live there; for instance, the tenant of the property. According to INE,[141] in 2012, in 75.1 per cent of the cases involving the custody of children, possession of the family home was granted to the mother, and only 9.7 per cent to the father; in the rest of the cases, possession of the family home was shared.

The estimated number of judicial evictions due to family situations for the whole of Spain remains very low, with only 549 in 2012.[142] However, these figures exclude the fact that each year approximately 96 000 divorced people (usually the man) leave the family home, either voluntarily or due to a court order, and go and find another property, normally rented.[143] Divorce is considered an important cause of default in paying for one's house, since the spouse that leaves the family home usually has to pay the mortgage on it, plus compensation/alimony to the other spouse, plus child support maintenance and other compensations;[144] all this in the context of a 26 per cent unemployment rate during the worst

---

[139]   Arts 90 c) and 96 CC.

[140]   Eg STS 7-7-2004 (RJ 2004\5108) and Art 234-8 CCC in Catalonia.

[141]   INE, *Estadísticas de nulidades, separaciones y divorcios* (2013) <http://www.ine.es/dyngs/INEbase/es/operacion.htm?c=Estadistica_C&cid=1254736176798&menu=resultados&idp=1254735573206>.

[142]   According to Consejo General Del Poder Judicial, *Nulidades, divorcios y separaciones 2007-2012* (2013) 2, 7 and 8.

[143]   Cáritas and Fundación Foessa, *La vivienda en España en el siglo XXI* (2013) 204.

[144]   As an example, in Catalonia there is another compensation related to the increase of each spouse's patrimony during the marriage.

years of the crisis.[145] According to DESC and PAH's survey,[146] divorce accounts for 15.1 per cent of eviction cases, and INE positions it as the third major cause of homelessness.[147] In fact, the loss of use of the family home due to a divorce, separation or nullity entails the right to apply for social housing.[148]

There is a perception since the beginning of the crisis in 2007 that sometimes divorced couples have no other option but to continue sharing the family home[149]: it is neither an adequate moment to sell it,[150] nor can the spouse that has to leave afford to pay the rent/mortgage of another property while he or she is obliged to continue paying the mortgage on the family home.[151] Even a court resolution in Mallorca decided that both spouses share possession of the family home (six months each), in order not to move the minor.[152]

3.6.2 Domestic violence cases

In cases involving domestic violence, specific mechanisms exist for the temporary relocation of the victim to, for example, a supervised flat or an emergency housing facility such as a shelter.[153] A victim can also seek a protection order[154] that includes the forced dispossession of family home

---

[145] It is worth mentioning that under art 227.1 Spanish Criminal Code, default in paying the pension to the former spouse or the alimony to the children is also a considered a criminal offence.

[146] DESC and PAH, *Emergencia habitacional en el Estado Español* (2013) 107.

[147] See below.

[148] Eg Art 11.2.a State Plan Housing 2013-2016 and Art 55.1.b. Catalan Decree 75/2014.

[149] See for example <http://www.diariovasco.com/v/20120921/al-dia-local/divorciados-bajo-mismo-techo-20120921.html>.

[150] Nearly 40 per cent depreciation in 2016 in relation to 2007. Data from TINSA, *Report IMIE* (November 2016).

[151] This is quite often the case because the contractual relationship of the couple with the bank is not altered in any way by the fact of the divorce; hence, if both signed as mortgagors, them both remain as such, regardless of who gets possession of the property after the divorce.

[152] <http://www.diariodemallorca.es/mallorca/2010/09/21/condenados-compartir-piso/604659.html>.

[153] Art 64.2 LO 1/2004, and, for example, in the Canary Islands, arts 21 and 22 c. and d. Act 16/2003.

[154] Art 64.2 LO 1/2004.

of the perpetrator and that prohibits the perpetrator from coming within a specified distance of the family home where the victim remains.

3.6.3   Declaration of ruin and other administrative actions

The firm declaration of ruin entails the removal of those living in the affected building (Article 22 RD 2187/1978). If there is a risk to those living in the premises, they can even be removed before the administrative process finishes (Article 26.1 RD 2187/1978). In addition, where there is a process of reparation, renovation or regeneration that affects first residences, those affected have the right to be provisionally relocated and the right to recover the dwelling once the works are finished (19.2 RDL 7/2015). If there is an expropriation, they have a right to be relocated to an owned or rented public dwelling of sufficient size (19.1 RDL 7/2015).

3.6.4   Other laws

For self-employed workers, Final Provision No. 5 of Act 14/2013 establishes a sort of moratorium on evictions due to Social Security debts. According to this provision, when Social Security has a debt against a self-employed worker and it encumbers his or her first residence, a minimum term of two years is needed between the notification of the first seizure and the auction, giving time to self-employed people to negotiate their debt with Social Security.

In addition, Draft Law of 17 November 2017 on contracts of real estate credit, transposing Directive 2014/17/EU, reduces the possibility of landlords effecting an early termination of the mortgage loan agreement due to non-payment (*vencimiento anticipado*). When the Draft Law is enacted, the position will be that the mortgagor must be in default to at least 2 per cent of the total value of the loan to be evicted or at least 4 per cent if he or she has already repaid half of the loan amount.

3.6.5   Soft law

As it has been pointed out above, a 'Good Banking Practices Code' was passed by Act 6/2012 and accepted by many lending institutions. This Code includes acquaintances, postponement of payments, reduction of interest rates, and a forced *datio in solutum* applicable to vulnerable mortgagors.

4. EXTENT OF EVICTIONS OVER THE PERIOD 2010–2015

4.1 Definition of Eviction

The eviction procedure depends on the type of tenure: mortgaged property and rented property.

Mortgaged property eviction procedure: once a mortgage loan has been defaulted (three months' default in 2017), the bank will file an executive claim (Article 685 LEC) before a judge, who will issue a decree accepting the enforcement. At this stage, the debtor may defend him- or herself (Article 695 LEC). If the mortgagor does not pay the debt, the auction of the dwelling will take place. The proceeds of the auction sale will be used to pay the debt and, if it is not sufficient, the debtor will continue being liable for the total amount (Article 1911 CC), except for cases of 'forced' *datio in solutum* (see above).

Rented property eviction procedure: the eviction procedure for rent arrears is an oral procedure (Article 250.1.1 LEC). After one month's arrears, the landlord can file the claim and the tenant may, within 10 days, pay to avoid the eviction (*enervación*) or defend him- or herself (for example, through evidencing the payment of the rent). In cases where a tenant does neither of the above, he or she will be evicted. This procedure also applies to social housing.

4.2 Evictions from Mortgaged Property

As noted earlier, exact figures for evictions from mortgaged property are available only for the period 2012 to 2015.[155] For 2010 and 2011, a projection has been made.[156] Thus, the numbers of actual evictions from mortgaged first residences are: in 2010, 39 849; 2011, 33 133; 2012, 39 051; 2013, 38 961; 2014, 30 056; 2015, 29 327.

---

[155]   This data was provided by the Bank of Spain <http://www.bde.es/bde/es/secciones/prensa/notas/Briefing_notes/>.

[156]   An approach to what happened in 2010 and 2011 is very difficult, because there is no reliable data on the 'General number of undertaken/actual evictions' just for residential mortgages. An unsatisfactory feeble way to address this could be to relate the number of first residence actual evictions (dwellings handed over) in 2012 (39 051) with the total commenced/filed first residence evictions, with the result that there were 49 175, ie 79.4 per cent. From this, it could be guessed that for the years 2010 and 2011, finished evictions on first residences were about 79.4 percent of those commenced.

4.3 Evictions from Private/Social Rented Housing

Evictions from private rented and public/social rented, in almost all cases, follow the same judicial procedure according to LAU and LEC (see above).[157] Disaggregated official data differentiating both is not available.

The numbers of court-ordered actual evictions of tenants from their first residences are: in 2010, 23 052; 2011, 19 036; 2012, 55 523; 2013, 38 141; 2014, 34 680; 2015, 35 677 (sources: INE, 2010 and 2011; CGPJ[158] 2012, 2013, 2014, 2015). Some limitations need to be pointed out however. Despite the vast majority of evictions being evictions from first residences, there are also dispossessions of garages, storage rooms, etc; most of which end in loss of possession of the dwelling for the tenant.[159] Additionally, the figure shown for each year is the combined number of evictions from private rented housing *and* public rented housing. There is no disaggregated official data available. Finally, it is important to note that the apparent increase in 2012 may have arisen from the fact that up to 2011 insufficient data was available from the courts, and therefore should be treated with caution.[160]

4.4 Evictions from Unauthorized Occupancies

In relation to the forced dispossession of those occupying other's land without title, including squatters but also authorized occupancies without consideration, there were 2323 such dispossessions completed in 2012 according to the CGPJ.[161] According to the same CGPJ, under 'other cases of actual evictions' (*lanzamientos*), including these same two cases (squatters and authorized occupancies), there were 3237 decisions in 2013; 3170 in 2014; 2457 in 2015; and 2447 in 2016.

---

[157] Elga Molina Roig, 'Spanish Report on residential leases' Project *Tenancy Law and Housing Policy in Multi-level Europe* (TENLAW), EU 7th Framework Programme (2013) <http://www.tenlaw.uni-bremen.de>.

[158] Consejo General Del Poder Judicial, *Una aproximación a la conciliación de los datos sobre ejecuciones hipotecarias y desahucios* (Boletín de Información Estadística, no. 35, June 2013) 5.

[159] Ibid 2, 5.

[160] Ibid.

[161] Ibid.

4.5 Other Evictions

In relation to divorces, it was stated that judicial removals due to divorces remain rather low in Spain, being 549 cases in 2012. But, in reality, about 96 000 divorced people (mainly men) lose the right to live in the family home every year.

Domestic violence cases were the main cause for urgent relocation both in Catalonia and the Basque Country in 2012 and 2013.

Information on the number of cases of declaration of ruin is not readily available. However, as an example, in the city of Gijón, out of approximately 275 000 inhabitants, there have been 59 such cases in the last 14 years.[162]

4.6 Commentary on the Statistics

Table 10.2 provides a summary of the different types of eviction discussed in the previous sections. It is noticeable that the number of evicted homeowners and tenants is higher than the ones from unauthorized occupancies. On average, evictions from mortgaged property and from rented housing are almost equal from 2010 to 2015; however, since 2012, the number of evictions from rented property is generally higher.

Table 10.2   Evictions in Spain from 2010–2015

	2010	2011	2012	2013	2014	2015
Evictions from mortgaged property	39 849	33 133	39 051	38 961	30 056	29 327
Evictions from private/social rented housing	23 052	19 036	55 523	38 141	34 680	35 677
Evictions from unauthorized occupancies	n/d	n/d	n/d	3237	3170	2457

Source: Own elaboration with data from CGPJ and INE, including projections for the early years.

---

[162] See further <http://www.elcomercio.es/v/20130822/gijon/urbanismo-tramito-expedientes-ruina-20130822.html>.

4.7 Profile of Those Evicted

According to the above-mentioned statistics and the data included in the following section (DESC and PAH, 2013), those evicted are both homeowners and tenants that are unemployed, since the main cause for defaulting repayments is unemployment (68 per cent for mortgagors and 75 per cent for tenants). They are usually couples with children, 51 years old on average and mostly immigrants (ie without a strong family network in Spain).

5. RISK FACTORS IDENTIFIED LEADING TO EVICTIONS FORM EACH HOUSING TENURE

The principal cause for defaulting in the repayment of a mortgage – the main cause for being evicted if you are a homeowner – is unemployment. In 2013, the rate of unemployment in Spain was almost 26 per cent and 20 per cent in 2015.

Unemployment has been highlighted as the cause for defaulting mortgage repayments in 70.4 per cent of the cases in the survey by DESC and PAH 2013.[163] This is also the case in the report of *Cáritas Barcelona* 2013,[164] which states that unemployment is very high (68 per cent for mortgagors and 75 per cent for tenants) among those attended to by intermediation services to prevent evictions.

Other causes for defaulting in mortgages that were identified in the DESC and PAH report are an increase in monthly mortgage repayments (32.8 per cent of cases) and the existence of other debts (21.3 per cent). Overindebtedness (correlated with unemployment) is also identified as a problem for mortgagors and tenants by *Cáritas Barcelona*. Separation and divorce are the cause for defaulting in 15.1 per cent of those surveyed in the DESC and PAH report.

To fully understand these circumstances, the INE 2012 survey[165] identifies that: there were a total of 22 938 homeless individuals (nearly 50 per cent of whom had been living more than three years without their own dwelling) in the whole of Spain in 2012 (4.7 per cent more than in 2005). Furthermore:

---

[163] Plataforma de Afectados por la Hipoteca and DESC, *Emergencia Habitacional En El Estado Español* (2013) 107.

[164] Ibid 80.

[165] INE, *Encuesta de personas sin hogar* (2012) <http://www.ine.es/prensa/np761.pdf>. This is a multi-choice survey.

1. Nearly half of them (10 328, 54.7 per cent more than in 2005) consider that they are homeless because they have lost their jobs and 17 835 remain unemployed[166]
2. 26 per cent consider that they are homeless because they have been unable to pay for their dwelling (11.4 per cent in 2005)
3. 20.9 per cent because they got divorced/separated (20.2 per cent in 2005)
4. 13 per cent because they moved to a new city
5. 12.1 per cent due to eviction from their dwelling (7.9 per cent in 2005)
6. 9.7 per cent because they or their children suffered violence
7. 7.5 per cent were imprisoned
8. 6.8 per cent were hospitalized
9. 5.8 per cent had reached the end of their lease
10. 3.7 per cent had become homeless due to their premises becoming uninhabitable (declaration of ruin, demolition, fire).

When considering the relationship between evictions and homelessness, there is no evidence that every evicted family sleeps rough immediately after the eviction.[167] Mechanisms to avoid this mainly come from the relatives of the evicted, the Public Administration and the third sector (charities).

There is a perception that mechanisms provided by the Public Administration (local, CA and state), such as the Emergency Tables, are insufficient, precisely due to the lack of adequate public/social housing for rent. Charities have intensified their activity in this field since the beginning of the crisis, as they have increased the number of dwellings they manage, which come from different public and private sources. In this regard, a report by *Cáritas Barcelona*[168] in 2014 asserts that 86.8 per cent of those attended to by their services stated that they faced economic problems, while 78.1 per cent stated that they were worried about not being able to feed themselves. The report also indicated that 20 per cent of those surveyed had at some point lived in a hostel, car, street or shelter; and that 53.1 per cent were living less than two years in the same dwelling and 36.6 per cent between two and six years.

---

[166] See Albert Sales i Campos, 'Crisi, empobriment i persones sense llar', I34 *Dossier Catalunya Social* (2014) 16.

[167] Ibid 13.

[168] Cáritas Diocesana de Barcelona, *Llar, habitatge i salut, acció i prevenci* (2014) 106.

Nevertheless, an essential source of support for many of the evicted are their relatives, especially their parents. Family ties in Spain are very important: 9 out of 10 elderly people are very happy with the relationship with their relatives and 81 per cent stay in touch nearly every day.[169] Elderly people, as stated, normally own their dwellings and have fully repaid their mortgages. There is some evidence of this:

1. 5.5 per cent of the expenses of the elderly are dedicated to their children and grandchildren. In fact, 1 out of 5 elderly left nursing homes to help relatives economically.[170]
2. 40.4 per cent have used their retirement pension to help relatives and friends (in 2009 it was only 15.1 per cent).
3. 1 387 000 families in 2016[171] have all their members unemployed, and some of them survive thanks to the retirement pensions of their elderly relatives.[172] One-fifth of all unemployed people live on the pension of an elderly relative. In addition to this, 70 per cent of elderly people take care of their grandchildren, allowing their sons and daughters to get a job.
4. The number of elderly people that live in their own dwelling with their sons and daughters (27.9 per cent) is more than double that of the opposite scenario.

Two more factors should be added to understand the situation in the studied period. On the one hand, the black economy and tax evasion represented 17.2 per cent of GDP in Spain in 2016, one of the highest rates in Europe.[173] On the other hand, Articles 143 and 144 CC guarantee a high level of compulsory solidarity on the part of relatives, which includes food, medical assistance and housing. This means that a relative (parent, grandparent, child, grandchild, and brother or sister) who has enough resources is obliged to provide the relative in need with such resources. Thus a relative with a spare room in his or her property will be

---

[169] Fundación Encuentro, *Informe España 2015* (2015) <http://www.carm.es/ctra/cendoc/haddock/16810.pdf>.

[170] Data from Educo Foundation <http://www.elmundo.es/espana/2015/09/07/55ed61b6268e3e5f118b457b.html>.

[171] INE, *Encuesta de población activa*. 2016.

[172] Miguel Laparra and Begoña Pérez Eransus (eds), *Crisis y fractura social en Europa. Causas y efectos en España* (Barcelona, Obra Social 'la Caixa' 2012).

[173] See <http://cronicaglobal.elespanol.com/graficnews/espana-economia-sumergida-2017_67942_102.html>.

obliged to accommodate a family member who has been evicted from their own place of residence. Moreover, the person in need of resources can seek the assistance of the court in acquiring them, regardless of his or her age or the duration of the need.[174]

6. LINKS BETWEEN EVICTIONS AND HOMELESSNESS

It is difficult to say to what extent the 2007 crisis and the increase of the number of evictions is contributing to homelessness, because:

1. First, according to INE 2012, there was an increase in the number of people left homeless due to eviction: they represent 12.1 per cent while it was 7.9 per cent in 2005. At the same time, 26 per cent stated they were homeless because they were unable to pay for their dwellings, compared to only 11.4 per cent in 2005.
2. There was a slight increase of homelessness in 2012 compared to 2005 (4.7 per cent), despite the severe economic crisis. As an example, the 2008 figures for Barcelona city[175] indicate that there were 2113 homeless people (658 of whom were sleeping rough) compared to 2799 homeless people (693 of whom were sleeping rough) recorded in 2015.
3. A 2016 report by Cáritas calculates approximately 40 000 homeless people in the whole of Spain, without taking into account situations of insecure or inadequate housing. However, the report considered that two out of three homeless people were in that situation before the beginning of the crisis in 2007.[176] In fact, the number of homeless in 2007, according to Cáritas, was 30 000.[177]
4. There is a significant difference between those evicted from first residences resulting from mortgage enforcements and defaulted leases (approximately 209 644 between 2010 and 2012), and the

---

[174] As long as he or she is taking proper measures to re-establish his or her situation.

[175] See Albert Sales, Joan Uribe and Inés Marco, *La situació del sensellarisme a Barcelona. Evolució i polítiques d'intervenció. Diagnosi 2015* (XAPSLL, 2015) 21.

[176] Cáritas, *Campaña de las personas sin hogar* (2016) <http://www.caritas.es/qhacemos_campanas_info.aspx?Id=850>.

[177] Cáritas, *Campaña de las personas sin hogar* (2007 <http://www.caritas.es/qhacemos_campanas_info.aspx?Id=559>.

number of homeless (about 22 938 in 2012) especially in relation to those that say that they have ended up homeless due to an eviction (2775) or because they were unable to pay their dwelling (5964).

To some extent, the measures described so far can explain this situation, especially the support of the family network, which might not work in relation to immigrants, who, instead, have returned to their countries of origin.[178]

However, there is a perception that some of the remedies (eg returning to the parental home) are not ideal situations (they are only temporary or palliative remedies), and without a follow up and professional support, the social integration of those affected will be difficult, especially for minors. Without a proper dwelling (permanent solution) people could be doomed to severe exclusion.[179] In addition to this, there is always a risk that public subsidies are withdrawn for the very long-term unemployed, that the elderly are incapable of continuing to help their (grand)sons and (grand)daughters, and that the mortgage enforcement moratorium might not be continuously extended and will instead end in 2020. Key factors to avoid this path from eviction to homelessness seem to be the end of long-term unemployment, the general economic recovery of the country, and an increase in the pool of affordable and public/social housing for rent.

There are groups that are perceived to be harder to be relocated by the Public Administration or charities, as they have special needs, such as the handicapped or families with many children. In addition to this, due to the low numbers of public housing available, there are areas (eg for emergency tables) or towns in which there are no dwellings available.

7. SIGNIFICANT CASES RELATED TO EVICTIONS IN THE PERIOD 2010–2015

In the case of *Ceesay Ceesay and Others v Spain*, the court suspended the eviction of 40 squatters because the Catalan government had not provided enough evidence on the measures it was going to take in relation to the squatters, and especially their children. While in the case of *Aziz v CatalunyaCaixa*,[180] the court held that a consumer should have

---

[178]   <http://www.rtve.es/noticias/20130422/poblacion-espanola-baja-primera-vez-desde-1996-regreso-inmigrantes-paises/646320.shtml> accessed 16-5-2014.

[179]   Sales i Campos (n 166) 13.

[180]   Case C-415/11.

the right to defend himself by raising arguments based on abusive clauses present in the guaranteed loan. In its turn, ATC 19-7-2011[181] stated that Article 47 CE on the right to housing cannot be used to prevent evictions resulting from mortgage enforcements, and STC 4-11-2013[182] established that the demolition of an illegally built house does not contravene intimacy and inviolability of domicile rights. (See also below the case of *Banco Primus v Gutiérrez García*,[183] on the early redemption.)

There has also been references to several cases, following the 'Robin-prudence' trend, that altered the legal system to help those about to be evicted, such as AAP Navarra 17-12-2010[184] (forced *datio in solutum*) or the Order of Criminal Court no. 4 Sabadell 8-5-2013[185] (denying a claim against squatters because the owner of the property was Sareb and it had not occupied the dwelling for housing purposes).

8. BEST PRACTICE MODELS FOR PREVENTING AND TACKLING EVICTIONS

8.1 Owner-occupied

Legislative measures such as the moratorium on evictions, 'forced' debt restructuring, and the relaxation of the requirements in respect to benefits granted to vulnerable mortgage debtors are examples of best practice models in the context of protection against eviction. Improved access to social housing and the supportive role played by relatives are similarly beneficial to those evicted or facing eviction. Despite these measures, however, many families are still at risk of eviction.

The forthcoming implementation of Directive 2014/17/UE,[186] which has the aim of preventing consumer overindebtedness and abusive banking practices, is another welcome development. However, the need to go beyond the provisions of the Directive is clear and this can be

---

[181]   RTC 2011\113.
[182]   RTC 2013\188.
[183]   C-421/14.
[184]   AC 2011\1.
[185]   JUR 2013\242758.
[186]   There is a draft law of its implementation (Draft Law 17.11.2017, on contracts of real estate credit), but the authors already consider that it does not cover the consumers' protection in the manner that the Directive envisages. See Klaus Jochen Albiez Dohrmann, 'Primerísimas observaciones al Anteproyecto de Ley reguladora de los contratos de crédito inmobiliario' (2016) 20 *CESCO* 55 ff.

achieved by, for example, including clear-cut messages alerting the consumer of the consequences of defaulting on a mortgage (a typical message would be 'Contracting and defaulting under this mortgage may result in the loss of your home and part of your personal estate'), clarifying when early redemption is permissible according to the ECJ case of *Banco Primus v Gutiérrez García* (C-421/14),[187] and making the involvement of a neutral professional a compulsory requirement of all mortgage transactions (for example: a notary who would advise the consumer of the legal and financial consequences that the mortgage arrangement would entail for him or her).

Reforms in procedural law should also be introduced to establish the obligation for the judiciary to contact social services as soon as there is a risk for a natural person to be evicted from his or her first residence. First steps have been taken in relation to squatters, since recent Act 5/2018 requires the Court to inform social services when evicting a squatter (Article 441.1 bis LEC). Existing local or CA protocols are also a first step; but only a general legal provision – both for squatters, tenants and homeowners – would actually compel social services to be proactive in advance in the case of evictions, thus preventing homelessness.[188]

There is a need for regulation of the proper functioning of intermediate tenures as a new sustainable way of accessing homeownership. Although high unemployment rates are behind the current number of mortgages in arrears and evictions, this is only the transitory effect of a more structural problem: the lack of a real alternative housing tenure to home ownership – a tenure that incentivizes sub-prime mortgaging and overindebtedness – in Spain. Tenancies have decreased since the 1950s regardless of the pro-landlord or pro-tenant legislation enacted, and despite the most recent reforms in 2013. Through Act 4/2013, tenancies have become even less attractive for tenants as they lose stability and do not gain either affordability or flexibility. This is the main reason to introduce a regulation of intermediate tenures for the whole of Spain, following the Catalan Act 19/2015 on shared ownership and temporal ownership, which would help families to avoid overindebtedness while increasing stability, especially when compared to the current regulation of leases. It is proposed that such a regulation could not only fill in this housing gap (as they are already achieving in at least six EU countries) but could also be used for helping those that have improved their economies. Better-off

---

[187] Case of 26 January 2017.
[188] See also UN Economic and Social Council, *Concluding observations of the Committee on Economic, Social and Cultural Rights-Spain*, 48th session (2012) 6.

households can no longer benefit from social rented housing. Indeed, the only option is to become indebted and buy, since they do not see private rented housing as a stable option.

8.2 Private Rented

Tenancies in Spain should be reformed in a new way to make them a true alternative to homeownership. From a landlord's perspective, while faster evictions are a reality since the beginning of 2014 due to legal reforms, the increase of tenants' stability, affordability and flexibility is still necessitated. The private rental sector remains unappealing and unaffordable to households. In this vein, Catalonia drafted, in 2017, a range of principles for a brand new legal framework for tenancies that make them more affordable, stable and flexible for tenants while keeping profitability and security for landlords; based on mature systems such as the German, Swiss and Austrian ones.[189]

In addition, benefits introduced by Act 1/2013 for mortgage enforcements have not been applied to tenancies; which seems unreasonable. These measures include the obligation for the credit institution to wait for three defaulted months before starting the mortgage enforcement; the moratorium on evictions until May 2020; the increase in the minimum unforeclosability threshold; and the possibility for the mortgage consumer to use abusive clauses of the loan contract to oppose the mortgage enforcement. It is submitted that it is difficult to see why these measures should not be applied to tenancy agreements, apart from the negative impact on landlords, especially when an increasing number of them are professional entities (REITs,[190] international funds, etc) engaged in a supplier–consumer relationship with tenants.

8.3 Social Rented

There is still a need for increasing the available stock of social rented housing and there are many measures available to achieve this. These include arrangements between NGOs and public administrations at all levels, right through to imposing penalties or increasing taxes on vacant dwellings and even promoting their expropriation in cases of evicted

---

[189] Nasarre-Aznar and Molina Roig, 'Parámetros para un nuevo marco de los arrendamientos urbanos, tras la Agenda Urbana de Habitat III 2016' (n 13) 19.

[190] 'Las socimis se reafirman como una de las nuevas estrellas del mercado inmobiliario' in *Diario el Mundo*, 5-1-2016 <http://www.elmundo.es/economia/2016/01/05/568b7679268e3e4b278b4663.html>.

vulnerable people and forcing the property owner to rent it back to them (though the latter is suspended by the Spanish Constitutional Court). Some of these measures exist at a local or CA level but only one at a national level, namely the creation of the Social Fund of Dwellings in 2012, which might be insufficient to have a real structural impact on the permanent stock of social housing.

Combined with the first proposal, proper management of rented social housing is also needed. Some indicators show that social rented housing in Spain is not properly managed: for example, the number of empty social dwellings in some regions (eg Catalonia) because they were built/acquired in an inconvenient location (eg in municipalities that there is no interest to live in). In addition, by mid-2013 about 4800 public rented dwellings in Madrid city and region were sold to international investment funds.[191] It is also commonly perceived that the low rate of circulation of new families accessing the system and the long waiting lists is partially due to the low numbers of social rented housing but partially due to the lack of supervision and mismanagement. It is proposed that the introduction of non-profit private entities as social housing managers, following the Dutch and English models of housing associations, might add efficiency and quality to the system.[192]

Finally, though there are already some practices of co-ordination between CAs and local authorities,[193] social services and housing services in the municipalities[194] and between public administration and NGOs, this still requires better coordination. It is suggested that the introduction of a general protocol establishing the obligations of each service provider and setting out the manner in which they should operate in a standardized manner would be of assistance.

---

[191]   About 1800 public dwellings by *Empresa Municipal de la Vivienda y Suelo (EMVS)* of city of Madrid (which was managing 17 000 public rented dwellings in 2012) were sold to the international investment fund Blackstone for €120 million <http://www.elconfidencial.com/economia/2013/06/24/madrid-dinamita-el-mercado-inmobiliario-vende-1800-viviendas-publicas-a-un-fondo-de-inversion-123614>. And the regional government of Madrid sold 2935 more public rented dwellings to Goldman Sachs <http://www.eldiario.es/sociedad/venta-vivienda-publica-pah-cavero_0_228527911.html>.

[192]   Núria Lambea Llop, 'Social housing management models in Spain' (2016) 52 *Revista catalana de Dret public* 115–128.

[193]   Competence on housing is shared between them, with general regulation by the Spanish central government.

[194]   They are often different services ruled by different city/town councillors; in many municipalities, housing is often confused with urban planning services.

9. CONCLUSION

Spain is still suffering the consequences of the housing crash of 2007 despite the number of evictions constantly decreasing since the worst years of 2011 and 2012. More and more regulations and policies are still being introduced at both the national and regional level to tackle the scarcity of affordable housing, including penalties for unoccupied dwellings and expropriations of properties enforced by banks.

The preponderance of homeownership jointly with the negative effects of the crisis (unemployment reached a 26 per cent in 2013; overindebtedness) have been highlighted as the main causes for evictions of mortgaged homeowners (an approximate total of 210 377 evicted households in the period 2010–2015), which coexist with other 'structural cases' of home dispossession such as divorces (96 000 per year) and domestic violence. The lack of a widespread system of intermediate tenures – with the exception of Catalonia since 2015, and the lack of affordable, flexible and stable tenancies are behind the high numbers of evicted tenants (an approximate total of 206 109 evicted households in the period 2010–2015, with only a share of 13.1 per cent of the rental sector in 2016).

Since the 'right to housing' cannot be adduced as a legal ground to prevent evictions, the legislator reactively addressed this phenomenon by introducing a number of transitory and structural measures; the former in the guise of the 'Good Banking Practices Code' (which includes acquittances, postponement of payments, *datio in solutum*, moratorium on evictions, and high minimum unenforceability threshold) and the latter via the passing of Act 1/2013 (following the ECJ case of *Aziz v CatalunyaCaixa* or a forced debt acquittance mechanism), with limited success. This is why 'Robinprudence' and squatting increased during these years. Directive 2014/17/EU has not been implemented as of February 2018, although this was due to happen in March 2016, and several ECJ sentences have compelled Spain to change its internal regulations to improve mortgage consumers' protection (eg to limit default interest rates, abusive floor clauses, early redemption, etc).

According to available data,[195] the link between evictions and homelessness in Spain remains relatively low, which would seem to indicate

---

[195] Barely 8739 homeless – in a multi-choice survey – out of 22 938 affirm that they have ended up as such due to a problem in paying for their home, taking into account that only between 2010 and 2012 there have been 209 644 households evicted.

that the combined efforts of the relatives of the evicted, the third sector, and the public social and housing services have reacted quite successfully and quickly to the problem.

11. Evictions in the UK: causes, consequences and management

Nicholas Pleace and Caroline Hunter

1. INTRODUCTION

Eviction in the UK is strongly associated with both poverty and with longstanding trends in housing policy. From the post-war period until the late 1970s, UK policies centred on reducing housing inequalities, through mass provision of affordable social housing with highly secure tenancies, financial support for owner-occupiers and regulation of the private rented sector. A 1977 law granted priority access to social housing for specific groups of homeless people, including families. From the 1980s to the present, policy has centred on promoting free market housing and enabling. Mortgage markets were deregulated, there were mass sales of social housing and rent controls in the private rented sector came to an end. Housing costs have spiralled upwards relative to income, the UK becoming one of the most unaffordable places to live in Europe. Poorer people for whom owner-occupation is at the limit of affordability now experience heightened risk of mortgage possession, while the rights of private rented tenants are restricted and time-limited. The 'lifetime' tenancies offered by social landlords are in the process of being replaced in England. Income is a predictor of housing security, with those on lower incomes facing increasingly unaffordable increases in rents and mortgages, while experiencing reductions in financial support and security of tenure.

2. POLICY BACKGROUND

2.1 General Housing Policy Related to Evictions

UK policy has placed protection of the interests of private landlords and mortgage lenders above that of renters and mortgagors, since the 1980s.

Deregulation of private rented sector markets and mortgage lending; that is, reducing consumer protections and rights, was pursued as part of a wider policy imperative to reduce the role of the state and promote a free market housing policy. The current legal settlement for the private rented sector was largely established in 1988, when the then Conservative government passed the Housing Act 1988, and effectively deregulated the previous system which had offered a high degree of security to tenants. Investment in new social housing development was effectively stopped and much of the social housing stock privatized through the 'Right to Buy'.[1]

2.2 Structural/Societal Factors Related to Evictions

In the 1980s the overwhelming majority of social tenancies were provided by local authorities (municipalities) under the Housing Act 1980 'secure' tenancies. There was also a small non-profit sector (generally referred to as 'housing associations'), whose tenants were also covered under the 1980 Act. By the time the Housing Act 1988 was introduced however, housing associations were no longer able to create secure tenancies. Instead the new framework for private tenants was applied to them. In the following decades, government policy has been to encourage the transfer of council-owned housing to housing associations and to fund any new building through associations. So while in England, in 1980, local authorities dominated the provision of social housing, accounting for 6.7 million units and 94 per cent of social rented stock, in 2015, this has decreased to 1.7 million dwellings, comprising 41 per cent of social rented stock.[2]

Although the UK shifted from neo-liberal administrations from 1979–1997, to a more broadly social democratic government from 1997–2010, the imperative on a market-based housing policy remained. This was because social housing had experienced residualization as a result of privatization and underinvestment, becoming associated with spatial concentration of socioeconomic disadvantage and was hence viewed as a 'failed' policy, replicating the nineteenth and early twentieth century

---

[1]   Peter Malpass and Alan Murie, *Housing Policy and Practice* (London, Palgrave Macmillan 1999).
[2]   Department of Communities and Local Government, *English Housing Survey: Headline Report, 2015–16* (hereafter DCLG, 2017a).

slums it was supposedly to replace.[3] Since 2010, neo-liberal governments have sought to reassert a free market-based housing policy. However, chronic shortages in affordable housing supply and high levels of housing exclusion and homelessness have generated a broad political, academic and housing practitioner consensus that the UK has pushed too hard at the limits of owner-occupation. The most recent housing proposals from central government were entitled *Fixing our Broken Housing Market* and included some attempts to lessen the more negative effects of earlier policies.[4] However, the longstanding emphasis on promoting a free-market housing policy in the UK will remain fundamentally unaltered, at least for the medium term.

The UK has seen marked increases in inequality since the 1980s. The UK state has pursued a policy of retrenchment in relation to the welfare and social housing. Health spending has varied, but has been cut sharply since 2010. Economic change has been marked – the UK has far less full-time, relatively well-paid and secure work than was the case a generation ago. The UK has seen spikes in child poverty, long-term unemployment, health inequalities and in housing inequalities, as the long-term association between income poverty and poor housing stand-ards, which social housing investment had greatly reduced, has now reappeared.[5] Housing affordability is low in much of the UK with the gap between income and housing costs growing in many areas. There is a chronic shortage of adequate, affordable housing across much of the UK.[6]

2.3 Specific Policies Related to Evictions

While the laws differ between the four current UK jurisdictions (England, Scotland, Wales and Northern Ireland), and particularly between Scotland and the rest of the UK, tenants currently have limited protections if a private sector landlord wishes to remove them. Social rented

[3] Roland Atkinson and Keith Kintrea, 'Area effects: what do they mean for British housing and regeneration policy?' (2002) 2 (2) *European Journal of Housing Policy* 147–166.

[4] H.M. Government, *Fixing our Broken Housing Market* (H.M. Government, 2017).

[5] Becky Tunstall, 'Relative housing space inequality in England and Wales, and its recent rapid resurgence' (2015) 15 (2) *International Journal of Housing Policy* 105–126.

[6] Danny Dorling, *All That Is Solid: How the Great Housing Disaster Defines Our Times, and What We Can Do About It* (Allen Lane, 2014).

sector tenants have traditionally had what are effectively lifetime tenancies, but there is a policy intention, in England, to remove these rights and recast social housing as an emergency/short term form of housing, providing a safety net function within a broader free-market housing policy. Policies were introduced to reduce the extent of mortgage possession following the subprime crisis, in part because house prices had fallen below the level of mortgage debt secured on them, these centred on a sustained cut in interest rates, lender forbearance and mortgage rescue schemes.

The UK is, while deeply iniquitous, an economically prosperous society which retains extensive welfare, public health and both social housing and welfare benefits targeted on allowing low-income households to manage housing costs. In the financial year 2016–2017, the Office for Budget Responsibility within central UK government projected a spend of £23 billion (€27 billion) on housing benefits, with some five million households receiving an average of £4700 (€5460) from the state, either paying their entire rent or helping them to pay their rent. This represented 3 per cent of total public spending and was equivalent to 1.2 per cent of national income.[7] The welfare system is likely to play a significant role in protecting households from eviction for financial reasons, as does the extensive provision of social housing, which still accounts for 17 per cent of housing stock in England, 16 per cent in Wales, and 23 per cent in Scotland.[8] Multiple safety nets exist for low-income and unemployed households whose housing security might otherwise be threatened by their economic status. The UK, despite the extreme concentration of wealth in a tiny proportion of the population experienced over the last 40 years, was still a welfare state in 2017, which meant there was no automatic association between job loss, other income reduction and the experience of eviction.

---

[7]   Office for Budget Responsibility, *Tax by tax, spend by spend: Welfare spending: housing benefit* (Office for Budget Responsibility, 2017).

[8]   Ministry of Housing Communities & Local Government (MHCLG), Live Tables- Table FT1101 (S101) <https://www.gov.uk/government/statistical-data-sets/live-tables-on-dwelling-stock-including-vacants>.

3. LEGAL AND CONSTITUTIONAL BACKGROUND TO PROTECTION AGAINST EVICTIONS

3.1 Housing as a Fundamental Right

The UK does not possess a written constitution and there is no universal, legal right to housing in UK law. The European Social Charter, which incorporates housing rights, was never passed into UK law. A series of housing related rights exist which broadly resemble those within the European Social Charter, as interpreted by the UN Committee on Economic, Social and Cultural Rights, which are justiciable.[9] These are:

- Protection from eviction, through various statutes that limit the right to evict mortgagors and tenants (discussed below) and a fall-back minimum right for all tenants and other occupiers to not be evicted without a court order: the Protection From Eviction Act 1977 or the Rent (Scotland) Act 1984;
- Social protection schemes (ie welfare benefits) which, subject to conditionality tests, provide support towards rent and mortgage payments in times of financial need;
- Minimum standards regarding overcrowding, safety and repairs in rented housing; and
- A statutory duty on local authorities to provide accommodation to certain groups of homeless people. This constitutes a legal right to accommodation in England, Wales and Northern Ireland and a right to settled housing in Scotland, but the right is conditional and is subject to passing a number of eligibility tests.

Certain homeless households were given conditional rights to housing in the original 1977 legislation, the Housing (Homeless Persons) Act 1977. These continue in various statutes, in each country of the UK. Each maintain the fairly broad definition of 'homelessness' found in the 1977 Act, so that an applicant who has accommodation may still be homeless if it is not reasonable for them to continue to occupy, for instance, because of domestic violence or the physical conditions of the accommodation.

Until recently, the main protections, effectively the closest equivalent to a legal right to housing in the UK, centred on families which include,

---

[9] Caroline Hunter, 'The right to housing in the UK' (2010) 3 (4) *Istituzioni del federalismo Rivista di studi giuridici e politici* 313.

or are about to include, one or more dependent children (ie school aged or younger). Conditional rights to housing also existed for 'vulnerable' groups. After a succession of legal interpretations in the lower courts, particularly *R v Camden London Borough Council, Ex p Pereira* [1998], that narrowed the definition on 'vulnerable', the Supreme Court in the case of *Hotak v Southwark LBC* [2015], re-considered the meaning of the word.[10] The word 'vulnerable' connotes necessarily some exercise of comparability and the applicant is not compared with (per *Pereira*) 'ordinary homeless persons' but with 'an ordinary person who is in need of accommodation', who is 'robust and healthy'.

Both vulnerable applicants and families containing, or about to contain, a dependent child, must demonstrate they are not 'intentionally homeless', ie have caused their own homelessness by deliberate action or inaction. Further, if they do not have a local connection to the local authority (municipality) from which they are seeking assistance, except where homelessness is associated with the risk of domestic violence, the duty to assist may be transferred to a local authority where there is a local connection. When criteria around the eligibility of household type (defined as being in 'priority need'), intentionality and local connection are satisfied, a household is defined as statutorily homeless.

Legislative reforms in Scotland, the Homelessness (Scotland) Act 2003, ended the focus on specific groups – a household no longer had to be in priority need, ie contain a 'vulnerable' person or contain dependent children, to be regarded as statutorily homeless. These changes came into effect in December 2012. Elsewhere in the UK, the requirements around 'priority need' remain in effect, although there are some variations as to how this is defined under the laws in England, Wales and Northern Ireland.

Under Scottish law, a statutorily homeless household has the right to 'permanent' accommodation. In England, Wales and Northern Ireland, the legal requirement is to provide temporary accommodation, until settled housing becomes available, either found by the household itself, or by the local authority. In practice, this has usually meant using the requirements to show 'reasonable preference' to statutorily homeless people in the allocation of social housing.[11] However, whereas the homelessness legislation used to be a potential route to a secure social rented tenancy (provided by a local authority or housing association),

---

[10] Jed Meers, 'A return to purer waters? "Vulnerability" under s. 189 Housing Act 1996' (2015) 37 (4) *Journal of Social Welfare and Family Law* 473.

[11] Joanne Bretherton and Nicholas Pleace, *Reasonable Preference in Scottish Social Housing* (Scottish Government, 2011).

legal changes now allow the discharge of duty to the private rented sector in England. Initially, consent was required before a statutorily homeless household could be placed in a potentially much less secure private rented tenancy, but this provision was removed. The other three jurisdictions all allow use of the private rented sector, though consent is required from a statutorily homeless household in Scotland.

3.2 Law Relating to Owner-occupation

The law in relation to eviction from owner-occupied housing provides some rights to mortgagors, but is heavily orientated towards protecting lender interests. Technically, under the relevant legislation, the Law of Property Act 1925 and the Land Registration Act 2002, a mortgagee always has the right to possess the property. In practice, many mortgages contain a clause whereby the mortgagee undertakes not to enforce the right to possession without default by the mortgagor.

Further, in the absence of vacant possession, or the mortgagor voluntarily surrendering their home, mortgagees tend to apply to the courts to get possession of a home. This situation exists because there are practical difficulties in obtaining possession of an occupied home without risk of contravening certain criminal or civil statutes, namely section 6 of the Criminal Law Act 1977, or section 1(3) of the Protection from Eviction Act 1977. Rather than run this risk, lenders will tend to seek a court order.

Section 36 of the Administration of Justice Act 1970, grants the courts some latitude around the type of order that can be made. The courts are given the power to adjourn cases or suspend possession orders:

> if it appears to the court that in the event of its exercising the power the mortgagor is likely to be able within a reasonable period to pay any sums due under the mortgage or to remedy a default consisting of a breach of any other obligation arising under or by virtue of the mortgage.

In practice, this usually means the mortgagor being given time to pay off arrears within a reasonable time period, rather than ordering immediate possession. Further, there is also a pre-action protocol (called a pre-action requirement in Scotland), in cases of arrears that places an obligation on the mortgagee to try to contact the mortgagor and attempt to agree repayment before starting any court action.

3.3 Law Relating to Private Renting

Originally, UK law in respect of eviction from the private rented sector was governed by the Housing Act 1988 (in Scotland the Housing (Scotland) Act 1988). The Housing Act 1988 was intended to revive and liberalize the rented market. It created two forms of tenancy: the assured tenancy and the assured shorthold tenancy. As originally enacted, the assured tenancy was the default tenancy, as landlords had to serve a notice before the start of the tenancy to create a shorthold tenancy. However, this was reversed by the Housing Act 1996, so that any tenancy to which the 1988 Act applies is a shorthold, unless the landlord gives notice otherwise.

The security position for shorthold tenants is relatively straightforward. Whether the tenancy is fixed-term or periodic, for the first six months of the tenancy the landlord can only seek possession as if it is an assured tenancy (see below). If, as is usually the case, the tenancy is a fixed-term, this limitation will continue throughout the period of the fixed term. However, provided the necessary two months' written notice is given, the landlord is entitled to apply for possession as soon as the fixed term ends, and the court *must* give possession. This automatic right to possession provides an incentive for landlords to utilize shorter fixed terms – generally 12 months or 6 months. In practice, private tenants tend to remain in their properties for longer than these fixed terms – within 2015/16, an average of 4.3 years in England,[12] but this legal regime and the need to continually renew tenancy agreements contributes heavily to a churning private rented sector market,[13] with around one-quarter of households having been in their current property for less than a year.[14]

For shorthold tenancies in England and Wales, the landlord can also use an accelerated procedure to evict. The accelerated procedure is rapid and does not usually require a court hearing. However, the accelerated procedure can only be used if the tenants have a written assured shorthold and the landlord has evidenced the two month notice has been properly served. The accelerated procedure also requires that tenants are not asked to leave before the end of a fixed-term tenancy and their deposit has been placed in a deposit protection scheme.

In Scotland, the Private Housing (Tenancies) (Scotland) Act 2016, will change private rented sector tenancies, removing the ability of landlords

---

[12] DCLG, 2017a (n 2).
[13] Julie Rugg and David Rhodes, *The Private Rented Sector: Its Contribution and Potential* (Centre for Housing Policy, 2008).
[14] DCLG, 2017a (n 2).

to require someone to leave their home, once the period covered by a tenancy agreement has ended. Protections for landlords remain extensive, but the law also allows for an element of rent regulation in the private rented sector. At the time of writing, possible revisions to the law relating to private tenancies are being contemplated for England, which may increase tenants' protections from eviction to some degree. But for the moment, the position of the private rented sector tenancies is very insecure and may have some association with homelessness (see below).

3.4 Law Relating to Social Renting

The assured tenancy, used primarily by housing associations, is more secure and closer to both the security available in the private sector before 1988, and the secure tenancy for social tenants. The starting point is that the tenancy cannot be terminated without a court order. The court cannot make an order unless first, a notice has been properly served by the landlord on the tenant and second, a ground for eviction has been proven. For some grounds, for example if the landlord needs the house for his own use, the court *must* give possession; for others, for example rent arrears (if not too great), the court has a *discretion* and may stay or postpone possession.

The main protection for all social tenants arrived with the Housing Act 1980, and is now found in the Housing Act 1985, the secure tenancy. However, this beguiling simplicity was shortlived. First, as noted, from 1989, any new housing association tenancy was an assured tenancy under the Housing Act 1988. This has led to housing associations using assured tenancies in the same way as secure tenancies. In Scotland, a single regime for all social tenancies was reinstated by the Housing (Scotland) Act 2001.

Secondly, over the last 20 years, two intertwined policy agendas have fragmented the protections in the 1985 Act: controlling anti-social behaviour[15] and a 'welfarist' model of social housing.[16] This has led to a plethora of new tenancy types with less security.

The secure tenancy operates in a similar way to assured tenancies, namely the tenancy cannot be terminated without a court order. The court

---

[15] Caroline Hunter, 'From landlords to agents of social control' in J Flint (ed) *Housing and Anti-social Behaviour: Theory, Policy and Practice* (Policy Press, 2006).

[16] Suzanne Fitzpatrick and Beth Watts, 'Competing visions: security of tenure and the welfarisation of English social housing' (2017) 32 (8) *Housing Studies* <http://dx.doi.org/10.1080/02673037.2017.1291916>.

cannot make an order unless first, a notice has been property served by the landlord on the tenant and secondly, a ground for eviction has been proven. The grounds are split into those where the court *may* order possession, for rent arrears or anti-social behaviour for example, and those it *may only make if suitable alternative accommodation is provided.* There were no mandatory grounds until an amendment to the Housing Act 1985 by the Anti-Social Behaviour, Crime and Policing Act 2014. This introduced a mandatory ground for certain serious anti-social behaviour.

Eviction is most usually sought for rent arrears. There is also a pre-action protocol (called a pre-action requirement in Scotland) that places an expectation on social landlords not to take repossessions for rent arrears to court, where this is possible. This provides for a range of managed repayment options to avoid eviction for rent arrears.

The forms of new tenancies for social tenants include probationary (introduction), demoted (both designed to manage anti-social behaviour) and flexible (time-limited tenancies for new tenants) tenancies. These build on the secure model, but with a move away from discretion residing in court to *mandatory* possession orders. In a number of cases (see *Manchester City Council v Pinnock* (2010); *Corby Borough Council v Scott, West Kent Housing Association Ltd v Haycraft* (2012); *Southend-on-Sea BC v Armour* (2014)) tenants have sought to challenge the enhanced power of social landlords to evict in these new tenancy types, through Article 8 of the European Convention on Human Rights (ECHR).[17] In order to comply with Article 8 ECHR, the Supreme Court in *Manchester City Council v Pinnock*, held that:

> ... where a court is asked to make an order for possession of a person's home at the suit of a local authority the court must have the power to assess the proportionality of making the order, and, in making that assessment, to resolve any relevant dispute of fact.[18]

---

[17]   Art 8 (1) ECHR provides that: 'everyone has the right to respect for his private and family life, his home and his correspondence'. The right is, however, a qualified one, which may not be interfered with by a public authority 'except as in accordance with the law and is necessary in a democratic society in the interests of national security, public safety or the economic well-being of the country, for the prevention of disorder or crime, for the protection of health or morals, or for the protection of the rights and freedoms of others.'

[18]   *Manchester City Council v Pinnock* [2010] UKSC 45; [2011] 2 AC 104 para 49.

On the face of it, this seems to reinstate discretion for the court. In practice, this discretion has been very limited.[19]

While the relatively protected status of social rented tenants in England is being brought into line with the lower protections offered against eviction for private rented sector tenants, this is not true throughout the UK. Again, Scotland differs from the rest of the UK in this respect – social tenancies are not under threat, and the Renting Homes (Wales) Act 2016 will radically change the position when it is brought into law in Wales.[20] Overall, most new social tenants in the UK will see a reduction in their rights, as the bulk of the population and of social housing stock is located in England.

3.5 Law Relating to Unauthorized Occupancy

Unauthorized occupancy, usually termed squatting, is a criminal offence in the UK, although in England and Wales only in residential buildings.[21] No protections exist in relation to eviction from a home or building when the occupants are squatters. This does not mean that landlords can use any means to evict squatters, for instance through force or violence. To ensure that they do not break the law, landlords can evict squatters using the procedure in the Civil Procedure Rules, including applying for an interim possession order.

3.6 Law Relating to Temporary Dispossession, Domestic Violence and Family Law Issues

The UK does not have a legal process relating to temporary dispossession. In cases of gender-based or domestic violence, an offending individual may be evicted from the social rented sector if they remain in their home after the partner and/or children subject to their abuse have left, using the processes detailed above. Sanctuary schemes and related service models, which enable a woman (almost all domestic violence is

---

[19] David Cowan and Caroline Hunter, '"Yeah but, no but" – Pinnock and Powell in the Supreme Court' (2012) 75 *Modern Law Review* 78–91; David Cowan and Caroline Hunter, '"Yeah but, no but", or just "no"? Life after Pinnock and Powell' (2012) 15 (3) *Journal of Housing Law* 58–62.

[20] Martin Partington, 'Wales' housing law (r)evolution: an overview part 2' (2016) 3 *Journal of Housing Law* 45–50.

[21] Lorna Fox O'Mahony, David O'Mahony and Robin Hickey (eds), *Moral Rhetoric and the Criminalisation of Squatting: Vulnerable Demons?* (Routledge, 2014).

directed by men against women) to remain in her home may combine physical and legal protections (in family law statutes and other general anti-harassment legislation), such as an injunction banning an offender from being in proximity to someone. However these injunctions to stay out of proximity are universally applicable, they are not restricted to temporary dispossession from specific housing.

3.7 Soft Law/Codes and their Effectiveness

Any soft law is linked to statutory measures, such as the provisions for homelessness. Thus local authorities must have regard for the Code of Guidance issued by the relevant national government.

4. EXTENT OF EVICTIONS OVER THE PERIOD 2010–2015

4.1 Definition of Eviction – Pre-court, Court and Post-Court Phases

The process of eviction begins when someone receives an instruction to leave their home and in the UK, as in many other European countries, households may lack the resources to contest a court case and will leave their home without a hearing taking place.[22] Court cases which result in physical eviction can and do happen, but, as described above, the UK's use of fixed-period private rented tenancies (assured shorthold tenancies), means that a private landlord usually only has to wait a comparatively short period; that is, until a fixed tenancy expires, before a tenant effectively has no right to remain (this practice is, as noted, coming to an end in Scotland). Similar tenancy arrangements are, as stated, being actively pursued in the social rented sector in England.

Pre-court actions are not recorded in the UK. These centre on various mechanisms to delay or prevent eviction by agreed management of rent or mortgage arrears, wherein a plan is agreed, between the tenant or mortgagor and their landlord or lender, sometimes directly and sometimes as a result of intervention from a homelessness prevention service.

---

[22] Padraic Kenna, Lars Benjaminsen, Volker Busch-Geertsema and Sergio Nasarre-Aznar, *Pilot Project – Promoting Protection of the Right to Housing – Homelessness Prevention in the Context of Evictions* Final Report (European Union, European Commission, Directorate-General Employment, Social Affairs and Inclusion 2016).

Courts may also issue suspended orders, requiring both parties to agree a payment plan to avoid eviction for rent arrears.

Floating support services, known as tenancy sustainment teams and the now emergent Housing First services, will negotiate with social or private landlords when they have rehoused a person with a history of homelessness and there has been an issue with arrears, nuisance or damage to a property, in an attempt to stop eviction. Activity to stop eviction that will trigger homelessness is led by Housing Option Teams in local authorities (municipalities), in England, Scotland and Wales and the Northern Ireland Housing Executive.

Some data is available on these activities, but it must be noted these are the homelessness-specific interventions only, not the total pre-court activity related to delaying or stopping evictions. Between 2010 and 2015, 43 710 households had rent arrears problems dealt with by homelessness prevention services in England, another 110 837 received other support to remain in their private or social rented home, including management of nuisance behaviour, using action or grants to improve living conditions or to make necessary adaptations to a home.[23] Similar services are operational in Scotland and a more extensive set of preventative interventions, which are more broadly available, have recently been introduced following legislative reform in Wales. Services are less developed in Northern Ireland, but were coming on stream at the time of writing.[24]

4.2 Evictions from Mortgaged Property

Repossession rates of mortgaged property reflect the level of decommodification in the UK; that is, income replaced by welfare systems when work is lost, or cannot be continued and is generally insufficient to maintain the repayment of a mortgage. As can be observed in Table 11.1, rates were relatively higher between 2010 and 2012, but then began to fall back again. It is important to note that the scale of mortgage possession seen during the previous housing market crash was not replicated following the 2008 crisis, rates exceeded 70 000 at one point in the early 1990s and the spike seen in 2010–2012 was short-lived, falling quite sharply by 2015, reflecting lender forbearance and other initiatives.

---

[23]   Department of Communities and Local Government, *Statutory homelessness and prevention and relief, October to December 2016: England* (hereafter DCLG, 2017b).

[24]   Fiona Boyle and Nicholas Pleace, *The Homelessness Strategy for Northern Ireland 2012-2017:An Evaluation* (Northern Ireland Housing Executive, 2017).

Table 11.1   Repossession of residential owner-occupied homes in England and Wales

Year	Claims	Claims leading to orders		Claims leading to warrants		Claims leading to repossessions by county court bailiffs	
		Actual number to date	% to date	Actual number to date	% to date	Actual number to date	% to date
2010	75 431	56 424	74.8	36 429	48.3	21 368	28.3
2011	73 181	53 187	72.7	32 338	44.2	18 284	25.0
2012	59 877	41 452	69.2	23 266	38.9	12 911	21.6
2013	53 659	35 127	65.5	18 404	34.3	9783	18.2
2014	41 151	23 604	57.4	10 575	25.7	5477	13.3
2015	19 852	10 682	53.8	3843	19.4	2042	10.3

Source: Ministry of Justice, *Mortgage and Landlord Possession Statistics in England and Wales, January to March 2017 (Provisional)* (Ministry of Justice, 2017).

Orders include suspended orders, which as noted, is a legal decision that the mortgage lender has the right to repossess a property due to arrears, but the judge has determined that more time should be allowed before this takes place; for instance, to allow repayment of debt and avoid eviction. Outright orders give a lender permission to repossess a property and that a person must leave their home by a set date (28 days after the decision), or be evicted under a warrant issued by the court. Physical evictions (repossessions by county court bailiffs) are relatively unusual and there is a downward trend from 2010–2015.

Comparable statistics are not available for Scotland, but the available data shows a sharp fall in the number of possession cases initiated. The figures (for 2010–11 to 2015–16) show a drop from 5224 to 1874,[25] with the figures for 2011–12, 2013–14 and 2014–15 being 6752, 5385, 4770 and 3268 respectively. Scotland has actively pursued a policy of minimizing repossession including the provision of the 'keeping your home' advice service.[26]

In Northern Ireland, the rate of repossession became relatively high compared to the rest of the UK. Policy interventions and an improving

[25] Scottish Government, *Civil justice statistics in Scotland 2015-2016* (Scottish Government, 2017).
[26] See <http://www.keepingyourhome.co.uk>.

economic situation have, as in Scotland, seen a downward trend emerge in applications (claims), from 3390 applications in 2010 to 1232 in 2015 (see Table 11.2).

Table 11.2 Applications for repossession received in Northern Ireland 2010–2015

Year	Applications received	Difference year-on-year (%)
2010	3390	−13
2011	3588	+6
2012	3732	+4
2013	3697	−1
2014	2910	−21
2015	1232	−58

Source: Department of Justice (Northern Ireland), *Mortgages: Actions for Possession Bulletin January to March 2017* (Department of Justice, 2017).

Debates about the economic consequences of Brexit at the time of writing, are characterized by ideological and political extremism, fuelled by a predominantly hard right, populist nationalist UK media. The scenarios of an economic boom following Brexit are not supported by most economists and businesses, and there is a broad consensus, outside politicians, supporters of nationalist and populist parties, and most of the media, that Brexit will cause a recession.[27] In mid 2017, house prices were starting to fall, but remained very high in relation to average incomes, so that the likely rises in unemployment from 2019 onwards may cause a spike in repossessions, possibly in the context of negative equity. The results of Brexit will, however, only become fully apparent once it actually occurs and the effects have had time to make themselves felt.

4.3 Evictions from Private/Social Rented Housing

Eviction claims by private and social landlords in England, including both the normal and accelerated procedures (see Table 11.3 below) broadly increased over the period 2010 to 2015 in England and Wales.

---

[27] Iain Begg and Fabian Mushövel, *The Economic Impact of Brexit: Jobs, Growth and the Public Finances* (London, London School of Economics 2016).

Actual evictions were markedly less common (see Table 11.4) in England, 36 628 took place in 2013, 40 641 in 2014 and 41 453 in 2015. Around 1300 evictions from rented property take place in Wales each year (1326 in 2014 and 1276 in 2015).[28]

Table 11.3   Landlord possession claims in the county courts of England and Wales by type of procedure and landlord

Year	Landlord type		Accelerated	Claims issued
	Private	Social		
2010	23 147	90 217	21 597	134 961
2011	22 740	93 631	25 712	142 083
2012	23 079	96 742	31 178	150 999
2013	23 196	113 175	34 080	170 451
2014	23 113	105 645	36 019	164 777
2015 (p)	20 712	94 577	38 402	153 691

Source: Ministry of Justice, *Mortgage and Landlord Possession Statistics in England and Wales, January to March 2017 (Provisional)* (Ministry of Justice, 2017); (p) provisional.

Table 11.4   Landlord possession workload in the county courts of England

Year	Social landlord	Private landlord	Accelerated	Repossessions
2010	15 983	5139	5641	26 763
2011	17 102	5681	7834	30 617
2012	16 180	5955	10 738	32 873
2013	18 404	5908	12 316	36 628
2014	19 983	6197	14 461	40 641
2015 (p)	19 095	5919	16 439	41 453

Source: Ministry of Justice, *Mortgage and Landlord Possession Statistics in England and Wales, January to March 2017 (Provisional)* (Ministry of Justice, 2017); (p) provisional.

---

[28] Ministry of Justice, *Mortgage and Landlord Possession Statistics in England and Wales, January to March 2017 (Provisional)* (Ministry of Justice, 2017).

Total evictions from rented property in Scotland were 13 905 in 2015–16 (see Table 11.5 below). The available figures cover both private and social rented housing, though it is reported that around two-thirds of evictions from rented housing in Scotland are from the social rented sector.[29] Levels have remained fairly constant both in terms of initiated cases (claims), and disposed cases where an eviction has occurred. Note that the figures for initiations and disposals do not necessarily refer to the same cases.

Ejectment cases; that is, evictions from rented housing, are not very common in Northern Ireland. Again, this has to be seen in the context of the use of time-limited tenancies by the private rented sector, where the tenant effectively has no right to remain once the agreed time period has ended, meaning it is cheaper and easier to simply wait for a tenant's right to occupy to come to an end. The available data covers three-month periods, October to December, which in 2015 saw 223 disposed ejectment cases, compared with 180 in the same period in 2016. Between 2010 and 2015, cases peaked in October to December 2013, at just over 450 disposed cases, with over 350 in the same period in 2012.[30]

Table 11.5   Evictions in Scotland

Year	Initiated	Disposed
2010–11	16 528	14 906
2011–12	14 160	13 972
2012–13	13 979	12 358
2013–14	10 532	11 613
2014–15	13 750	12 892
2015–16	14 690	13 905

Source: Scottish Government, *Civil justice statistics in Scotland 2015–2016* (Scottish Government, 2017).

4.4   Evictions from Unauthorized Occupancy

Squatting, as noted, is a criminal offence in the UK. Criminal justice system statistics are of limited utility, the laws relating to squatting are

---

[29]   Scottish Government (n 25).

[30]   Department of Justice (Northern Ireland), *County Court Bulletin October to December 2016: Research and Statistical Bulletin 05/2017 Provisional quarterly figures* (Department of Justice, 2017).

not necessarily used when someone is removed from what is defined as the illegal occupation of a dwelling; that is, they may be arrested for other offences. There are no statistics regarding civil actions against squatters.

4.5   Other Evictions – Family Law, Redevelopment

Statistics for applications for family law remedies – either a non-molestation or an occupation order – in England indicate a recent steady trend (2010–2017) for the latter, while for non-molestation orders the recent trend, although fluctuating, has been slowly upward.[31]

4.6   Commentary on the Statistics

Statistics are available for each of the four jurisdictions of the UK (England, Wales, Northern Ireland and Scotland) but not for the UK as a whole. The data collected across the different jurisdictions are not always directly comparable.

4.7   Profile of Those Evicted

The profile of those households who experience evictions varies across the tenures.

5.   RISK FACTORS IDENTIFIED LEADING TO EVICTIONS FROM EACH HOUSING TENURE

Eviction is linked to socioeconomic position. Job loss and relationship breakdown which causes a loss of income are obviously a major driver of eviction. Although the UK's welfare systems are comparably extensive and relatively generous, housing costs are very high relative to what most people earn and, in areas of high housing stress, can be higher than the level of support offered by welfare payments. As noted, welfare systems do not tend to replace lost income from paid work at a sufficient level to allow someone with a mortgage to maintain payments. There are situations in which eviction is triggered by unmet support and treatment needs, which may be associated with later homelessness.

Research on repossession of mortgaged homes shows, as would be expected, a strong association between loss of income and arrears.

---

[31]   Ministry of Justice, *Family Court Statistics Quarterly, England and Wales, July to September 2017* (Ministry of Justice, 2017).

Research in England found that nearly half of a surveyed group with mortgage arrears cited loss of work as a reason why they had gone into arrears, while 27 per cent of the 451 people surveyed, reported multiple reasons why arrears had occurred, such as relationship breakdown alongside job loss.[32]

Where repossession takes place, there is evidence of the same trigger factors, all centring on reduction of income, through unemployment, relationship breakdown or a combination of factors. There is evidence that job loss or ill health can be associated with higher rates of repossessions than for those whose arrears had arisen for other reasons. Where a suspended order or informal arrangement to manage and repay arrears had been put in place, but broken down, the risk of eviction also increased. Sustained loss of income, whether in the medium or long term, is correlated with an increased risk of possession.[33]

Private rented sector evictions are also associated with loss of income and with rent levels that present a high housing cost burden to lower and middle income households in many parts of the UK. There are problems with abusive behaviour by landlords and substandard housing within the lower end of the private rented sector. The key challenge from the perspective of some academics, researchers and housing professionals is that the private rented sector with its high rents, limited regulation and restricted legal protections for tenants is an inherently insecure tenure. There is an argument that lessons must be learned from more successful private rented sector markets in other countries.[34]

In the social rented sector, there is evidence of an over representation of women, lone parents and those in employment within eviction cases. Problems in the administration of Housing Benefit (a subsidy designed to help welfare benefit reliant low income households with rent) can be a factor in arrears cases as it is paid in arrears causing issues with amassing arrears. Problems in paying rent often stem from moving from out-of-work benefits into insecure, erratic employment, a process which the benefit system has always been ill-equipped to manage[35] and which the recent welfare reforms have sought to correct. However, the introduction

---

[32] Andrew Gall, *Understanding Mortgage Arrears* (Building Societies Association, 2009) 10.

[33] Ibid.

[34] Shelter, *Time for reform: How our neighbours with mature private renting markets guarantee stability for renters* (Shelter, 2016).

[35] Liz Phelps, *Unfinished Business: Housing associations' compliance with the rent arrears pre-action protocol and use of Ground 8.* (Citizens Advice Bureau, 2008); Hal Pawson, Filip Sosenko, Dave Cowan, Jacqui Croft, Matthew

of the Universal Credit system, designed to respond more flexibly to modern labour markets, has been coupled with heavy cuts to welfare support, including support for young people, disabled adults and people with limiting illness, and for low income families, which seem likely to exacerbate experience of eviction.[36]

6. THE LINKS BETWEEN EVICTION AND HOMELESSNESS

There is evidence that the associations between eviction and homelessness, in the UK context, are limited. Analysis of government homelessness statistics in England has highlighted the rising number of homeless people reporting the end of a time-limited assured shorthold tenancy as a trigger factor for their homelessness.[37]

Despite the cuts in welfare budgets, the reason why eviction in general, and repossession in particular, are not more clearly associated with homelessness causation, centres on the extent of social protection and social housing systems in the UK. In spite of the ongoing retrenchment across UK social policy, these systems remain extensive relative to much of Southern and Eastern Europe. There is an extensive safety net; social protection systems will pay all, or a large proportion of the private or social housing rent for many low income and unemployed people.

There are, however, clear restrictions: benefits will only cover a bedroom in a shared house for most people under 35, support for young people is being cut, and a lone adult over 35 will not normally receive enough benefit to pay the rent for more than a one-bedroomed property. Equally, a family will not receive more financial support than is required to provide them with sufficient space. Provision of social housing is shrinking, with the private rented sector now the second tenure, but the social rented sector is still a significant tenure and meets a huge amount of housing need.

Finally, of course, there are the statutory homelessness systems in England, Scotland, Wales and Northern Ireland. These have, since their

---

Cole and Caroline Hunter, *Rent Arrears Management Practices in the Housing Association Sector* (Tenants Services Authority, 2010).

[36]   S Moffatt, S Lawson, R Patterson, E Holding, A Dennison, S Sowden and J Brown, 'A qualitative study of the impact of the UK "bedroom tax"' (2015) 38 (2) *Journal of Public Health (Oxford)* 197–205.

[37]   Suzanne Fitzpatrick, Hal Pawson, Glen Bramley, Steve Wilcox and Beth Watts, *The homelessness monitor: England 2017* (Crisis, 2017).

inception, broken the link between eviction and homelessness by inter-ceding before sustained homelessness can occur, most evidently and most successfully in respect of homeless families, by providing temporary accommodation and then settled housing. The scale is not inconsiderable: 3 517 350 households were found statutorily homeless in England between 1979 and 2015. Since the mid 2000s, the role of homelessness prevention systems has become increasingly important. These systems are reported as stopping eviction from occurring at a significant scale in England, prevention is becoming equally extensive in Scotland and has undergone an expansion, outstripping provision elsewhere, as a result of the introduction of recent Welsh legal reforms and is growing in Northern Ireland.[38]

7. SUMMARY OF SIGNIFICANT CASES AND REPORTS RELATED TO EVICTION IN THE PERIOD 2010–2015

On the face of it the most significant case on eviction in the UK between 2010–2015 is *Manchester City Council v Pinnock* [2010] UKSC 45; [2011] 2 AC 104, on the applicability of Article 8 of the ECHR on possession hearings. However, for the reasons explored above, the effect of the case has been muted.[39]

8. BEST PRACTICE MODELS FOR PREVENTING AND REACTING TO EVICTIONS

8.1 Preventing Eviction

The prevention of eviction centres on legal advice, mediation and the provision of financial support. These different elements can be summar-ized as follows:

- Legal advice and support when a private or social landlord is not adhering to the law correctly, or is attempting to illegally intimidate a tenant. This might include support with taking a landlord to court. Legal advice and support can, of course, be offered when a lender

---

[38] Boyle and Pleace (n 24) 26.
[39] Cowan and Hunter (n 19).

is trying to repossess an owner-occupied property without following the correct procedure.

- Mediation services, which facilitate negotiation between a tenant and a landlord or between a mortgagor and a lender. Negotiation can, as described above, be ordered by a court, but these services can be brought in before the legal process of seeking an eviction has started. In many cases, this will involve an agreed rescheduling of arrears. In rented housing, there will be instances where a tenancy is under threat because of nuisance or damage to a property and an agreement is developed to ensure nuisance does not recur or to rectify damage, to prevent eviction.

- Financial support, either in the form of a grant or a highly affordable loan, can be the most effective and quickest way to end the possibility of an eviction which is linked to arrears. Landlords or lenders may, in certain circumstances, be persuaded to write off arrears, or, more commonly a fund can be provided that simply pays off arrears directly and/or makes affordable loans available. Lender forbearance can prevent eviction in the owner-occupied sector, though this may not involve actual reduction of debt, merely the postponement of repayment.

Where an individual or household has high support and treatment needs that are associated with housing instability, for example, problems managing money, nuisance behaviour or damage to a rented property, the UK employs 'tenancy sustainment teams'. These teams, which can be used to stop an eviction or other potential homelessness triggers from occurring, employ a low to mid intensity case management model. A peripatetic support worker, who visits a formerly or potentially homeless person or household in their home, provides housing advice, practical support and makes referrals to whatever services may be required by an individual, including health, social work, education, training, drug and alcohol and specialist or legal advice services. The model is a common part of local authority homelessness strategies in the UK, it may be focused entirely on homelessness and potential homelessness or have a broader remit to support potentially vulnerable people living as independently as possible in the community. Tenancy sustainment teams are also used where a formerly homeless person has been resettled and is assessed as at risk of repeated homelessness.

Certain models of homelessness service can also be employed in a preventative way, particularly where eviction is likely to be triggered if high support and treatment needs are not met. One model, which is still emergent in the UK, is Housing First, which can be targeted at known 'at risk' groups, such as former offenders with complex needs who are leaving prison without a settled home to go to, people with comorbidity of problematic drug and alcohol use and severe mental illness, and vulnerable young people at the point they leave the care of social services. Such services can stop eviction in the sense that they can meet the complex needs that if unaddressed, are likely to trigger eviction, though this is of course just one aspect of what they seek to achieve.[40]

8.2 Reacting to Eviction

The core response to eviction is to provide services that facilitate rapid, ideally immediate, access to alternative housing, or at the very least to temporary accommodation. Where a household is eligible, the statutory homelessness systems provide this immediate response, assuming help is sought at the point of eviction or prior to eviction taking place. In England, Scotland and Northern Ireland, households can seek assistance 28 days in advance of eviction or other triggers for potential homelessness occurring. In Wales, help can be sought 56 days in advance of possible homelessness and the other jurisdictions may soon adopt this practice. In every part of the UK, there is an emphasis within statutory homelessness systems to use preventative services to avoid the use of these provisions, which can include effectively by-passing the statutory system to provide rehousing through another route, such as the local lettings schemes which are described below.

Outside the statutory systems, the main responses to eviction also centre on providing access to housing as rapidly as possible. This can be through orchestration of all available social housing in an area, using a communal allocation system, such as the points and bidding-based Choice Based Lettings model, which is widespread throughout the UK, to ensure void properties are re-let as rapidly as possible (which is also in social landlords' interest).

Another model is the use of a local lettings scheme, which is designed to maximize and expedite access to adequate and affordable private rented sector housing. This system works by offering private landlords what is in effect, a full management service for their property; that is, a tenant will occupy the housing, all housing management issues, including any problems, will be handled by the local lettings scheme. In some cases, private landlords will also receive guaranteed rent payments, even when their property is void and awaiting re-letting. A local lettings

---

[40] Nicholas Pleace, *Housing First Guide Europe* (FEANTSA, 2016).

scheme can be self-financing; that is, adopt a social enterprise model, charging a competitive rate for management services that is enough to cover running costs and perhaps generate a small profit.

In return for the local lettings scheme management service, private sector landlords, who essentially have nothing to do other than receive their rent, give up control of allocation and the local lettings agency decides the allocation of the private rented stock that it manages. A key role of local lettings agencies is to support potentially vulnerable groups, prevent homelessness and the recurrence of homelessness.[41]

Finally, there is also a network of county court duty schemes in England, Wales and North Ireland. The schemes provide: '"on-the-day" emergency face to face advice and advocacy to anyone facing possession proceedings. Anyone in danger of eviction or having their property repossessed can get free legal advice and representation on the day of their hearing, regardless of their financial circumstances.'[42]

In England and Wales such schemes are funded by the Legal Aid Agency. Although Bright and Whitehouse found that advice was not available in all courts, they did conclude that:

> ... representatives are often able to negotiate repayment agreements with the claimant at court prior to the hearing ... [and they provide a] significant role ... in assisting some occupiers to avoid losing their homes ... .[43]

If these systems, ranging from the statutory homelessness systems, to choice-based lettings schemes for social housing, local lettings agencies for the private rented sector, to advice at court, work properly, then eviction should rarely if ever lead to homelessness. Transitions should occur from the home someone is being evicted from, into a new home, rather than a transition from eviction to homelessness. These systems are, of course, reliant on a welfare system that enables someone to meet basic housing and living costs when they are out of work or unable to work. A local lettings scheme cannot function if the target population cannot afford any of the rents in the private rented sector properties the scheme is able to secure.

---

[41]   Shelter Scotland, *Social Models of Letting Agencies: Scoping Study* (Shelter Scotland, 2015).

[42]   Ministry of Justice, *Housing Possession Court Duty Scheme Commissioning Sustainable Services* (Ministry of Justice, 2017) 3.

[43]   Susan Bright and Lisa Whitehouse, 'Information, Advice & Representation in Housing Possession Cases' Oxford Legal Studies Research Paper No. 25/2014 (2014) 77.

8.3 Improving Responses to Eviction

The key to success in stopping homelessness or housing exclusion following eviction, lies in producing a strongly integrated strategy in which housing advice, homelessness prevention and homelessness reduction services are working together seamlessly. An integrated system should share data, flagging an individual or household as at risk of eviction as soon as possible, conducting a coordinated assessment and ensuring that eviction is prevented where possible. Where there is a risk of recurrent homelessness, triggered by eviction, that must be minimized, which is where homelessness services become important. Bringing together support, prevention and rapid re-housing services can greatly reduce the impact of eviction.

The UK does not compare very well with Finland, where preventative services and services to reduce homelessness are part of an integrated strategy, which includes anti-eviction measures, centred around collaborative working and case management. In the context of an integrated homelessness strategy, eviction in Finland is minimized and experience of homelessness is reduced to a functional zero; that is, very few people become homeless and those who do, do not experience it for long.[44]

It is important to remember that whether or not eviction constitutes a social problem is strongly related to housing markets, social protection (welfare) systems and the roles occupied by social housing in the UK. Eviction is related to housing costs and housing costs are high because the supply of affordable housing is insufficient in the UK, indeed the housing shortage is chronic.[45] Exorbitant rents, poor standards and inherent insecurity of tenure in the private rented sector are ultimately a function of inadequate housing supply in the UK. The inherent dysfunction of the private rented sector itself needs to be addressed, because in delivering often difficult to afford housing, with restricted tenancy rights, the nature of this element of the housing market potentially exacerbates the risk of eviction.

Equally, the high cost of home ownership relative to income means that job loss or other reductions in income is often a potential trigger for repossession. Again, the nature of the housing market itself is an issue here, more affordable housing options would reduce the risk of eviction from owner-occupied housing.

---

[44] Nicholas Pleace, Dennis P Culhane, Riitta Granfelt and Marcus Knutagård, *The Finnish Homelessness Strategy: An International Review* (Ministry of the Environment, 2015).

[45] Dorling (n 6) 6.

Finally, there are the structural risks of increased eviction stemming from the reform to the social protection system in the UK. These welfare reforms have potential advantages, but have been introduced in the context of very large and sustained cuts to welfare budgets, restricting the accessibility and level of welfare benefits. Any reduction in the capacity of poor and low income people to afford rents and mortgages and, by extension, to pay other household bills, which will also reduce their capacity to pay rent or the mortgage, is likely to risk an increase in eviction. Inefficiencies and inequities in the administration of welfare benefits are associated with evictions from the social rented sector, but might equally have an impact on eviction levels from the private rented and owner-occupied sectors.

9. CONCLUSION

The experience of the UK shows that eviction is not necessarily a trigger to housing exclusion or homelessness where multiple systems and services are in place, both to counteract poverty and to prevent homelessness. There are, as noted, at least some associations between the end of an assured shorthold tenancy and homelessness in England, although the numbers involved are much smaller than those experiencing the end of an assured shorthold tenancy and other causal factors may be involved.

There is a need for greater coordination in terms of responses to eviction in the UK. Systems do need to work together to minimize the risk that eviction occurs and that when it does occur, to ensure that an evicted household or person is housed, ideally by simply moving into new housing before a physical eviction can take place, or as soon as possible thereafter.

Law plays a central role in eviction in the UK. Law determines the framework in which eviction occurs. While market forces create pressures in the private rented sector that raise the risk of eviction, it is the law that makes the private rented sector an inherently insecure tenure for tenants, limiting their rights in relation to private sector landlords. It will be interesting to see how far the legal changes in Scotland and the planned reforms in England rebalance control of security of tenure towards tenants. The protections against eviction built into social tenancies, a home for life unless tenancy conditions are breached, are being systematically removed in England, although this pattern may not be repeated elsewhere. Again, the creation and extension of laws that make social housing less secure will do nothing to reduce the frequency of eviction in the UK.

For owner-occupiers, the risk of eviction is determined by lender forbearance or by the decision of a court, as to whether or not an order is suspended, and time given to pay off arrears. The rights of the mortgagor are less well protected than those of the lender, again reflecting the market orientated housing policy of the UK over the last 40 years.

An argument to introduce legal protection from eviction is probably not something that is tenable in the current political climate in the UK. The dominance of the neo-liberal, pro-market Right seems unlikely to end and the many small private landlords, and of course the financial sector, constitute a considerable lobby.[46] Yet the humanitarian and practical arguments are strong, the UK is economically disadvantaged by unaffordable housing (labour mobility is restricted) and poverty, which had been alleviated by social housing and the welfare system, is becoming an increasingly destructive experience as the old association between low income and poor, indeed extremely poor, living conditions reasserts itself.[47] Both the laws and the levels of inequity in the UK need to change, if levels of eviction are to be brought down.

---

[46] Dorling (n 6) 2.
[47] Tunstall (n 5) 105.

Index

ELGAR LAND AND HOUSING LAW AND POLICY

Titles in the series include:

Tenancy Law and Housing Policy in Europe
Towards Regulatory Equilibrium
Edited by Christoph U. Schmid

Loss of Homes and Evictions across Europe
A Comparative Legal and Policy Examination
Edited by Padraic Kenna, Sergio Nasarre-Aznar, Peter Sparkes and
Christoph U. Schmid